Teaching LGBTQ Politics

SUNY series in Queer Politics and Cultures

Cynthia Burack and Jyl J. Josephson, editors

Teaching LGBTQ Politics

Edited by

EDWARD F. KAMMERER JR.,
ROYAL G. CRAVENS III, *and*
ERIN MAYO-ADAM

SUNY
PRESS

Published by State University of New York Press, Albany

EU GPSR Authorised Representative:
Logos Europe, 9 rue Nicolas Poussin, 17000, La Rochelle, France
contact@logoseurope.eu

For information, contact State University of New York Press, Albany, NY
www.sunypress.edu

Library of Congress Cataloging-in-Publication Data

Names: Kammerer, Edward F., Jr., 1979– editor. | Cravens, Royal G., III,
    1986– editor. | Mayo-Adam, Erin, editor.
Title: Teaching LGBTQ politics / edited by Edward F. Kammerer, Jr.,
    Royal G. Cravens III, and Erin Mayo-Adam.
Description: Albany : State University of New York Press, [2025] | Series:
    SUNY series in queer politics and cultures
Identifiers: LCCN 2025000928 | ISBN 9798855803556 (hardcover : alk. paper) |
    ISBN 9798855803563 (ebook) | ISBN 9798855803549 (pbk. : alk. paper)
Subjects: LCSH: Gay and lesbian studies—Study and teaching—United States. |
    Sexual minorities—History—Study and teaching—United States.
Classification: LCC HQ75.16.U6 T44 2025 | DDC 323.3/26071073—dc23/eng/20250213
LC record available at https://lccn.loc.gov/2025000928

Contents

Introduction

ERIN MAYO-ADAM, ROYAL G. CRAVENS III,
AND EDWARD F. KAMMERER JR.

In recent years, a resurgence of Christian nationalism has led to a movement against diversity, equity, and inclusion (DEI) education in both K–12 and college classrooms. Since Florida passed its infamous "Don't Say Gay" law in 2022, which sought to significantly limit the discussion of LGBTQ topics in K–12 schools, a concerted effort by far-right politicians and adherents of the political ideology known as white Christian nationalism has catapulted around the country (Izaguirre 2022; Thoreson 2022; Izaguirre and Farrington 2023). Leading Republicans have called on K–12 schools to eliminate books that "might make students feel discomfort, guilt, anguish, or any other form of psychological distress because of their race or sex" and "sexually explicit material," which includes books written by women, people of color, and LGBTQ people (Shivaram 2021; Chappell 2021). In higher education, as part of the effort to eliminate perceived "divisive concepts," states have moved to eliminate DEI education altogether, closing entire DEI offices and restricting tenure (see, e.g., Confessore 2024; Flaherty 2022; Kruesi 2022).

Alongside the growing political fervor against inclusive curricula, colleges are in the midst of an inclusive curricula renaissance, spurred by social movement activism that has emphasized the need to elevate minority voices in the classroom, and an increase in acceptance of LGBTQ people (Pew 2013). There now are hundreds of LGBTQ centers on college campuses nationwide, many in states whose anti-discrimination laws do not mention sexual orientation or gender identity, including in Alabama and

Oklahoma (Pratt 2014), and at many private religious institutions (Coley 2018). Against this backdrop of increased acceptance amidst heightened attacks on inclusive curricula, there are virtually no resources available for college faculty who wish to engage with LGBTQ content on their campuses. This is particularly true of political science, where LGBTQ people are rarely centered in research and LGBTQ scholars and their scholarship face individual-level and structural discrimination (Ayoub 2022). How should a political science classroom incorporate LGBTQ materials? What does an LGBTQ politics class entail? How can faculty and students encourage their campuses to create and support inclusive classrooms?

Teaching LGBTQ Politics provides a blueprint for navigating the contested environment that is queer higher education in the United States, with a focus on the political science classroom. Political science as a discipline does not take LGBTQ politics as seriously as it should. Not all departments offer LGBTQ politics courses, nor do all faculty include relevant LGBTQ content in their courses. This volume helps rectify that failing by providing a resource to faculty considering teaching LGBTQ political issues. The chapters collected here span the entire discipline of political science. This broad coverage is designed to help all faculty make their courses more inclusive, an important goal that colleges and universities regularly struggle to meet. Identity politics are a crucial component of the political science curriculum. This is particularly true as greater numbers of people identify as members of the LGBTQ community and as colleges face calls from students and experts to adopt more racially and ethnically inclusive materials (Jones 2021). While public opinion on LGBTQ issues has become significantly more positive over time, recent laws targeting the transgender community, in particular, remind us that LGBTQ political debates, and the real-world impact of those debates, are far from settled (Feliciano 2021). This volume seeks to provide instructors with the tools necessary to help navigate the teaching of LGBTQ politics in this contested terrain.

Expanding the Field: Scholarship on Inclusive Curricula

In 2007, the American Political Science Association (APSA) Committee on the Status of LGBTQ Individuals in the Profession published a survey of introduction to US politics textbooks that found that most books inadequately addressed LGBTQ issues and frequently treated LGBTQ people as "another structurally disempowered group, often grouped with the disabled, and listed after longer substantive sections on race and gender" (Novkov and Gossett 2007, 393). Since the publication of this report, and in response to widespread student-driven protests calling for more intersectionally inclusive courses, universities around the country have engaged in broader efforts to incorporate LGBTQ issues and struggles in their curricula. Yet much work remains to be done, especially in light of a well-funded and powerful movement to abolish education on race, ethnicity, sexual orientation, and gender expression and identity in the classroom (Brandel 2020). *Teaching LGBTQ Politics* contributes to the growing body of research on the need to expand the study of politics to include racial, gender, and sexual minorities.

Although there is burgeoning scholarship on the need to incorporate LGBTQ community experiences in the study of politics, there are no volumes available that focus on how faculty, instructors, and members of the general population who are interested in LGBTQ-inclusive education can engage with the subject. Scholarship on the need to expand curricula includes several symposia. For example, with the support of the APSA's LGBT Status Committee, Paisely Currah edited a symposium in 2011 that included works from five scholars in sexuality and politics who both emphasized how the study of sexuality and politics deepens our understanding of core concepts in political science and is sidelined in a profession that assumes heteronormativity in research (Brettschneider 2011; Currah 2011; Doan 2011; Mucciaroni 2011; Rollins 2011; Smith 2011). In another symposium edited by Tungohan et al. (2020), scholars argue that intersectionally informed political science courses enhance the college experience by making curricula more applicable and relevant in contemporary society (see also Levac 2020). *Teaching LGBTQ Politics* contributes to this research both by highlighting the need to expand the field to include LGBTQ identities, issues, and struggles and by showing scholars how to do so.

In addition to research on the need to expand political science curricula to include intersectionally marginalized populations, *Teaching LGBTQ Politics* also includes scholarship on LGBTQ politics generally. The book thus speaks to the growing number of volumes on LGBTQ politics, including one by Brettschneider et al. (2017) on LGBTQ politics, which has a compilation of contemporary political science research on LGBTQ politics for use in the undergraduate and graduate classroom. In addition, Haider-Markel et al. (2021) recently created a handbook on LGBTQ politics and policy that offers a wide array of chapters examining the contributions of LGBTQ scholarship in political science. Finally, both *PS: Political Science & Politics* and *Politics, Groups, and Identities* have special editions on LGBTQ politics that compile contemporary research on the topic and speak to the growth of the field in recent years. These volumes begin to lay out an emerging field of LGBTQ politics. *Teaching LGBTQ Politics* builds on this field and explores how academics might incorporate LGBTQ research both in LGBTQ-specific and non-LGBTQ-specific courses, including courses on American government, international relations, comparative politics, political theory, public administration, and public law.

Outside of political science, other disciplines are also publishing new volumes on teaching LGBTQ issues in order to address increased demand for courses in higher education. For example, Rupp and Freeman (2014) have published a volume on how to integrate LGBTQ history into the standard college curriculum. This shows the importance of taking social equity, including LGBTQ issues, more seriously. Works like this are part of a renewed effort to encourage instructors to adopt inclusive curricula in college settings. However, there is a dearth of research on this topic in political science. *Teaching LGBTQ Politics* is the first volume to address teaching and researching LGBTQ issues in the college classroom. Consequently, the book enhances the field of political science and aligns the field with what is happening in other disciplines.

In addition to research on inclusive education and the emergence of LGBTQ politics as a disciplinary subfield, a growing body of work now focuses on how to advocate for inclusive education in the classroom. According to the National School Climate Survey report released by GLSEN in 2019, only 19.4 percent of LGBTQ people were taught positive representations of LGBTQ people and history in the classroom in the United States (Kosciw et al. 2018). The dearth of LGBTQ-inclusive education in the country has spawned a national movement to diversify K–12 and college curricula. This movement has fostered a national audience interested in LGBTQ education, in addition to a variety of books on the subject. These include books on inclusive education in the K–12 setting (see, e.g., Sadowski and Jennings 2016; Ryan et al. 2018; Shane 2020; Dellenty 2019). *Teaching LGBTQ Politics* contributes to this body of research and enhances it by illuminating how the movement for LGBTQ-inclusive education can impact the college and graduate school classroom. In doing so, the book contributes to an ongoing political debate about the need for inclusive curricula at all education levels during a moment when the right of minority students to see themselves reflected in classroom material is at risk.

Despite the book's many contributions to the field, *Teaching LGBTQ Politics* also illuminates how the field of political science continues to silo the study of identity politics in ways that do not reflect the broad array of intersectional identities that exist in the real world. Identity politics is divided into different subfields in research and in professional associations (e.g., race and ethnic politics, LGBTQ politics, and gender politics). As a result, it remains common for political science to sideline the experiences of those who are intersectionally marginalized. This failing is apparent in the teaching of LGBTQ politics, where instructors who hold white gay and lesbian identities are significantly overrepresented. As with the field as a whole, more advantaged LGBTQ identities are overrepresented in this volume's contributing authors, despite the editors' best efforts to diversify submissions. In order to address this shortcoming, this volume includes chapters that directly address how to incorporate more marginalized people within the LGBTQ community in the class-room and contributes to calls for intersectional diversity in the college setting.

Outline of the Book

Teaching LGBTQ Politics is divided into three parts. The first examines LGBTQ politics-centered courses. Courses that focus on LGBTQ politics are varied in the field, and part 1 reflects this variation, providing a blueprint for adapting LGBTQ politics courses in a number of different subfields. Topics in part 1 include whether an LGBTQ politics cannon exists, how to center the struggle for LGBTQ-inclusive schools in college curriculum, how to address the historical evolution and contested nature of the LGBTQ political movement, how to teach LGBTQ politics in specific environments, and how to design a graduate seminar on LGBTQ rights. These chapters cover a wide range of specific issues, depending on instructor preferences and abilities.

Part 2 focuses on how to incorporate lessons from LGBTQ politics into classes where LGBTQ issues are not the focus, such as introductory public administration, methods, comparative politics, and international relations courses. For example, when teaching Introduction to American Politics, including a course framework that actively incorporates LGBTQ people and history enhances the course coverage. Courses on public law and social movements similarly lend themselves to LGBTQ-inclusive courses, but LGBTQ issues belong, and can be incorporated into, every subfield in political science. *Teaching LGBTQ Politics* shows how even quantitative methods classes can include LGBTQ politics by teaching students how to properly count LGBTQ people in survey design.

Part 3 shifts the focus to broader pedagogical issues that face LGBTQ scholars and researchers, such as training LGBTQ researchers for conducting fieldwork and how to engage with students on identity topics in a manner that incorporates students' own activist interests and an intersectional approach to teaching. Chapters in part 3 also examine pedagogical issues that arise when teaching LGBTQ politics in hostile environments and how to use librarians to expand curricula to make it more intersectionally inclusive.

Teaching LGBTQ Politics concludes with an afterword by Dorothee Benz that examines the rise of anti-LGBTQ legislation in the twenty-first century, places it in historical context, and contemplates how LGBTQ politics courses might approach this historical moment going forward. Benz's afterword argues that queer politics courses must resist the urge to respond with a "domesticated—homonormatized—non-threatening addition to capitalist-compatible politics" as the LGBTQ politics movement so often does when it faces attacks from Christian nationalists. Instead, Benz contends that courses must integrate a queer-inclusive, transformative politics modeled off the larger liberation projects of Black feminists. This volume urges readers to do just that and provides a framework teachers and academics can use to accomplish this.

References

Ayoub, Phillip M. 2022. "Not That Niche: Making Room for the Study of LGBTIQ People in Political Science." *European Journal of Politics and Gender* 5 (2): 154–72. https://doi.org/10.1332/251510821X16345581767345.

Beck, Bob. 2022. "Gender Studies Funding Restored During Final Budget Vote." *Wyoming Public Media*, March 7. https://www.wyomingpublicmedia.org/politics-government/2022-03-07/gender-studies-funding-restored-during-final-budget-vote.

Brandel, Shawna M. 2020. "It's (Not) in the Reading: American Government Textbooks' Limited Representation of Historically Marginalized Groups." *PS: Political Science & Politics* 53 (4): 734–40.

Brettschneider, Marla. 2011. "Heterosexual Political Science." *PS: Political Science & Politics* 44 (1): 23–26.

Brettschneider, Marla, Susan Burgess, and Christine Keating, eds. 2017. *LGBTQ Politics: A Critical Reader*. New York University Press.

Confessore, Nicholas, 2024. "'America Is Under Attack': Inside the Anti-D.E.I. Crusade." *New York Times*, January 20. https://www.nytimes.com/interactive/2024/01/20/us/dei-woke-claremont-institute.html.

Currah, Paisley. 2011. "The State of LGBT/Sexuality Studies in Political Science: Editor's Introduction." *PS: Political Science & Politics* 44 (1): 13–16.

Chappell, Bill. 2021. "A Texas Lawmaker Is Targeting 850 Books That He Says Could Make Students Feel Uneasy." *WNYC*, October 28. https://www.npr.org/2021/10/28/1050013664/texas-lawmaker-matt-krause-launches-inquiry-into-850-books.

Coley, Jonathan. 2018. *Gay on God's Campus: Mobilizing for LGBT Equality at Christian Colleges and Universities*. University of North Carolina Press.

Dellenty, Shaun. 2019. *Celebrating Difference: A Whole-School Approach to LGBT+ Inclusion*. Bloomsbury Education.

Doan, Alesha E. 2011. "'What's Wrong with Being Sexy?' Why Political Science Needs to Get Serious About Sexuality." *PS: Political Science & Politics* 44 (1): 31–34.

Feliciano, Ivette. 2021. "Pride: 2021 Has Set a Record in Anti-Trans Bills in America." *PBS News Hour*, June 6. https://www.pbs.org/newshour/show/pride-2021-has-set-a-record-in-anti-trans-bills-in-america.

Flaherty, Colleen. 2022. "'A New Low' in Attacks on Academic Freedom." *Inside Higher Ed*, February 21. https://psuaaup.net/blog/entry/a-new-low-in-attacks-on-academic-freedom.

Friedman, Adam. 2022. "Senate Passes Critical Race Theory, 'Divisive Concepts' Bill Aimed at Tennessee Colleges." *Tennessean*, March 21. https://www.tennessean.com/story/news/politics/2022/03/21/tennessee-senate-passes-critical-race-theory-bill-colleges-universities/9349486002/.

Haider-Markel, Donald P., Carlos Ball, Gary Mucciaroni, Bruno Perreau, Craig A. Rimmerman, and Jamie K. Taylor, eds. 2021. *The Oxford Encyclopedia of LGBT Politics and Policy*. Oxford University Press.

Izaguirre, Anthony. 2022. "'Don't Say Gay' Bill Signed by Florida Governor Ron DeSantis." *AP News*, March 28. https://apnews.com/article/florida-dont-say-gay-law-signed-56aee61f075a12663f25990c7b31624d.

Izaguirre, Anthony, and Brendan Farrington. 2023. "Florida Expands 'Don't Say Gay': House Expands Anti-LGBTQ Bills." *AP News*, April 1. https://apnews.com/article/desantis-florida-dont-say-gay-ban-684ed25a303f83208a89c556543183cb.

Jones, Jeffrey M. 2021. "LGBT Identification Rises to 5.6 Percent in Latest U.S. Estimate." *Gallup*. https://news.gallup.com/poll/329708/lgbt-identification-rises-latest-estimate.aspx.

Kosciw, Joseph G., Caitlin M. Clark, Nahn L. Truong, and Adrian D. Zongrone. 2019. "The 2019 National School Climate Survey: The Experiences of Lesbian, Gay, Bisexual, Transgender, and Queer Youth in Our Nation's Schools." GLESEN. https://www.glsen.org/sites/default/files/2021-04/NSCS19-FullReport-032421-Web_0.pdf.

Kruesi, Kimberlee. 2022. "Tennessee's 'Divisive Concept' Bill Targeting Colleges Advances." *AP News*, March 1. https://apnews.com/article/education-lawsuits-tennessee-5b6942ef990b5139c70ee383dfd60178.

Levac, Leah. 2020. "Negotiating Tensions in a Community Engaged and Intersectionally-Informed Political Science Course." *Politics, Groups, and Identities* 8 (1): 194–202.

Mucciaroni, Gary. 2011. "The Study of LGBT Politics and Its Contributions to Political Science." *PS: Political Science & Politics* 44 (1): 17–21.

Novkov, Julie, and Charles Gossett. 2007. "Survey of Textbooks for Teaching Intro to U.S. Politics: How Do They See Us?" *PS: Political Science & Politics* 40 (2): 393–98.

Pew. 2013. "A Survey of LGBT Americans." Pew Research Center, June 13. https://www.pewresearch.org/social-trends/2013/06/13/a-survey-of-lgbt-americans/.

Pratt, Timothy. 2014. "Colleges See Gay Students as a New Market." *Hechinger Report*. https://hechingerreport.org/colleges-see-gay-students-new-market/.

Reilly, Kate. 2022. "Republicans Are Increasingly Targeting 'Divisive Concepts' at Colleges and Universities." *Time*, March 2. https://time.com/6162489/divisive-concepts-colleges/.

Rollins, Joe. 2011. "Political Science, Political Sex." *PS: Political Science & Politics* 44 (1): 27–30.

Rupp, Leila J., and Susan K. Freeman. 2014. *Understanding and Teaching US Lesbian, Gay, Bisexual, and Transgender History*. University of Wisconsin Press.

Ryan, Caitlin L., Jill M. Hermann-Wilmarth, and Mariana Souto-Manning. 2018. *Reading the Rainbow: LGBTQ-Inclusive Literacy Instruction in the Elementary Classroom*. Teacher's College Press.

Sadowski, Michael, and Kevin Jennings. 2016. *Safe Is Not Enough: Better Schools for LGBTQ Students*. Harvard Education Press.

Shane, Kryss. 2020. *The Educator's Guide to LGBT+ Inclusion: A Practical Resource for K–12 Teachers, Administrators, and School Support Staff*. Jessica Kingsley Publishers.

Shivaram, Deepa. 2021. "More Republican Leaders Try to Ban Books on Race, LGBTQ Issues." *WNYC*, November 13. https://www.npr.org/2021/11/13/1055524205/more-republican-leaders-try-to-ban-books-on-race-lgbtq-issues.

Smith, Charles Anthony. 2011. "Gay, Straight, or Questioning? Sexuality and Political Science." *PS: Political Science & Politics* 44 (1): 35–38.

Thoreson, Ryan. 2022. "Florida Advances 'Don't Say Gay Bill': Censoring Discussions Jeopardizes Children's Rights." Human Rights Watch, February 17. https://www.hrw.org/news/2022/02/17/florida-advances-dont-say-gay-bill.

Tungohan, Ethel, Leah Levac, and Kimala Price. 2020. "Introduction to Dialogues Section on Socially Engaged Research and Teaching in Political Science." *Politics, Groups, and Identities* 8 (1): 160–63.

Part 1

LGBTQ Politics Courses

Faculty choosing how to create courses centered on LGBTQ politics may approach the task in a variety of ways, as evidenced by the chapters included in this section. As Kammerer and Cravens show in chapter 1, there is little agreement on an LGBTQ politics canon, at least as far as specific texts are concerned. They do, however, find some agreement on topics that should be considered. And some of the examples offered in part 1 of *Teaching LGBTQ Politics* demonstrate ways to do that. But others go beyond and ask us to question the coverage that tends to dominate courses on LGBTQ politics. These chapters push the field further, both in content and in teaching techniques. The chapters included in part 1, we hope, will provide faculty with a solid foundation upon which to build a new LGBTQ politics course from the ground up or modify an existing course with new topics or materials.

In chapter 1, "Is There an LGBTQ Politics Canon?," Edward F. Kammerer Jr. and Royal G. Cravens III use data from a survey of political science faculty members who teach LGBTQ politics courses to assess whether this particular subfield has coalesced around a set canon of readings or texts that should inform our courses. They begin by discussing the role of canons in setting disciplinary boundaries and norms. Next, they discuss the findings from their survey, which shows that while a core set of readings has not yet formed into a concrete canon, there exists broad agreement on the topics that should be covered in LGBTQ politics courses. This presents faculty with both challenges and opportunities. Faculty, especially those new to teaching LGBTQ politics courses, may struggle to determine which readings to assign. Conversely, the open-ended nature of LGBTQ politics gives faculty immense freedom in choosing those topics and readings. The chapters that follow can help faculty navigate as they decide how to construct these courses. As such, this chapter acts as a foundation to part 1 by providing a starting point to think about ways to advance and expand what is traditionally covered in LGBTQ politics topics.

Next, chapter 2, "Centering Schools in LGBTQ Politics" by Richard S. Price, invites us to think about high schools as sites of LGBTQ political contestation and the need to include education law and policy in our conceptualization of LGBTQ politics. Their chapter makes a compelling case for expanding our courses to include schools, even though they are not commonly included and did not show up in the canon survey from Kammerer and Cravens discussed in chapter 1. Price's chapter also draws on issues that are directly relevant to the lived experiences of many college students, which can help increase student engagement and make the material relevant to their lives.

In chapter 3, "Teaching LGBTQ Politics in and of Newark," Jyl Josephson discusses her experience teaching a course grounded in oral history sources and infused with active learning strategies. Josephson's practical suggestions can help faculty find ways to use this type of teaching technique to bring stories of LGBTQ people directly into the LGBTQ politics classroom. In this chapter, Josephson uses locally available resources in Newark, New Jersey, like the Queer Newark Oral History Project, to teach basic qualitative research methods, while helping students make connections between the study of specific LGBTQ histories and the study of politics. Drawing on queer archives, particularly local archives, brings the study of queer politics to life and connects students directly to the community.

Julian Applebaum and Patrick Schmidt's "The Historical Horizons of LGBTQ+ Politics," chapter 4, asks us to rethink the way we teach LGBTQ rights by encouraging a historical perspective. They argue that the dominant approach to teaching LGBTQ rights, focused on the major cases in the LGBTQ rights canon, focuses too narrowly. This leads students to miss important historic contexts and parallels to earlier eras. In order to rectify this, Applebaum and Schmidt argue that instructors should widen the chronological frame for LGBTQ rights in their courses and, in doing so, fully embed LGBTQ experiences in American institutions and history. This chapter could be useful to faculty as they seek to enrich a standard civil rights–type course or to develop a course focused explicitly on LGBTQ rights. Many of the issues raised in this chapter echo concerns raised in chapter 9 (Kammerer).

Chapter 5, "Queer Politics as Movement Formation" by Erin Mayo-Adam, offers an example of how LGBTQ politics courses can adopt some of Applebaum and Schmidt's suggested approach. Mayo-Adam's chapter provides an outline of a law, policy, and politics course that embeds LGBTQ experiences of sexual regulation, immigration, and federal exclusion in a history that extends well before the mid-twentieth century. Her chapter also offers another framework for designing LGBTQ politics courses—one that centers an unstable political movement that is in constant flux with the goal of encouraging students to imagine new futures for the movement for queer and trans justice in their own lives and to actively consider the intersection of race, gender, and class when thinking through queer issues.

Part 1 ends with a chapter from Cyril Ghosh entitled "Designing a Graduate Seminar on LGBTQ+ Rights," shifting focus to the graduate classroom. Ghosh wrestles with the difficulty inherent in designing courses on LGBTQ rights due to the lack of a clear canon. Using his own experience, Ghosh explores how to make choices between breadth and depth, and the extent to which queer theory can and should be included in graduate seminars.

Chapter 1

Is There an LGBTQ Politics Canon?

Edward F. Kammerer Jr. and Royal G. Cravens III

How does the study of LGBTQ identity fit into the study of politics? In this chapter we attempt to answer that question by exploring the idea of an LGBTQ political science canon. Academic disciplines and fields of study can be difficult to pin down, particularly at the margins or as new ideas and emerge. Political science, for example, blends into sociology when talking about political socialization and social movements. New disciplines emerge out of existing ones. International relations can be seen as either a subset of political science or a discipline in its own right (see Rosenberg 2016). International relations may be in the process of spawning the new, distinct field of international political economy as scholars in that area define their own core set of questions (Dickins 2006).

The shifting of disciplinary lines is, in general, a good thing. New knowledge can be gained when disciplines break free from their historic silos. But as disciplinary boundaries weaken, other challenges may arise. Distinct disciplines have different doctrines that define expected bodies of knowledge. Core concepts and shared understandings, coming from a clearly defined canon, allow the ongoing scholarly conversation that drives research forward to continue. Without an agreed upon foundation, building on previous knowledge becomes difficult. Can a discipline even exist without a canon?

Before turning to the specific questions and challenges an LGBTQ canon raises, we first examine the broader political science canon and its role in disciplinary education. Canons, as scholars across many disciplines have noted, define through exclusion. Canons focus a discipline's attention on the most important works, leaving the rest behind. But that process can produce inequalities and create limitations. Whose voices are canonized and whose voices are ignored has significant implications for the creation of knowledge. For too long, the canon (in most, if not all fields) has been largely structured to privilege the views of straight white men at the expense of women and other marginalized people. When other perspectives and other voices are excluded, the discipline suffers and the production of knowledge is diminished (Smith and Lee 2015).

In this chapter, we explore whether the study of LGBTQ politics has, or could potentially have, a clearly defined canon. Within LGBTQ political and social movements, white men have long dictated movement agendas, placing their concerns before those of lesbians, trans people, and LGBTQ people of color (Boykin 2000; Adler 2018). Assuming a clearly defined LGBTQ politics canon exists, does that canon incorporate the breadth of voices that study LGBTQ politics? Or instead does it, like canons traditionally have, continue to privilege the voices of white men?

This of course raises an important question: Is it better to diversify the canon, drawing in previously excluded voices, or, in the alternative, to abandon the concept of a single canon entirely? Canons can be useful. But they are also dangerous. Even if a canon is broadened to include new, previously marginalized perspectives, it will still set boundaries and mark some ideas as important while others remain on the fringe. That is, by definition, what a canon exists to do. But defining a canon may perpetuate hierarchies even in disciplines like queer theory that are often committed to disrupting and dismantling hierarchy. This suggests some disciplines may be better served by existing without a canon, an issue we will explore further.

It is not our purpose here to answer the broadly philosophical question of whether there *should* be an LGBTQ politics canon. Instead, we are examining whether or not such a canon is emerging and, if so, which topics and works are included. Whether or not this should be called a canon, having a foundational understanding of what works are regularly assigned in LGBTQ politics courses can help new faculty as they prepare syllabi and help more senior faculty assess the state of the discipline. LGBTQ topics arise across the political science curriculum, and more and more of our students are identifying as members of the LGBTQ community (see Rivera et al. 2022). It is imperative that we adapt to these things to ensure that political science remains relevant for all our students and adjusts to the realities of politics today. As we discuss below, we suggest two ways to teach political science in a more LGBTQ inclusive way: queering the existing political science canon and teaching dedicated LGBTQ politics courses.

We turn next to a discussion of the idea of a political science canon or canons generally.

The Political Science Canons—and Why They Matter

Defining a single political science canon may be impossible. The discipline of political science, historically, was most concerned with studying the state and government. Many political science scholars have moved away from that focus to studying politics more broadly (Grant 2011). Early political science scholarship was also concerned more with governance than with politics. Politics is more than just government; it focuses on power relationships in a variety of contexts. Shifting from a focus on governance to a focus on politics broadens areas of inquiry and can expand what is considered canon. Grant (2011, 90) gives the example of Marx. Lacking a theory of government, Marx was outside the political theory canon until the shift in focus made that work relevant to political science. As political science's focus expanded to include a broader analysis of power and society, Marx's work was seen as relevant and thus moved into the theory canon. Thus as the disciplinary focus shifts, more works become important and potentially canonical.

Political science, as a broad discipline with many subfields and even more specializations within those subfields, more accurately has multiple canons. Political theory, American politics, comparative politics, and international relations each have their own canonical works. And of course there is no single accepted way to divide the discipline into smaller subfields to determine how to outline those multiple canons (see Jensen and Moses 2021, 15). Even when there is agreement on the labels for a subfield, agreement on that subfield's canon is not assured. Within any subfield, individual assessment of the important foundational works may generate significant disagreement about what is properly canon and what is merely supplementary (Diament et al. 2017).

Examining the readings assigned in graduate level courses is one way to determine if a clear canon exists and what it contains. The readings assigned in graduate courses play an important role in shaping the discipline. The scholarship assigned in graduate political science courses signals to the students both what is important in terms of content and whose work is important in that area (Diament et al. 2017; Kammerer and Estrella-Luna 2020). Both of these messages are important in defining the future of the discipline.

Graduate seminars matter. As Diament and co-authors (2017, 257) note, "Faculty who teach these seminars thus occupy a uniquely influential gatekeeping position, able to perpetuate or challenge prevailing modes of thought in the field." This gatekeeping is part of how a canon gets defined, including both the topics and scholars that are central to the field. Unfortunately, the research analyzing what this canon is remains limited. One study, looking at the American politics subfield, did find "substantial agreement on what works make up" the foundations of that subfield. But that agreement was not universal. Significant variation also exists (Diament et al. 2017, 270). Research in other subfields will likely find similar patterns.

Another way to measure a field's canon is to look at citation counts. Works that are heavily cited clearly have some level of importance. Of course, how to determine which citations, from which journals, in which fields, is also a challenging question (Jensen and Moses 2021). But it is safe to assume that citations matter. More citations, generally, means more influence and more importance. Of course, not all citations are equal. Future scholars demonstrating a previous work's faults may increase the citation count, particularly in the short term. But over time, works that continue to be cited and engaged with are, by definition, important—even if the meaning of that importance may be unclear.

Sigelman (2006), in honor of the *American Political Science Review*'s centennial, examined the frequency of citations to high-impact articles published in the *APSR* (those with more than one hundred citations). Sigelman notes that while most articles go uncited and/or forgotten, even those by "illustrious political scientists" of the past, some are more widely cited and remain relevant (667). Sigelman provides a list of the twenty articles in the journal's history with the highest citation counts. These could form the basis for a canon, or part of one. But interestingly, Diament et al. (2017) find that none of the top twenty articles from *APSR* are present on the core American politics graduate syllabi they reviewed, despite the fact that articles from the *APSR* are assigned more than any other journal. This shows a disconnect between the work cited and the work assigned in the American politics subfield that may warrant further exploration. Which measure better marks the bounds of a canon, if either does, remains unclear.

It is also important to think critically about whose voices continue to be excluded from whatever political science canon may exist. Diament et al. (2017), building on their earlier study of American politics seminars, examined gender representation in the core courses. Unsurprisingly, they find limited representation of women authors on core graduate syllabi. Only 18 percent of the works in their data include a female author; only 11 percent have women listed as first author. More troubling is that they found women authors tended to be concentrated in a small number of topics, like identity politics and gender. Hutchings and Owens (2021), looking at the international relations canon, find clear evidence of women's exclusion, despite their ideas meeting the traditional criteria of influence and importance. Jensen and Moses (2021, 29) also found women to be overlooked in political science broadly. These authors used citation counts in top political science journals as a metric for influence; only two of the top twenty-three cited authors in their data were women.

Political science is not alone in failing to recognize women's contributions. Other disciplines have also wrestled with their historic marginalization of women (e.g., Berges 2015; Maddrell 2015). Scholars of color across academia similarly remain marginalized. Looking specifically at political theory, Omar (2016, 154) notes the eurocentrism that permeates the field because of the emphasis on the classic Western canon. This demonstrates, Omar argues, a need for decolonization of the existing canon. Yet efforts to rectify these historic exclusions are often met with fierce resistance.

Beyond privileging certain voices and perspectives, canons also determine the questions a discipline deems to be important for study. Political science is no different. Research on issues central to women, people of color, and other minoritized communities has often been ignored. When this research is done, it is often done in such a way to avoid challenges to the canon. Caiazza (1997) noted that when political science included research on sex and gender, for example, it did it in such a way as to avoid disturbing mainstream political science—to avoid undermining the canon. Research on these communities is often relegated to specialized journals because it is deemed too niche for the flagship journals. This belief is predicated on the assumption that other research (involving issues central to white men) is more important, with broad appeal and greater generalizability. Thus, the canon resists redefinition and the marginalization of ideas and of scholars continues.

LGBTQ Politics in the Political Science Canon?

There are two ways to think about the possibility of LGBTQ political science work being part of the canon. One is to queer the existing canon by infusing existing bodies of political science literature with critical LGBTQ perspectives. The other is to define a distinct LGBTQ canon. In this section, we examine the advantages, disadvantages, and challenges inherent in both approaches. We then explore preliminary findings from an original survey to assess a potential LGBTQ political science canon.

Incorporating LGBTQ topics in the general political science canon may prove difficult. Political science, as a field, has historically been hostile to, or at best uninterested in, LGBTQ-focused research (Smith and Lee 2015). This is particularly true when that research is conducted by LGBTQ scholars (Novkov and Barclay 2010). These challenges persist, despite significant progress having been made (Ayoub 2022). Scholars still have difficulty trying to publish LGBTQ political work in top journals, although that trend may be changing (Tadlock and Taylor 2017). Conference panels provide another avenue for sharing research, but Ayoub (2022) notes that even when LGBTQ research is included in conferences, it tends to be siloed in LGBTQ-themed panels rather than integrated with similar research on non-LGBTQ topics. A paper on LGBTQ legal advocacy could be included on a law and courts panel, for example, rather than one focused solely on LGBTQ activism. Presenting this research on a non-LGBTQ exclusive panel helps diversify the discipline and integrate new perspectives by exposing the research to a wider audience. Unfortunately, this work tends to remain siloed, sending a signal that LGBTQ political science is a niche field, with limited interest or relevance to the broader work of political science. This, however, could not be further from the truth (Ayoub 2022).

Research on LGBTQ topics helps illuminate many of the questions central to political science, across all its subfields. The chapters in part 2 of this volume illustrate just some of the myriad ways the study of LGBTQ politics achieves this. Opening the mainstream political science canon in this way, like the way the literary canon has been broadened to include once marginalized perspectives, is a good plan. But the resistance to this will likely be strong—as it was during the canon wars in literary studies.

The other way of thinking about an LGBTQ political science canon sees LGBTQ politics as its own area of specialization. Thus, LGBTQ politics has its own core canon, largely distinct from other areas of political science. By viewing LGBTQ politics as a distinct specialization, concerns about siloed panels and specialized courses become less important. That is, as an area of research unto itself, LGBTQ politics *should* have its own panels at conferences and courses focused entirely on LGBTQ issues.

These features of a specialization are easy to achieve in large part because they already exist, at least in some academic departments and professional organizations. However, LGBTQ politics does lack a dedicated journal in which to publish its scholarship. This is harder to achieve but may be a worthwhile goal to pursue in light of the continuing struggle to have LGBTQ research accepted at highly ranked, more "generalist" journals. While some journals, like *Politics, Groups, and Identities*, are very welcoming of LGBTQ scholarship, the lack of a dedicated journal raises questions about LGBTQ politics' status as a specialized subfield.

Considering LGBTQ politics as its own specialization also raises new challenges. The boundaries of what is considered an LGBTQ political issue or subject is contested, shifting over time and across different research studies. Schulenberg (2013, 455) explains the boundaries of the term "homosexual," showing that it remains essentially contested; researchers rely on different definitions and categories depending on the focus of the research. Some focus on identity, some on actions and behaviors, others incorporate culture.

Queer is an even more complicated term (Berlant et al. 1994). For some, it is an umbrella term referring broadly to the LGBTQ community and, by extension, excluding cisgender heterosexuals. Some view it differently, including all non-normative sexual practices, like BDSM, even if engaged in by otherwise heterosexual couples. For others, queer carries a political, generally leftist, connotation. Still others see queer as inherently resisting categorical definition. What identities, individuals, cultures, and behaviors are relevant to an LGBTQ politics canon remains hard to define.

Smith (2011) notes the lack of nuance in how political science tends to study sexuality. He writes, "Political science frames the world as straight or gay, heterosexual or not, a 1 or a 0, and the nuance of sexuality is essentially lost in the analysis of the predominantly hetero-normative lens through which research is projected to the world" (35). Capturing that nuance is necessary but difficult. For LGBTQ politics (or queer politics) to develop as a discipline with boundaries and potentially a canon, attention to these definitional issues is essential.

After addressing definitional concerns, other challenges emerge. LGBTQ political issues span subfields and specializations, which makes defining any one LGBTQ politics canon challenging. For example, important queer theory work, while certainly relevant, may be perceived as secondary to American politics work focused on political mobilization and legal change. The reverse may also be true: Empirical research on LGBTQ voting behavior in American elections may not be perceived as central to many queer theory projects. Comparative politics and international relations also raise their own specific queer concerns that may be distinct from those asked in other areas of research. While these issues are all important, how they relate to each other and their relative importance in a specific LGBTQ politics specialization is difficult to determine.

Is it possible, or even desirable, then, to speak of a single LGBTQ politics canon? If not, how do we navigate a world of multiple, distinct queer canons? Is LGBTQ politics inherently resistant to the concept of a canon? Having acknowledged these questions as challenges, we also acknowledge the importance of a foundational canon. For LGBTQ political science to be seen as a distinct field of study, an agreed upon, foundational series of readings or topics is important. Without a canon, defining "LGBTQ politics" as a truly distinct area of research animated by its own distinct questions seems improbable.

We do not want to imply that these two approaches, queering the existing canon and creating a distinct LGBTQ canon, are mutually exclusive approaches to studying LGBTQ politics. Both are possible. Creating a distinct LGBTQ politics specialization does not negate the need to add LGBTQ-focused scholarship into the core canons of political science's existing subfields. Both of these approaches are important, and likely should be done in tandem. But before any LGBTQ canon can exist in either form, there must be agreement among scholars as to which works constitute what might become that canon. This is the question to which we turn in the next section.

Toward a Canon of LGBTQ Political Science Scholarship?

In this section, we explore the results of a survey of faculty who teach LGBTQ politics to determine which authors and concepts are regularly assigned. This, we think, can serve as a preliminary foundation from which a specialization may be emerging with its own canon. This research can also provide suggestions for queering the existing canon across the discipline of political science by highlighting LGBTQ works that address concerns relevant to other subfields in the discipline. We first explain the data collection and analysis before discussing the findings.

METHODS

In 2021, we fielded a survey[1] asking respondents several questions about teaching LGBTQ politics, both as a stand-alone course and through incorporating LGBTQ concepts into other courses in the political science curriculum. To explore whether an LGBTQ canon exists, we asked respondents two distinct questions. First, we asked what topics or issues are most important to include in LGBTQ politics courses. This, we believe, sheds light on the role of a canon in determining what ideas or questions are most relevant to a discipline. For this question, we provided a selection of possible topics, but also left open-ended response options to allow respondents to add their own topics. Second, we asked respondents to list up to five specific works that are essential to include when creating an LGBTQ politics course. This gets at the core readings that could function as the basis of a canon. This question was open-ended, without any suggestions provided to respondents. We also requested, if respondents wanted, that they share their syllabi with us. Only a few respondents emailed syllabi to be included in the analysis.

We distributed our survey via both the American Political Science Association's LGBTQ Caucus and the Sexuality & Politics section email lists. The LGBTQ Caucus is a group for LGBTQ political scientists, regardless of field of study; the Sexuality & Politics section is for anyone who studies sexuality, regardless of their own orientation or gender identity (Newton et al. 2022). We also posted the survey links on Twitter (which were reposted by both the Sexuality & Politics and the LGBTQ Caucus accounts) and to the LGBTQ Caucus's Facebook page. This allowed us to reach faculty who teach and research in LGBTQ politics at a variety of institutions. Survey responses were collected via Qualtrics. We acknowledge that our sample is not representative of the full breadth of LGBTQ politics scholars, despite our best efforts to recruit a diverse pool of respondents. Thus, our findings should be viewed as preliminary. We hope, with this initial survey, to begin a conversation about the possibility of an LGBTQ canon existing or being formed.

Respondent Demographics

We received fifty-nine complete responses to the survey. Respondents were diverse in gender (twenty-eight male, twenty female, nine nonbinary, one genderqueer, one non-response). Some respondents identified as transgender (n = 6), but most did not (n = 52). Most respondents identified as gay, lesbian, or bisexual (n = 43). While eleven respondents identified as straight, additional potential responses included queer and asexual.

Respondents were nearly all white, with only four respondents indicating a race other than white. This limits the conclusions we can draw from this survey, particularly since questions of canon already tend to skew toward white voices. We did attempt to address this by actively soliciting additional responses from scholars of color through targeted outreach. Unfortunately, we did not receive many responses to our targeted outreach. Thus, the sample remains skewed. As noted below, however, even with this sample, respondents emphasized the importance of including works centering more marginalized communities.

Respondents came from a variety of institutional types and different professional ranks. The majority of respondents work or study at public research universities, with twenty-four coming from Carnegie classification R1s and another eight from R2s. The remaining responses included private liberal arts colleges, private research institutions, and public teaching-focused colleges. Respondents came from all academic ranks, with a plurality of assistant professors (n = 18), followed by associate professors (n = 14), and graduate students (n = 12). Fewer respondents were full professors, lecturers, postdocs, or adjuncts. Most faculty respondents were either tenured (n = 20) or tenure track (n = 16). Some held non–tenure track positions (either visiting or permanent). The fact that the majority of respondents are earlier in their careers may reflect both the relative newness of LGBTQ politics as a field of study and the method of survey distribution.

We also asked respondents whether they had taken an LGBTQ politics course during their educational career. The overwhelming majority of respondents (n = 44) had not. Of the respondents who had taken an LGBTQ politics course, less than one-third (n = 11) took a course in graduate school and a smaller proportion (n = 9) took a course as an undergraduate. Some respondents did report taking courses at both levels. This is unsurprising. Few universities have faculty specializing in LGBTQ politics to offer such a course. For faculty who do offer LGBTQ politics courses, the lack of specialized training presents challenges, especially when faculty design their syllabi. While it is not necessary for teaching an LGBTQ politics course, having a clear canon to draw from can alleviate some of these challenges.

FINDINGS

We first asked respondents what topics they think are most important to cover in LGBTQ politics courses. Respondents were asked to limit their choices to the five topics they felt were most important. The survey included a list of suggested topics and space to add up to five additional topics. The list of suggested topics and open-ended responses are presented in table 1.1, with the frequency counts for each option.

Table 1.1. Topics to Include in an LGBTQ Politics Course

Suggested Topics	Frequency
Transgender issues	38
Race and racism in the LGBT movement	25
Assimilation vs. liberation	20
LGBT political participation (voting behavior, lobbying)	20
Anti-LGBT movements	19
Movement organizations (Mattachine, GLF, HRC, ACT UP)	19
Nondiscrimination law	13
LGBT political representation (elected officials, movement leaders)	13
Marriage equality and family	12
HIV/AIDS	11
Religious liberty	6
LGBT people in the criminal justice system	5
Healthcare	5
Sodomy laws	5
Other legal issues (free speech, freedom of association)	4
Hate crimes laws	1
Military service	0
Other (see Below)	

continued on next page

Table 1.1. Continued.

Open-Ended Responses Supplied by Respondents	Frequency
LGBTQ movements and relationships with other liberation frameworks	3
Legal rights across different states	1
Non-Western concepts of sexuality and gender	1
Identity politics (bisexual erasure/lesbian feminist politics)	1
Immigration	1
International sexual politics	1
LGBT history	1
Spatial politics (gayborhoods, zoning)	1
Mobilization/counter-mobilization	1
Queer mobilizations in Africa	1
Religion (other than religious liberty)	1

In table 1.1, we can see some broad areas of agreement. Transgender issues, race/racism within the LGBTQ movement, and LGBTQ political behavior received strong support for inclusion. Healthcare, military service, hate crimes, and sodomy laws all received weak support. In the middle, topics like nondiscrimination law, movement organizations (and counter movements), marriage equality, and the debate between assimilation and liberation strategies received noticeable support.

We also asked respondents to rank the choices they selected in terms of importance. Not all respondents who named a topic ranked its importance in the same way. For example, transgender issues were named by the most respondents (n = 33). Of that group, more than one-third (36 percent) said the topic was the most important topic to cover (ranked either 1 or 2). Fewer respondents named race/racism within the LGBTQ movement as an important topic to cover (n = 20). However, of the respondents who named the topic, two in five (40 percent) said it was the most important topic to cover (ranked either 1 or 2). A larger proportion of those who named nondiscrimination law (n = 18) also said it was the most important topic to cover (61 percent). Taken together, the results suggest that although more respondents view transgender issues and race/racism as topics that should be covered in LGBTQ politics courses, not all respondents lend the same weight to these topics in their courses.

In addition to asking questions on general topics, we asked respondents to indicate up to five specific works that they felt were essential to include in LGBTQ politics courses. Respondents, generally, provided specific information about individual works that we could identify and code. Both of the co-authors reviewed each response submitted and coded the work for its main topics. Where there was disagreement, the coders discussed the work to come to consensus; thus both authors agreed on the final coding for all the works included. We also noted when the suggested books were edited volumes, particularly when the chapters included span a wide range of topics, like with *LGBTQ Politics: A Critical Reader* (Brettschneider et al. 2017).

Eleven books were edited volumes or readers. Some respondents suggested authors, rather than specific works. In these examples, we coded the authors based on their primary area of research. Some works were coded with more than one subcode. This happened when works spanned coding categories. For example, a work on ACT UP would be coded both as being about AIDS and social movements. A work on legal activism would be coded as both law and social movements. This expands the total number of possible topic codes beyond the number of works provided. We think this best reflects the ways that different faculty may use a single work to emphasize different concepts. A single book or article may fit many different approaches to teaching LGBTQ politics.

In terms of individual works, we saw far less agreement here than in the broad topics in the previous section. Of the nearly one hundred different works suggested, only a small number (n = 12) appeared more than once, with even fewer appearing more than twice. This may indicate that individual canonical works have not yet emerged for LGBTQ politics as a subfield. The works that did get included more than once focused on transgender issues, law and social movements, and queer theory. This aligns with the topics suggested in the previous section, where transgender issues was the most frequent topic suggested. Only one work listed more than once specifically focused on international relations/comparative politics. Table 1.2 lists the works that were mentioned more than once.

Looking at all of the individual works suggested, we see that they align somewhat, but not exactly, with the topics suggested for inclusion

Table 1.2. LGBTQ Works Referenced Multiple Times

Title	Author
Out of the Closets, Into the Courts	Andersen, Ellen
When States Come Out	Ayoub, Philip
LGBTQ Politics: A Critical Reader	Brettschneider et al.
Gender Trouble	Butler, Judith
The Straight State	Canaday, Margot
Punks, Bulldaggers, and Welfare Queens	Cohen, Cathy
Beyond Trans: Does Gender Matter	Davis, Heath Fogg
History of Sexuality	Foucault, Michel
Normal Life	Spade, Dean
Transgender History	Stryker, Susan
The Remarkable Rise of Transgender Rights	Taylor, Jami K. et al.
Case law	Supreme Court

in LGBTQ politics courses. The most frequent single topic code is "social movements." Works addressing transgender issues or gender issues more broadly are also among the most frequently suggested. Law and civil rights also appear near the top of the frequency list. These topics were also suggested as among the most important for inclusion, so it makes sense that works addressing these topics would also be frequently included. But works focused on queer theory, public policy/administration, and history are also frequently suggested as among the most important to include. These topics were, however, not among the most important topics suggested. Similarly, topics that were suggested as important, like race and marriage, did not appear as frequently on the list of individual works. Table 1.3 presents the topic codes that appeared most frequently.

Discussion: Is There a Queer Canon?

There are broad thematic areas of agreement among the responses for what constitutes important content in an LGBTQ politics course. Queer theory, transgender issues, social movements, public policy, and law are all widely reported as important topics to include. Other topics, like marriage, were

Table 1.3. Highest Frequency Topic Codes on Individual Works

Topic Code	Frequency
Social movements	27
Theory	24
History	18
Policy/admin.	18
Queer theory	16
Comparative/IR	15
Transgender	15
Law	14
Civil rights	12
Gender/feminism	12
Sex/sexuality	11

less important. Marriage being less important may change given Justice Thomas's call to reconsider *Obergefell v. Hodges* and the new wave of anti-LGBTQ policies spreading across the United States.

There is less agreement on specific works. As noted above, only a handful of individual works came up multiple times in the survey responses. This does not mean that other works do not appear widely on syllabi. Since we asked about the most important works, not an exhaustive list of works, other works perceived as less important may still be foundational enough to appear on multiple course syllabi. Future research should investigate how well syllabi, as actually designed and used, align with faculty perceptions of important works.

Importantly, what agreement we find takes into account the need to center intersectionally marginalized experiences. That is, this majority white, cisgender sample indicated that topics related to gender and race are among the most important to include in courses on LGBTQ politics. This reflects the lesson from queer theory that there is value in learning from the intersections of marginalization because understanding how politics works for those at the margins and intersections defines how it works for everyone else.

This agreement, of course, could stem from the current salience of topics confronting these communities. We fielded our survey during a time when conservative states largely began enacting laws targeting trans youth in school sports and gender-affirming healthcare. Trans issues are central to LGBTQ politics and should always have been so. But that centrality is particularly heightened at the current moment and potentially played a role in how respondents thought about structuring LGBTQ politics courses. This could also show the potential for LGBTQ politics courses to adapt as new issues rise on the political and policy agendas.

Our results also show the diversity of subfields and approaches in which LGBTQ political scholars already operate and the efforts underway to incorporate LGBTQ scholarship into those subfields. LGBTQ issues span the political science discipline and, as such, are incorporated across curricula. This diversity also highlights the reality that there is no one single way to teach LGBTQ politics. Approaches vary. This gives faculty incredible flexibility. It does, however, mean that there is not yet a singular LGBTQ politics canon.

For faculty new to teaching LGBTQ politics, this lack of a clear canon may pose challenges as they design courses. But the topics highlighted by our respondents and the works they suggested can help new and continuing faculty construct LGBTQ politics courses. Even though a single canon has not yet formed, there is agreement on broad directions for LGBTQ politics. Faculty, then, have both a point from which to start and the freedom to choose where they go. We hope that this study, and the other chapters in this volume, will provide faculty with guidance as they design LGBTQ politics courses and bring LGBTQ-relevant issues into the broader curriculum.

Note

1. The survey was approved by Idaho State University Human Subjects Committee, Study Number IRB-FY2021-79.

References

Adler, Libby. 2018. *Gay Priori*. Duke University Press.

Ayoub, Phillip M. 2022. "Not That Niche: Making Room for the Study of LGBTIQ People in Political Science." *European Journal of Politics and Gender* 5 (2): 154–72.

Berges, Sandrine. 2015. "On the Outskirts of the Canon: The Myth of the Lone Female Philosopher, and What to Do About It." *Metaphilosophy* 46 (3): 380–97.

Berlant, Lauren, Michael Warner, Eric Clarke, et al. 1994. "FORUM: On the Political Implications of Using the Term 'Queer,' as in 'Queer Politics,' 'Queer Studies,' and 'Queer Pedagogy.'" *The Radical Teacher* 45:52–57.

Boykin, Keith O. 2000. "Where Rhetoric Meets Reality: The Role of Black Lesbians and Gays in 'Queer' Politics." In *The Politics of Gay Rights*, edited by Craig A. Rimmerman, Kenneth D. Wald, and Clyde Wilcox. University of Chicago Press.

Brettschneider, Marla, Susan Burgess, and Christine Keating. 2017. *LGBTQ Politics: A Critical Reader*. New York University Press.

Caiazza, Amy B. 1997. "Inclusion and Exclusion: Feminism's Relationship with Political Science." *Southeast Political Review* 25 (4): 659–83.

Diament, Sean M., Adam J. Howat, and Matthew J. Lacombe. 2017. "What Is the 'Canon' in American Politics? Analyses of Core Graduate Syllabi." *Journal of Political Science Education* 13 (3): 256–78.

Diament, Sean M., Adam J. Howat, and Matthew J. Lacombe. 2018. "Gender Representation in the American Politics Canon: An Analysis of Core Graduate Syllabi." *PS: Political Science & Politics* 51 (3): 635–40.

Dickins, Amanda. 2006. "The Evolution of International Political Economy." *International Affairs* 82 (3): 479–92.

Donadio, Rachel. 2007. "Revisiting the Canon Wars." *New York Times*, Sept. 16.

Grant, Judith. 2011. "Forget the *APSR*: The Politics of Political Science." *New Political Science* 33 (1): 87–91.

Hutchings, Kimberly, and Patricia Owens. 2021. "Women Thinkers and the Canon of International Thought: Recovery, Rejection, and Reconstitution." *American Political Science Review* 115 (2): 347–59.

Jensen, Magnus Rom, and Jonathon W. Moses. 2021. "The State of Political Science, 2020." *European Political Science* 20 (1): 14–33.

Kammerer, Edward F., and Neenah Estrella-Luna. 2020. "Law & Public Policy: A Gap Between Theory and Teaching?" *PS: Political Science & Politics* 53 (2): 292–97.

Maddrell, Avril. 2015. "To Read or Not to Read? The Politics of Overlooking Gender in the Geographical Canon." *Journal of Historical Geography* 49:31–38.

Newton, Monique, Brian Harrison, and Edward F. Kammerer Jr. 2022. "Political Science & LGBTQ Identity: Thoughts & Advice for Graduate Students." In *Strategies for Navigating Graduate School and Beyond*, edited by Kevin G. Lorentz II, Daniel J. Mallinson, Julia Marin Hellwege et al. American Political Science Association.

Novkov, Julie, and Scott Barclay. 2010 "Lesbians, Gays, Bisexuals, and the Transgendered in Political Science: Report on a Discipline-Wide Survey." *PS: Political Science & Politics* 43 (1): 95–106.

Omar, Ayesha. 2016. "Moving Beyond the Canon: Reflections of a Young African Scholar of Political Theory." *Arts and Humanities in Higher Education* 15 (1): 153–59.

Rivera, David P., Roberto L. Abreu, and Kirsten A. Gonzalez, eds. 2022. *Affirming LGBTQ+ Students in Higher Education*. American Psychological Association. https://doi.org/10.1037/0000281-000.

Rosenberg, Justin. 2016. "International Relations in the Prison of Political Science." *International Relations* 30 (2): 127–53.

Schulenberg, Shawn. 2013. "Essentially Contested Subjects: Some Ontological and Epistemological Considerations When Studying Homosexuals and Terrorists." *New Political Science* 35 (3): 449–62.

Sigelman, Lee. 2006. "The *American Political Science Review* Citation Classics." *American Political Science Review* 100 (4): 667–69.

Smith, Charles Anthony. 2011. "Gay, Straight, or Questioning? Sexuality and Political Science." *PS: Political Science & Politics* 44 (1): 35–38.

Smith, Nicola J., and Donna Lee. 2015. "What's Queer About Political Science?" *British Journal of Politics and International Relations* 17 (1): 49–63.

Tadlock, Barry L., and Jami K. Taylor. 2017. "Where Has the Field Gone? An Investigation of LGBTQ Political Science Research." In Brettschneider et al., *LGBTQ Politics*.

Chapter 2

Centering Schools in LGBTQ Politics

RICHARD S. PRICE

I've been teaching LGBTQ politics for a decade now and I often struggled to balance historical context, which I love, with modern experience that students often gravitate toward. As my research drifted into the history of queer educational activism, I realized that I had overlooked an important governmental institution: the public schools. Public schools are powerful political actors. They exist, in part, to generate the next generation of citizens. Of course, this political enterprise requires choices as to what makes a good citizen, and straightness has long been a key component. Queerness was something to be expunged from the school environment because it posed an existential threat to the ideals of American citizenship that centered a (white) straight, cisnormative world. With roots back to the 1960s, queer educational activism slowly began to contest this straight school. Today there is no question that things have improved, especially in comparison to decades ago, but it is also fair to say that educational activism has resulted in fairly minimal accommodation within the still straight school. Much of the educational activism amounted to carving out relatively small spaces where queerness can exist in schools, but not too much of it. A teacher might be allowed to be out, but not too out. Queer kids are allowed to meet after school and wear buttons, but not learn any queer history or inclusive sex ed. A curriculum might toss references to Harvey Milk and Tammy Baldwin as "firsts" in elected offices, but not engage with the nature of gender and sexuality oppression in the American past and present. In this way, queer educational activism represents the struggles of the broader movement in achieving major societal changes in the US.

I realized that including the schools as a central part of LGBTQ activism had two major benefits. First, the battles of LGBTQ teachers and students to gain inclusion within these straight institutions allows us to explore dynamics of activism, institutional responses, and legal and political strategies in various times and institutional contexts. Second, our students bring personal experience with the school system and can relate to this material in a way that many may struggle with when it comes to other issues. Utilizing experiences of teachers, students, and in curriculum struggle, I illustrate some of the ways in which LGBTQ politics has challenged and altered the straight school. Sadly, I cannot do the complexity of these issues justice here but hope that this overview demonstrates how inclusion of schools in LGBTQ politics can be effective and engaging.

The Straight School

Margot Canaday (2009, 3) demonstrated the ways in which the federal government built a straight state through military, welfare, and immigration politics and how a "homosexual-heterosexual binary . . . was being inscribed in federal citizenship" at mid-century. Stephen Engel's (2016) framing of the lesbian and gay rights movement around the concept of citizenship builds upon this constructed binary. Rather than see citizenship as limited to bundle of rights, "the citizen is a person subject to the state's sight or recognition, identification, and classification." This shifts focus "away from the rights claimant and toward those institutions that constitute, exercise power over, and enable the citizen" (7). The question, thus, turns upon how the government sees subjects within its control and influence. Engel's theory is particularly apt for exploring the place of queer people within schools. It directs attention to the institutional treatment of queer people, to how the school sees its space and what identities have legitimate place within it. Canaday and Engel speak to the ways in which governing structures sought to construct citizenship in a way to exclude queerness.

Whereas Canaday points us to the federal government as a prime actor in embedding this binary into public policy, less well studied is the role of state and local government in maintaining and policing the sexual boundary. Anna Lvovsky (2021) explored the nature of law enforcement's regulation of queer existence and the varied ways that regulatory and criminal systems sought to enforce this binary. The public education system, however, is an often-overlooked governing structure, even though schools have long sought to replicate a straight citizenry. Catharine Lugg (2016, 5) noted that a foundational scholar in educational sociology wrote, in 1932, that "nothing is more certain than that homosexuality is contagious," and thus the school must purge all homosexuality from the school environment. Historically, this focused on teachers, mostly women, who were subjected to various formal and informal gender and sexual norms to ensure that they presented the appropriate (straight) image to students (Blount 2005). By eliminating queer teachers, the school sought to preserve its mission of producing straight students. After all, for much of the late twentieth century, "according to authoritative declarations by parents, teachers, preachers, psychiatrists, and courts, gay kids are not gay but merely 'confused'" (Ruskola 1996, 270). The idea of gay contagion would linger for many decades, with antigay activists frequently echoing the claim that "exposing children to homosexuality will turn them into homosexuals" (Rosky 2013, 608). An education dean in 1977 stated this openly: If we hire a gay teacher, a child will think that "if it's okay to hire a sex pervert to teach in a public institution and it it's okay to pay a sex pervert with tax money and if it's okay to put a sex pervert in charge of the educational destinies of schoolchildren, then it's just got to be okay to be a sex pervert," but this cannot be allowed "because the actual survival of our country in the years ahead will depend upon a generation that will grow up straight" (Rafferty 1977, 92). As Catherine Lugg (2016, 2) summarized it, "For nearly a hundred years, these opponents have argued that *all queer identity and information must be erased* within the public school's walls to protect innocent children—who are all presumed to be non-queer. Quite simply, queerness in the public school is viewed as contagious."

The public school system, thus, is an integral element of the straight state. Contesting this straight space has occurred in multiple dimensions and through different forms. In this chapter, I will outline some key disputes in three areas: teachers, students, and curriculum. Obviously, the engagement will be necessarily limited, but the goal is to illustrate some of the ways that exploring LGBTQ educational activism can enhance the study of LGBTQ politics. This, of course, is an ongoing struggle that is still resisted to this day in dramatic fashion.

Teachers

Jackie Blount (2005) examined the ways in which teaching has long been coded as a straight, female profession. In the early days of public education, the focus was on hiring "women teachers thought to be chaste and pure guardians of virtue" (15). This ensured proper modeling of behavior that was supplemented "with curricula overtly intended to shape young people into properly heterosexual women and men well-versed in middle-class courtship rituals" (16). Interestingly, this structure gave queer women greater flexibility as they often could live openly with another teacher, at times for years or decades, and be read as two single straight spinsters serving the public. Post–World War II public expectations began to shift with the rising discussion of the dangers of homosexuality and juvenile delinquency. Schools responded by "filling the ranks of educators with persons meeting culturally idealized representations of men and women" (78). One key to this change was that teachers were to be married to ensure proper modeling of good, straight citizens. Schools also actively purged any teacher from their ranks if even rumors of homosexuality reached administrators. At times this could be as simple as learning that a teacher was on a mailing list for gay periodicals (Johnson 2019, 118–19). In some places the campaigns were far more formal. For example, Florida's Johns Committee spent the late 1950s to mid-1960s investigating and entrapping gay and lesbian college faculty and public school teachers (Graves 2009).[1]

Against this background, it is unsurprising that gay and lesbian teachers hid themselves. Even if involved in the gay politics of the 1970s, they would try and build a wall between their personal and professional selves. The 1970s saw a number of high-profile lawsuits over gay and lesbian teachers being fired even though they were typically closeted at work. Peggy Burton was only a few months into her first teaching position in 1970 when her principal called her into his office to report that there were rumors of her being a lesbian. When she admitted that she was, an emergency school board meeting terminated her "based on her admitting to be a homosexual." This language was later altered to "Peggy Burton be dismissed . . . because of her immorality of being a practicing homosexual" to bring the dismissal in line with Oregon law that allowed teacher dismissal for immorality (Harbeck 1997, 229–33, 246). Joe Acanfora[2] was fired from his Maryland junior high school in 1972. Acanfora had just graduated from Penn State, where he was active in organizing the Homophiles of Penn State student group, which had to sue to force recognition at the university. Because of this litigation, Acanfora was described in the press as gay, and his student teaching positioned was threatened—he retained it through another lawsuit—and the teacher evaluation committee of the university refused to certify him as morally upstanding for Pennsylvania teacher credentials. Ultimately, Acanfora went to Maryland and obtained a job but lost it when national news covered the final decision to issue him credentials in Pennsylvania. It was this coverage that outed him, and Acanfora was dismissed. James Gaylord[3] was not out at the school where he was employed in Tacoma, Washington, but was approached by a student who said he was struggling with his sexuality. Although Gaylord did not confirm his sexuality, the student took it as a given and later told a principal. Gaylord was terminated in 1972.

Curriculum Connection 1

I like to utilize this teacher material when I discuss the battle to overturn sodomy laws leading up to *Bowers v. Hardwick* (1986). While sodomy laws had increasingly receded from criminal enforcement, at least as it applied to sex in private between consenting adults, such laws were often invoked in other ways. One was to justify the firing of public employees, such as teachers.

The courts were largely unreceptive to claims of employment discrimination. Though it issued some language supportive of Acanfora, the district court ultimately concluded that "to some extent every teacher has to go out of his way to hide his private life, and that a homosexual teacher is not at liberty to ignore or hold in contempt the sensitivity of the subject to the school community."[4] While Acanfora denied mentioning his sexuality at all in school, his being out and public in his private life was a legitimate subject of regulation. Similarly, the Washington Supreme Court rejected Gaylord's lawsuit, declaring that his "homosexual conduct must be considered in the context of his position of teaching high school students. Such students could treat the retention of the . . . teacher by the school board as indicating adult approval of his homosexuality."[5] In both cases, the justification was that a publicly gay teacher was seen as a danger to the future of the straight students the schools were trying to produce. Burton did win a declaration that the statute was unconstitutionally vague and she was granted back pay, but the courts refused to order her reinstated.[6] In these early days, only California provided some degree of legal protection, as the California Supreme Court, in a 4–3 decision, held that simply being gay was not sufficient to show unfitness without evidence of some other conduct.[7]

Trans teachers were far less visible in this early wave, but the few examples show a similar trend of exclusion with little recourse. The most famous example is Steven Dain, who took leave to transition in 1977 and intended to seek a new teaching position where he would be able to present as himself without the baggage of old memories. His superintendent, however, encouraged him to return to his existing district because he was a great teacher.[8] Unfortunately for Dain, a new superintendent took office and the public uproar over his transition proved intense. The school board fired him initially for immorality, but after an adverse court decision it altered the grounds to his supposed misuse of sick leave for this medical transition. Ultimately, Dain never taught again. As Blount (2005, 119) noted, "These teachers violated their gender roles" in the eyes of their school districts and "they could damage the psychological well-being of their students." Importantly, trans teachers were left to their own devices in these fights as mainstream lesbian and gay rights groups generally ignored trans teachers.

Some local governments passed civil rights protections covering sexual orientation in the 1970s, triggering fierce counter-mobilization. Most famously, Anita Bryant led a campaign against Miami-Dade's 1977 civil rights expansion, complaining that the law "discriminat[ed] against my children's right to grow up in a healthy, decent community that we're proud to be a part of" (Bryant 1977, 16). These homophobic campaigns highlighted gay teachers as a particular danger. Bryant, for example, explained that she was troubled by two aspects of gay teachers: "First, public approval of admitted homosexual teachers could encourage more homosexuality by inducing pupils into looking upon it as an acceptable life-style. And second, a particularly deviant-minded teacher could sexually molest children" (114). She thus built upon the long-standing myth of the gay male sexual predator but also warned that even a non-predatory gay teacher was a danger because they could serve as a role model to children who had to be straight only. The presence of gay teachers thus undermined the entire purpose of the straight school. In Eugene, Oregon, a group inspired by Bryant warned that the gay agenda in education was to have gay guidance counselors, students encouraged to explore "alternative lifestyles," textbooks ceasing to ignore homosexuality or referring to it as a mental illness, homosexual books and studies programs, and homosexual student clubs. Thus, they warned parents that "your children will be more exposed to the homosexual lifestyle in school" if the ordinance was allowed to stand (Gay Writer's Group 1983, 89–90). Bryant's campaign, and

Christian right campaigns inspired by her, won a series of quick victories overturning civil rights ordinances in Miami-Dade, Eugene, Wichita, and St. Paul. Gay teachers always played a role in these campaigns, but it was nothing compared to the Briggs Initiative.

California State Senator John Briggs latched onto the issue of gay teachers as a way to strengthen his campaign for governor. He announced his measure in San Francisco, describing the city as being "in a captured nation status and wanting to be liberated" from the homosexual hordes (Blount 2005, 135). The Briggs Initiative, on the 1978 ballot as Proposition 6, would negate the legal protections of gay teachers who engaged in public homosexual activity, an act of non-private sex that became known, or "public homosexual conduct," which included "the advocating, soliciting, imposing, encouraging or promoting of private or public homosexual activity directed at, or likely to come to the attention of, schoolchildren and/or other employees." This last item forbade hiring not only out employees but also any straight allies who dared to support gay rights. In the early days of the campaign, Briggs seemed destined to win easily, but a strong anti-Briggs organization built across the state ultimately defeated the initiative. As Smith-Silverman (2020, 93) discussed, teacher unions were key to the campaign; this was not only about their own jobs, but gay teachers "knew that this would have devastating consequences for their students, many of whom were struggling to come to terms with their sexual orientation in a hostile world." Thanks to a broad coalition, Briggs failed by a wide margin, but the legal position of gay and lesbian teachers was still tenuous.[9]

Curriculum Connection 2

I like to utilize the Byrant and Briggs campaigns as a type of reoccurring motif in queer politics. The idea of the dangerous gay predator had long been deployed in American life. The 1961 *Boys Beware* educational film presented this in stark terms. Briggs and Byrant reinvigorated this trope, which was then expanded in the 1980s and 1990s to include claims that the gay movement harbors pedophiles through the occasional presence of the North American Man/Boy Love Association (NAMBLA) in gay spaces, mostly classified ads in gay and lesbian newspapers. In the 2020s antigay push, this was raised in a slightly different way. Now the assault is less directly aimed at LGBTQ teachers themselves but instead the claim that any discussion of sexuality or gender is "grooming" and "sexualizing" kids. As the conclusion notes, this represents many of the themes of this chapter coming back into play.

Despite this backlash, some gay teachers and straight allies organized in the 1970s and 1980s. In San Francisco, Tom Ammiano came out in 1975 at a press conference and organized gay teachers and friends to put pressure on the district. He recalled only having eight people turn out for the first meeting (Ammiano 2020, 38). They organized a speakers bureau because, as they said, "we thought it was important for students to see us" (52). In one of the group's flyers they stressed the need to provide accurate information, share their personal experiences, and undermine stereotypes because there was "very little responsible and meaningful dialog" about homosexuality.[10] In 1972, Warren Blumenfeld organized a speakers bureau in Boston for colleges before later expanding it to high schools. Lane (2019, 85) concluded that Blumenfeld's bureau was designed to "present a relatively conservative, mainstream image of homosexuality for students' consumption." Or as Blumenfeld described it, "We couldn't send drag queens or 'Dykes on Bikes' to a high school" (Lane 2019, 85). These programs were certainly not without controversy despite being designed to be as "mainstream" as possible, but this was the first time openly gay people spoke in these schools.

Gay teachers organized in some major cities, such as Los Angeles, San Francisco, and New York City, where the legal protections were stronger. These groups seemed to share many functions. Importantly, regular socials were held that surely offered support and networking for teachers who were marginalized in their work spaces, to say nothing of their personal lives. But gay teachers also spent significant time trying to strengthen their unions' position on gay rights and nondiscrimination; ultimately, unions would be instrumental in both the defeat of Briggs and the support of teachers in the decades going forward (Smith-Silverman 2020). Many of these teachers were the first to push for school reforms to improve the environment for queer students as well. There was certainly little doubt that schools were hostile spaces, as most teachers, school workers, or prospective teachers generally tended to hold mild to drastic homophobic views. (See Sears 1992 for a summary of this research.)

While there is no doubt that queer teachers in the new millennium were in a far better position than their predecessors, the evidence suggests that they are still in a precarious position made more difficult by issues of race and job security. Catherine Connell's (2015, 3–4) study of lesbian and gay teachers in Texas and California in 2008 found significant tension, driven in part "by a fundamental incompatibility between the demands of contemporary LGBT politics, which center on the ethos of gay pride, and the norms of teaching professionalism, which expect teachers (gay and lesbian teachers in particular) to be cautious and self-disciplining about their personal—and sexual—lives." Connell (2015) found that teachers tended to fall into one of three categories: Some sought to split their sexual/personal identity and isolate it from the school environment; others sought to knit the identities together by being out in class; and a third group simply could not handle navigating the tension and quit teaching (58–93). Interestingly, she found that many of the teachers interviewed were hesitant even when they had legal protections in their district, and some were ignorant of the protections that they did have (105–11). Coming out was often described as important not only to the teacher but also to the students: "I did it for the kids. When I see what they go through, I had to come out" (132). Being out still came with limits, however. Connell concluded that as marriage and family issues dominated gay rights discourse, "gays and lesbians are increasingly expected to look and act the same as their straight counterparts and even to have the same desires" (134). Teachers were, thus, still constrained by conventional norms, or as one teacher put it, "It's up to the gay or lesbian teacher to act like a person, and not have bizarre or flamboyant character" (141).

Unfortunately, few studies of trans teachers exist, especially in any broad representative manner. In 2018, NPR surveyed seventy-nine trans and gender nonconforming teachers in the US and Canada (Kamenetz 2018). While the sample was skewed younger and to new teachers, with thirteen in New York City alone, the findings are largely unsurprising, with 20 percent reporting verbal harassment typically from administration and other faculty, 17 percent being asked to change their gender presentation in some way, and two who were fired. More than half reported trying to introduce LGBTQ topics into their curriculum and an unspecified number mentioned working with LGBTQ student groups. This limited data indicated that trans people face some challenges that overlap with lesbian and gay teachers who Connell focused on, but additional research is sorely needed.

Connell's findings suggest teachers respond to a broad set of factors before coming out in school. The 1970s experience certainly served as a cautionary tale, but a major element of gay rights organizations over the next decades was the adoption of nondiscrimination laws covering sexual orientation and, at times, gender identity. In some sense this should provide stronger legal protections but the actual experience is unclear because, as Connell discovered, many are rightfully skeptical that such job protections are meaningful given the barriers to legal recourse and the imbalance of resources between a teacher and school district. Stuart Biegel (2018) explored the mixed outcomes LGBTQ teachers faced when trying to deploy various constitutional claims to protect their positions (79–108). The high-water mark of legal protection is *Bostock v. Clayton County* (2020), where the Supreme Court found that Title VII of the Civil Rights Act of 1964 protected against discrimination in employment on the grounds of gender identity and sexual orientation.[11] One lesbian teacher in Texas was able to use a *Bostock*-type argument against her school when she was asked to resign, got suspended, and then was reassigned for showing a picture and of her and her fiancé to elementary students; she won a significant settlement shortly before *Bostock* was decided (Aviles 2020). Of course, the meaning of this rule will depend significantly on its application in future cases by a federal judiciary deeply altered by President Trump's tenure in office.

Curriculum Connection 3

Connell's (2015) findings that teachers were often unaware of legal protections and indifferent to their existence is a good opportunity to explore the limits of nondiscrimination law. The teachers displayed an impressive understanding of these limits, noting in their own comments that such policies meant little in practice and that an administration that wanted to get rid of a teacher would find a way around the policy.

Students

The enforced invisibility of queer students makes their history hard to track. There is little doubt that being gay, whether actually being out or just being perceived as gay, led to a difficult experience in schools. GLSEN, an activist group that emerged out of the 1990s as the leading LGBTQ education voice, only began its survey in 2001 and found a widespread frequency of verbal abuse from staff and students, as well as less frequent physical violence. Earlier studies reached similar conclusions. For example, Kathleen Malinsky (1997, 39) interviewed twenty-seven out queer teen girls and young women about high school experience in the mid-1990s, and only two reported no firsthand harassment. In 1992, the Massachusetts Governor's Commission on Gay and Lesbian Youth held hearings throughout the state and took testimony from students. The resulting report detailed high levels of verbal harassment and physical assaults that drove a mental health crisis among gay youth.[12]

Queer youth received little institutional or movement support until the 1980s and 1990s. As seen in the discussion of teachers, decades of public discourse had centered on gay adults as a danger to youth, so it is unsurprising that the early gay rights organizations steered away from too much engagement. And within schools, queer students were treated as nonexistent, and thus any problems they faced were similarly invisible. Stephen Lane (2019, 78) recounts one Massachusetts teacher's story of lobbying for school support in the late 1980s, and a board member opined that "to his knowledge, homosexual students were not a problem at the school." The teacher, however, knew that the board member's son was gay. As straight spaces, schools simply could not easily accept the idea that queer kids existed. Breaking this barrier of invisibility was made possible, in significant part, by the teen suicide crisis of the 1980s. The Department of Health and Human Services (HHS) commissioned a major report on youth suicide that included the first significant governmental attention to gay and lesbian youth suicide. This inclusion, however, led to the HHS secretary effectively disowning the report and burying it (Lane 2019, 142–43).

Virginia Uribe created the first visible program for gay and lesbian youth in 1980s Los Angeles (Uribe and Harbeck 1992, 9–28). A science teacher at Fairfax High School, Uribe remembered the tipping point being the disappearance of a student from her classes. Upon investigating, she discovered that he had been kicked out of his home, at fourteen, for being gay and bounced between the foster system and the street. Uribe began to investigate the situation for gay youth in her school and was troubled by the discovery of similar stories, as well as student and faculty harassment of those students. She created Project 10—reflecting the idea from the Kinsey Reports that about 10 percent of the population was gay—in 1984 as a support program for queer kids that included counseling, social support, and educational efforts. Uribe described the mission as "not only to keep kids in the classroom, but to keep them alive and claiming their right to be who they are" (Lane 2019, 96). In 1988, the Los Angeles Unified School District supported Uribe bringing Project 10 to the whole district, marking the first broad institutional support to queer youth and sparking counter-mobilization from conservative Republicans in the legislature who threatened the school with budget cuts. Despite this public controversy, Project 10 expanded and became a model for similar programs that emerged in the late 1980s and early 1990s in the San Francisco Bay Area and Massachusetts.

Unfortunately, few students had access to such affirming school projects. Many faced mental and physical abuse every time they entered the school building. Some students turned to the law to fight back. Jamie Nabozny pioneered this strategy. For nearly five years, beginning when he was twelve, Nabozny faced an onslaught of abuse from fellow students, ranging from persistent verbal harassment to escalating physical harassment (which included a mock rape in a science class with dozens of students watching) to a beating that was so severe he required surgery to stop internal bleeding. When Nabozny's parents repeatedly sought assistance from school officials they were largely ignored, with warnings that if Jamie insisted on being openly gay, he could expect similar incidents to occur. One assistant principal even laughed at him for reporting incidents of verbal harassment as well as shoves and getting tripped in hallways (Ball 2011, 75). Nabozny eventually filed a lawsuit, arguing that his constitutional rights were violated by the school when it failed for years to protect his safety. After the court of appeals found the claim sufficient,[13] the school settled for just under a million dollars. Over the next decade, schools would pay out more than four million dollars to LGBTQ students in similar cases, and these are just the publicly known cases—there are an unknown number that may have been settled confidentially (Ball 2011, 96–97; Biegel 2018, 67–71 discusses two other prominent examples). Lawsuits are limited in achieving major institutional change, but this kind of constitutional tort action has been shown to alter institutional practices as administrators adapt to the changing environment (Epp 2009). Luckily, other actors also sought to alter school environments.

Queer students themselves hit on one key change to schools by seeking to create space within them. Out student activists turned to the creation of Gay Straight Alliances (GSAs).[14] Lane traced these developments to Massachusetts private schools in the late 1980s. For example, a lesbian student at Philips Andover Academy posted an announcement for a gay discussion group in February 1989 with the support of a straight teacher who decided it was easier to hold the meeting rather than ask permission (Lane 2019, 115, 117). Lane explored how this eventually grew into the model for GSAs that some other schools adopted. GSAs received a major boost when the 1993 Massachusetts Governor's Commission on Gay and Lesbian Youth Report endorsed them as one of the four items that schools should adopt to provide better support for struggling students. GSAs spread rapidly through Massachusetts and became a significant part of GLSEN and other educational activist groups. The most common justification for GSAs proved to be the evidence that queer students face higher risk of bullying, mental health struggles, and suicidal thoughts and actions (Lane 2019, 143).

Curriculum Connection 4

I often ask my students to guess what the likely "gay" club was in the days before students were out in large numbers. In my experience, they pretty much all go drama/theater. I find this to be an interesting discussion about stereotypes and finding space.

As the GSA model spread, however, and out students began challenging their invisibility, GSAs encountered greater resistance. When a lesbian student in Salt Lake City tried to organize a GSA in 1995, one method of dealing with the shock of queer students organizing was to simply ignore it and instead suggest the influence of outside groups, raising the specter of pedophilia. The senate president announced that this was not a gay and lesbian issue and that he had no problem with the right of gay people to live as they wanted "as long as they don't inflict that on others," suggesting that some outside group was really pushing the drive to organize (Semarad 1996). When students at two other high schools tried to start GSAs, an education department attorney opined that the "more fuss that is made, the more exciting it becomes for kids to tweak the administration and their parents. The fastest way to get kids to wear strange clothes is to tell them they can't" (Groutage 1996). Thus, the claim was that this was not genuine queer kids organizing and calling for change, but kids looking for another way to rebel. After the city board of education voted to ban all extracurricular clubs to avoid the reach of the Equal Access Act, one member announced that he did not "believe our young people should be placed in a position to deal with these kinds of issues" and that "this is a moral issue" (Autman 1996), presenting a mindset that fundamentally rejected the existence of queer youth.

GSA organizers, however, had an unexpected source of support: the federal Equal Access Act (EAA).[15] Passed in 1984 to protect Bible study and prayer clubs, the EAA became the strongest support for LGBTQ students seeking to organize. In brief, the EAA states that secondary schools who have extracurricular clubs must allow all such clubs to organize unless they present a material disruption to the school environment. In 1990, the Supreme Court interpreted curricular clubs narrowly, as clubs directly tied to the curriculum, those that mirrored the course content, or those in which students received credit.[16] Attempts to ban all extracurricular clubs generally failed because the district nearly always tried to fudge the lines between curricular and extracurricular in such a way that only the GSA was excluded.[17] Other schools attempted more creative arguments that similarly failed, such as a Florida school district that framed the GSA as a sex-based club that would interfere with abstinence-only education.[18] Another Florida district went through extraordinary measures to avoid having a middle school GSA recognized, going so far as to successfully lobby the legislature to delete a definition of middle school as secondary education, but the courts again found that middle schools provided secondary education in Florida.[19] GSAs have been virtually unbeaten in this litigation,[20] so much so that now the American Civil Liberties Union (ACLU) can provide a form letter to superintendents, noting the list of cases finding that differential treatment of GSAs was legally invalid.[21] GLSEN surveyed students nationally and found that in 2001 only 30 percent reported a GSA, but by 2019 that number doubled to 61 percent. However, in 2021, this dropped again to 41 percent. The most likely reason was the difficulty of clubs in the COVID-induced closure period, though the anti-LGBTQ wave in recent years likely played a role.

In addition to restrictions on organizing GSAs, queer kids have had to contest a number of other restrictions put on them. In some ways this speaks to the attempt of the straight school to force kids into invisibility. Just under 60 percent of students in GLSEN's 2019 climate survey reported a range of differential treatment, such as being punished for displays of affection that straight students are not punished for (28 percent), being prohibited from discussing LGBTQ issues in school or extracurricular activities (16 percent), being prohibited from wearing clothing with LGBTQ slogans (10.7 percent), and even being prevented from going to dances (7.6 percent).[22] When students litigate these issues they almost always win; students have forced schools to settle and revoke rules prohibiting wearing shirts about day of silence events[23] and shirts saying "Jesus is not a homophobe,"[24] "Gay pride,"[25] and "Nobody knows I'm a lesbian."[26]

Proms and dances have become particularly interesting places of exclusion, especially for out students. K. K. Logan was prevented from

---

Curriculum Connection 5

One of the more difficult elements is asking students to share their experiences in school. Many have stories ranging the spectrum discussed above, and often I hear a lot of stories about the ways in which things have changed for the better. This is a short writing assignment that I have them submit only to me; they can share publicly if they want, but I do not force it. It is a good opportunity for them to see the course reflected in their own lives.

---

entering her school prom because she was trans and wearing a typical evening gown. The school spent years dragging out the litigation without explaining this decision beyond noting a school rule against advertising one's sexual orientation, but it eventually settled for an undisclosed sum.[27] The most famous modern prom dispute occurred when Constance McMillen tried to bring her girlfriend to the 2010 prom in Fulton, Mississippi. School rules required a date of the "opposite sex" and she was denied a couple's ticket. Further, McMillen was informed that if they brought boys but then danced with each other, they would be ejected if it made others uncomfortable. When ACLU lawyers made a demand to cease the discriminatory treatment or face a lawsuit, the school canceled the prom, and a parent-led prom was announced but also then canceled when McMillen tried to get tickets. The school then held a sham prom on the same night as the private event so that McMillen showed up to a nearly empty ballroom. The publicity around this event caused the school's insurer to force a settlement.

The fact that the students in these cases overwhelmingly win should be considered carefully, especially given GLSEN's data on the degree that students continue to report such differential treatment. Litigation is difficult and requires either the resources to pursue court action or the assistance of a public interest legal firm, most commonly the ACLU. Even then, for minors it also requires supportive parents or guardians. Finally, schools prevent the development of a strong body of law supporting queer kids by settling these lawsuits before a dispositive court action.

In recent years, the inclusion of trans kids in schools has garnered public attention. While for many knowledge of trans children began with Barbara Walters's 2007 interview of six-year-old Jazz Jennings, as Jules

Gill-Peterson (2018) demonstrated there has been a long history of trans kids largely invisible to the broader society. The earliest known reported legal battle gives a glimpse of what life was like for these trans kids when they went public. Trina Harrington[28] began to transition in 1998, during seventh grade, at her junior high school. Her principal harassed her in a variety of ways and told her grandmother that Trina would have to undergo therapy before returning the next year. She returned with a diagnosis and medical support for her transition, something the principal ignored as he required Trina to come to his office every day where he would send her home to change if she wore what he considered to be too girly clothing; she reported that as little as a butterfly barrette in her hair was sufficient for this. He claimed her clothing was disruptive but never explained how—little else other than Trina's trans existence disrupted his notions of the gender binary. The Gay and Lesbian Alliance Against Defamation (GLAAD) brought suit on her behalf, and in 2000 the superior court issued the first reported legal victory for a trans student. GLSEN's 2019 survey suggests that this kind of school-based surveillance still occurs, as 18.3 percent of respondents reported such gender "inappropriate" clothing regulation.[29] Though in late 2021, discriminatory dress codes reentered the discussion as some schools in Texas were sued for policies limiting nail polish and long hair to female students (Ebrahimji 2021).

By far the most attention in recent years on trans kids in schools has revolved around bathrooms, locker rooms, and sports. As Kristen Schilt and Laurel Westbrook (2015) illustrate, the concern for private spaces such as bathrooms and locker rooms represent "penis panics." Critics argue that in these private spaces restriction is necessary to protect women and children, with the notion being that trans women and girls are an existential threat. School polices are notoriously complex because school management is largely dispersed and local in nature. And of course, written policies can be quite different from the policies in practice, both in support of and opposition to trans and gender nonconforming students based on staff implementation. Much of the attention has focused on federal Title IX policy, as trans kids and their legal allies invoke sex discrimination provisions to assert their space within the straight, cis school. Title IX, however, has been subject to the vagaries of national politics. In May 2016, the Obama administration issued a "dear colleague" letter to public schools asserting, in part, that it would interpret sex as including the gender identity of students as expressed. This policy, however, was reversed in February 2017 by the new Trump administration, which declared only "biological" sex was covered by Title IX, a directive that itself was revoked by the Biden administration in 2021. The situation was also complicated by the Supreme Court's *Bostock* decision, holding that Title VII sex discrimination includes sexual orientation and gender identity within its reach.[30] The trend appears to be moving toward applying *Bostock* broadly. Gavin Grimm sued his Virginia school when it refused to let him use the boy's bathroom in 2015, and his case traveled up and down the appellate court system, as the administrative decisions changed the situation frequently. Ultimately, in August 2020, the Fourth Circuit held that the school's policies violated Title IX.[31] Transphobic groups have attempted to litigate trans-inclusive policies as supposed violations of Title IX. The Ninth Circuit, in 2020, rejected such a suit against an Oregon district for trans-inclusive policies including for bathrooms and locker rooms.[32] The exact reach of this will likely depend on the composition of the federal judiciary, especially as many Trump-appointed judges were quite hostile to trans people in their careers.

School sports have taken on a high profile in recent years, as transphobic campaigns frame their attacks in terms of support for cisgender girls in sports. This campaign relies on the erasure of trans boys completely (let alone nonbinary kids) and seeks to present inclusion of trans girls in competitions as unfair. In fact, many proposed statutory bans on trans participation are titled Save Women's Sports Acts. Trans participation in sports is similarly complicated by the decentralized nature of schools, as discussed above. State athletic associations in some states have issued guidance, with fifteen cataloged as friendly to trans participation and the remaining states classified as hostile, to varying degrees, from requiring birth certificates/sex assigned at birth to surgical requirements to various discriminatory limitations, and a few states have no clear guidance.[33] Transphobic groups have sought to leverage Title IX against trans inclusion in sports. Most significantly, three cis female athletes in Connecticut sued the state athletic association for allowing trans inclusion, claiming that it put them at a competitive disadvantage. In April 2021, the case was dismissed because the plaintiffs could not identify any actual trans athletes in the state since recent graduations.[34] Laws passed in 2021 and 2022 limiting trans participation in sports are being litigated.

Curriculum

While schools have always been straight spaces, some states, and potentially individual districts, further institutionalized this by adopting antigay, or no promo homo, curriculum laws. Rosky cataloged five different forms of such antigay curriculum laws. In some states, schools were simply forbidden from mentioning "alternate sexual lifestyles from heterosexual relationships," in essence a "Don't Say Gay" law (Rosky 2017, 1469, quoting South Carolina law). The classic no promo homo law, such as Arizona's, forbid any "instruction which . . . promotes a homosexual lifestyle," "portrays homosexuality as a positive alternative life-style," or suggests that gay sex can be safe (Rosky 2017, 1470, quoting Arizona law). Some states, such as Texas and Alabama, affirmatively required that sex education courses include "an emphasis . . . that homosexuality is not a lifestyle acceptable to the general public" and that it is a crime in the state (Rosky 2017, 1470–71, quoting Alabama and Texas laws). Oklahoma adds a requirement to these antigay laws by instructing sex ed courses to teach that "homosexual activity" is responsible for HIV spread (Rosky 2017, 1471, quoting Oklahoma law). Some states require the promotion of heterosexuality explicitly, and this influences the last category of abstinence-until-marriage politics. The last is included because marriage was always defined to exclude queer couples in these states (Rosky 2017, 1472–74). In 2017, Rosky (2017, 1475) found that twenty states had one or more of these antigay curriculum laws. No promo homo laws were an attempt to reinforce the straight school when it was finally facing some degree of activism toward LGBTQ inclusion.

No promo homo laws may seem like a relatively small impediment to inclusive education as they only existed in a minority of states and often were narrowly focused, say in health education. The straight school, however, has a strong inclination to path-dependence. Having been designed to reinforce straight citizenry, it resisted queer inclusion often by simply ignoring it. Outside of health class, where gay people might be mentioned in regard to HIV/AIDS information, or misinformation, you would find almost no education about gay or lesbian people in the 1990s, and none about trans folk. For example, one prominent health textbook in the 1990s asserted that HIV was spread mostly by gay men and that students should never have gay sex in order to avoid sexually transmitted infections (Kielwasser and Wolf 1994, 64). In the 1990s, attempts to change this largely focused on just getting books with lesbian and gay characters or themes into school libraries. This was met, at times, with strong public hostility.

In 1990, the Bay Area Network of Gay and Lesbian Educators (BAN-GLE), Contra Costa chapter, developed a book donation project to alter the dynamics of school life for gay teens. They specifically tied this to the recent findings that gay teens were far more likely to attempt suicide than straight kids and that book donations "providing role models and information not otherwise available to gay teens will positively impact this needless waste of human life."[35] This project would win financial support from the United Way for the next five years, as BANGLE described its project as seeking to allow for the establishment of a gay, lesbian and bisexual book section in each high school library in the county.[36] It appears that the Bay Area schools were relatively open to the donations, though the first set did see some minor local scandal. Both *Annie on My Mind* by Nancy Garden and *All American Boys* by Frank Mosca disappeared from the schools in one town without any explanation other than that a recently resigned vice principal had taken them (Clark 1991). The relative success of the project in California inspired a move to take it national.

Multiple groups in the San Francisco Bay area combined to co-found Project 21 to pressure California to develop gay- and lesbian-inclusive curriculum. Robert Birle then took the project to the Midwest, basing himself in Kansas City, Missouri. He immediately began contacting schools in the Kansas City area, offering donations of *Annie on My Mind* and *All American Boys*. A group burned the books publicly, with one speaker warning that "they are here to seduce your son and recruit young men and women into the gay and lesbian lifestyle" (Sanchez 1993). A number of schools in the area not only rejected the donations but removed existing copies of *Annie on My Mind*[37] to try and mollify public opposition to even minimal gay and lesbian representation in the library collection. After nearly two years of litigation, in which school board officials ultimately made clear that the book was removed only because it showed lesbian teens in a positive light, the Olathe School District's removal was found unconstitutional.[38] In 1998, a Wisconsin school district similarly removed a copy of *One Teenager in Ten*, a groundbreaking book of stories by gay teens themselves, after parents complained it was inappropriate. In settling an ACLU lawsuit, the school agreed to purchase the second edition of the book to replace it (Rupnow 1999). These legal victories should not, however, suggest that gay and lesbian inclusion was any easier. The controlling legal precedent is vague and allows schools significant leeway to work around using pretexts, and LGBTQ books would be a prime target of book challengers in schools for decades (Price 2021).

GLSEN data suggest that inclusive curriculum is hard to find for most queer students. The 2019 report found that two-thirds of respondents had no classroom inclusion and for the remaining third almost half reported negative representations overwhelmingly. Undoubtedly, some unknown numbers of individual teachers have taken steps to rectify this, but there was relatively little evidence that districts took any serious action. In recent years, however, some states have taken broader steps. In 2011, California adopted the Fair, Accurate, Inclusive, and Respectful (FAIR) Education Act, which mandates that contributions of LGBTQ and disabled people be included in K–12 instruction. Unfortunately, as Don Romesburg (2015, 488–94) and Stacie Brensilver Berman (2022, 101–13) found, the state provided no guidance or funding, leaving most districts to perhaps throw in some token mention of cisgender gay men and lesbians a few times. Information about implementation is hazy, but it seems likely that districts with a stronger history of inclusion adapted well and others likely dragged their feet. As of 2021, five other states—New Jersey, Colorado, Oregon, Illinois, and Nevada—have adopted similar inclusion requirements, but all are were adopted since 2019, and given the COVID-19 pandemic, evidence of implementation is lacking.

Curriculum Connection 6

Curriculum provides an interesting example for creative student work. I require students to write a medium-length paper identifying one thing they wish a school did, taught, or offered. I like this assignment because it asks students to think of a way to apply what they are learning and in a context that they are deeply familiar with, even if they were always the student in this environment.

Conclusion

This chapter, I hope, illustrates some of the important themes one can address in LGBTQ politics around educational activism. While I presented them as distinct areas, it is important to consider the linkages across all of them. Gay teachers often framed their activism as being as much about the children as about themselves; after all, who knows better than queer teachers the challenges faced by queer youth? The activism of both students and teachers was integral to supporting efforts to broaden the curriculum in even minimal ways. And GLSEN's data strongly suggest that schools with more aspects of inclusion, from accepting teachers to GSAs to curriculum, have reduced the harassment and bullying faced by queer students tremendously.

Sadly, this experience is not a thing of the past. In recent years, beginning most clearly in the 2021–22 school year, anti-LGBTQ activism in schools exploded in frequency. At the end of March 2022 *NBC News* reported that 238 anti-LGBTQ bills were filed in state legislatures so far that year, where only forty-one were introduced in the whole of 2018 (Lavietes and Ramox 2022). While much of this was targeted at trans students' healthcare and sports access, it also spilled over widely into a host of vague education laws. The most famous was Florida's HB 1557, dubbed the "Don't Say Gay" law. The law states that schools could provide no "instruction" in K–3 on sexual orientation or gender identity in addition to any such instruction "that is not age-appropriate or developmentally appropriate for students in accordance with state standards." This law came with a financial bounty, allowing community members to sue schools broadly for supposed violations—complete with a right to attorney's fees if they won; the teacher or school sued did not have that right. Supporters noted that this was an intentional effort to prevent LGBTQ topics from being discussed in school, representing again the idea that only queer people have sexual orientation or gender identity (Diaz 2022). The law's vague terms, however, especially what counts as age-appropriate beyond K–3, has already demonstrated significant expansion beyond this supposed purpose. After parents harassed a sixth-grade teacher for mentioning that he recently married his husband, he and other queer teachers decided they could not continue teaching in Florida schools with this law hanging over their heads that allowed parents to sue them simply because their existence was treated as propaganda (Lavietes 2022a). This has also been helped by the political rhetoric that again embraces the language of the pedophile myth that Anita Bryant deployed so effectively. However, now it is framed in terms of "grooming." The idea is that the very mention of LGBTQ people in school is inherently sexual and thus grooming children to become gay. This rhetoric has contributed to the attacks on LGBTQ people in schools (Block 2022).

Moreover, this hostility is not limited to teachers. In Davis County, Utah, teachers were prohibited from having Pride flags in their classrooms or any pins, stickers, or the like that demonstrated support for LGBTQ people, students, or rights (Tanner 2021). This was justified by the need to be politically neutral; the straight school is once again coded as the "neutral" option while any acknowledgment of sexual or gender diversity is dangerous indoctrination. A district in Irving, Texas, went so far as to scrape off all rainbow stickers on teachers' doors intended to signal to queer students that the rooms were safe spaces for them. The school argued that all spaces were safe for students, which of course proved not to be true. When a small group of teachers pushed back, one was fired, another decided it was better to just leave, and another was removed from the classroom. Students reported an increase in homophobic bullying and slurs that the school refused to address, and two GSA members were interviewed about their involvement with the GSA (Kingkade 2022). Some school board members have used this "grooming" language to criticize the very existence of GSAs in schools. In Texas, this hostility has resulted in the removal of LGBTQ-centric suicide prevention websites and resources from state sites (Yurcaba 2022), and some districts are blocking access to an array of LGBTQ websites (Childers 2021). The Grapevine-Colleyville school district in Texas adopted a total ban on any mention of "gender fluidity," appearing to prohibit any acknowledgment of trans people or even of a student or staff member transitioning (Branigin 2022). Finally, and it is because of limited space that I've only touched on the full extent of these attacks, there has been a dramatic increase in demands to censor books from school classrooms and libraries (and sometimes public libraries). As PEN America's *Banned in the USA* 2022 report details, this issue is broader than just censoring LGBTQ books and resources, but queer-inclusive materials are a particular target, with about one-third of the report's banned books having LGBTQ characters (PEN America 2022).

Sadly, this short list of examples demonstrates the continued relevance of schools for LGBTQ politics. In many ways, it echoes many critiques of the movement where some were quick to declare victory after marriage equality won in 2015 (Burns 2019). There was a time where the anti-LGBTQ political right seemed to be receding, as explicitly homophobic campaigning became unpalatable to the general public. For years, however, the Christian right and its allies shifted the focus to trans people, and especially kids, for years and then used the successes there to springboard back to broader anti-LGBTQ activism. The 2021–22 swell of anti-LGBTQ actions has demonstrated the success of this strategy. Now we are facing a reassertion of the straight school that decades of educational activists and students had just barely begun to alter. The fight against this new wave will require a reinvigoration of activism, which luckily many youth have taken the lead in (Lavietes 2022b). In fact, my last curriculum connection is to consider ways in which our students can both participate in and understand the political dimensions of this anti-LGBTQ education backlash. Our students may have to join the front lines of this battle sooner than we expect.

Notes

1. The Florida committee produced the infamous *Homosexuality and Citizenship in Florida* report, https://ufdc.ufl.edu/UF00004805/00001/images.

2. Facts taken from *Acanfora v. Board of Education*, 359 F. Supp. 843 (D. Md. 1973).

3. Facts taken from *Gaylord v. Tacoma School Dist. 10*, 559 P.2d 1340 (Wash. 1977).

4. *Acanfora*, 359 F. Supp., at 856–57.

5. *Gaylord*, 559 P.2d, at 1347.

6. *Burton v. Cascade School Dist.*, 512 F.2d 850 (9th Cir. 1975).

7. *Morrison v. State Board of Education*, 461 P.2d 375 (Cal. 1969).

8. *Vaults*, podcast, episode 34 "Gym Class," May 23, 2020.

9. Oklahoma did pass a law identical to the Briggs Initiative. Ultimately, the law was held unconstitutional to the extent that it limited the free speech of teachers to advocate for public change in their private lives. However, the ban on gay teachers was left intact. This decision was affirmed by the Supreme Court only because it deadlocked 4–4. *National Gay Task Force v. Board of Education of the City of Oklahoma*, 729 F.2d 1270 (10th Cir. 1984).

10. The Gay Speakers Bureau of Northern California, undated flyer. Hank Wilson Papers, carton 1, Gay Speakers Bureau of Northern California, GLBT Historical Society.

11. *Bostock v. Clayton County*, 590 U.S. 644 (2020).

12. Governor's Commission on Gay and Lesbian Youth. 1993. "Making Schools Safe for Gay and Lesbian Youth," education report.

13. *Nabozny v. Podlesny*, 92 F.3d 446 (7th Cir. 1996).

14. In recent years, these are often titled gender and sexualities alliances or queer straight alliances, as well as some other versions. I will just use GSA as a generic term.

15. 20 U.S.C. §4071.

16. *Westside Community Board of Education v. Mergens*, 496 U.S. 226 (1990).

17. *Gay-Straight Education (PRIDE) v. White County School Dist.*, 2006 U.S. Dist. LEXIS 47955 (N.D. Ga. 2006); *East High School Prism Club v. Seidel*, 95 F. Supp. 2d 1239 (D. Utah 2000).

18. *Gay-Straight Alliance v. School Bd. of Okeechobee*, 483 F. Supp. 2d 1224 (S.D. Fla. 2007).

19. *Carver Middle School Gay-Straight Alliance v. School Board of Lake County*, 842 F.3d 1324 (11th Cir. 2016).

20. The only exception is *Caudillo v. Lubbock Ind. Sch. Dist.*, 311 F. Supp. Ed 550 (N.D. Tex. 2004). Frankly, the reasoning in this case is bizarre. The District Court relied upon two justifications. First, that sodomy was a crime at the time when the GSA refusal was issued. Second, that some literature the GSA distributed led, through a series of online links, to "adult" content in some way and thus it undermined the abstinence-only education. It is unclear why this case was not appealed, but I suspect the lawyers felt that the recent invalidation of the sodomy law, along with more careful flyers, would overcome the school district. While this case was oft cited by other schools, other courts did not take it seriously.

21. https://www.aclu.org/letter/open-letter-schools-about-gay-straight-alliances.

22. GLSEN. 2020. *The 2019 National School Climate Survey*, xix–xx, https://www.glsen.org/sites/default/files/2021-04/NSCS19-FullReport-032421-Web_0.pdf.

23. *Hatcher v. DeSoto County School District Board of Education*, 939 F. Supp. 2d 1232 (M.D. Fla. 2013).

24. *Couch v. Wayne Local School District* (S.D. Ohio, filed April 3, 2012) Docket no. 1:12-cv-00265.

25. *Gillman v. School Board of Holmes County*, 567 F. Supp. 2d 1359 (N.D. Fla. 2008).

26. *T.V. v. Beukelman* (E.D. Cal., filed October 15, 2015) Docket no. 2:15-cv-02163.

27. *Logan v. Gary Community School Corporation* (N.D. Ind., filed December 12, 2007) Docket no. 2:07-cv-00431.

28. I borrow the facts from *Doe v. Yuntis*, 2000 WL 33162199 (Mass. Super. 2000) and Trina's podcast interview. https://www.glad.org/cases/pat-doe-v-yunits/.

29. GLSEN. 2020. *The 2019 National School Climate Survey*, 41. https://www.glsen.org/sites/default/files/2021-04/NSCS19-FullReport-032421-Web_0.pdf.

30. *Bostock v. Clayton County*, 590 U.S. 644 (2020).

31. *Grimm v. Gloucester Cty. Sch. Bd.*, 972 F.3d 586 (4th Cir. 2020). Note that the failure of the Supreme Court to review a case does not technically express anything about the merits, but it does mean that at least at this point there were not four votes to take up the issue.

32. *Parents for Privacy v. Barr*, 949 F.3d 1210 (9th Cir. 2020).

33. "K–12 Policies," *Transathlete.com*, https://www.transathlete.com/k-12.

34. Lori Riley, "Federal Judge Dismisses Lawsuit That Sought to Block Transgender Female Athletes from Competing in Girls High School Sports in Connecticut," *Hartford Courant*, April 26, 2021, https://www.courant.com/sports/high-schools/hc-sp-hs-transgender-case-dismissed-20210425-twgpmkmsrvhnhl64u2tr32tg3y-story.html.

35. BANGLE letter to librarian, October 1992, BANGLE Collection Carton 2, Book Project, GLBT Archive.

36. BANGLE United Way Funding Proposal, FY 1992. BANGLE Collection Carton 2, United Way Proposals, GLBT Archive.

37. No school had copies of *All American Boys* already. This book was largely obscure and not well reviewed.

38. *Case v. Unified School Dist.*, 908 F. Supp. 864 (D. Kan. 1995).

References

Ammiano, Tom. 2020. *Kiss My Gay Ass: My Trip Down the Yellow Brick Road Through Activism, Stand-Up, and Politics*. Bay Guardian Books.

Aviles, Gwen. 2020. "Lesbian Teacher Suspended for Showing Photo of 'Future Wife' Gets $100,000 Settlement." *NBC News*, Feb. 26. https://www.nbcnews.com/feature/nbc-out/lesbian-teacher-suspended-showing-photo-future-wife-gets-100-000-n1143736.

Autman, Samuel A. 1996. "Gay Clubs Are Out, but So Are Others." *Salt Lake Tribune*, Feb. 21, A1.

Ball, Carlos. 2011. *From the Closet to the Courtroom: Five LGBT Rights Lawsuits That Have Changed Our Nation*. Beacon Press.

Biegel, Stuart. 2018. *The Right to Be Out: Sexual Orientation and Gender Identity in America's Public Schools*. 2nd ed. University of Minnesota Press.

Block, Melissa. 2022. "Accusations of 'Grooming' Are the Latest Political Attack—with Homophobic Origins." *NPR*, May 11. https://www.npr.org/2022/05/11/1096623939/accusations-grooming-political-attack-homophobic-origins.

Blount, Jackie M. 2005. *Fit to Teach: Same-Sex Desire, Gender, and School Work in the Twentieth Century*. State University of New York Press.

Branigin, Anne. 2022. " 'Don't Say Trans': Texas School Board's New Policies Spark an Outcry." *Washington Post*, August 24. https://www.washingtonpost.com/nation/2022/08/24/texas-school-dont-say-trans/.

Brensilver Berman, Stacie. 2022. *LGBTQ+ History in High School Classes in the United States Since 1990*. Bloomsbury Academic.

Bryant, Anita. 1977. *The Anita Bryant Story*. Fleming H. Revell.

Burns, Katelyn. 2019. "The LGBTQ Civil Rights Fight Is Far from Over." *Vox*, July 17. https://www.vox.com/first-person/2019/7/17/20697174/lgbtq-civil-rights-fight-not-over.

Canaday, Margot. 2009. *The Straight State: Sexuality and Citizenship in Twentieth-Century America*. Princeton University Press.

Carter, Wayne. 2022. "Grapevine Students Walk Out of Class Over New Anti-LGBTQ School Policies." *NBC DFW*, August 26. https://www.nbcdfw.com/

58 | Richard S. Price

news/local/grapevine-students-walk-out-of-class-over-new-anti-lgbtq-school-policies/3058103/.

Childers, Shelly. 2021. "Katy ISD Continues to Block LGBTQ+ Resource Websites as Student Appeals for Change Again." *ABC 13*, December 14. https://abc13.com/katy-isd-lgbtq-sites-blocked-school-board-resources-inaccessible/11336566/.

Clark, Keith. 1991. "Gay Youth Novels Vanish from Contra Costa Schools." *Bay Area Reporter*, September 26.

Connell, Catherine. 2015. *School's Out: Gay and Lesbian Teachers in the Classroom*. University of California Press.

Diaz, Jaclyn. 2022. "Florida's Governor Signs Controversial Law Opponents Dubbed 'Don't Say Gay.'" NPR, March 28. https://www.npr.org/2022/03/28/1089221657/dont-say-gay-florida-desantis.

Ebrahimji, Alisha. 2021. "This Teenager's Painted Nails Got Him Suspended." CNN, April 23. https://www.cnn.com/2021/04/23/us/nail-polish-texas-school-gender-neutral-trnd/index.html.

Engel, Stephen M. 2016. *Fragmented Citizens: The Changing Landscape of Gay and Lesbian Lives*. New York University Press.

Epp, Charles R. 2009. *Making Rights Real: Activists, Bureaucrats, and the Creation of the Legalistic State*. University of Chicago Press.

Gay Writer's Group. 1983. *It Could Happen to You*. Alyson Publications.

Gill-Peterson, Jules. 2018. *Histories of the Transgender Child*. University of Minnesota Press.

Graves, Karen L. 2009. *And They Were Wonderful Teachers: Florida's Purge of Gay and Lesbian Teachers*. University of Illinois Press.

Groutage, Hilary. 1996. "West, Highland Seek OK for Gay Clubs." *Salt Lake Tribune*, February 6, B1.

Harbeck, Karen M. 1997. *Gay and Lesbian Educators: Personal Freedoms, Public Constraints*. Amethyst Press and Productions.

Johnson, David K. 2019. *Buying Gay: How Physique Entrepreneurs Sparked a Movement*. Columbia University Press.

Kamenetz, Anya. 2018. "More Than Half of Transgender Teachers Surveyed Tell NPR They Are Harassed at Work." NPR, March 8. https://www.npr.org/sections/ed/2018/03/08/575723226/more-than-half-of-transgender-teachers-face-workplace-harassment.

Kielwasser, Alfred P., and Michele A. Wolf. 1994. "Silence, Difference, and Annihilation: Understanding the Impact of Mediated Heterosexism on High School Students." *High School Journal* 77 (1/2): 58–79.

Kingkade, Tyler. 2022. "A Texas Teacher Faces Losing Her Job After Fighting for Gay Pride Symbols in School." *NBC News*, April 7. https://www.nbcnews.com/news/us-news/lgbtq-students-texas-school-rainbow-stickers-rcna23208.

Lane, Stephen. 2019. *No Sanctuary: Teachers and the School Reform That Brough Gay Rights to the Masses*. ForeEdge.

Lavietes, Matt. 2022a. "'I Cannot Teach in Florida': LGBTQ Educators Fear Fallout from New School Law." *NBC News*, April 1. https://www.nbcnews.com/nbc-out/out-politics-and-policy/-cannot-teach-florida-lgbtq-educators-fear-fallout-new-school-law-rcna22106.

Lavietes, Matt. 2022b. "Florida Students Stage School Walkouts Over 'Don't Say Gay' Bill." *NBC News*, March 3. https://www.nbcnews.com/nbc-out/out-politics-and-policy/florida-students-stage-school-walkouts-dont-say-gay-bill-rcna18600.

Lavietes, Matt, and Elliott Ramox. 2022. "Nearly 240 Anti-LGBTQ Bills Filed in 2022 So Far, Most of Them Targeting Trans People." *NBC News*, March 20. https://www.nbcnews.com/nbc-out/out-politics-and-policy/nearly-240-anti-lgbtq-bills-filed-2022-far-targeting-trans-people-rcna20418.

Lugg, Catherine A. 2016. *US Public Schools and the Politics of Queer Erasure.* Palgrave Macmillan.

Lvovsky, Anna. 2021. *Vice Patrol: Cops, Courts, and the Struggle Over Urban Gay Life Before Stonewall.* University of Chicago Press.

Malinsky, Kathleen P. 1997. "Learning to Be Invisible: Female Sexual Minority Students in America's Public High Schools." *Journal of Gay & Lesbian Social Services* 7 (4): 35–50.

PEN America. 2022. "Banned in USA." PEN America. https://pen.org/banned-in-the-usa/.

Price, Richard S. 2021. "Navigating a Doctrinal Grey Area: Free Speech, the Right to Read, and Schools." *First Amendment Studies* 55 (2): 79–101.

Rafferty, Max. 1977. "Should Gays Teach School?" *Phi Delta Kappan* 59 (2): 91–92.

Romesburg, Don. 2015. "There's No T in FAIR? Implementing a Trans-Inclusive K–12 History Law." *Transgender Studies Quarterly* 2 (3): 488–94.

Rosky, Clifford J. 2013. "Fear of the Queer Child." *Buffalo Law Review* 61 (3): 607–97.

Rosky. Clifford. 2017. "Anti-Gay Curriculum Laws." *Columbia Law Review* 117 (6): 1469.

Rupnow, Chuck. 1999. "Barron Schools Will Keep Banned Books." *Leader-Telegram*, October 8, 1.

Ruskola, Teemu. 1996. "Minor Disregard: The Legal Construction of the Fantasy That Gay and Lesbian Youth Do Not Exist." *Yale Journal of Law and Feminism* 8:269–331.

Sanchez, Mary. 1993. "'Books' Gay Theme Protested Parents, Others Burn a Copy of One at KC School Offices." *Kansas City Star*, October 8, C1.

Sears, James T. 1992. "Educators, Homosexuality, and Homosexual Students: Are Personal Feelings Related to Professional Beliefs?" In *Coming Out of the Classroom Closet: Gay and Lesbian Students, Teachers and Curricula*, edited by Karen Harbeck. Routledge.

Schilt, Kristen, and Laurel Westbrook. 2015. "Bathroom Battlegrounds and Penis Panics." *Contexts* 14 (3): 26–31

Semarad, Tony. 1996. "Lawmakers Looking at Anti-Gay Club Bill." *Salt Lake Tribune*, February 3, A4.

Smith-Silverman, Sara. 2020. "'Gay Teachers Fight Back!': Rank-and-File Gay and Lesbian Teachers' Activism Against the Briggs Initiative, 1977–1978." *Journal of the History of Sexuality* 29 (1): 79–107.

Tanner, Courtney. 2021. "This Utah School District Has Banned LGBTQ Pride and Black Lives Matter Flags, Saying They Are 'Politically Charged.'" *Salt Lake Tribune*, September 21. https://www.sltrib.com/news/education/2021/09/21/this-utah-school-district/.

Uribe, Virginia, and Karen M. Harbeck. 1992. "Addressing the Needs of Lesbian, Gay, and Bisexual Youth: The Origins of Project 10 and School-Based Intervention." In Harbeck, *Coming Out of the Classroom Closet*.

Waller, Allyson. 2021. "Houston-Area School District Suspends Gender-Based Provisions of Its Dress Code After Being Sued Over Its Long-Hair Policy." *KHOU 11*, November 5. https://www.khou.com/article/news/education/texas-tribune-magnolia-isd-dress-code-hair-policy-suspended/285-8988cd21-785d-4341-86f1-1c7838476dee.

Yurcaba, Jo. 2022. "Texas Continues to Remove LGBTQ Suicide Prevention Resources from State Websites." *NBC News*, March 2. https://www.nbcnews.com/nbc-out/out-news/texas-continues-remove-lgbtq-suicide-prevention-resources-state-website-rcna18376.

Chapter 3

Teaching LGBTQ Politics in and of Newark

JYL JOSEPHSON

The upper-level undergraduate LGBTQ politics class is both exciting and challenging to teach. Students come with different levels of knowledge about the LGBTQ movement in the US and internationally. Developments in the movement require ongoing changes to key materials and choices about what to include and exclude are always difficult. And as Edward F. Kammerer Jr. and Royal G. Cravens III note elsewhere in this volume, there is not necessarily a settled "canon" of texts to teach in the course, even as there is some consensus on the topics that should be covered.

This chapter addresses teaching LGBTQ politics as a community-engaged course, an approach that I have developed over the last several years and iterations of the class. The course draws on materials of local relevance to students and that reflect the diversity and specific history of the LGBTQ community in Newark. Developing and using these materials has made the course content more engaging and relevant to my students at Rutgers University–Newark, whose identities reflect the racial, ethnic, class, and religious diversity of Newark and northern New Jersey. This approach of community-engaged teaching using locally relevant resources can be adapted to many different contexts, as I suggest briefly in the conclusion of the chapter.

I begin by outlining the specific pedagogical innovations that I have developed over the last several iterations of the course and the reasons that I have done so. This is followed by more specific discussion of the course content, and how I have used materials from the Queer Newark Oral History Project (QNOHP), including the ways that I use the materials to teach students some very basic qualitative research techniques. I discuss both the interdisciplinary materials on which I draw to teach the course and the ways that students are challenged to see the connections between the study of specific LGBTQ histories and the study of politics.

Origin of the Course and Its Location in the Curriculum

I first developed this course in the early 2000s as an upper-level undergraduate elective class in the political science major and minor, and cross-listed with women's and gender studies. The course now also serves as an elective in the minor in LGBTQ studies. Thus, there are usually students in the class from each of those courses of study, as well as students taking the course as a general studies elective. The course focuses on LGBTQ movements and politics in the US context but needs to respond to this interdisciplinary range of student backgrounds. In this sense, the fluid nature of the political science sources for this course makes it possible to draw more connections with the movements as well as with literature in women's, gender, and sexuality studies and LGBTQ studies.[1]

Core Subject Matter

As the movements and political context have changed, I have changed some of the course learning objectives and adapted the course content. In the early 2000s, much of the course content was focused on the LGBTQ movement in the US, including a range of policy issues such as military service, local and state human rights ordinances and nondiscrimination laws, K–12 curriculum and equity and inclusion policies, and marriage equality. I also usually included some material on international movements for SOGIE (sexual orientation, gender identity, and expression) human rights and/or some comparative public policy material.[2] I included political science and public policy sources, and there was indeed plenty of such material available, though not nearly as much as has developed in the two decades since I began teaching the class.

As the movement changed, I added to and changed the specific materials included. The context for the course has also changed significantly; as the political science literature on public attitudes in the US and elsewhere regarding LGBTQ+ people has shown, there has been a significant shift during this time period (Garretson 2017). Certainly, students' attitudes and background knowledge will vary in different university settings, yet it is very different to teach this course in the third decade of the twenty-first century than it was two decades earlier. Now students are learning in the context of a society in which many people not only are aware of the existence of LGBTQ+ people but have relationships with and commitments to the well-being of people who identify as part of the LGBTQ+ diaspora, and a society in which the legal system has shifted to policies of greater equality and inclusion. I have also found that the current generation of students are much more comfortable being vocal about their commitments as members of or allies of the LGBTQ+ community than were students of previous generations.

I should note that throughout the time that I have been teaching this class I have also included material about backlash to the movement. The nature of the backlash has also changed as there have been movement successes as well as setbacks. I believe that it is important for students to understand some aspects of the opposition and backlash to LGBTQ+ rights for them to understand movement strategies and why the movement has been more successful in some policy areas than in others. This is helpful because students may only be familiar with conversations around LGBTQ+ politics that are current at the time that they are taking the class. Since there is a common structure to the types of backlash that occur, it is helpful for students to understand this aspect of contemporary social movements as well.

I usually introduce the course with multiple readings about issues of inclusion and exclusion in the LGBTQ+ community and in the movement. For example, most recently I have included essays about how the acronyms used by movement activists have changed over time, reflecting changes in who is included under the umbrella. This unit includes readings that address the issues of categorization and identity. This helps introduce students to the complexity of the movement and the power differences among different groups in the LGBTQ+ community. This then leads into a unit on intersectionality that focuses on alliances and rifts with other, overlapping movements and organizations, such as reproductive justice, gender equality, civil rights and racial justice, and movements against mass incarceration and for prison abolition. Other units in the course include materials from trans studies, usually focusing on policy-oriented literature, and units that address SOGIE human rights in the international sphere. These key topics shift somewhat as the movement changes, for example focusing on policy debates that are most salient at the time of the class. Most recently, however, I have developed a more engaged pedagogy, and I have found this to be a successful way to enhance student learning.

Over the last several decades there has been a movement across the disciplines in higher education to develop more effective pedagogy. One way to do this is to increase opportunities for active learning in the classroom as well as student engagement in both classroom and community. This movement has been based on the strong evidence that hands-on learning, when thoughtfully integrated into course goals and subject matter, can aid student learning, increase students' interest in course materials, and enhance retention of course content. In political science there has been a focus on community-engaged learning for civic engagement, but this pedagogical approach can be helpful for courses on a wide variety of topics (Bennion and Laughlin 2018; Finley 2011). While there are many approaches to incorporating active learning, one way is through building in a component of community-engaged research (see Levac 2020).

My university has actively encouraged faculty to develop more community-engaged pedagogy and programming. Rutgers University–Newark has always seen itself as an urban university, but over the last decade in particular the university went through a strategic planning process that has led to many new initiatives for community engagement. The motto "In Newark and of Newark" exemplifies the goals of attracting and supporting more students from the city of Newark and engaging more with community partners.[3] This community engagement is based on the idea of the "outside-in university," that the university has much to learn from the community, and that universities and communities should be reciprocal partners in the creation of a learning community (Cantor 2021). The Queer Newark Oral History Project (QNOHP) is an example of bringing these elements together.

As a result of this national movement for engaged pedagogy, as well as the support for such initiatives at Rutgers, I have developed a community-engaged pedagogy for the LGBTQ+ politics class that draws on the QNOHP. The development of the QNOHP and the related materials developed by faculty, students, staff, and community members have made it possible to focus the course on these materials while relating them to the historical context and politics of LGBTQ movements for change. These materials, drawing on the stories of people in our local community, deepen student interest. In the next section I describe QNOHP in more detail and outline how the class draws on the resources available about Newark from the QNOHP.

Basic Features of the Course and the Approach to Pedagogy

Course description (from the spring 2021 course syllabus): This course explores LGBTQ political movements and related public policies in the United States and locates these within historical contexts and with reference to theories about gender and sexuality. The importance of intersecting identity categories such as race, class, sex, gender, sexual orientation, and gender identity will be explored as they impact political mobilization and public policy strategies and impacts of the movement. We will also look to the specific context of LGBTQ life and politics in Newark and use the resources of the Queer Newark Oral History Project, including working with the oral histories as part of the main research project for the class.

The QNOHP began in 2011 with collaboration between writer and activist Darnell Moore, historian and Rutgers University–Newark (RU–N) faculty member Beryl Satter, and RU–N staff member Christina Strasburger. The initial collaboration led to a one-day conference during the fall semester of 2011 that brought together several generations of queer Newark activists for a public conversation.[4] At the conference, participants and attendees were invited to sign up to have their oral history recorded or to donate documents or other materials to the Queer Newark archive.

Following this event, the history department, in conjunction with the American Studies PhD program and the women's and gender studies program, began the project of collecting oral histories. Faculty began to teach students how to conduct oral histories and to curate the archive and received university support through a chancellor's seed grant and through research assistantships in the American studies program. There have been multiple additional events, and to date more than seventy-five oral histories have been collected, curated, and made available publicly through the QNOHP website.[5]

University funding also helped to support a visual exhibit created by students in faculty member and public historian Mary Rizzo's class, collaborating with graphic arts students led by faculty member Chantal Fischzang. This exhibit was first displayed in the Newark Public Library, and it happened to be on display as I was implementing the community-engaged section of my LGBTQ politics class.[6] There were several interactive elements to the exhibit that made it especially useful for students to explore.[7] I built in a visit to the library during a class session; fortunately, this is a short walk from campus. In addition, there were several campus events that featured speakers of interest to the class, some of whom had been interviewed for the project. These also became field trips for the class.

Guest speakers from the project were another highlight of the engaged portion of the class. Several of the graduate students who were writing about the oral history project for their research or whose graduate assistantships involved conducting some of the interviews visited my class to speak about their work. One of the faculty who was co-curator of the project, Whit Strub, also gave a guest talk; he has since published an edited volume about the project that includes some of the oral history materials (Strub 2024).

To unify these experiences for students, I assigned a field notes project. Students were not required to attend every event but were required to complete field notes for the events that they did attend. I was able to schedule some of these during our regular class period. The field notes project was simple: to take detailed notes during the event and then spend about ten minutes at the end of the event writing up observations, questions, and ideas about how this related to course reading material or other course elements. Students also completed field notes for guest speakers as well as for the occasional film shown in class. Students could use these field notes as research material for their final paper project.

The field notes assignment served several purposes for the class. First, as happens when one uses field notes in research, the process of taking the field notes, and the requirement to do so, helped students notice specific details about the experience. It helped to focus their attention. Second, it also provided a very basic introduction to the ways that students would be using their own original data as they developed their research projects for the course. These notes could be used as a source in their final paper. Third, having field notes for other aspects of the course, and not just their research projects, helped students integrate their own research observations with their observations about other course materials and experiences. Fourth, field notes provided a way for students to document some of the more ephemeral experiences of the course, such as guest speakers, so that they could return to those notes as they completed other assignments. Students were required to submit their notes to the instructor; the grading was primarily on the completeness or thoroughness of the notes and not on the observations themselves.

I should note that before the availability of the QNOHP, I had used some Newark-related material in my class, primarily related to the murder of Sakia Gunn in 2003 and the activism in the community that resulted from that terrible event.[8] Students related to this material; however, it also focused the Newark portion of the class around violence and trauma in a way that was not always healthy for students and likely gave them a distorted view of the community. QNOHP and all the rich cultural resources that the project has made possible has given students a set of people and ideas with whom to engage and with whom they can relate, and this has shown up in class discussions as well as in students' work and writing in interesting ways. It has also helped to put Sakia Gunn's murder in the context of community visibility and invisibility. And it helps to highlight the subsequent community activism and advocacy that led to the creation of more community resources and public recognition for the queer community in Newark.

QNOHP is of course a significant contribution to the story of Newark, but it also contributes to LGBTQ+ history more generally. As one example, Newark had an active ballroom scene, and some of the respondents were part of that scene. Ballroom culture is perhaps most familiar from the film *Paris Is Burning*, but there were ballroom practices in many cities outside of New York. Marlon Bailey's (2013) in-depth study of the Detroit ballroom scene illustrates how important such sites and practices were and are, especially to Black queer culture. Karen McCarthy Brown (2001) discusses some aspects of the ballroom scene in Newark based on interviews and observations conducted in the 1990s. Many narrators in the QNOHP mentioned clubs and ballroom spaces and houses as an important part of Newark's queer scene and as crucial safe community spaces.[9] Many of the physical locations no longer exist, but they have been documented through the oral histories and the digital document archive of QNOHP.

The QNOHP has various materials in addition to the oral histories. There is an archive that includes materials about the city of Newark's first LGBTQ commission, the QNOHP conferences, and the Newark Pride Alliance formed after the murder of Sakia Gunn. There are also materials about the history of Queer clubs and other spaces in Newark. In working on their projects, students could use any of these materials in addition to their chosen oral history.

The Assignment for the Oral Histories: Goals and Details

The major writing project that students complete over the course of the semester is a research paper on an oral history in the QNOHP. This project involves teaching students some basic research skills, requiring them to engage with one of the oral histories in the project, and bringing in course materials as well as their original analysis to write the final paper. Here I describe the project in detail; it could certainly be adapted to other LGBTQ politics courses, but this project could also be used in other political science courses, such as for a unit in a qualitative methods course.[10]

The initial assignment is simple: Students are asked to look through the oral histories on the site, choose an individual (hereafter "narrator") and their oral history that constitutes their main material for the final paper, and write a brief proposal describing why and how they have chosen that particular narrator's oral history.

The project then involves working with the oral history itself. Some of the histories are available only as audio recordings and transcripts, while others also include video footage. I teach students some very basic social science methods for analyzing qualitative interviews, and they use these methods to analyze their oral history. First, students complete the field notes exercise the first time they listen to the interview. Then, students read some basic materials about qualitative coding methods and choose a portion of the transcript to apply those methods. The first time I used this project, I had students choose which coding methods to use. However, this proved a bit confusing for students, so the second time that I taught the course I chose two specific coding methods, and this worked much better.

Students are asked to select any five-page section of the transcript and code it with one method, and then code the same section with the other method. The first method is "in vivo" coding, which uses the narrator's own language to create codes. I ask students to use this method first so that they can become more acquainted with the narrator's own way of speaking and expressing themselves. This helps students identify some of the unique characteristics and ideas of the narrator. The second method involves selecting terms and themes from one of the class readings by coding it and then coding the same section of the oral history text using those themes. This method, called descriptive coding, helps students to link other materials from the class with the oral history they are analyzing. For example, narrators did not always use terms such as "intersectionality," but they often spoke of multiple aspects of their identity. Students are required to submit their actual coding and a research memo discussing what they learned from each method of coding. Although not a requirement, some students also code other parts of the transcript or use additional coding methods in order to develop their papers.

For the final paper, students draw on this analysis as well as on course readings and other course materials to write about the narrator, their oral history, and how the person's story relates to LGBTQ history, movements for change, and Newark. For example, some course readings cover the topic of coalitions with other social movements. Some of the narrators have also been very active in the LGBTQ movement and in advocacy for greater inclusion in Newark. Students who write about these narrators can draw on reading materials that links their analysis of the interview with the LGBTQ rights movement. Other narrators discuss the multiple aspects of their identity and how this has shaped their life, and students can draw on reading materials on intersectionality to analyze their narrator's story.

The core of the paper is the student's analysis of the interview, relating the material in the interview to some key themes of the class. Students are required to discuss their research methods and coding in their analysis. They can also draw on any of the other course materials, including the guest speakers, the exhibit, other materials that are part of QNOHP, and readings, films, and class discussions. Students write a draft and final essay; the draft is necessary as most students are not familiar with using this kind of original analysis in a research paper. Student feedback on the course has been very positive; most students enjoyed doing this kind of original research and many were excited and inspired by the stories of their narrator, made even more meaningful that these were stories of Newark.

Adapting to Virtual Instruction

In the spring of 2021, I taught the LGBTQ politics course virtually due to the global pandemic. Many aspects of the course worked quite well in a virtual format. In what follows I discuss both how I adapted the course materials and subject matter to teaching and learning under the conditions of the pandemic and how I taught the course remotely and asynchronously.

Given the pandemic, I wanted to adapt some of the course content to respond to the situation. I found several sources that brought together analysis or discussion of the HIV/AIDS pandemic and the COVID-19 pandemic. Jackson Davidow (2020) wrote an excellent essay on the "Day Without Art" for the *Boston Review*. The *Kitchen Sisters* podcast did a wonderful story on Gert McMullin, a seamstress and longtime curator of the HIV/AIDS quilt project, who was sewing masks during the COVID-19 pandemic. Anthony Fauci wrote a remembrance of Larry Kramer, who passed away in May of 2020. These all helped to give students a bit of perspective and history, as well as to see some parallels between the way that both pandemics were devastating to marginalized communities. We watched a film about ACT UP and read an interview with Sarah Schulman. Students also spent time looking through the oral history archives of ACT UP to compare with the QNOHP.

Most of the course translated well to remote learning. The oral history project worked well with virtual instruction, given that all the materials are available on the QNOHP website. I adjusted some of the reading assignments and used more visual materials, especially films, for the virtual class. The field notes assignments still worked in the virtual format. The most challenging part of the course to teach virtually was the process of coding, and I prepared several explanatory video lectures to make sure that students understood the assignment. Students could turn in the assignment in whatever format worked for them, given that their access to technology varied. Some students were able to do their coding using highlights and comments within a document. Other students manually marked up printed documents and then scanned them.

One element that I adapted was the guest speakers. I did not invite as many guest speakers, and the presentations were done through a prerecorded video conversation between the speaker and the instructor. The course was taught asynchronously, and so it was not interactive with the students, and this likely made it much less effective as an instructional approach. I have brought back the interactive element to the course now that it is taught in person again, including the guest speakers. This could also be done in a synchronous virtual format.

I have found that students really engage with the material about Newark and the Newark community. This engagement seemed to be heightened by the conditions of the pandemic. Perhaps due to how isolated people were feeling, students found it encouraging that people in their own community had been successful in making changes in the local political and social climate for LGBTQ+ people.

These materials and assignments would likely work well for instructors in a variety of institutional settings. Students should find the oral histories very relatable even without the local connection to the community. Instructors could also integrate other oral history projects in this way, such as the ACT UP archive, which is also publicly available.[11] I would also urge instructors to look for oral history archives in their own communities as well, since there have been many projects of this kind and having local connections has certainly enhanced students' engagement with the course.

Reflections on Oral Histories and LGBTQ Politics

I originally developed a pedagogy of community-engaged teaching for a different course and had not imagined that I would adapt other courses to use this type of pedagogy. However, what I found with the other course was that students really responded to the hands-on aspects of the course and enjoyed hearing from community leaders (Josephson 2018). This made me think about adapting other courses, such as this one, to use this kind of engaged pedagogy. As noted, there is a good deal of evidence that hands-on learning, when thoughtfully integrated into the course goals and subject matter, can really aid student learning and interest. Working with colleagues in my department, we have developed several community-engaged courses, generally by partnering with a community organization (Allam et al. 2021).

A challenge with community-engaged classes is how to integrate more traditional course materials with the engaged activities. Using the oral histories does mean that I focus the reading material and films more on local activism than I might in a generic LGBTQ politics course. The oral histories cover such a wide range of topics and experiences, however, that in some ways this has opened the course in terms of subject matter. For example, we can read materials about the movement for marriage equality and then relate those to some of the oral histories and implementation of marriage equality in New Jersey and in Newark. This works with most of the standard topics in an LGBTQ politics class.

The focus on oral histories also provides the opportunity to address topics that might not be as commonly addressed in an LGBTQ politics course. For example, Patreese Johnson is one of the people featured in the oral histories. She is a poet and public speaker. Johnson is also one of the New Jersey Four, a group of young women who were wrongly charged with assault after themselves being assaulted in the west village in New York City. The film *Out in the Night* features the story of these young African American lesbian women from Newark whose lives were turned upside down by this incident, by police misconduct (which Johnson likens to the methods used by the police in the Central Park Five cases), and by her subsequent incarceration for assault, when in fact she and her friends were the ones who were assaulted. Johnson's story links to issues such as mass incarceration, police misconduct and over-policing, and the demonization of African American lesbian women by the press, all of which are a significant part of her life story as related in the oral history.

Another person whose story students find particularly engaging is that of Tracey "Africa" Norman, a model who grew up in Newark and, in the 1970s, became the first African American transgender woman model featured on a box of Clairol. She modeled for and was featured in a number of magazines including *Essence* and *Harper's Bazaar*. Students are often surprised to learn that this kind of success was even possible in the 1970s. I would not necessarily cover the fashion industry as related to issues of exclusion and inclusion in a political science class, but Norman's story links these issues in a way that engages students' interest.

Focusing on the oral histories does mean that I spend less time addressing literature produced by political scientists about LGBTQ politics. For example, although the empirical evidence on changes in public attitudes in the US toward members of the LGBTQ+ community is interesting, and there is a good deal of this kind of work, I generally do not draw on this literature for this class. This is because while there are some QNOHP public figures, public opinion is not closely related to any of the oral histories. Thus, the class does not really address elections and electoral politics, nor do we read about LGBTQ+ public officials or candidates. On the other hand, the class does draw on literature that addresses public policy relating to some of the issues that narrators discuss. So for example I have used Heath Fogg Davis's (2017) book *Beyond Trans*, as well as Paisley Currah's (2022) *Sex Is as Sex Does* in the class.

I also draw on some literature about local politics and policy. A number of the QNOHP respondents were instrumental in creating a more supportive community in Newark through institutions such as the

Unity Fellowship Church, the Newark LGBT Community Center, and the Newark LGBTQ Concerns Advisory Commission. Thus, the focus is often on public policy, especially local and state policy, and civil society infrastructure, rather than on elected officials or elections.

This focus on policy and the oral histories also has made the course more appealing to students with interdisciplinary backgrounds. Political science literature, especially the literature that focuses on elections and public opinion, in my experience is not very interesting to students from fields outside of the discipline. However, the focus on stories and their connections to local politics and policy makes the course more interesting to students from gender and sexuality studies, as well as from the humanities disciplines. Given the location of the course as an elective in several interdisciplinary programs as well as in political science, this has made the course more intelligible and has enhanced conversations between students.

Conclusion

Developing courses with engaged pedagogy can be more labor-intensive for faculty. However, the benefit to students and to course engagement is well worth the effort. I have greatly enjoyed using the materials from the QNOHP. I have found that using the oral histories engages students both with the local LGBTQ movement and with basic approaches commonly used in social science research. The students' enthusiasm for the material has made teaching the course quite satisfying.

Many of the approaches and assignments that I described could be adopted in part or as a whole by others who teach about LGBTQ+ politics in political science and in interdisciplinary majors and minors. Some of this material could also be used as a unit within a course on a variety of topics in political science, such as a gender and politics course, an upper-level course on public policy, or a course on methodology.

The QNOHP is an ongoing project, and new oral histories continue to be collected and added to the website. Scholars have drawn on this resource for their research, and I expect this to continue and add to the material for courses on LGBTQ+ politics. This resource promises to continue to engage students and scholars for the foreseeable future, and I am glad to be able to use it in my teaching.

Notes

1. For more on some of these issues, see also chapter 6 by Cyril Ghosh and chapter 5 by Erin Mayo-Adam in this volume.

2. For more ideas on how to incorporate materials on SOGIE human rights, albeit in a different kind of course, see chapter 10 in this volume by Seth J. Meyer, Nicole M. Elias, and Maria J. D'Agostino.

3. Rutgers University–Newark Office of the Chancellor. 2014. "Rutgers University–Newark: Where Opportunity Meets Excellence," https://www.newark.rutgers.edu/sites/default/files/run_strategic_plan_-final.pdf.

4. "Queer Newark: Our Voices, Our Histories," Queer Newark Oral History Project, November 12, 2011, https://queer.newark.rutgers.edu/events/queer-newark-our-voices-our-histories.

5. Queer Newark Oral History Project, https://queer.newark.rutgers.edu.

6. "At Home in Newark: Stories from the Queer Newark Oral History Project," https://queer.newark.rutgers.edu/about/at-home-in-newark.

7. For more information, see the exhibit page on the QNOHP website, https://queer.newark.rutgers.edu/about/at-home-in-newark.

8. For a brief discussion, see Timothy Stewart-Winter and Whit Strub, "The Murder of Sakia Gunn and LGBT Anti-Violence Mobilization," Out History, https://outhistory.org/exhibits/show/queer-newark/murder-of-sakia-gunn.

9. See this summary on the QNOHP site, https://queer.newark.rutgers.edu/resources/history-queer-club-spaces-newark.

10. See chapter 11 in this volume, by Andrew R. Flores, for ideas on quantitative methods courses; certainly if one were teaching both qualitative and quantitative methods, the assignment I describe could be adapted for the qualitative methods portion.

11. "Interviews (in Numerical Order)," Act Up Oral History Project, https://actuporalhistory.org/numerical-interviews.

References

Allam, Nermin, Janice Gallagher, Jyl Josephson, and Mara Sidney. 2021. "Outside-In Political Science: Implementing Community-Engaged Pedagogy Across the Political Science Curriculum." *PS: Political Science & Politics* 54 (2): 377–80.

Bailey, Marlon. 2013. *Butch Queens Up in Pumps: Gender, Performance, and Ballroom Culture in Detroit*. University of Michigan Press.

Bennion, Elizabeth A., and Xander E. Laughlin. 2018. "Best Practices in Civic Education: Lessons from the Journal of Political Science Education." *Journal of Political Science Education* 14 (3): 287–330. https://doi.org/10.1080/15512169.2017.1399798.

Brown, Karen McCarthy. 2001. "Mimesis in the Face of Fear: Femme Queens, Butch Queens, and Gender Play in the Houses of Greater Newark." In *Passing: Identity and Interpretation in Sexuality, Race, and Religion*, edited by María Carla Sánchez and Linda Schlossberg. New York University Press.

Cantor, Nancy. 2021. "Building the Inclusive Academy from the Outside In." Remarks given at the Rutgers Biomedical and Health Sciences Faculty Development Symposium, Developing and Empowering Diverse Communities in Higher Education, held virtually on June 21, 2021.

Currah, Paisley. 2022. *Sex Is as Sex Does*. New York University Press.

Davidow, Jackson. 2020. "Museums and Mourning in COVID-19." *Boston Review*, December 1.

Davis, Heath Fogg. 2017. *Beyond Trans: Does Gender Matter*. New York University Press.

Finley, Ashley. 2011. "Civic Learning and Democratic Engagements: A Review of the Literature on Civic Engagement in Post-Secondary Education." Washington, DC: US Department of Education.

Garretson, Jeremiah. 2017. "The How, Why and Who of LGBTQ 'Victory.'" In *LGBTQ Politics: A Critical Reader*, edited by Marla Brettschneider, Susan Burgess, and Christine Keating. New York University Press.

Josephson, Jyl. 2018. "Teaching Community Organizing and the Practice of Democracy." *Journal of Political Science Education* 14 (4): 491–99.

Levac, Leah. 2020. "Negotiating Tensions in a Community Engaged and Intersectionality-informed Political Science Course." *Politics, Groups and Identities* 8 (1): 194–202. https://doi.org/10.1080/21565503.2019.1605297.

Nelson, Davia, and Nikki Silva, hosts. *The Kitchen Sisters*. Podcast, episode 144, "95,000 Names: Gert McMullin, Sewing the Frontline." https://kitchensisters.org/present/95000-names-gert-mcmullin-sewing-the-frontline/.

Strub, Whit. 2024. *Queer Newark: Stories of Resistance, Love, and Community*. Rutgers University Press.

Chapter 4

The Historical Horizons of LGBTQ+ Rights

Julian Applebaum and Patrick Schmidt

The past half century has been a remarkable time for the progress of LGBTQ+ persons toward full citizenship in society. Although the road has been long, and there are miles to go—with backsliding yet possible—the turnabout has been nothing short of remarkable. Indeed, the dramatic developments in decriminalizing sexual practices and legalizing same-sex marriage have presented scholars with a puzzle: How did so much change within one generation, all while public support for rights in other areas of social and cultural freedom, such as reproductive rights, remained steady? Scholars have pursued many fruitful lines of inquiry, from the media to movements to litigation.

What makes for intriguing research has also made for compelling teaching. The modern cases in which the US Supreme Court expanded LGBTQ+ rights, including marriage equality, are now part of the canon for teaching US civil liberties. Contemporary college students, who display deeper and more bipartisan support of LGBTQ+ rights than their parents and grandparents, embrace the task of explaining this shift. Although there are many other courses in which LGBTQ+ politics can be explored, law-centered courses are common in curricula, and the framework of constitutional law has been a ready way to bring questions of identity, citizenship, and inclusion to the table.

There's much to celebrate and learn from in these materials. Still, we take pause to consider the limits of the dominant approach to LGBTQ+

rights as it gets introduced in many political science courses, especially those with an emphasis on law. Simply put, too often the topic of LGBTQ+ rights has been inserted into textbooks by selecting just a few judicial decisions concerning sexual privacy and same-sex marriage. LGBTQ+ rights, equality, inclusion, and citizenship is much bigger than that. But how can instructors make moves in that direction? Instructors are always limited in what can be packed into a course, especially one as expansive as the US constitutional tradition. We understand why modern treatments may begin at *Bowers v. Hardwick* (1986), or if lucky, Stonewall.

In this chapter, we argue that for teachers of American politics, the most generative next step is to widen the chronological frame for LGBTQ+ rights, and secondarily, to introduce issues related to LGBTQ+ equality that spring from beyond bedrooms and bathrooms. We make this case in two steps. First, we explain the damage done when we treat the modern quest for equality as a narrow set of challenges to the legal order, like a question for marriage equality. Second, if we have convinced you of that, we offer some idiosyncratic suggestions of ways to historicize and diversify the modern story of LGBTQ+ rights. Our hope is that we will have encouraged some instructors to interrogate their approach.

The Hazards of Half Measures

What learning objectives can motivate the inclusion of LGBTQ+ rights into political science courses? There may have been a role, at one point, simply for inclusion and exposure, as an anecdote from one of this chapter's authors (Schmidt) suggested. Teaching American constitutional politics at a university in a southern state, I assigned Daniel Piniello's *Gay Rights and American Law* when it was published in 2003. His impressive study, coding nearly four hundred decisions from federal and state courts, usefully illustrated numerous facets of the judicial process, from the judges to interest groups. As a young teacher, I had a lot to learn about pedagogy, as became clear one day in particular. Whereas Piniello's statistical models and analysis of cases could be considered somewhat dry for undergraduates, a class discussion about the role of case facts and legal distinctions turned uncomfortable as students avoided at all costs using the language rife in Piniello's text. A student who did manage to utter the word "homosexual" ended up flustered and red-faced. It dawned on me after that class period that many of my students had never experienced such a blunt discussion of sexual orientation, at least with an authority figure in the room and without recourse to slang and slurs. While pedagogically this class session was naive and risky, in retrospect it did accomplish something important: It was part of a period in which American society was breaking down barriers.

Twenty years later, college students have different levels of awareness, albeit in a system that still tries to drive discussion out of the classroom. Still, students can speak fluidly about sexuality and sexual identities. What, then, are the pedagogical possibilities of teaching LGBTQ+ rights? Some conversations are still challenging and vitally necessary, most notably around trans identities and conceptions of gender, especially in more conservative climates. But as the scope for sexual and relational freedom has gained wider purchase, another opportunity presents itself: the goal of making more complex the meaning of LGBTQ+ rights. The harm of how LGBTQ+ rights is frequently taught, we argue, is that we risk reducing and erasing the complexity of citizenship and the struggle for full inclusion.

As we describe in this chapter, a canon of key legal decisions has narrowed the story of LGBTQ+ rights to a selection of concerns. The key to unlocking the complexity of full citizenship is fortunately available in the historical record. By widening the historical record, we can offer students new ways of thinking about the present and future of inclusivity. As Marcel Proust wrote, "The real voyage of discovery consists not in seeking new landscapes but in having new eyes." To further tease out the problems we aim to address, in the following subsections we tease out the problems of erasure, reductivism, and the narrowed horizons for what LGBTQ+ politics must be.

ERASURE

Telling LGBTQ+ history by surveying the progress made in the past half century is appealing, and in its triumphalism it risks serious misrepresentations. The selection and elevation of some issues, those that are front and center in contemporary awareness, frames the history of LGBTQ+ activism through a received tradition that is itself the product of historical violence. What has been erased is not only the people whose stories can be told but the ambiguities in and challenges to the social and political order that were erased from our conscious understanding. What can be emphasized today is how much work historians and other scholars have done to uncover and recover the sense of possibilities that were lost.

In the context of LGBTQ+ history, the much vaunted and inspiring victory of *Obergefell v. Hodges* (2015) is too often presented unmoored from the rich, lengthy threads of activism through decades and even centuries. Taking one leading textbook as an example, the authors arrive at *Obergefell* from a distinct path: reproductive rights and its reliance on privacy rights. The "hook" is to show that "the right to privacy, as it follows from the 'liberty' guaranteed in the due process clauses, has implications for many other activities, including private sexual activity, same-sex marriage, the right to die, drug testing, and communication in the information age" (Epstein et al. 2022, 372). In this telling, the Court's decision in *Bowers v. Hardwick* (1986) "energized the gay community" and inspired major efforts to overturn such laws (372–73). Although the authors are careful to note that arguments based on Fourteenth Amendment equal protections were woven in, they locate the case among privacy doctrines, nod toward the many other cases adjudicating privacy, and move on to the right to die. Another textbook, among the deepest and most historically-minded, goes no further, except to fill in the space between *Bowers* and *Lawrence v. Texas* (2003) with the Defense of Marriage Act of 1996 and developments at the state level around the same time (Gillman et al. 2020). In these leading examples, *Obergefell* is adjacent to a societal debate about privacy, bookended by reproductive rights and the right to die. The case has been removed from the sphere of LGBTQ politics and relocated as a segment of other doctrines. In this narrative, *Obergefell* is less about the rights of political equality for same-sex couples and more about how that victory was leveraged into other political struggles.

Furthermore, these texts isolate *Obergefell* from its revolutionary and historical contexts. A curriculum forwarding these LGBTQ+ political victories pins the movement with a specific, sometimes even singular objective. Erased are the branches of a sprawling tree of resilience, strength, and activism. The street fighting around the Stonewall Inn is not mentioned in the texts just discussed, perhaps because the political significance of protest movements is difficult to square with this court-centered, focused agenda—and even more difficult to square with an account that makes same-sex marriage the teleological vision. Even stretching to Stonewall complicates this narrative with the recognition of resisting police brutality, oppressive violence toward transgender and gender nonconforming identities, and criminalization of sex workers. Further (lest an account that makes Stonewall a foil for contemporary politics reinforce its own erasures), pre-Stonewall LGBTQ+ resistance and mobilization, such as the

1966 Compton Cafeteria Riot, urges us to dig below the surface of history to place the "revolutionary moment" into the context of more systemic oppression and struggle (see Bronski 2011, 209). As noted later, much of the struggle had other issues in mind.

Abbreviating LGBTQ+ history in this way has broader cultural and moral implications as well. For one, though we hope it doesn't need to be said, portraying gay rights as a history only decades old reinforces the false claim that being gay and trans is a fad. Recency bias erases not only the multiplicity of issues and desires of LGBTQ+ persons but their very existence. Students may well observe in wider discourse how LGBTQ+ identities are portrayed as novel aberrations, curable conditions afflicting confused and perverted individuals, or trendy labels hijacking our youth via peer pressure. In constitutional discourse, this argument has a tangible bite: Since equal protection analysis invites consideration of historical marginalization as a factor when organizing legal provisions into suspect categories, the uncontextualized arrival of LGBTQ+ rights alienates LGBTQ+ persons from that conversation. It becomes easier to give credence to Justice Antonin Scalia's oft-published quips that rather than being a "discrete and insular minority," the modern turn in the law was the creation of a newly "politically powerful minority" (*Romer v. Evans* [1996]) that had hoodwinked law schools and courts with the "so-called homosexual agenda" (*Lawrence*). When gay rights are a flash in the pan, the quick emergence and victory of same-sex marriage gives little indication of any pattern of oppression.

The attempts to erase identities in the present often mirror erasures of the past and are even directly aided by them. Homophobes and transphobes weaponize a shallow historical frame to delegitimize the LGBTQ+ community in the eyes of the heterosexual cisgender public. The surge in "Don't Say Gay" bills reflects a desire to invalidate and stamp out LGBTQ+ history to undermine recognition of gender and sexual minorities. In the 2020 book *Irreversible Damage: The Transgender Craze Seducing Our Daughters*, Abigail Shrier calls being transgender a "social contagion" among adolescent girls that materialized less than twenty years ago (Shrier 2021, 15). Her book generated thousands of sales and was named an *Economist* book of the year. Similarly, Rosaria Butterfield (2022) begins her article "What Is Transgenderism?" by finding significance in the term being "such a new concept that the 1973 Oxford English Dictionary that sits open on [her] desk has no entry." At best, thin accounts of LGBTQ+ rights are a missed opportunity to offer historical touchstones at a time when high school curricula are unlikely to venture there. At worst, instruction in LGBTQ+ politics can reify erasures being actively promoted.

REDUCTIVISM

Related to erasure is the problem that students are too often presented with LGBTQ+ politics only through legal materials. By pointing at the "reductivism" of LGBTQ+ politics, we mean the tendency of contemporary materials to overly simplify both the substance and processes by which issues are contested.

The opinions in *Lawrence, Obergefell,* and select others were written in the justices' anticipation that their words would enter into the national media and be read as part of the wider "culture wars." They are approachable, exciting, frustrating, and engaging texts. Despite the aphorism of Alexis de Tocqueville that "scarcely any political question arises in the United States that is not resolved, sooner or later, in a judicial question," court cases do, in fact, make some issues more legible than others. The breadth of issues found in the judicial record mirrors the injuries that have been brought to court (Felstiner et al. 1980–81). With a little more digging, one can find claims for gay rights that preceded *Bowers*. Even so, one such effort (Fisher and Harringer 2013) to describe the percolating challenges to sodomy statutes in the early 1970s still built toward a 1976 dissent that linked the appeal for privacy in "sexual intimacies" to the effect of *Griswold v. Connecticut* (1965). These are the claims that made it to court, but they still represent the tip of an iceberg. Much more went unraised, much less unaddressed. Some oppressive acts, such as workplace discrimination, remain hidden. In fact, LGBTQ+ rights claims struggled to gain traction in the US courts, and the law was usually weaponized to suppress gay, lesbian, and transgender Americans' voices. For one, LGBTQ+ people facing discrimination also faced barriers finding legal representation. A 1956 study found that lawyers were the most hostile of all the professions to homosexuality (Canaday 2009, 248), and suits were more quickly dismissed by biased legal officials. Even powerhouse civil rights activists have wavered on including gay rights in their work. In 1957, the American Civil Liberties Union (ACLU) concluded it was "not within the province of the Union to evaluate the social validity of laws aimed at the suppression or elimination of homosexuals" and approved of Eisenhower's purges of homosexuals from government offices (Cervini 2020, 61). The social ramifications of being open about one's sexuality or gender also curbed the desire of LGBTQ+ citizens in seeking legal solutions to discrimination.

Furthermore, the canon of LGBTQ+ rights suffers from a survival bias, where only cases representing a narrow set of identities, issues, and ideologies make it inside the courtroom and into the textbooks. Since legal cases are undertaken with the desire to win, the logics and strategies deployed in court are influenced by what is most tactically effective. Most cases concerning transgender litigants have tended to rely on logics that perpetuated the pathologization of gender variance, to the point where the litigants have deployed narratives of mental anguish and medical emergencies to increase their likelihood of legal success (Applebaum 2023, 135). In other cases, judges begin with the assumption that sex/gender is natural, immutable, and assigned at birth and interpret the litigant within that framework. This too has led transgender litigants to portray themselves in conformity to that narrative so that they can persuade judges to view them favorably (139). However, while studying these arguments can be valuable for understanding the power of law to (mis)understand marginalized communities and the legal conditions transgender people have faced, they are not representative of the much broader transgender political movement that has aimed to dismantle these very ideas. This is true even for *Bostock v. Clayton County* (2020) where the Supreme Court delivered a victory to a trans woman based not on her gender identity but rather on her assigned sex at birth. The trans legal rights movement has been criticized for undercutting larger objectives of trans freedom and self-determination and, as Dean Spade (2012, 11) says, "fail[ing] to deliver meaningful change to trans people." Teaching trans politics through only its legal footprint risks reducing it to the legal arguments that have been most effective before judges, which have neglected and even undermined large swaths of activism and political organizing.

Oppressive policies and activities materialized beyond the courts and legislatures, emerging in forms like the US park police's Sex Perversion Elimination Program (Adkins 2016), the exclusion of gay men and women from veterans benefits (Canaday 2009, 150), and deportation of gay immigrants as "psychopaths" (Canaday 2009, 222). Even among contemporary "mainstream" LGBTQ+ issues, most have not found a foothold within appellate decision making. Civil rights for transgender people did not reach the Supreme Court until *Bostock v. Clayton County* was decided in 2020, which was a consolidation of two claims of sexual orientation discrimination and one claim of gender identity discrimination (Bove 2019).

The most talked about transgender rights issues of today, namely women's sports inclusion, bathrooms, and gender-affirming healthcare, only just started to be litigated in appellate courts within the last decade, and the highest court has said precious little about these issues. Many enterprising instructors will reach for materials that can present these to students, whether briefly (opinion pieces) or excerpts of briefs in lower court appeals, but this illustrates how so many issues, past and present, must be made legible without a ripe case of parties clashing. Constitutional questions are found outside of the courtroom. Municipalities and even school districts show a wider range of contemporary battlefronts: Housing and workplace nondiscrimination policies (as reflected in *Romer*), healthcare, service from public accommodations, and more are negotiated within states and cities before breaching the national sphere. In 1972, East Lansing, Michigan, became the first city in the country to prohibit discrimination based on sexual orientation when the city council approved a policy outlining that the council would "employ the best applicant for each vacancy on the basis of his qualifications for the job and without regard to race, color, creed, national origin, sex or homosexuality" (Cosentino 2012). Ann Arbor passed the nation's first comprehensive nondiscrimination ordinance covering employment, housing, and public accommodations that same year.

The impulse within legal circles to "locate" a case within a certain line of doctrine is a reductivist tendency, one that gives a dispute meaning for its contribution to a conceptual framework on some question, stripped of the identities of the participants. Looking back to a textbook from 1990, when *Bowers* stood alone from the now-canon, the "issue of laws criminalizing homosexual conduct" was tucked into a chapter on privacy and autonomy under a section titled "Other Issues"—along with *Moore v. City of East Cleveland* (1977) concerning a single-family zoning ordinance that prevented a grandmother from living with her grandchildren (Feeley and Krislov 1990). Over time, "gay rights" appears to have been constructed out of the thread of canonical cases—*Bowers, Romer, Lawrence, Windsor, Obergefell*—though it is still placed as subsections of chapters on privacy and equality. This phenomenon happens for other groups as well. The rights of African Americans are overwhelmingly taught through the issue of equality in education: from *Brown v. Board of Education* to school busing to affirmative action in higher education. A personal anecdote makes the point: One day, a decade ago, a Black student raised her hand and asked why her civil liberties casebook had no cases on police violence, because, she said, "that's my experience of civil liberties in America." Two answers became obvious. First, the material on criminal justice in the casebook was framed as Fourth Amendment or Fifth Amendment issues with little mention of their differential impact on Americans of color. Second, critically, police violence produces few issues that rise to the Supreme Court, much less in now-canonical cases.

In short, the richness of LGBTQ+ activism is distorted by being reduced to a few cases. Even among LGBTQ+ litigation, there is a deep well of challenges. Many times these cases are placed within different doctrinal lines, such that they escape recognition as part of a constellation of rights swirling around an identity collective. In *One Inc. v. Olesen* (1958), credited as the first case before the US Supreme Court dealing with homosexuality, the justices reversed a circuit court decision that allowed the post office to refuse service to *One: The Homosexual Magazine* on the grounds of the obscenity of the material. The Court's one-sentence per curiam decision merely invoked the six-month-old landmark *Roth v. United States* (1957). The twenty-eight years between *One Inc.* and *Bowers* saw another eight cases involving LGBTQ+ issues, including immigration and employment. The available materials, especially the lack of highly visible, digestible appellate decisions, affects how the issues are framed to students.

CHANGED LANDSCAPE, WIDER HORIZONS

Most broadly, we observe that the absence of historical depth constrains students in their ability to understand and analyze emerging and issues yet to emerge in American society. Sometimes the issues that students are considering come from students themselves, who can be more plugged into the strains circulating in popular discourse. These issues can provide a gateway to historic questions, though sometimes instructors are simply unaware of the questions that have currency, especially on social media.

For example, the umbrella of LGBTQ+ advocacy itself has been contested in a number of places. One of the most widely recognized is TERFs, or trans-exclusionary radical feminists (see, e.g., Burns 2019), which has had particular traction, not least of which because of controversial comments by bestselling author J. K. Rowling. Infighting can be found at numerous historical and geographic moments among those in the LGBTQ+ community as well. The notion of a "politics of respectability," where there is division about the goal of assimilation within a dominant culture, plagues all movements in which a marginalized group may marginalize some of their own in order to win acceptance (Strolovitch and Crowder

2018; Dazey 2021; Jones 2022). The effect appears no less vividly merely because a society appears to evolve along on a more inclusive path. In London, a new lesbian, gay, and bisexual alliance group formed in 2019 and purposely excluded the transgender community from its platform. The LGB Alliance launched with the mission of serving the same-sex-attracted population, claiming that the gay and transgender communities should be divorced due to the lack of common struggle and shared identities. Co-founder Kate Harris explained, "The main difference is that lesbians, gays, and bisexuals have something in common because of our sexual orientation, that has nothing to do with being trans" (Gluck 2019). The organization rapidly gained international attention and expanded to over a dozen countries.

As the component identities are understood today, disagreements and separation within the umbrella might appear sensible or obvious. The distinction between gender identity and sexual orientation is simple: You can be gay without being trans and vice versa. Gay and trans people use different pride flags, have different terminology specific to their experiences, and face different forms of oppression. Nevertheless, before casting away the umbrella, a historical approach offers a caution: Untangling same-sex attraction from gender variance is a contemporary phenomenon. In the late nineteenth century, sexologists theorized that same-sex desire was "the result of physical, emotional, or psychological 'inversion.' In other words, the gender of persons who desired their own sex was somehow reversed. When a man desired a man, it was actually a woman—presumably existing within the man's body—who was desiring a man. When a woman desired a woman, it was actually a male essence within the woman's body who felt that desire" (Bronski 2011, 94). In other words, same-sex attraction was a form of gender variance. The line between being homosexual and being transgender was non-existent because both were considered men trapped in women's bodies or women trapped in men's bodies. Therefore, they formed a community of "inverts" based on shared struggle and a state-imposed identity that later evolved into the LGBTQ+ community. Neglecting the category's historical roots erases the meaning of these identities and limits understanding the origins of LGBTQ+ politics as an umbrella.

A struggle over the composition of the movement reflects disagreement about the issues that can claim the weight of the movement behind it—along with allies, media attention, and public support. Trans rights, as the most recent phase of struggle, has had a more ambiguous place.

The historical work to understand movement agendas can pay off in the ability to critique the roads taken and not taken. Front and center, the canonical narrative of privacy and same-sex marriage might strike many students as an unlikely focus. Most often, among the vast majority of students eighteen to twenty-two years old who support same-sex marriage, the thread leading to *Obergefell* is read triumphantly, with the remaining questions being how to defend these gains (in the context of expanding precedents for religious freedom) or the directions yet taken.

But revisiting the horizons, we might ask why same-sex marriage was never seen as the crux of the radical LGBTQ+ rights agenda. Some activists have criticized the focus on same-sex marriage as a kind of assimilation into a category of relationship that has value precisely because it is exclusionary and heteronormative (Kim 2010). Rather than address ongoing struggles of survival through disproportionate homelessness, hate crimes, lethal denial of healthcare, or radical missions of deconstructing systemic homophobia and transphobia, society elevated the desire of some gay couples to replicate legally and socially sanctioned heterosexual marriage. From a civil rights perspective, of course gay couples should not be excluded from the legal benefit of marriage. But its success as the only LGBTQ+ rights issue to be victorious in high courts highlights its utility to society, which can tolerate homosexuality because it can imitate heterosexuality rather than because gay people are in and of themselves worthy of protection. Calls to end "Don't Ask, Don't Tell" and valorize brave LGBTQ+ soldiers instead gained traction among heteronormative media spaces, and advocates pursuing institutional paths to change came to represent the movement itself. In short, by replicating visions of suburban monogamy, the rise of same-sex marriage failed to give voice to queer futures. As Lisa Duggan (2003, 44) notes, by the turn of the millennium, "multicultural" diversity within the neoliberal mainstream cooperated with the corporate neoliberal, leaving a "rhetorical commitment to diversity, and to a narrow, formal, non-redistributive form of 'equality' politics."

POSSIBILITIES

This critique admits of several caveats. Most obviously, this critique aims at a common part of the American curriculum: instruction in law. American political scientists have long benefited and then maintained the myth of American constitutional law; courses, often as a two-course sequence, in the institutions and rights provided by the American constitution, are standard.

So is the style of the instruction, which often replicates professional law schools (see Graber 2005). There are many, even within the subfield, who escape this problem by teaching focused courses on LGBTQ+ politics and rights. This strategy answers a second limitation of our account, namely that the choices made in courses are often the product of time limitations. Even when teachers are willing to explore historical rabbit holes, it is impossible to do so. If nothing else allows, perhaps it is still desirable to introduce LGBTQ+ politics through the *Bowers*-to-*Obergefell* line of material and then to use discussion to push against the dominant approaches.

That may be the case. Nevertheless, we hope that this critique opens up some new directions for instructors and students. In what follows, we advance some ideas that have expanded our vision of LGBTQ+ rights and equality and that might generate discussions that will undo erasures, avoid reductivism, and widen horizons.

Moving Beyond the Moment

The past decade has been a daunting time for teachers of politics, public policy, and more. Norms have been shaken at the same time that pedagogy has been upturned by the intersection of technology and pandemics. But perhaps the party deserving the most credit for challenging the reactionary tendencies of contemporary politics are historians. The increasing diversity of the field in the past half century has had dividends for historical inquiry itself, as scholars have tapped into overlooked material and asked new questions of old archives. In this section, we offer an idiosyncratic look at work that exemplify strategies for widening the historical scope of the struggle for LGBTQ+ rights. Our goal here is to offer an instructor of American politics or constitutional law a few resources that have been useful.

THE QUESTIONS WE ASK

An enduring problem for much teaching in American politics, including but well beyond LGBTQ+ politics, is the insularity and limited horizons of its exposition by "Americanists"—namely political scientists who specialize in US politics, usually without reference to the frameworks and methods from the comparative politics subfield. Possessing the critical mass necessary to stay siloed, buoyed by the US' global stature in the twentieth century such that the inquiry needs no justification, and distanced from scholars in other nations, the study of American politics took a long turn into more specialized and narrow research questions, often of a behavioral persuasion. A key reply took shape in the scholarly agenda of American political development (APD). Then, in discussions of rights and law, a comparative turn increasingly opened up questions that are now paying off in an era of democratic backsliding. These questions include What is a constitution after all? What exists beyond liberal ideologies? And what drives revolutions? These are questions that may have been momentarily useful for discussing the foundations of American politics (i.e., the American Revolution) but seemed irrelevant to end-of-millennium politics in a mature democracy. Like the project of APD, which has been synthesized with LGBTQ+ politics in works such as Engel (2016), our first call is for critical reflection on the questions we forward to students. Within constitutional law, fascination with the development of privacy short-circuits questions about the mental maps of doctrines themselves (Schmidt 2016) and about how doctrine is both an output and an input into discourse and structures of contestation.

Even though historical perspectives may provide a ready antidote to the limited gaze of the contemporary canon, we can add that comparative investigation is often equally useful for displacing assumptions students may hold about the political world. It can surprise students, for example, who assume that advocacy for LGBTQ+ inclusivity must come from the progressive left of the political spectrum, that in the past generation of European politics the demand for tolerance and inclusivity has come from the political right, including some of the far-right politicians—such as the Netherlands' Geert Wilders—who spark disgust for their crusades against ethnic diversity. The inversion performed by Wilders's PVV party (Partij Voor de Vrijheid; "Party for Freedom") is that a platform of conserving of Dutch values, especially liberal tolerance, allowed Wilders to position the LGBT insiders against the true threat to the nation from Muslim outsiders/immigrants who were unwilling to support gay rights and marriage equality. Thus, the comparative turn upsets the "given" quantities of liberal and conservative in the same way that a historical turn can, and in a wider vein we would argue that teachers of American politics continue to look at ways of teaching American politics from a vantage point on other shores.

DEEP HISTORIES OF DECENCY

The payoff of historical perspectives is sometimes greatest when you make a big chronological jump. Taking students to a period of time that is far removed, and then showing the parallels to the present, sets the stage for the age-old work of making the strange familiar and the familiar strange.

A concrete example illustrates. Among the hundreds of proposed anti-transgender laws in American states, a number have focused on drag performances and cross-dressing. Doctrinally, challenges to these laws are expected to generate lengthy litigation, first in light of First Amendment principles of expression and second as equal protection claims, both against the statues on their face and as applied in enforcement. Beyond the question "Are these constitutional?" the light of contemporary politics might illuminate questions about where and why these bills have emerged. Why are "culture wars" such a popular agenda item at this point in time? Who stands to gain? How are these laws resisted?

A historical perspective resists the idea that transgender individuals are newly emergent in society, fashioned by changes in medical technologies (hormones and surgery) or by radical changes of norms driven by activists. We suggest two scholars whose work offers an accessible entry point into the debate. Ruthann Robson's book *Dressing Constitutionally* connects constitutional case law concerning dress in an array of ways. Chapter 3, "Dressing Sexily," offers three discrete sections detailing how the state has policed clothing in order to maintain sexual hierarchies. In Robson's telling, statutes designed to maintain gender-segregated clothing have been challenged since such laws first appeared in New York in 1845, but they were met with mixed success until "social change in dress made the notion of gender-appropriate dress incoherent, rendering cross-dressing laws unconstitutionally vague." But, she adds, "the direct imposition of gender-appropriate dress remains a vital strategy for controlling certain segments of the population, especially the young" (Robson 2013, 64). Instead of a unique modern panic, then, gender segregation in clothing becomes a cyclical phenomenon, raising different questions of causality and social forces.

Swirling within macro-level questions about when and why threats to LGBTQ+ rights emerge, a complementary reading can bring into focus micro-level practices concerning gender fluidity. The work of sociologist Clare Sears offers a wide-ranging tour through cross-dressing in the law, showing how it was entwined at various points in prostitution, vagrancy, vaudeville theater, freak shows, and more. Her book-length treatment of the subject, *Arresting Dress*, reorients our attention to the ways that laws construct "normality" (Sears 2015). For a shorter, more classroom-friendly entry into her work, "All That Glitters" (2008) has for years captivated students with a portrayal of the "Old West" in which all-male dances in gold mining camps were decidedly more camp than anyone today might have imagined. But Sears does much more than show that cross-gender practices "flourished" among migrants to the West. In the decades that followed, attacks on immigrant labor from China flipped that script to use the supposedly "feminized" Chinese laborer as part of the justification for discrimination and eventual exclusion. Should any students need an introduction to intersectionality, Sears's article provides that along cleavages of ethnicity and gender expressions. This historical account does more than just connect contemporary questions of gender identity and the law with a long history of the same. It also renders hypocrisy and political agendas shockingly familiar.

POLICING ACROSS POLICY DOMAINS

The regulation of LGBTQ+ lives is well understood from the direct assault on the intimacies of the bedroom, especially criminal sodomy statutes. While one may argue that more indirect means of oppression ultimately grow from the same source and target the same ends, examining the ways that law has policed sexual identities across a wider range of policy fields has several effects. For one, it demonstrates how ongoing regulation was both possible and practiced. This contrasts with the facts of *Bowers* and to a lesser extent *Lawrence*, in which it is unclear whether police can enforce proscriptions that happen behind closed doors. Surveillance and mechanisms of control find many expressions, and the bureaucratic machines devoted to this work have been far more extensive than students know. That is, the machinery of regulation was built and running long before the modern age. Also, rather than remaining within the criminal field with its emphasis on penal prescriptions, penalties appear in many forms, particularly the denial of benefits or loss of access.

The Republican-led states of Texas and Florida have inspired a new wave of work that is prime for discussion. As just one example, the *Chronicle of Higher Education* produced a series of articles that simply move to a pre-Stonewall era of persecution of LGBTQ+ persons in higher education. The works give credit to archival material and oral histories, and they are able to portray the victims and perpetrators of the campus inquests in their full humanity (Pettit 2022a, 2022b). As rights movements do not emerge from nowhere, such works can invite students to look more closely at the ways that the voices of LGBTQ+ activists were being heard. The groundwork for later development is laid by people with agency, not simply in a welling up of victimization. One longer, though readable, account of pre-Stonewall activism is Eric Cervini's *The Deviant's War* (2020), which charts the work of the Mattachine Society of Washington as it fought the persecution of LGBTQ+ employees of the federal government.

Margot Canaday offers an especially robust tour through policy domains that can be useful for questioning how contemporary discourse in the making centers on select issues to the exclusion of others. Canaday's *The Straight State* (2009) highlights how sexuality played a role in immigration, military affairs, and welfare policy from 1900 to 1983. To offer a shorter snippet of her material suitable for class discussion, Canaday's study of the GI Bill describes how the highly significant benefits offered to World War II veterans were denied to any soldier with an undesirable discharge on account of "homosexual acts or tendencies" (Canaday 2003). The effect was, she writes, to "build a closet within federal social policy" (956) while conferring significant benefits on the normatively "deserving" type of citizen. Consider then: What is the horizon for gay rights? In historical perspective, the post–World War II boom was one of the most significant moments for a changing America, and in higher education and social welfare, exclusion was explicit. These works speak to what the nation values, in addition to what is being denied at individual points in time.

The historical development and lived experiences look more complicated with the turn to employment offered by Canaday's more recent work, *Queer Career: Sexuality and Work in Modern America* (2023). Her interview-based book puts focus on law, civil rights, and liberation in both public and private sector employment from the 1960s to the 1990s. Central to her account is that gay and lesbian workers weren't "hidden," as one might assume if only studying privacy, sex, and police investigations. Instead, she describes a different experience: employers who knew and took advantage (sometimes coercively) of employees' sexual orientation.

CASES BEYOND THE CANON

The works discussed here open up periods of time and policy fields that usually never see the light of an undergraduate syllabus. A last strategy for bringing students into new discussions about LGBTQ+ rights involves a personal rebellion against the canon of constitutional law as given to most instructors by the casebooks of the field. The canons, like the top tourist attractions in major destinations, usually get attention for a good reason. But the serendipitous discoveries while traveling are often the most memorable, and likewise inserting an uncommon case or two into the canon can be enormously generative.

As Canaday writes, some of the contemporary social construction of homosexuality comes out of mid-twentieth-century immigration law. In her account, immigration laws are intended to police persons as wanted or unwanted, and the state wields immense power against noncitizens, who lack the right to due process in the American legal system. In the 1952 McCarran–Walter Act, state officials sought to deport and exclude homosexuals at the border under provisions concerning "crimes of moral turpitude" and "psychopathic personality." Homosexuality became a legal construct; someone who committed homosexual acts was assigned the status of a homosexual person and therefore a psychopath. The state devised, implemented, and enforced a legal homo-hetero binarism based on a constellation of perceived traits, actions, and behavior. However, the two sides of this binary were not on equal footing. Homosexual acts proved homosexuality, but heterosexual acts did not a heterosexual make. The National Organization of Women (NOW) reported that at its height, perhaps around two thousand immigrants per year were medically excluded for homosexuality.

With Canaday as an instructor's tour guide, a few cases make illustrative additions to the usual suspects. The 1956 case *United States v. Roberto Flores-Rodriguez* posed the first challenge to the moral turpitude and psychopathic personality provisions. Roberto Flores-Rodriguez, an immigrant from Cuba, had been arrested for exposing himself to other men in a New York City restroom and convicted of disorderly conduct. His imprisonment sentence was suspended so that he could return to Cuba. When he reentered the United States two years later, he failed to report that he had been previously convicted of disorderly conduct. He was later arrested and convicted again of disorderly conduct, and the Immigration and Naturalization Service (INS) claimed his reentry was invalid due to his failure to disclose the previous conviction and ordered him deported. Flores-Rodriguez appealed, arguing that there was a technical distinction between a "crime" of moral turpitude and, as it was classified under New York State law, the "offense" of disorderly conduct for which he had been convicted. The Second Circuit Court of Appeals ruled against him, writing in its opinion that not only did his offense conviction count as a crime of moral turpitude but also the offense itself made him susceptible to exclusion as a psychopathic inferior. This marks a shift from regulating homosexuality as a class of activities to policing homosexuals as a class of person.

Fleuti v. Rosenberg was a turning point when it reached the Ninth Circuit in 1962. George Fleuti, who admitted to partaking in homosexual relationships for twenty-two years and was set to be deported as a psychopathic personality, successfully argued that the statute for psychopathic personality was void for vagueness by highlighting that the Public Health Service (PHS) surgeon and Fleuti's own doctor disagreed as to the meaning of the term, and that Fleuti would not have engaged in such behavior if he had been properly warned. The court canceled the deportation and legally recognized homosexuality as a form of conduct rather than an unshakable status. The government appealed the case to the Supreme Court, asking the Court to reassert the notion that homosexuality was a condition or status rather than a behavior. The Court let the Ninth Circuit's ruling stand, and Chief Justice Earl Warren wrote in a note to himself, "It was conceded by the government doctors that all homosexuals are not medically psychopaths."

Boutilier v. INS in 1966 concerned Clive Michael Boutilier, who disclosed a dismissed sodomy charge during his naturalization application process. The Second Circuit recognized that "Congress utilized the phrase 'psychopathic personality' not as a medical or psychiatric formulation, but as a legal term of art designed to preclude the admission of homosexual aliens into the United States" to support the INS in deporting Boutilier (Canaday 2009, 242). In the Supreme Court appeal, Boutilier's lawyers attempted to disrupt the notion that homosexual behavior condemned someone to homosexual status: "The source of the evil lies in an apparent belief that there is some kind of recognizable human being that is a homosexual, like one might recognize a red-head. . . . By and large homosexuality is a kind of behavior, evidently very wide spread, and not the manifestation of a particular kind of person" (244). They pointed to instances of Boutilier having heterosexual sex and displaying markers of good citizenry like working, attending mass, and bowling. The Court upheld his deportation, concluding that homosexuality was an identity that could be extrapolated from homosexual activity and incompatible with citizenry.

The usual presentation of rights movements needs a jolt. Too often, the ascendance of Thurgood Marshall and the National Association for the Advancement of Colored People (NAACP) in the 1950s sets the stage for Ruth Bader Ginsburg's work in the 1970s. But movements overlapped and demands were present. That point can be made with reference to numerous groups and issues. Like what Ian Haney Lopez's excellent *White by Law* (1997) does for our understanding of race, one or more of these cases can take LGBTQ+ rights out of the contemporary struggle and cut fundamentally to the question of how law understands and constructs identity. A corpus of outstanding work doing the same for sexuality is now emerging (see, e.g., Vogler 2021; Engel and Lyle 2021). Here are the foundational questions for rights and citizenship for LGBTQ+ individuals in the United States, exposed with just a short step outside the canon.

Conclusion

We are sympathetic to anyone teaching constitutional law today. The range and amount of wonderful material available for classroom use allows for nearly limitless choices. It can feel irresponsible or unforgivable to offer a course in American civil liberties and civil rights but to admit that there are whole units that must be cut for simple lack of time. In any given course, vital questions such as the death penalty, gerrymandering, and numerous free speech puzzles have hit the cutting room floor. In that context, it is a difficult message to send at the same time: that there's something that should be added. Leaving out a substantive area of law involves something different than leaving out historical perspectives, however, because the recency bias afflicting many courses about American rights jurisprudence do damage to how students understand the struggle. At its worst, it leaves younger learners prone to the myths that are propagated about LGBTQ+ persons, including the erasure of those who have been persecuted across the whole of the American experience. We have argued here for some interventions that can be economical and high value by showing students the fuller light of history in the struggle for LGBTQ+ rights.

References

Adkins, Judith. 2016. "'These People Are Frightened to Death': Congressional Investigations and the Lavender Scare." *Prologue Magazine* 48 (2), https://www.archives.gov/publications/prologue/2016/summer/lavender.html.

Applebaum, Julian. 2023. "Transgender in Court: Judicial Interpretations of Gender Identity from 1966 to 2022." *Bulletin of Applied Transgender Studies* 2 (3/4): 129–49.

Bove, Jared. 2019. "SCOTUS Hears First Transgender Civil Rights Case." NCSL Blog, Oct. 8. https://www.ncsl.org/blog/2019/10/08/scotus-hears-first-transgender-civil-rights-case.aspx.

Bronski, Michael. 2011. *A Queer History of the United States.* Beacon Press.

Burns, Katelyn. 2019. "The Rise of Anti-Trans 'Radical' Feminists, Explained." *Vox,* Sept. 5. https://www.vox.com/identities/2019/9/5/20840101/terfs-radical-feminists-gender-critical.

Butterfield, Rosaria. 2022. "What Is Transgenderism?" Ligonier, Apr. 4. https://www.ligonier.org/learn/articles/transgenderism.

Canaday, Margot. 2003. "Building a Straight State: Sexuality and Social Citizenship Under the 1944 G.I. Bill." *Journal of American History* 90 (3): 935–57.

Canaday, Margot. 2009. *The Straight State: Sexuality and Citizenship in Twentieth-Century America.* Princeton University Press.

Canaday, Margot. 2023. *Queer Career: Sexuality and Work in Modern America.* Princeton University Press.

Cervini, Eric. 2020. *The Deviant's War: The Homosexual vs. The United States of America.* Farrar, Strauss and Giroux.

Cosentino, Lawrence. 2012. "A Gay Rights First." *Lansing City Pulse,* Mar. 7. https://www.lansingcitypulse.com/stories/a-gay-rights-first,9267.

Damhuis, Koen. 2019. "Why Dutch Populists Are Exceptional." Brookings, https://www.brookings.edu/articles/why-dutch-populists-are-exceptional/.

Dazey, Margot. 2021. "Rethinking Respectability Politics." *British Journal of Sociology* 72 (3): 580–93.

Duggan, Lisa. 2003. *The Twilight of Equality? Neoliberalism, Cultural Politics, and the Attack on Democracy.* Beacon Press.

Engel, Stephen M. 2016. *Fragmented Citizens: The Changing Landscape of Gay and Lesbian Lives.* New York University Press.

Engel, Stephen M., and Timothy S. Lyle. 2021. *Disrupting Dignity: Rethinking Power and Progress in LGBTQ Lives.* New York University Press.

Epstein, Lee, Kevin T. McGuire, and Thomas G. Walker. 2022. *Constitutional Law for a Changing America: Rights, Liberties, and Justice.* 11th ed. CQ Press.

Gillman, Howard, Mark A. Graber, and Keith E. Whittington. 2020. *American Constitutionalism.* Vol. 2, *Rights and Liberties.* 2nd ed. Oxford University Press.

Graber, Mark A. 2005. "Constitutionalism and Political Science: Imaginative Scholarship, Unimaginative Teaching." *Perspectives on Politics* 3 (1): 135–48.

Feeley, Malcolm M., and Samuel Krislov. 1990. *Constitutional Law.* 2nd ed. Harper Collins.

Felstiner, William L. F., Richard L. Abel, and Austin Sarat. 1980–81. "The Emergence and Transformation of Disputes: Naming, Blaming, Claiming . . ." *Law and Society Review* 15 (3/4): 631–54.

Fisher, Louis, and Katy J. Harringer. 2013. *American Constitutional Law.* Vol. 2, *Constitutional Rights.* 10th ed. Carolina Academic Press.

Gluck, Genevieve. 2019. "What's Current: Dispute Over Gender Identity Splits Stonewall, Creating LGB Faction." *Feminist Current*, Oct 23. https://www. feministcurrent.com/2019/10/23/whats-current-dispute-over-gender-identity-splits-stonewall-creating-lgb-faction/.

Haney Lopez, Ian. 1997. *White by Law: The Legal Construction of Race*. New York University Press.

Jones, Philip Edward. 2022. "Respectability Politics and Straight Support for LGB Rights." *Political Research Quarterly* 75 (4): 935–49.

Kim, Suzanne A. 2010. "Bridging Marriage Skepticism and Marriage Equality." *Tulane Journal of Law & Sexuality* 19:170–74.

Pettit, Emma. 2022a. "The Inquisition." *Chronicle of Higher Education*, Oct. 11.

Pettit, Emma. 2022b. "Private Little Hell." *Chronicle of Higher Education*, Nov. 28.

Piniello, Daniel R. 2003. *Gay Rights and American Law*. Cambridge University Press.

Robson, Ruthann. 2013. *Dressing Constitutionally: Hierarchy, Sexuality, and Democracy from Our Hairstyles to Our Shoes*. Cambridge University Press.

Schmidt, Christopher W. 2016. "The Civil Rights-Civil Liberties Divide." *Stanford Journal of Civil Rights & Civil Liberties* 12 (1): 1–41.

Sears, Clare. 2008. "All That Glitters: Trans-ing California's Gold Rush Migrations." *GLQ: A Journal of Lesbian and Gay Studies* 14 (2–3): 383–402.

Sears, Clare. 2015. *Arresting Dress: Cross-Dressing, Law, and Fascination in Nineteenth-Century San Francisco*. Duke University Press.

Shrier, Abigail. 2021. *Irreversible Damage: The Transgender Craze Seducing Our Daughters*. Regnery Publishing.

Siegel, Scott. 2017. "Friend or Foe? The LGBT Community in the Eyes of Right-Wing Populism." *Europe Now*. https://www.europenowjournal.org/2017/07/05/friend-or-foe-the-lgbt-community-in-the-eyes-of-right-wing-populism/#_ftnref4.

Spade, Dean. 2012. "What's Wrong with Trans Rights?" In *Transfeminist Perspectives in and Beyond Transgender and Gender Studies*, edited by Anne Enke. Temple University Press.

Strolovitch, Dara Z., and Chaya Y. Crowder. 2018. "Respectability, Anti-Respectability, and Intersectionally Responsible Representation." *PS: Political Science & Politics* 51 (2): 340–44.

Vogler, Stefan. 2021. *Sorting Sexualities: Expertise and the Politics of Legal Classification*. University of Chicago Press.

Chapter 5

Queer Politics as Movement Formation

How Activism and History Shape Law and Policy

Erin Mayo-Adam

This chapter explores how to create an inclusive LGBTQ law and politics course by structuring the course around the idea that movements are constantly forming and never formed, that they are continually contested and contestable, and that they are composed of constantly shifting coalitions rather than singular identities. This allows each class to delve into laws and policies from a variety of viewpoints while simultaneously highlighting tensions within the LGBTQ community that are at the heart of the queer liberation movement. It also enables discussions around not only how queer and trans people shape the law, but how the law shapes identity and belonging. By treating the queer liberation movement as one that is constantly forming and never formed, each section of the course features the voices of intersectionally marginalized groups within the movement whose stories are often mis-historicized in linear assemblages of law and social change.

Many sexuality, law, and politics courses at the undergraduate level focus on law and social change through the lens of mostly white gay and lesbian civil rights cases. This has resulted in the exclusion of more marginalized LGBTQ voices in the undergraduate legal studies classroom, especially LGBTQ people of color and transgender people. The focus on more advantaged members of the LGBTQ community generally occurs because many legal studies courses are built around major Supreme Court cases, which inevitably results in the centering of those who have the most access to the courts. In progressive social movements, large social movement organizations have the most access to the courts, and these organizations have long centered issues that matter to the most advantaged members of minority communities (Strolovitch 2007; Cohen 1999b) and large funders (Francis 2019). The emphasis on more advantaged LGBTQ people is even more pronounced in the LGBTQ movement because movement histories also often prioritize them. For example, many histories begin with the Mattachine Society, the Daughters of Bilitis, and the homophile movement, which had white leaders with middle-class and affluent backgrounds. In popular culture, much of the history of the AIDS epidemic has been told through the lens of white male activists like Peter Staley and Larry Kramer, who have produced bestselling books, plays, documentaries, and movies. In the 1990s and 2000s, marriage equality dominated the agenda of the movement, largely because of religious conservatives and Republicans who saw outrage over same-sex marriage as a way to mobilize voters. An emphasis on marriage equality also resulted in a focus on more advantaged community members who benefited the most from marriage (Spade 2015; Kandaswamy 2008).

The overwhelming focus on more advantaged LGBTQ people in the courts and in popular culture creates a conundrum for undergraduate legal studies classes today. How can an undergraduate course that emphasizes law and policy be fully inclusive when many of the major works on the LGBTQ movement are not? To make matters even more complicated, LGBTQ history is virtually non-existent at the K–12 level in the United States. Only six states require at least some LGBTQ history, while a growing number of states censor or ban discussions of LGBTQ people in the classroom (MAP 2023). This means that when students come to college, they often do so without any prior knowledge of LGBTQ issues other than what they've gleaned from movies, television, and social media. How can an undergraduate course accommodate the complexities of the LGBTQ movement for students who have never been taught LGBTQ history?

The following pages delineate how to construct a course around the theme of movement formation in two parts. Part 1 is an outline of my course Queer Policy & Politics that includes core course themes. The outline illuminates how to construct a course that intentionally challenges the linear narratives so common in law and politics courses that focus on progressive movements. Part 2 examines the assignments, cultural outings, and guest speakers that have become integral to the course. This section demonstrates how a variety in-class and out-of-class activities can help shape a class that incorporates the lived experience of LGBTQ students today.

Part 1: Queering Law, Policy, and Politics

I teach Queer Policy & Politics at Hunter College in New York City, which has one of the most diverse student bodies in the country. Hunter boasts over twenty thousand undergraduate students and a majority minority student body with a relatively large LGBTQ student population. The college itself holds a special place in LGBTQ history. The college recently renamed its main street Audre Lorde Way after notable alumna Audre Lorde, who graduated from Hunter in 1959, taught at the college, and went on to become a leader and activist in the queer liberation movement. While places like Hunter College in New York City are important to the LGBTQ movement, and the state is more accepting of LGBTQ people than many other states in the country, New York is not as welcoming as it may at first seem. New York currently does not mandate LGBTQ history in its K–12 curriculum. As a result, only 28 percent of K–12 students in New York State are taught positive representations of LGBTQ people in the classroom and only 18 percent receive LGBTQ-inclusive sex education (GLSEN 2019). Every year, when I ask my Queer Policy & Politics class if they have ever been taught LGBTQ history, only one student usually raises their hand. When I teach this class at Hunter, it usually fills with a diverse set of students who identify with the LGBTQ community and are taking the class to learn more about themselves.

Queer Policy & Politics embraces these students with a shifting curriculum that centers movement formation—or the idea that movements are always constantly forming. The curriculum is "shifting" because, though it is set before the class begins, I generally update and slightly alter the reading materials after the first day of class in order to ensure that they address the backgrounds and experiences each new set of students brings to the classroom. For example, during one iteration, the class included a large number of South Asian LGBTQ students. In response, I altered the syllabus to include more readings from South Asian LGBTQ academics and activists.

The course allows for novel changes and updates because it is not structured in a linear progression or chronologically. Instead, the course emphasizes key themes and concepts. I begin by introducing students to the idea that the LGBTQ movement is contested—both from outside actors and from within. The first readings, like Cathy Cohen's "What Is My Movement Doing to My Politics?," emphasize this. Cohen's (1999a) speech identifies a dominant divide in the LGBTQ movement between the mainstream, which consists of more advantaged organizations and community members who seek to assimilate into society, and the radical, which consists of more disadvantaged and intersectionally marginalized LGBTQ people who seek to undo and reimagine core political institutions around queer and trans liberation. This divide is followed throughout the course, including within each course theme.

After I introduce students to the idea that the LGBTQ movement is contested, the course usually dovetails into the theme "othering in immigration." I like to open with this theme because it destabilizes the idea that the LGBTQ movement begins in the mid-twentieth century as a response to the oppression of the McCarthy era and the reverberating quests for liberation initiated by the civil rights movement. Instead, the course shows how LGBTQ exclusion and oppression are deeply embedded in American political institutions, like the US immigration system. For instance, in class, I show how racial exclusions like the Chinese Exclusion Act of 1882, which prevented Chinese laborers from entering the United States, were passed alongside immigration laws that excluded those who had committed crimes of "moral turpitude," sex workers, and the mentally ill—exclusions that would have included LGBTQ people in the late 1800s. Assigned readings include excerpts from Margot Canaday's (2009) *The Straight State* as well as Canaday's (2003) article "Who Is Homosexual?: The Consolidation of Sexual Identities in Mid Twentieth-Century American Immigration Law," which document the various ways that LGBTQ exclusion and oppression are part of the American administrative state.

This segment of the course follows LGBTQ immigration exclusions from the late twentieth century through today, ending with a discussion of the treatment of transgender migrants and asylum seekers in migrant shelters and US immigration detention centers (Balaguera 2018; Human Rights Watch 2016). I usually also include readings that speak to the diversity of immigrant experiences that Hunter College students bring to the classroom. For instance, in one recent iteration of the course, I assigned an article written by Shweta Majumdar Adur (2018) entitled "In Pursuit of Love: 'Safe Passages' Migration, and Queer South Asians in the US." The "safe passages" piece examines the experiences of queer and trans

South Asians who immigrate to the US, including the disappointments of the American dream, the isolating experiences of immigration to rural America, and islamophobia in the aftermath of the 9/11 attacks.

The two course themes that follow the section on immigration similarly tackle LGBTQ oppression in state institutions. The discussion of islamophobia and the 9/11 attacks nicely leads into the next section, which focuses on military and federal exclusion from World War I through today. Readings in this part of the course include the 1950 Congressional Subcommittee report *Employment of Homosexuals and Other Sex Perverts in Government* and Liz Montegary's (2015) "Militarizing US Homonormativities: The Making of 'Ready, Willing, and Able' Gay Citizens." The former details the official policy during the Lavender Scare, the historical moment when gay men and lesbians were investigated and expelled from all federal employment. Montegary's piece examines how military service and the campaign for LGBTQ inclusion in the military had harmful effects on the LGBTQ community. It is this portion of the course where the tension between assimilation and radical resistance to problematic institutions begins to fully take shape. Students simultaneously grapple with the wrongs of military exclusion, which culminated in the "Don't Ask, Don't Tell" policy in the 1990s and 2000s—a policy that created a great deal of pain and trauma for LGBTQ servicepeople, including brutal beatings and suicides—and the horrors of a military industrial complex that relies on working-class people of color in its war-making and has intensified xenophobia and islamophobia domestically. The juxtaposition of the two effectively teaches students who are unfamiliar with LGBTQ history about an important historical period where LGBTQ people were legally excluded from federal employment. However, it also encourages students to think critically through that historical moment and activist responses to exclusion.

The next segment of the course takes up the theme of exclusion as well, but through a different lens—the criminalization and regulation of sexuality in US history. This portion of the course includes *Lawrence v. Texas*, which is often taught in more traditional sexuality, law, and politics courses. However, it expands beyond this case by beginning with a deep dive into the history of criminalization of sexuality in America. This approach is more novel because it includes a discussion of how the criminalization of sodomy is connected to the same movement that pushed for criminalizing birth control and abortion in the late 1800s. The easing of criminalization also tracks alongside the elimination of abortion restrictions at the state level in the 1960s, a few years prior to the *Roe v. Wade* decision. This approach to teaching the history of criminalization of sexuality emphasizes the various ways that the regulation of sodomy is connected to the regulation of reproductive rights. For this reason, *Roe v. Wade* and *Planned Parenthood v. Casey*, the two major Supreme Court cases that established the right to abortion before they were overturned in *Dobbs v. Jackson Whole Women's Health*, are taught alongside *Lawrence v. Texas*.

The discussion of *Lawrence v. Texas* ends with a segment on Katherine Franke's (2004) "The Domesticated Liberty of *Lawrence v. Texas*," which delves into the problem of ending the criminalization of consensual sodomy through the constitutional umbrella of the right to privacy. According to Franke, framing sexual freedom through the right to privacy reinforces that sodomy is something to be shamefully hidden within the confines of a private bedroom. This framing is also problematic because for decades following *Roe v. Wade*, conservatives on the Court were incrementally creating case law that dismantled the right to privacy, culminating in *Dobbs v. Jackson Whole Women's Health*, which eliminated the right to abortion. The segment on criminalization of sodomy ends with *Dobbs* and an examination of the potential of the expansion of *Dobbs* beyond abortion. This encourages students to grapple with *Dobbs* as a historical moment akin to previous decades when criminalization reached beyond abortion and into other reproductive and sexual freedoms.

The section on the criminalization of sexuality and reproductive care leads into a larger discussion of healthcare and the AIDS epidemic—the next part of the course. This segment examines the AIDS crisis and the right to healthcare within the LGBTQ community. Students begin this section by reviewing and discussing the documentary *United in Anger: A History of ACT UP* alongside a lecture on the history of the AIDS crisis and excerpts from Cathy Cohen's (1999b) *Boundaries of Blackness* (see also Brier 2018). This combination of course materials helps students think through the tragedies of the AIDS crisis and the empowering responses from LGBTQ organizations like ACT UP. Students are also encouraged to think critically about responses to the crisis, through excerpts from Cohen's book, helping illuminate the racially disproportionate response to the epidemic, which ultimately centered the experiences of white gay men over LGBTQ people of color. This has created problems that have continued within these communities through today, where HIV still has a disproportionate impact. The discussion in this portion of the course also revives themes from earlier segments on community and belonging by encouraging students to grapple with who is left out of more mainstream responses to crises.

The classes on the AIDS crisis lead into a general discussion of the right to healthcare for LGBTQ people, with an emphasis on gender-affirming care for transgender people. For this segment of the course, I assign a variety of readings on the politics of trans healthcare. Because this is such a large issue politically at the moment, I have expanded this part of the course in recent years and usually invite a guest speaker to talk with the class about anti-trans legislative efforts. Many LGBTQ activists and academics argue that issues like same-sex marriage became the focal point of queer activism for two decades because of the decisions of a few, well-funded national LGBTQ organizations and networks of attorneys (see, e.g., Spade 2015; Arkles et al. 2010). While it is certainly the case that these groups benefited financially from the struggle for marriage equality and eventually made same-sex marriage the focal point of their policy struggles, social scientists tell a more complicated story. Dorf and Tarrow (2014), for instance, argue that same-sex marriage came to dominate the LGBTQ movement because religious conservatives fixated on the issue in the 1990s when the Hawaii same-sex marriage case *Baehr v. Miike* presented a constitutional argument for the right to same-sex marriage. Even though the case ultimately failed to legalize same-sex marriage in Hawaii, the conservative hysteria it inspired pushed everyday LGBTQ people, who bore the brunt of the misinformation and homophobia of anti-same-sex marriage campaigns that followed, to demand a response from LGBTQ organizations, according to Dorf and Tarrow.

Following the nationalization of same-sex marriage in 2015, a similar dynamic began to emerge on trans issues at the local level. Many of the organizations that had pursed marriage equality lost their major funders and as a result were ill-equipped to pursue other issues impacting the LGBTQ community after winning same-sex marriage, despite assurances made to local trans activists that they would do so (Mayo-Adam 2020). At the same time, organizations that represent religious conservatives began releasing policy briefings and model legislation limiting trans rights, likely in an attempt to maintain their own funding after they lost the marriage wars. Although their campaigns largely lost in 2016, they gained larger public support among conservatives during the Trump presidency and in the aftermath of the coronavirus pandemic. While the anti-trans legislation religious conservatives targeted a whole slew of trans rights, the largest and most successful campaigns in red states have been laws banning gender-affirming care for trans youth.

The readings assigned in this section of the course detail this history. They include an article from *Harvard Law Review* entitled "Outlawing Trans Youth: State Legislatures and the Battle Over Gender-Affirming Healthcare for Minors" and a selection of academic readings from political scientists who are experts on trans rights, like Joanna Wuest (2019), Zein Murib (2022), Health Fogg Davis (2017), Paisley Currah (2022), and Libby Sharrow and Isaac Sederbaum (2022). Collectively, these readings teach students about the rise of attacks on trans healthcare and how these fit into a broader network of exclusionary gender policies that are part of American government bureaucracy. Students are also encouraged to think through who shapes the evolution of gender policy and how responses to community attacks, even responses that begin with the best intentions, can have rippling negative effects years after a policy struggle is resolved.

The tensions among mainstream and marginalized constituencies within the LGBTQ community and religious conservatives outside of it give way to a portion of the course that illuminates how divergent policy outcomes can emerge among LGBTQ activists. The topics covered here include hate crimes activism and prison policy. Mainstream LGBTQ organizations have long pursued more robust hate crimes laws alongside many leaders of civil rights organizations in response to horrific crimes that target LGBTQ people and Black Americans. These laws generally punish hate crimes by enhancing the sentences of those who commit violent crimes against someone because of their race, gender, sexual orientation, and/or gender expression. The national push for federal hate crimes legislation gained broad public support in response to the violent murders in 1998 of James Byrd Jr. (by white supremacists) and of Matthew Shepard. The legislation was broadly supported by LGBTQ people and Black Americans because of the history of violence aimed at these communities. However, it also spurred criticism among those who were concerned that hate crimes legislation that increased prison sentences would contribute to mass incarceration and fail to fully address violence against these communities because the legislation did not also call for inclusive education or increased social services designed to mitigate intercommunity violence (Spade and Willse 2000).

The class then explores the problem of mass incarceration and how mainstream LGBTQ organizations have responded to prison violence and LGBTQ inmates by advocating for separate prison facilities for LGBTQ people. I assign Russell Robinson's (2011) "Masculinity as Prison: Sexual Identity, Race, and Incarceration" and Dean Spade's (2012) "The Only Way to End Racialized Gender Violence Is to End Prisons" in order to examine the implications of separate prison facilities. Robinson's article argues that one separate prison facility for gay and bisexual men and transgender people in the Los Angeles men's jail, which had been lauded as a model by many mainstream LGBTQ organizations, actively excluded gay, bisexual, and trans Black and Latino men by requiring familiarity with white gay male culture as a condition of placement. While Robinson presents a series of recommendations for improving the facility, Spade argues that even improvements will not resolve the core problem of prison violence. It is during this segment of the course that the idea of shifting coalitions of LGBTQ activists is fully revealed. Prior sections of the class primarily introduced the idea that the LGBTQ community is not always united, by presenting students with exclusive laws and policies and critiques of how these came to an end. By contrast, this section of the course shows students that there are genuine political differences within the LGBTQ community and these differences generate multiple coalitions within the population that support divergent policy outcomes.

The course ends by having students examine arguably the largest LGBTQ victory of the twenty-first century: the nationalization of same-sex marriage. As with many other sections of the course, these classes begin by outlining the history of marriage in the US and of exclusion from marriage. There are a wealth of academic readings critiquing marriage that I have assigned in the past alongside this historical lecture, including Melissa Murray's (2012) "Marriage as Punishment" and Priya Kandaswamy's (2008) "State Austerity and the Racial Politics of Same-Sex Marriage in the US." More recently, I have also assigned materials that point out how the case *Obergefell v. Hodges*, which nationalized same-sex marriage, simultaneously created problems for LGBTQ families by failing to recognize reproductive and parental rights for LGBTQ people. Other cases have even further limited these rights by allowing corporations to discriminate in healthcare coverage on the basis of religion (*Burwell v. Hobby Lobby*) and forcing municipalities to continue to work with religious organizations that refuse to place foster children with LGBTQ people (*Fulton v. City of Philadelphia*).

Together all of these topics create a narrative arc that emphasizes tension and difference amidst a constantly forming queer liberation movement composed of shifting coalitions of activists. The course also provides a history of regulation and criminalization of sexuality and gender alongside the recognition of tensions within activist communities over how to respond to the tragedies that homophobic and transphobic laws, policies, and institutions create. I do also often swap out some sections of the course with other topics if another topic is particularly pertinent in the public consciousness. For example, past iterations of these course have extended this narrative to an analysis of the history of anti-discrimination policy and antigay curriculum laws in the US as well. However, the dominant themes—that law and policy both shape and are shaped by identity, that the queer liberation movement is composed of a multiplicity of unstable coalitions, and the narrative of queer history is one of nonlinear movement formation—generally does not change.

Assignments, Guest Speakers, and Cultural Outings

Because Hunter College is based in New York City, there is a unique opportunity in my Queer Policy & Politics course to include experiential learning activities that encourage the exploration of queer and trans law and policy outside of the classroom. This has been aided in recent years by the generous support of the New York City Council and the CUNY LGBTQ Consortium, which have provided funds to support these activities. The course includes these activities alongside more traditional assignments. The main course assignments include a short paper assignment, an extended research project, and weekly response papers. The short paper assignment functions as a take-home midterm that asks students to create a short essay that uses the materials from the first half of the course to connect law and policy to LGBTQ identity. The longer research paper includes three component parts: a research proposal, research paper, and research presentation. For the past few years, I have had students select a law or policy that in some way impacts LGBTQ people and to research its historical and political development and tell me how it has shaped social norms. The structure of the research paper is meant to mirror the structure of some of the segments of the course, like the section on the criminalization of sexuality, which examines the history of the criminalization of same-sex sexual intercourse and how this has shaped LGBTQ identity and activism. The course ends with student presentations of their class research papers. This fulfills the public speaking part of the class, which is a core requirement of classes taught at the Roosevelt House.

The guest speakers and cultural activities are integrated into the course through the assigned topics and response papers. Because the class is taught through the Roosevelt House's LGBTQ Policy Center, students are encouraged to attend policy center events as part of the class. Every semester, the LGBTQ Policy Center hosts two to three major events that feature local policymakers, attorneys, activists, and community organizers discussing current issues that impact the queer and trans community. For example, in the spring of 2022, the center hosted three events—one on the struggle for human rights within queer and trans South Asian communities, one on the rise in anti-trans legislation, and one on LGBTQ homelessness in New York City. The event on queer and trans South Asian human rights featured professor and civil rights activist Glenn Magpantay, Tashnuva Anan Shishir (a Bangladeshi trans activist who is now based in New York City), and Hunter College student government leader Ariana Ahmed. The event addressed human rights concerns that are specific to the queer and trans South Asian community, including the rise in violence in the aftermath of the 9/11 attacks and in response to the COVID pandemic. The event on the rise in anti-trans legislation featured academics and attorneys, including Bobby Hodgson (a supervising attorney at the New York Civil Liberties Union), Zein Murib (a professor at Fordham University and expert in gender, race, and public policy), Ryan Thoreson (then a researcher in the LGBTQ rights program at Human Rights Watch), and Joanna Wuest (a professor at Mount Holyoke College and expert on trans legal rights). The final event, on LGBTQ homelessness, featured Joe Pressley (then the CEO of the Hetrick–Martin Institute, the nation's oldest LGBTQ youth services organization) and Daniel Tietz (the commissioner of the New York State Office of Temporary and Disability Assistance). Students attended these events to hear from the perspectives of contemporary policymakers and activists while simultaneously learning the history behind each major policy discussion in the classroom.

In addition to the events held each semester by the LGBTQ Policy Center, I also often bring guest speakers into the classroom to discuss past and present issues and struggles in addition. For instance, in one past iteration of the course, students watched the documentary *The Lavender Scare* in the section on LGBTQ exclusion in the military and federal government. After watching the film, producer and director Josh Howard spoke with the class about the film. In another iteration, Lambda Legal senior attorney Carl Charles spoke with the class during the section on gender policy. Carl Charles's work focuses on expanding federal civil rights for transgender people and includes serving as counsel on some of the biggest transgender rights cases in the country.

In addition to panels and events, the class also regularly attends cultural outings in New York City. In the past, these have been Broadway plays. For example, early in the spring of 2020, the class took a trip to see the Broadway show *The Inheritance*. *The Inheritance* won four Tony Awards that year, including for Best Play. The play was billed as an "epic examination of survival, healing, class divide, and what it means to call a place home" (Playbill 2019). It worked well in the class because it featured three generations of gay men grappling with past tragedies decades after the AIDS epidemic. Topics included the tension between assimilation and liberation across generations, the ongoing struggle for community and belonging, and how the tragedy of the AIDS epidemic continues to shape gay life today. More recently, students saw the Pulitzer Prize–winning comedy *Fat Ham*, a Black queer reimagining of Shakespeare's *Hamlet*. For each of these shows, questions were prepared for students to think through how major themes connected to the course. Students turned in their answers to the questions as part of their weekly response reading grade and then discussed their answers and reactions to the plays in class. LGBTQ law and politics classes that are not based in New York City might consider including virtual sessions with speakers and historians from other areas of the country and include digitized collections of LGBTQ museums and archival centers as part of the class materials. These classes might also consider collaborating with local and on-campus LGBTQ centers and nonprofit organizations to enhance the course experience.

Conclusion

Queer Policy & Politics is a unique class for a number of reasons. It destabilizes the linear narrative through which the LGBTQ movement is traditionally constructed. Most histories of the movement begin with the police raid of Stonewall Inn in 1969 and the ensuing rebellion that inspired the gay liberation movement of the 1970s. By contrast, Queer Policy & Politics imagines queer people as part of the rich fabric of American history that extends well before 1969. The class does not construct history from one identity, but from a variety of perspectives. In order to accomplish this, major court cases are taught alongside academic and activist readings, and the class is encouraged to think about queer life beyond the classroom. At its core, Queer Policy & Politics is a legal and political history of the queer liberation movement—a movement that is in a continual process of formation.

Given the unique location of Queer Policy & Politics at Hunter College in New York City, there are some significant limitations to holding a class like this in other environments, especially in places that are more rural and that have less diverse student bodies. With this said, it is possible to adapt parts of this course in other contexts. For example, every state has organizations devoted to LGBTQ rights, including areas that are more conservative. In fact, some of the most active organizations in the country are located in these areas. Classes held in more rural and conservative areas might invite leaders and community organizers from these organizations into the classroom. For example, one of the most active and influential organizations in the South is Southerners on New Ground. Although the organization is based in Atlanta, it operates throughout multiple Southern states, including in more rural areas. Classes held in this part of the country might invite community organizers into the classroom to discuss how they are combating anti-trans and anti-LGBTQ legislative efforts and providing local community supports.

In addition to more marginalized organizations like Southerners on New Ground, mainstream organizations like the American Civil Liberties Union (ACLU), Planned Parenthood, the Equality Federation, and Lambda Legal have offices throughout the country. For example, Lambda Legal has offices that cover different regions of the country, while the ACLU has local affiliates in every state. The ACLU is often part of the core network of LGBTQ organizations advocating for LGBTQ rights and dignity at the local level. Other adaptations of this course might bring in speakers from these organizations to help ground the course in a local context that recognizes the diversity of voices in the state where the class is based.

Finally, outings to an LGBTQ-specific performance in New York might be replaced with a tour of a local LGBTQ resource center or LGBTQ youth center. Many localities throughout the country have local centers like these. If one is too far away to visit during the college semester, affiliates from the resource center might be invited into the classroom or for a virtual event. One of the benefits of framing the LGBTQ movement as a movement never formed but always forming is that it provides the opportunity to adapt the class to different contexts in ways that suit the variations of

LGBTQ identity and belonging across the country—from urban to rural, from conservative to liberal, and across the diversity of class, racial, and ethnic identities and experiences that exist throughout the US.

References

Arkles, Gabriel, Pooja Gehi, and Elena Redfield. 2010. "The Role of Lawyers in Trans Liberation: Building a Transformative Movement for Social Change." *Seattle Journal for Social Justice* 8 (2): 579–641.

Balaguera, Martha. 2018. "Trans-Migrations: Agency and Confinement at the Limits of Sovereignty." *Signs: Journal of Women, Culture, and Society* 43 (3): 641–64.

Brier, Jennifer. 2018. "AIDS and Action (1980s–1990s)." In *The Routledge History of Queer America*, edited by Don Romesburg, 95–106. Routledge.

Canaday, Margot. 2011. *The Straight State: Sexuality and Citizenship in Twentieth-Century America*. Princeton University Press.

Canaday, Margot. 2003. " 'Who Is Homosexual?' The Consolidation of Sexual Identities in Mid-Twentieth Century American Immigration Law." *Law & Social Inquiry* 28 (2): 351–86.

Cohen, Cathy J. 1999a. "What Is This Movement Doing to My Politics?" *Social Text* 61, *Out Front: Lesbians, Gays and the Struggle for Workplace Rights*: 111–18.

Cohen, Cathy J. 1999b. *Boundaries of Blackness: AIDS and the Breakdown of Black Politics*. University of Chicago Press.

Currah, Paisely. 2022. *Sex Is as Sex Does: Governing Transgender Identity*. New York University Press.

Dorf, Michael C., and Sidney Tarrow. 2014. "Strange Bedfellows: How Anticipatory Countermovement Brought Same-Sex Marriage into the Public Arena." *Law & Social Inquiry* 39 (2): 449–73.

Francis, Megan Min. 2019. "The Price of Civil Rights: Black Lives, White Funding, and Movement Capture." *Law & Society Review* 53 (1): 275–309.

Franke, Katherine M. 2004. "Commentary: The Domesticated Liberty of *Lawrence v. Texas*." *Columbia Law Review* 104:1399–1426.

Fogg Davis, Heath. 2017. *Beyond Trans: Does Gender Matter?* New York University Press.

GLSEN. 2019. "School Climate for LGBTQ Students in New York." *Gay, Lesbian, and Straight Education Network*, accessed June 26. https://www.glsen.org/sites/default/files/2021-01/New-York-Snapshot-2019.pdf.

Government Printing Office. 1950. "Employment of Homosexuals and Other Sex Perverts in Government." Senate Congressional Committee on Expenditures in the Executive Departments, Subcommittee on Investigations, S. Res. 280, 81st Congress.

Harvard Law Review. 2021. "Outlawing Trans Youth: State Legislatures and the Battle Over Gender-Affirming Healthcare for Minors." *Harvard Law Review* 134:2163–85.

Human Rights Watch. 2016. "'Do You See How Much I'm Suffering Here?' Abuse Against Transgender Women in US Immigration Detention." Human Rights Watch, accessed June 26. https://www.hrw.org/report/2016/03/23/do-you-see-how-much-im-suffering-here/abuse-against-transgender-women-us.

Kandaswamy, Priya. 2008. "State Austerity and the Racial Politics of Same-Sex Marriage in the U.S." *Sexualities* 11:706–25.

Majumdar Adur, Shweta. 2018. "In Pursuit of Love: 'Safe Passages,' Migration, and Queer South Asians in the US." *Current Sociology Monograph* 66 (2): 320–34.

MAP. 2023. "Healthcare Laws and Policies." Movement Advancement Project, accessed June 26. https://www.lgbtmap.org/equality-maps/healthcare_laws_and_policies.

Mayo-Adam, Erin. 2020. *Queer Alliances: How Power Shapes Political Movement Formation*. Stanford University Press.

Montegary, Liz. 2015. "Militarizing US Homonormativities: The Making of 'Ready, Willing, and Able' Gay Citizens." *Signs: Journal of Women in Culture and Society* 40 (4): 891–915.

Murib, Zein. 2022. "Laws Targeting Transgender Youths Lean on Myths About White Childhood Innocence. This Explains How." *Washington Post*, March 23. https://www.washingtonpost.com/politics/2022/03/23/anti-transgender-laws-race/.

Murray, Melissa. 2012. "Marriage as Punishment." *Columbia Law Review* 112 (1): 1–65.

Playbill. 2019. *The Inheritance*. https://playbill.com/production/the-inheritanceethel-barrymore-theatre-2019-2020.

Robinson, Russell. 2011. "Masculinity as Prison: Sexual Identity, Race, and Incarceration." *California Law Review* 99:1309–1408.

Sharrow, Elizabeth, and Isaac Sederbaum. 2022. "Texas Isn't the Only State Denying Essential Medical Care to Trans Youth. Here's What's Going On." *Washington Post*, March 10. https://www.washingtonpost.com/politics/2022/03/10/texas-trans-kids-abortion-lgbtq-gender-ideology/.

Spade, Dean. 2012. "The Only Way to End Racialized Gender Violence Is to End Prisons: A Response to Russell Robinson's 'Masculinity as Prison.'" *California Law Review Circuit* 3:184–95.

Spade, Dean. 2015. *Normal Life: Administrative Violence, Critical Trans Politics, and the Limits of Law*. 2nd ed. Duke University Press. Originally published in 2009.

Spade, Dean, and Craig Willse. 2000. "Confronting the Limits of Gay Hate Crimes Activism: A Radical Critique." *Chicano-Latino Law Review* 21:38–52.

Strolovitch, Dara Z. 2007. *Affirmative Advocacy: Race, Class, and Gender in Interest Group Politics.* University of Chicago Press.

Wuest, Joanna. 2019. "The Scientific Gaze in American Transgender Politics: Contesting the Meaning of Sex, Gender, and Gender Identity in Bathroom Rights Cases." *Politics & Gender* 15:336–60.

Chapter 6

Designing a Graduate Seminar on LGBTQ+ Rights

CYRIL GHOSH

Since 2016, I have periodically offered a graduate seminar on international LGBTQ+ rights at The New School's Julien J. Studley Graduate Program in International Affairs (GPIA). Given the nature of this program, the course intentionally includes interdisciplinary as well as international perspectives. Elsewhere, I teach similar material using a domestic, United States–based, framework. The course was originally titled International LGBT+ Rights, but since summer 2022 it has been renamed Global Politics of LGBT+ Rights.[1]

In this chapter, I describe the course schedule as I originally designed it for summer 2022. One of my aims here is to explain to the reader how I came to decide on this specific set of readings and visual texts for the course. As I explain in some details below, there is no established canon as of yet in the (sub)field of sexuality and politics that a political science instructor can unproblematically rely on when building their syllabi for courses such as the one being analyzed here. In addition, in this chapter I offer some reflections on my experience teaching the course virtually from June 1 to July 13, 2022. I begin, however, with a discussion of the context in which the course was being offered.[2]

Background

The Julien J. Studley Graduate Programs in International Affairs at The New School is an interdisciplinary program that focuses on the study of contemporary problems affecting the globe, ranging from climate change to refugee crises to authoritarianism. It integrates theory, policy, and practice through field-based learning, developing intellectual communities, and integrative research. The New School defines international affairs as "processes, interactions and institutions that shape economy, society, politics and culture." The pedagogical approach is "rooted in critical social enquiry and engaged learning with a commitment to the values of global solidarity."[3]

The nature of the program, together with the fact that courses offered in this program are open to students across divisions at The New School, necessitated that I adopt a trans/interdisciplinary approach and an international perspective in designing the syllabus. In addition, the course also fulfills a requirement for the gender and sexuality studies certificate. I routinely get graduate (but also sometimes advanced undergraduate) students from a number of different disciplines taking the course. The assigned readings were therefore drawn from the social sciences, the humanities, law, and media studies, as well as gender and sexuality studies.

In addition, Global Politics of LGBT+ Rights takes seriously GPIA's emphasis on critical social inquiry and, consequently, a major focus of the course is the interrogation of contemporary discourses on the rights of sexual minorities[4] and postcolonial/decolonial thought. It thus includes a significant amount of material that investigates things like policies related to admission of transgender students to single-sex (particularly women's) colleges; masculinity and homoeroticism in Asia; the assimilationist rhetoric of marriage equality; queer (decolonial) theory; pinkwashing; transgender individuals' participation in athletics; the rights of *hijras*; queer Muslim intersectionality; and so on.

In the next section, I offer an account of the kind of thinking and reasoning that went into the design of the course's schedule and reading list. Teaching a class on sexuality and politics is always tricky because there is, as of yet, no easily accessible, obvious, "go-to" introductory textbook or cannon that an instructor can draw upon to compile a set of core readings for the seminar. Nevertheless, as Kammerer and Cravens have shown (chap. 1 of this volume), when asked, instructors who teach courses on sexuality and politics do frequently rely on one core set of readings. I am not an exception to this. The list of LGBTQ works referenced multiple times (chap. 1) has eleven works listed in addition to case law. As it turns out, in my courses on sexuality and politics, I include seven of the eleven authors listed here. For Global Politics of LGBT+ Rights, I include four of the authors from that list of eleven. In the next section, I offer a detailed discussion of the process of building the course schedule. I focus here on the absence of an established canon and describe the reasoning behind how and why I picked this particular set of readings for the seven weeks of the course.

Designing the Course Schedule

I begin here, first, by offering a description of the course (the complete syllabus can be found in the appendix to this chapter). I am a political scientist by training, and my students need to have some sense of my positionality before they take a course such as this one with me. Given the hyper-interdisciplinarity of both the field of sexuality studies (sometimes called gay and lesbian studies or queer studies) and the program in which I am offering this course, I think it is important for my students to get an accurate sense of what they are signing up for, and so I try very hard to make it clear that this is ultimately a class on sexuality *and politics*. In addition, the focus of the course is international. While I obviously discuss some material on domestic US policy, that is not the main point of the course. In addition to clarifying some of these things in the "course description" as it appears on the syllabus, I also disambiguated all this verbally on the first day of class when I introduced myself and the course. I explained to the students that if they were looking for material drawing upon, say, literary criticism or anthropology, this was not the sort of class they should be enrolled in. In the remainder of the discussion in this section, following a description of the course, I explain the rationale and thinking that informed all the decisions I made as I selected the readings and other material, such as visual texts, for this course. Here, the discussion is divided into seven parts, each representing one week of this summer semester. For each of these weeks, I furnish a detailed account of the course materials and the pedagogical choices I made.

COURSE DESCRIPTION

This is a survey class on the rights, recognition, and struggles of lesbians, gays, bisexuals, transgender people, queer-identified people, and other nonheterosexual individuals and sexual-orientation and gender-identity minorities in both the Global North and the Global South. I designed the course in a way such that it would proceed in three segments. We would begin with a broad overview of the discourse of human rights in international law and then survey the literature on the rights of sexual minorities. In doing so, we would familiarize ourselves not only with the Universal Declaration of Human Rights but also the International Covenant on Civil and Political Rights, the Yogyakarta Principles, and so on. In addition, we would analyze the scholarship on both the marriage equality movement and the claims of radical/queer critics of marriage. In the remaining two segments, we would examine the rights, accomplishments, and struggles of LGBTQ+ individuals, first in the Global North (with a focus on the United States) and then in the Global South (particularly South Asia and the Middle East and North Africa).

COURSE READINGS AND RATIONALE

As the course description indicates, I organized this course in three modules. Part I would be an overview of some main themes in the field of LGBTQ+ rights. Parts II and III would focus on the Global North and Global South, respectively. The segmentation here would be for heuristic purposes only. I knew that a number of topics, or their close cousins, discussed in each of these modules would reemerge in the others. The course would meet for three hours and forty minutes, every Wednesday, for seven weeks during summer 2022. I describe below the choices I made regarding what materials to assign. But I should clarify here, again, that I was not designing this course from scratch. I had taught versions of this seminar before. As a result, some of the choices I made here are informed by my experiences; others are entirely new.

Week 1

For week 1, I assigned readings that focused on extant discourses of human rights and the rights of sexual minorities. For a course on the global politics of LGBTQ+ rights, I don't have much wiggle room about what I assign on the first day of class. Two of the texts I assigned for this week, the Universal Declaration of Human Rights and the Yogyakarta Principles and the Y+10 (additional Yogyakarta principles), are foundational to the study of transnational LGBTQ+ rights. Most contemporary LGBTQ+ rights claims are predicated on, or share affinities with, the Yogyakarta Principles. In 2006, frustrated by international human rights tribunals' reluctance toward taking up their cause and the tribunals' chronic deference to arguments about cultural autonomy and sovereignty emanating from nation-states with sodomy (and other homophobic) laws, a group of scholars, policymakers, intellectuals, activists, and human rights lawyers convened at Gadjah Mada University in Yogyakarta, Indonesia, and drafted the Yogyakarta Principles (2007). This has, over time, become the only existing standardized document that codifies the application of human rights law to sexual orientation and gender identity (SOGI) minorities.

In 2017, the Yogyakarta Principles were expanded to also include "gender expression" and "sex characteristics" to the list of prohibited grounds for discrimination. This yields the now widely used acronym SOGIESC (sexual orientation, gender identity and expression, and sex characteristics). The principles themselves build upon the rights enumerated in the Universal Declaration of Human Rights (UDHR). Many international tribunals currently cite them as the canonical document enumerating the rights of SOGIESC minorities.

For this week, I also assigned Ryan Thoreson's piece "Queering Human Rights" and an excerpt from Jack Donnelly's *International Human Rights* as complements to these two foundational texts. The UDHR states that each of us is bestowed with a set of human rights on account of our "humanity." Donnelly's expanded treatment on some theories of what, precisely, the sources of these human rights are is a rich complement to the UDHR. Thoreson's assessment of the Yogyakarta Principles and their accomplishments and adoption, published in the *Journal of Human Rights* a few years after the principles were published, is, again, a useful complement to the Yogyakarta Principles themselves. Together, these readings lay the groundwork for everything that is to follow in the course.

However, I also made a deliberate choice to include a chapter on the first day of classes from Cynthia Weber's *Queer International Relations* (2016). Two kinds of reasoning motivated me here not only to include Weber's work on the first day but also to pick this precise chapter for this week. The first was this: Given that this was a course being offered in an international affairs program, it made sense to get my students acquainted with queer international relations, and no one has done more foundational work in this particular sub-subfield than Cynthia Weber. *Queer International Relations* offers groundbreaking theorization. Second, most of the other readings are quite somber—some might even say lugubrious—in tone. So I wanted to introduce a text that could offer something quirky as a topic of discussion that would offset some of the heaviness accompanying the substance of the remainder of the readings. Based on this reasoning, I assigned a chapter from *Queer IR* on the "bearded drag queen," in which Weber reads the Tom Neuwirth/Conchita Wurst character, who won the 2014 Eurovision song contest, as a metonymic stand-in for the politics of European integration. I also played a YouTube clip in class from the original performance itself. This is not to say that Weber's work is frivolous compared to the rest of the material. On the contrary, it is densely theoretical. But because it is an analysis of pop culture, there is at least a feeling of lightheartedness about the text that serves as a useful accompaniment to everything else assigned for that day.

Week 2

Week 2 concluded the overview module, and in it we discussed contemporary theoretical interventions about the rights of LGBTQ+ folks. Having set up the contours of the course on the first day of class, my goal in the second session was to focus on theory, particularly theories that deconstruct the concepts of gender and sexuality. Two of the texts I selected for this week were obvious choices. I would not know how to teach this survey class on the rights of sexual minorities without giving my students some training in Foucauldian and Butlerian thought. It would not be an exaggeration to say that Foucault's *History of Sexuality* and Butler's *Gender Trouble* are canonical interventions in the study of sexuality and gender. However, in the past my students have found that *Gender Trouble* is not the most accessible of texts. On the other hand, they find *Undoing Gender*, at least the parts that I assigned here, vastly easier to grasp. I should also mention another choice that is almost an obvious one, especially when one is thinking about the social constructionist nature of sexuality: Eve Kosofsky Sedgwick's *Epistemology of the Closet*. But, given that this text is primarily a work of literary criticism, I decided that it was not a good fit for this course.

I decided to supplement Foucault and Butler with a couple of other readings that also investigate the social construction of gender and sexuality. One of these texts is Francisco Valdes's pathbreaking law review piece "Queers, Sissies, Dykes, and Tomboys," a withering critique of the social and legal conflation of sex, gender, and sexual orientation, as well as androcentrism in the domain of the law. I also assigned for this week my own critique of Kenji Yoshino's analysis of the sociological phenomenon of "gay covering." Much of the analysis in this text is about how gender is "performed" in specific ways that either signal/flaunt the transgression of gender norms or allow people to "cover" their gender expression and sexual orientation to assimilate into a heteronormative mainstream. A foundational understanding of the Butlerian concept of performativity (also assigned this week) is wonderfully helpful in thinking through some of these issues.

Finally, I assigned a very specific visual text for this week. I complemented the theoretical analyses in the textual materials that were assigned with David France's somewhat grim documentary *Death and Life of Marsha P. Johnson*. One of the main themes running through this documentary is the sidelining of the queer and the radical from mainstream, assimilationist gay rights politics, which dovetails with the discussion on "covering" and also sets up nicely the discussions that ensue in week 3.

Week 3

Having read some of the foundational documents relating to the global politics of LGBTQ+ rights and some of the core theorists whose work has structured sexuality studies since the late twentieth century, my students moved on to the next module during weeks 3 and 4. For this segment, my thinking was that we would focus on some of the main controversies in the US particularly but also generally in the Global North. The core idea for this week was that we would delve into the topic of internecine strife between assimilationists and radicals.

All the texts assigned this week address the assimilationist politics and "norm-ification" of the lived experiences of LGBTQ+ folks in the Global North as well as the rights politics that are associated with sexual minorities. Thus, I use Jasbir Puar's "Mapping US Homonormativities," which critiques the neoliberalism, patriotism, domesticity, and docility of gay assimilationist practices and norms. Equally, Michael Warner's "Beyond Gay Marriage" is a celebrated and provocative critique of gay marriage and gay norm-ification. My own piece, "Marriage Equality and the Injunction to Assimilate," is an interrogation, very much in the tradition of Warner's queer theoretic critique, of the US Supreme Court's *Obergefell v. Hodges* (2015) decision that instituted same-sex marriage nationwide. Finally, I included among this week's readings another chapter from Cynthia Weber's *Queer International Relations* that analyzes who gets cast as normal and who gets characterized as queer in international human rights discourse. One of the things Weber investigates here is Hillary Clinton's speech at the United Nations where she declared that LGBTQ+ rights were, in fact, human rights.

In addition to these readings, I also decided that starting this week and running until the end of the summer session I would assign yet another visual text: a web series produced in India called *Made in Heaven* (2019). This series offers a richly textured examination of the politics of gender, sexuality, and socioeconomic class in South Asia. Students would be expected to watch the entire series (one or two episodes per week) for the remainder of the semester. I recognize that the discussions catalyzed by viewing this web series should typically belong to the module called "the Global South." However, the reason I decided to start assigning this web series this week is that it would be unmanageable to attempt to cram a discussion of all nine episodes into the three weeks of the semester dedicated to the Global South.

Week 4

In week 4, my goal was to move away from the politics of assimilation and to take a close look, instead, at those sexual- and gender-identity minorities who are on the margins, as it were. But on these margins reside a plural and variegated set of controversial issues. Consequently, it was not easy to choose which ones to include and which ones to omit. I had to make difficult choices and many important issues, unfortunately, were not included because there simply wasn't enough time in one semester (let alone in one intensive summer class!) to cover every controversy relating to the rights of sexual- and gender-identity minorities. Some such issues (again, this is not an exhaustive list) are bathroom bills and the politics of race;[5] bio-essentialism and bio-determinism in the politics of transgender rights;[6] queer reproductive justice;[7] homelessness among queer youth;[8] (queer) intersectionality;[9] cruising and consent;[10] "PrEP whores and HIV prevention";[11] queer incarceration;[12] queer of color critique;[13] (queer) utopianism and anti-utopianism;[14] and so on.

Picking readings for this week was, in some ways, the hardest set of decisions I made for this course. As the syllabus appended below indicates, in the end the selections I finally made for this week relate to the following themes:

- queer migrants;

- bisexuals;

- nonbinary folks;

- bans on trans athletes;

- gender markers on official identification (especially the politics of single-sex colleges); and

- the mental health establishment's responsibilities toward transgender children.

Am I perfectly happy with my choices? For the most part, yes. As indicated above, I am fully aware that I cannot possibly include every controversial issue as a topic for a single day under the rubric of "margins." But such is the nature of any survey course—one has to make difficult decisions about what to include and what to exclude. If it were the case that there already existed a well-established canon, I would not have to make elaborate decisions about what topics to include and what to exclude. On the other hand, I also think that as much as this was a challenge, it was also an opportunity to be creative about what readings to assign, to make decisions about what thematics to include in the training of graduate students, and in turn to influence the future of the discipline itself.

Eventually, for this week, I selected an extract from Erin Mayo-Adam's *Queer Alliances*, which focuses on the concept of "intersectional translators" and the work these translators do in building a politics of solidarity among immigrants' rights organizations and queer social movements. The extract also includes thinking about those who identify as the "undocuqueer." In addition, I assigned a piece by Chassitty N. Fiani and Christine R. Serpe that discusses nonbinary identity and offers a nuanced analysis of the politics of globalization, cultural imperialism, and the challenges and possibilities associated with transnational internet-based connectivity. One of the insights here is that while these phenomena lead to negative externalities like cultural appropriation and cultural imperialism, the internet also offers havens of refuge where a diverse range of individuals can express their identity under conditions of relative safety.

It is not easy to find academic work on bisexuality, particular in the domain of sexuality and politics. It is widely known that the "B" and the "T" in the abbreviation "LGBTQ" are frequently marginalized both discursively and in terms of visibility. The same is true, particularly in the case of bisexuals, in academic literature (much, much more has been written about transgender rights). One interesting piece that investigates bisexual identity is Charles Anthony Smith, Shawn Schulenberg, and Eric A. Baldwin's "The 'B' Isn't Silent: Bisexual Communities and Political Activism." This piece appears in *LGBTQ Politics: A Critical Reader* (2017), an edited volume that anthologized some of the major concerns in the field of sexuality and politics. Edited by Marla Brettschneider, Susan Burgess, and Christine Keating, *LGBTQ Politics* has been truly a gift for those among us who teach and learn about sexuality and politics. If there is a budding, but still hazy, canon emerging within this subfield, this anthology ought to be central to it.

A range of issues related to transgender rights could have made it onto this syllabus. But in the end I decided to stay with three specific themes. The first is drawn from *LGBTQ Politics*: Heath Fogg Davis's analysis of the politics of single-sex colleges. This piece questions the need for identity markers on official documentation, such as the Free Application for Federal Student Aid (FAFSA) form, and advances the argument that perhaps the time has come to relinquish sex-segregated spaces such as women's colleges and recharacterize them as "historically female colleges" that, presumably, now have a gender-inclusive admissions policy. I also included a piece by Libby Sharrow critiquing cisgender supremacy through an interrogation of initiatives to prohibit transgender athletes' participation in women's sports categories. Finally, I included Laura Edwards-Leeper and Erica Anderson's *Washington Post* piece that calls for a greater emphasis on and inclusion of psychological assessment in the diagnosis of gender dysphoria among adolescents and before any material steps are taken toward gender transition.

Week 5

In the last three sessions of the course, we addressed LGBTQ+ rights issues related to the Global South. First, in week 5, we focused on the themes of pinkwashing and the decolonial queer. These last three sessions were necessarily a bit messy because I was trying to cover quite a few regions of the world and, at the same time, stay within reasonable limits of my own expertise on some of the themes. This is complicated because, while I want to offer a broad survey of issues to my students, I also want to stay far away from misrepresenting myself as what Said[15] excoriated as an "expert" on an entire "hemisphere" (that eternally haunted figure: the Orientalist).

It also made sense for me to focus on those areas of the Global South about which I have some knowledge and expertise. These are South Asia and the West Asian/Middle Eastern region. One of the things I have written about in quite some detail is pinkwashing. In recent years, pinkwashing has been used as an analytical term to describe the following phenomenon: a state using its progressive record on LGBTQ+ rights to advance the idea that they are liberal, tolerant, and morally superior to those states that don't "protect" their gays. Israel has been involved in an aggressive pinkwashing campaign to elevate its status among Western powers and to vilify neighboring, frequently Muslim-majority, countries for being illiberal havens of persecution.

While pinkwashing is not always a phenomenon that occurs in western Asia, it frequently does occur there. Nevertheless, I have tried, in this session, to primarily focus on West Asia and, relatedly, on queer Muslims. Assigning Katherine Franke's piece "Dating the State" was an obvious choice for this week because, as a critique of the phenomenon of pinkwashing, especially although not exclusively as it relates to the case of Israel, this piece is a foundational and incisive text. My own piece "Radical Theory Creep" complements the Franke piece, or so I fervently hope, and takes issue with some other extant analyses of pinkwashing, while pointing out that others, such as Franke's piece, represent a more sophisticated and successful tradition of interrogation.

A canonical debate on the study of Arab men who have sex with men is the one between Joseph Massad and Arno Schmitt. Given our focus on the West Asian region for this class session, it made sense to assign the original piece by Massad, which investigates the difficulties of transposing or superimposing a Western-oriented gay rights discourse onto a non-Western, in this case West Asian, context. Schmitt's response to Massad's original piece is also assigned here. In addition, I assigned Momin Rahman's discussion of the intersectional subjectivity of the queer Muslim because it is a useful complement to the preceding texts as well as an effort to decolonize international relations methodology. Finally, contiguous with the latter theme of decolonial thought, I assigned Pedro Paulo Gomes Pereira's chapter on the decolonial queer in which he addresses the possibilities as well as difficulties (particularly linguistic and translational) associated with imbricating queer theory with decolonial thought. While this last piece is not directly about West Asia, the theme of colonialism represents a throughline across the texts assigned this week.

Week 6

In week 6, we focused particularly on (human and other) rights rhetoric and "Western"-style LGBTQ+ rights politics, including things like pride parades. Since the course is about LGBTQ+ rights in general, it made sense to discuss the rights rhetoric in the Global North (and its tension with the radicals/queers who do not necessarily find a rights-based discourse/ politics emancipatory). My students read about all this in week 3. But I wanted them to also have a glimpse of what a rhetoric based on rights might *do* in the world, as it were. For this reason, I assigned a range of texts for week 6 that address the politics of LGBTQ+ rights struggles across various parts of the Global South.

Omar Encarnación's piece "A Latin American Puzzle" distinguishes between a human rights–based, universalist discourse on LGBTQ+ rights in Argentina and compares that to a more specific, civil rights argument advanced in Brazil. He shows us how these two types of social movements have catalyzed two somewhat different trajectories of LGBTQ+ rights advances in these two countries. Equally, I assigned two pieces, one by Michael Bosia and the other by Deepika Jain and Debanuj Dasgupta, that throw into relief the paucity of a Western-style rights discourse in alleviating the circumstances in which sexual minorities live in the Global South, with Bosia taking an expansive global approach and Jain and Dasgupta focusing on the particular experiences of transgender persons living in the South Asian region.

Rights rhetorics can cut in all sorts of ways. I wanted my students to grapple with what it means to make demands for "LGBTQ+ rights": Are these rights sometimes about something as basic as survival? Are they sometimes about the right to what Nancy Fraser[16] has called, and Paisley Currah[17] has critiqued as, a politics of "recognition"? To think through some of these issues, I assigned for this week, in addition to the texts discussed, a podcast of a conversation with the late Ugandan activist David Kato, in Cambridge, UK—a few months before he was brutally killed in his home—in which he offers a virulent critique of the Ugandan state's extreme homophobia toward its sexual minorities.

Keeping in mind that one major instantiation of recognition politics in the domain of LGBTQ+ rights is the pride parade, I also assigned for this week a piece by Phillip M. Ayoub, Douglas Page, and Sam Whitt on the localized effects of pride parades on gay rights movements in the

Balkans. (I realize that the Balkans do not fit extremely well in a module on the Global South, but I nevertheless included it in this segment rather than the one on the Global North because it worked better for what I wanted my students to be thinking about during this week.)

Week 7

In the last session of the course, I decided to focus on the theme of "other masculinities." One of the reasons why I did this is because we live in a world in which much of what gets culturally coded as homophobia and transphobia is really an artifact of a global obsession with androcentrism and a global anxiety about emasculation. It is widely known, for example, that in many regions of the world it is acceptable for men to have sex with men as long as they are the active partners. This kind of conduct is less, and in some cases not, frowned upon because they are not markers of emasculation. I wanted to make sure that before we wrapped up the course, we had a detailed discussion of the role of masculinity in the global politics of LGBTQ+ rights.

One of the domains where we frequently see individuals complaining of homo- and transphobic persecution is that of gender expression. Nowhere is there a clearer example of this phenomenon than in the sphere of asylum. My piece "Dancing Around Gender Expression,"[18] assigned for this week, is a critique of current US policy on LGBTQ+ asylum. I interrogate here, among other things, the United States Citizenship and Immigration Services' difficulties in navigating the terrain of gender expression when it deals with asylum cases. It is vital that there is a comprehensive understanding of the role of masculinity and perceptions about emasculation in how persecution plays out around the world. Yet, US immigration policy is inadequately equipped to engage, at least as of now, with the category of gender expression as an axis of persecution.

The other pieces assigned for this week examine, in diverse ways, the category of the masculine in various other parts of the world. Thus, I included Hongwei Bao's autoethnography of a gay Chinese man's pre- and post-immigration experiences and his subsequent efforts at assimilation in Australia; Helen Gao's formidable critique of the Chinese government's attempts to regulate the gender expression of effeminate men in *The New York Times*; and Dredge Kang's "Surfing the Korean Wave," an ethnographic investigation of the politics of nationalism and gender expression in Thailand through an analysis of the overnight success of a Thai dance cover band, the Wonder Gays. Finally, I assigned a text by R. Raj Rao, who offers a commentary on the homoeroticism of the legendary Indian actor Amitabh Bachchan's films from the 1970s and the 1980s. Just as was the case with Cynthia Weber's text on the bearded drag queen, Conchita Wurst/Tim Neuwirth, assigned for week 1, the discussion of pop culture here in week 7 is also both profound and lighthearted.

Reflections

There were thirteen students enrolled in the course, including one auditor. Only ten, however, attended the class regularly and completed all the coursework. One of the first things I would like to observe here is self-critical: I assigned more readings than I should have. This may seem surprising because what I have listed above does not seem extraordinarily burdensome for a graduate seminar—at least at first glance. This would have been true, I think, for a regular semester, but for an intensive summer session such as this one, particularly in a period when we all still felt a pervasive "Covid fatigue" (it was, after all, summer 2022), this turned out not to be the case. On a few occasions, I felt like my students, although really motivated, had not been able to get through the readings or catch up on the visual texts (documentary and web series) assigned. To be sure, though, one student said to me that they did not think there was too much reading and that they had just completed a course in which the instructor had assigned about three hundred pages a week!

Another thing to observe, and I feel ambivalent about this, is that the classroom presentations[19] and discussions were quite good. In fact, they were generally excellent. But the negative externality of this ordinarily good thing was that I struggled a few times to cover all the material in the sessions. A few times I had to tell my students that we would cover the residual matter from that day's session during the following week. Consequently, I had to readjust the syllabus to drop some readings. This happened mostly in the latter half of the semester. Thus, despite my elaborate thinking and motivations in selecting the assigned readings, I ended up dropping the Schmitt reading from week 5, the Bosia and Ayoub et al. readings from week 6, and the Bao reading from week 7. In each case, I eliminated the reading that was the least "contiguous" with the others. Going forward, I will have to be mindful of this and assign fewer readings when I am teaching a summer version of this course. One additional interpretation is that I had only six class sessions to slot all the presentations (I couldn't assign students to present during the first week, obviously), and as a result many presentations got crowded into the last three days. In the future, I will distribute the presentations more skillfully throughout the six sessions. Finally, I very strongly feel that I could have lectured less and facilitated more discussion during class time.

Having said all this, however, the course was also immensely rewarding. I can sincerely say that I genuinely enjoyed the class discussions throughout the seven sessions. The group presentations were particularly fascinating. As indicated in the syllabus (see appendix A), this assignment is one in which students work in groups or pairs and present on some theme related to LGBTQ+ rights in a particular region of the world. I made an unorthodox decision to do an improvised lottery in class to determine which group would end up with what region. In the end, we had the following five group presentations (I had several other options listed but we didn't need more than five groups):

- Central America

- Sub-Saharan Africa

- Southeast Asia

- South Asia

- Eastern/Central Europe and Russia

I have assigned this exercise in class before and it is always one of the things I am most excited about in a course like this. My students and I learn a great deal from these group research projects, and this semester was no exception. On at least two occasions, at least one member of the group ended up with a region with which they had native familiarity (Central America and South Asia). This was a bonus for all, given that they were assigned the topics by lottery. I am also delighted to report that the vast majority of the individual presentations were incredibly fascinating. Here are some examples of topics my students elected to present on (these were their ideas, not mine):

- An LGBTQ+-run food pantry in Mexico City

- A proposed ban in Texas on minors watching drag shows

- Chinese masculinity

- LGBTQ+ youth mental health

- Rights advances in India for *hijras*

- Gay rights in Nepal

- Racial discrimination within LGBTQ+ dating contexts
- New York State's Gender Recognition Act (permitting the gender marker "X" on official documents)
- Pinkwashing in Israel
- LGBTQ+ rights and FIFA siting of the football world cup in Qatar

What I found particularly uplifting was the global breadth of the choices made by my students. Every single one of these presentations taught me and the others in class a number of things we didn't know. While these student research projects and presentations are usually quite rewarding for me (I invariably learn many new things!), I think the topics my students selected in this semester constituted a particularly edifying mix.

I will conclude this set of remarks with a note on a set of reflections from the last day of class. On this day, July 13, I did a little exercise with my students. I created a Google Doc that I shared with them. In it were three prompts:

- Something you learned in this course that you will remember for one additional semester, for sure
- One good thing about this course
- One not-so-good thing about this course

I asked them to verbally share this feedback with me but also invited them to write it down in the Google Doc. I told them that I was currently in the process of writing this chapter. And I also alerted them that, just like their verbal comments in class, the written feedback was not anonymous because the shared document would reveal their names against the text they entered.

I also let them know that they were not at all required to write anything in this document and that, if they did indeed write something, they were certainly not required to respond to all three prompts. I will conclude this chapter with a transcription of my students' responses, copied from the Google Doc on July 15. The feedback, presented in table 6.1, indicates a high level of satisfaction with the course among my students. And, generally, I concur with most of their opinions about the course.

Table 6.1. Student Responses

Something you learned in this course that you will remember for one additional semester, for sure:
• The role of intersectional translators in human rights/political movements.
• LGBT asylum policies.
• Background knowledge of the Yogyakarta Principles.
• Ghosh, Cyril. 2018. "Marriage Equality and the Injunction to Assimilate: Romantic Love, Children, Monogamy, and Parenting in *Obergefell v. Hodges*."
• That the LGBTQ+ rights/human rights format can be harmful and oppressive in some cases.
• Learning about the concept [of] pinkwashing and how it's been capable of distracting communities from legitimate violence and issues.
• How many countries attempt to offer LGBTQ folks more rights, but they are still not quite inclusive or written from the perspective of LGBTQ folks, so they fall short much of the time.
One good thing about this course:
• Lots of homework and feedback, a chance to practice critical writing and receiving feedback. Very rich discussions.
• The opportunity for open discussions, and learning about different countries each week.
• Presentations about other regions in the world, something I have never had the opportunity to look into in detail.
• The class discussions and group presentations allow us to learn pretty comprehensively about how LGBTQ folks are being treated around the world.
One not-so-good thing about this course:
• Too short — would love to process this info over a longer period of time.
• Similar note as above, the course was very condensed and I wish it could have been spread out over more time (but I understand the limitations of a summer course in that regard).
• Craving more international politics and Global South perspectives.
• Lectures are long, but I would also like to take more classes in this course.
• A little too much reading! It was hard to keep up during some weeks.

Appendix A: Syllabus (Edited)

Global Politics of LGBT+ Rights

Cyril Ghosh

Summer 2022

NINT 5039

CRN 3090

Note: This syllabus is subject to alterations.

COURSE DESCRIPTION

This is a survey class on the rights, recognition, and struggles of lesbians, gays, bisexuals, transgender people, queer-identified people, and other nonheterosexual individuals and sexual-orientation and gender-identity minorities both in the Global North and the Global South. The course proceeds in three segments. We will begin with a broad overview of the discourse of human rights in international law and then survey the literature on the rights of sexual minorities. In doing so, we will familiarize ourselves not only with the Universal Declaration of Human Rights but also with the International Covenant on Civil and Political Rights, the Yogyakarta Principles, and so on. In addition, we will analyze the scholarship on both the marriage equality movement and the claims of radical/queer critics of marriage. In the remaining two segments, we will examine the rights, accomplishments, and struggles of LGBTQ+ individuals, first in the Global North (with a focus on the United States and Britain) and then in the Global South (particularly South Asia, the Middle East and North Africa, sub-Saharan Africa, and Latin America).

For undergraduate students, this course also counts toward the gender studies minor.

TEXTS

No required texts. However, you are expected to have access to Netflix and Amazon Prime.

REQUIREMENTS

Participation (20 percent)

Students are expected to actively participate in class. Participation includes speaking up in class in order to engage with the instructor *and* with other students. You should be prepared to demonstrate a willingness to offer your comments, draw attention to insights from the readings, and ask questions related to the topic of the day. Discussion of current events and media reports that relate to the topics relevant to the course is strongly encouraged.

Classroom presentation (10 percent)

Each of you will make one fifteen-minute in-class presentation on a recent news story (US or international) that relates to the themes discussed in the week's readings. You are expected to provide a background to the story and introduce the various points of view that are in circulation. In addition, you are expected to express your own opinion about the topic, argue for a side, and describe how the topic relates to the themes discussed in that week's readings.

Response paper (10 percent)

Once during the semester, you will turn in a response paper on any one of readings for that day. The paper should be approx. two to three pages long. Give me a brief synopsis of the readings and then your reactions to it. This is intended as a reflective writing exercise. Extensive citations are not required.

Midterm exam (20 percent)

There will be take-home midterm examination (four to five pages). You will receive the prompt(s) on June 8. The exam is due on June 15. You will be asked to write an argumentative essay. In it, you will take a position on a controversial topic and provide evidentiary as well as logical reasons for your decision to take that position. You are also expected to engage with opinions that conflict with yours. More details of an argumentative essay may be found here: https://owl.purdue.edu/owl/general_writing/academic_writing/essay_writing/argumentative_essays.html

Group presentations (10 percent)

Once during the semester, students will work in pairs or groups of three and do a group project on a preassigned topic related to LGBTQ+ rights and human rights in a specific region of the world. The presentations should be twenty to twenty-five minutes long, including a discussion/ Q+A session. You are allowed to use slides, short videos, images, etc. Each group will be asked to write a memo discussing the most urgent interventions required in the region and make recommendations for funding and other support. Ideally, this memo should be about five to six pages long (single-spaced). You should email the memo to me by 11:59 p.m. on the Friday following your group presentation. It should be addressed to me: Cyril Ghosh, part-time assistant professor, The New School. More details on this will be provided in class. Here is a helpful link that gives you some basic instructions on how to format a memo. https://web.ics. purdue.edu/~jbay/419/memotemplate.doc

Final paper (30 percent)

The final research paper (ten to twelve pages) is worth 30 percent of the grade. The topic for these papers will be decided in consultation with the instructor. More details on this in class. The paper is due on July 13.

Note: Undergraduate students will have the option to do a final take-home exam. This exam will be a second iteration of the midterm argumentative essay.

COURSE SCHEDULE

PART I—OVERVIEW

Week 1—June 1: The International Human Rights and Queer International Relations

Readings:

- Universal Declaration of Human Rights. http://www.un.org/ en/universal-declaration-human-rights/

- Yogyakarta Principles and Additional Yogyakarta Principles. http://www.yogyakartaprinciples.org/

- Thoreson, Ryan Richard. 2009. "Queering Human Rights: The Yogyakarta Principles and the Norm That Dare Not Speak Its Name." *Journal of Human Rights* 8 (4): 323–39.

- Donnelly, Jack. 2013. "Theories of Human Rights." In *International Human Rights*. Westview Press.

- OutRight Action International. 2021. "UN New Yorker: December 2021." https://outrightinternational.org/content/un-new-yorker-december-2021

- Weber, Cynthia. 2016. "The 'Normal *and/or* Perverse Homosexual' in International Relations: The 'Eurovisioned Bearded Drag Queen.'" In *Queer International Relations: Sovereignty, Sexuality, and the Will to Knowledge*. Oxford University Press.

Week 2—June 8: History of Sexuality and Performativity

Readings:

- Foucault, Michel. 1978. "We 'Other Victorians' & 'The Repressive Hypothesis.'" In *History of Sexuality. Vol. 1, An Introduction*. Vintage/Random House.

- Butler, Judith. 2004. "Gender Regulations." In *Undoing Gender*. Routledge.

- Ghosh, Cyril. 2018. "Covering's Other Hidden Assault." In *De-Moralizing Gay Rights: Some Queer Remarks on LGBT+ Rights Politics in the US*. Palgrave.

- Valdes, Franciso. 1995. "Queers, Sissies, Dykes, and Tomboys: Deconstructing the Conflation of 'Sex,' 'Gender,' and 'Sexual Orientation' in Euro-American Law and Society." *California Law Review* 83 (1): 1–377. [Selections.]

Video:

- *Death and Life of Marsha P. Johnson*. 2017. Dir. David France. [Available on Netflix.]

Group Presentation 1 (Catherine and Tamar)
Individual Presentations 1 and 2 (Olive)

PART II—FOCUS: GLOBAL NORTH

Week 3—June 15: Homonormativity and Marriage Equality

Readings:

- Puar, Jasbir K. 2006. "Mapping US Homonormativities." *Gender, Place & Culture: A Journal of Feminist Geography* 13 (1): 67–88.

- Warner, Michael. 1999. "Beyond Gay Marriage." In *The Trouble with Normal: Sex, Politics, and the Ethics of Queer Life.* The Free Press.

- Ghosh, Cyril. 2018. "Marriage Equality and the Injunction to Assimilate: Romantic Love, Children, Monogamy, and Parenting in *Obergefell v. Hodges.*" *Polity* 50 (2): 275–99.

- Weber, Cynthia. 2016. "The Normal Homosexual in International Relations: The 'Gay Rights Holder' and the 'Gay Patriot.'" In *Queer International Relations: Sovereignty, Sexuality, and the Will to Knowledge.* Oxford University Press.

Videos:

- *Made in Heaven.* 2019. [Available on Amazon Prime.] Episodes 1 and 2.

Group Presentation 2
Individual Presentations—3 and 4 (Catherine; Gustavo)
Midterm exam due

Week 4—June 22: The Margins: BTQ+

Readings:

- Davis, Heath Fogg. 2017. "Single-Sex Colleges and Transgender Discrimination: The Politics of Checking a 'Male' or 'Female' Box to Get into College." In *LGBTQ Politics: A*

Critical Reader, edited by Marla Brettschneider et al. New York University Press.

- Sharrow, Elizabeth A. 2021. "Sports, Transgender Rights and the Bodily Politics of Cisgender Supremacy." *Laws* 10 (3): 63.

- Smith, Charles Anthony, Shawn Schulenberg, and Eric A. Baldwin. 2017. "The 'B' Isn't Silent: Bisexual Communities and Political Activism." In *LGBTQ Politics: A Critical Reader*, edited by Marla Brettschneider et al. New York University Press.

- Edwards-Leeper, Laura, and Erica Anderson. 2021. "The Mental Health Establishment Is Failing Trans Kids." *Washington Post*, November 24.

- Mayo-Adam, Erin. 2020. Introduction and "Chapter 4: Thwarting Division Through Intersectional Translation." In *Queer Alliances: How Power Shapes Political Movement Formation*. Stanford University Press.

- Fiani, Chassitty N., and Christine R. Serpe. 2020. "Non-Binary Identity and the Double-Edged Sword of Globalization." In *Trans Lives in a Globalizing World: Rights, Identities and Politics*, edited by J. Michael Ryan. Routledge.

Videos:

- *Made in Heaven*. 2019. [Available on Amazon Prime.] Episodes 3 and 4.

Group Presentation 3 (Gustavo and Olive; Vanessa and Grant)
Individual Presentations 5 and 6 (Ramnik; Bree)

PART III: FOCUS—GLOBAL SOUTH

Week 5—June 29: Pinkwashing and the Decolonial Queer

Readings:

- Ghosh, Cyril. 2018. "Radical Theory Creep." In *De-Moralizing Gay Rights: Some Queer Remarks on LGBT+ Rights Politics in the US*. Palgrave.

- Franke, Katherine. 2012. "Dating the State: The Moral Hazards of Winning Gay Rights." *Columbia Human Rights Law Review* 44 (1): 1–46.

- Pereira, Pedro Paulo Gomes. 2019. "Decolonial Queer." In *Queer in the Tropics: Gender and Sexuality in the Global South.* Springer.

- Massad, Joseph. 2002. "Reorienting Desire: The Gay International and the Arab World." *Public Culture* 14 (2): 361–85.

- Schmitt, Arno. 2003. "Gay Rights Versus Human Rights: A Response to Joseph Massad." *Public Culture* 15 (3): 587–92.

- Rahman, Momin. 2020. "Queer Muslim Challenges to the Internationalization of LGBT Rights: Decolonizing International Relations Methodology Through Intersectionality." In *The Oxford Handbook of Global LGBT and Sexual Diversity Politics*, edited by Michael J. Bosia, Sandra M. McEvoy, and Momin Rahman. Oxford University Press.

Videos:

- *Made in Heaven.* 2019. [Available on Amazon Prime.] Episodes 5 and 6.

Group Presentation 4 (Rthvika and Ramnik)
Individual Presentations 7 and 8 (Tamar; Grant)

Week 6—July 6: Rights Rhetoric: Human/Gay/Transgender

Readings:

- Encarnación, Omar. 2018. "A Latin American Puzzle: Gay Rights Landscapes in Argentina and Brazil." *Human Rights Quarterly* 40: 194–218.

- Jain, Deepika, and Debanuj Dasgupta. 2021. "Law, Gender Identity, and the Uses of Human Rights: The Paradox of Recognition in South Asia." *Journal of Human Rights* 20 (1): 110–26.

- Podcast: "David Kato: A Matter of Life and Death: The Struggle for Ugandan Gay Rights."

- Centre for Gender Studies and the Centre of Governance and Human Rights, Cambridge, UK, http://www.cghr.polis.cam.ac.uk/events/events_archive/events_2010/events_2010_catouganda.

- Bosia, Michael J. 2020. "Global Sexual Diversity Politics and the Trouble with LGBT Rights." In *The Oxford Handbook of Global LGBT and Sexual Diversity Politics*, edited by Michael J. Bosia, Sandra M. McEvoy, and Momin Rahman. Oxford University Press.

- Ayoub, Phillip M., Douglas Page, and Sam Whitt. 2021. "Pride Amid Prejudice: The Influence of LGBT+ Rights Activism in a Socially Conservative Society." *American Political Science Review* 115 (2): 467–85.

Videos:

- *Made in Heaven*. 2019. [Available on Amazon Prime.] Episodes 7 and 8.

Group presentations 9 and 10 (Vanessa; Seth)

Week 7—July 13: Other Masculinities

Readings:

- Ghosh, Cyril. "Dancing Around Gender Expression: LGBTQ+ Asylum Policy in the US." Draft manuscript.

- Bao, Hongwei. 2018. *Queer Comrades: Gay Identity and Tongzhi Activism in Postsocialist China*. NIAS Press.

- Gao, Helen. 2021. "China's Ban on 'Sissy Men' Is Bound to Backfire." *New York Times*, December 31. https://www.nytimes.com/2021/12/31/opinion/china-masculinity.html?referringSource=articleShare.

- Kang, Dredge Byung'chu. 2018. "Surfing the Korean Wave: Wonder Gays and the Crisis of Thai Masculinity." *Visual Anthropology* 31 (1–2): 45–65.

- Rao, R. Raj. 2000. "Memories Pierce the Heart: Homoeroticism, Bollywood-Style." *Journal of Homosexuality* 39 (3–4): 299–306.

Video:

- *Made in Heaven.* 2019. [Available on Amazon Prime.] Episode 9.

Group Presentation 6
Individual Presentations 11, 12, 13 (Ellie; Rthvika; Tanya)
Final paper/exam due

Notes

1. The name of the course being analyzed here is Global Politics of LGBT+ Rights. Throughout the text, when I refer to the course, I use the term "LGBT+" as opposed to "LGBTQ+." To the best of my knowledge, there is no rule about whether or not the symbol "+" in the abbreviation "LGBT+" subsumes categories such as queer; questioning; intersexed persons; allies; asexual persons; two-spirit people; those who self-identify as members of the third gender; *hijra, kothi, aravani, kathoey,* and *waria* communities; nonbinary persons; gender nonconforming persons, and so on. But, over the years, for various reasons, I have come to value what can be said to be included in the category of "queer" (both in the sense of queer theory and in the sense of queer lived experience) enough that I am interested in centering it here (and elsewhere).

2. This article was written in July 2022—immediately after the course had been offered.

3. "Julien J. Studley Graduate Programs in International Affairs," The New School, https://www.newschool.edu/international-affairs/.

4. The term "sexual minority" is one shorthand for SOGIESC (sexual orientation, gender identity and expression, and sex characteristics) minorities.

5. Neil Young, "How the Bathroom Wars Shaped America," *Politico,* May 18, 2018; Zein Murib, "Laws Targeting Transgender Youths Lean on Myths About White Childhood Innocence. This Explains How," *Monkey Cage, Washington Post,* March 23, 2022.

6. Jo Wuest, "The Scientific Gaze in American Transgender Politics: Contesting the Meaning of Sex, Gender, and Gender Identity in the Bathroom Rights Cases," *Politics & Gender* 15 (2019): 336–60.

7. Kimala Price, "Queering Reproductive Justice: Toward a Theory and Praxis for Building Intersectional Political Alliances," in *LGBTQ Politics: A Critical Reader*, eds. Marla Brettschneider, Susan Burgess, and Christine Keating (New York University Press, 2017), 72–88.

8. Jason Stodolka, "You Don't Belong Here, Either: Same-Sex Marriage Politics and LGBT/Q Youth Homelessness Activism in Chicago," in Brettschneider et al., *LGBTQ Politics: A Critical Reader*, 414–35.

9. See, for example, Cathy Cohen, "Punks, Bulldaggers, and Welfare Queens: The Radical Potential of Queer Politics?," *GLQ* 3 (1997): 437–65.

10. Spencer Kornhaber, "Cruising in the Age of Consent," *Atlantic*, July 15, 2019.

11. Andrew Spieldenner, "PrEP Whores and HIV Prevention: The Queer Communication of HIV Pre-Exposure Prophylaxis (PrEP)," *Journal of Homosexuality* 63, no. 12 (2016): 1685–97.

12. Che Gossett, "We Will Not Rest in Peace: AIDS Activism, Black Radicalism, Queer and/or Trans Resistance," in *Queer Necropolitics*, eds. Jin Haritaworn, Adi Kuntsman, and Silvia Posocco (Routledge, 2014): 31–50.

13. See, for example, R. A. Ferguson, *Aberrations in Black: Toward a Queer of Color Critique* (University of Minnesota Press, 2003).

14. See, e.g., Leo Bersani, *Is the Rectum a Grave? And Other Essays* (University of Chicago Press, 2010); J. E. Muñoz, *Cruising Utopia: The Then and There of Queer Futurity* (New York University Press, 2019); Lee Edelman, *No Future: Queer Theory and the Death Drive* (Duke University Press, 2004); J. Halberstam, *The Queer Art of Failure* (Duke University Press, 2011).

15. Edward Said, *Orientalism* (Vintage, 1979).

16. Nancy Fraser, "From Redistribution to Recognition: Dilemmas of Justice in a 'Postsocialist' Age," *New Left Review* 1, no. 212 (July–August 1995): 68–93.

17. Paisley Currah, *Sex Is as Sex Does: Governing Transgender Identity* (New York University Press, 2022).

18. The title of this piece, in its (later) published form, is this: "Dancing Around Gender Expression and Sex Talk: LGBTQ+ Asylum Policy in the United States," *Journal of Human Rights* 23, no. 3 (2024): 253–66.

19. A complete list of assignments appears on the syllabus (appendix A).

Part 2

Bringing LGBTQ Issues into Other Political Science Courses

In part 2, we turn to an examination of how best to incorporate lessons from LGBTQ politics into courses that are traditionally designed without consideration for LGBTQ people or topics. The chapters in this section provide insight across political science subfields and include practical tips for structuring political science courses that align with critical pedagogies.

While LGBTQ inclusion is a key theme of the chapters in this section, the authors share the perspective that issues of curricular exclusion are systemic. That is, the exclusion of LGBTQ politics, like the study of most marginalized groups, from political science curricula is not just the product of reluctant instructors. It is also a function of reticence within the discipline and its institutions (e.g., textbook publishers and professional organizations) to recognize the value of LGBTQ political studies to our shared understanding of power and politics. Because the structures and institutions of higher education—many controlled by politicians aligned with interests hostile to the promotion of diversity, equity, and inclusion—limit how instructors do their jobs, LGBTQ curricular exclusion is baked into course preparations and reflected in the course offerings and materials instructors can teach or adopt.

Because teaching LGBTQ politics is itself a political endeavor, there is an inherent tension over how to bring LGBTQ issues into other political science courses. The tension is similar to that described by Kammerer and Cravens in chapter 1 (i.e., "Is it better to diversify the canon, drawing in previously excluded voices, or, in the alternative, to abandon the concept of a single canon entirely?").

The task of teaching LGBTQ politics, then, manifests in complementary approaches. On the one hand, inclusion of LGBTQ politics is the end goal for some instructors interested in bringing LGBTQ issues into their other political science classes. On the other hand, inclusion is just the water's edge for some instructors. Regardless of the perspective adopted, the chapters in part 2 all offer robust structural critiques of LGBTQ curricular exclusion and offer practical examples, like coursework and assignments, that will help new and seasoned instructors either create new courses focused on LGBTQ politics or incorporate LGBTQ politics into their existing course structures. The chapters also foreground additional questions explored in part 3 including how disparate educational environments affect course development.

Part 2 opens with Cravens's contribution, titled "So Proudly We Hailed." This chapter explores how LGBTQ politics can be incorporated into introductory American government courses, despite the lack of representation in almost every major textbook on the subject. The chapter extends some of the analysis Kammerer and Cravens offer in chapter 1 related to LGBTQ representation in the political science canon and posits several strategies for instructors to overcome the systemic LGBTQ content deficit in introductory American government textbooks. Beginning with course design and development, Cravens draws a through line for instructors to link their course goals and objectives with assignments and assessments that use LGBTQ politics to teach the foundational lessons of the class Introduction to American Government.

Chapter 8, "Thinking Sex: Why Every Political Science Major Should Read Gayle Rubin" by C. Heike Schotten, argues that no political science major should be allowed to graduate without having had Gayle Rubin's pivotal "Thinking Sex" assigned in at least one course during their undergraduate career. The author argues that the text provides important lessons, skills, analytic frameworks, and political positionings that remain understudied and underappreciated in the political science curriculum. In this way, the author offers an attempt at "transformation of political science from a discipline wherein questions of sex/gender/sexuality get tacked onto its back end, like the embarrassment many political scientists may feel them to be, to one wherein questions of sex/gender/sexuality are considered central to its disciplinary inquiry."

Edward F. Kammerer Jr. follows Schotten with chapter 9, "Integrating LGBTQ Issues into to Law-Themed Courses: Moving Beyond Marriage and Nondiscrimination." In this chapter, Kammerer offers suggestions for expanding the LGBTQ content in courses covering law and legal advocacy. Importantly, he shows that sex, sexuality, and gender are central to a multitude of legal issue areas, not just the usual topics of marriage equality and nondiscrimination law. Kammerer discusses free speech and obscenity, asylum and immigration law, criminal law and prison reform, education, healthcare, and more. He also draws on critiques of the overreliance on equal protection framing to expand the scope of what can and should be considered an LGBTQ legal issue.

Seth J. Meyer, Nicole M. Elias, and Maria J. D'Agostino also engage with pedagogical strategies that incorporate LGBTQ politics into courses in public administration. In chapter 10, titled "Reading Is Fundamental: Pedagogical Strategies for Including SOGIE in Public and Nonprofit Administration Education," the authors explore the most effective strategies to teach LGBTQ topics in public administration by focusing on course policies, pedagogical practices, and substantive content. In addition, the authors offer an overview of the ways in which LGBTQ people interact with public organizations, and how these organizations can be more welcoming of LGBTQ people.

Part 2 ends with chapter 11 by Andrew R. Flores titled "Using LGBTQ Politics and Policy to Teach Quantitative Methods." In this chapter, Flores explores how LGBTQ people, who often resist rigid characterizations, present a unique opportunity to teach quantitative research methodologies. Specifically, the author addresses the dual pedagogical challenges of incorporating diverse sexualities and genders in teaching quantitative social science and incorporating quantitative social science in teaching LGBTQ politics. Flores shows that in both contexts, particular appreciation should be paid to the fluidity of identity, the role of institutions in constructing and reconstructing groups, individual (yet constrained) agency in self-categorization, and the intersectional differences that accurately describe and explain the lived experiences of LGBTQ people.

Chapter 7

So Proudly We Hailed

Incorporating LGBTQ Politics into American Government Courses

Royal G. Cravens III

As Richard Shaull argues in the forward to the thirtieth edition of Paulo Freire's (2014, 34) *Pedagogy of the Oppressed*, "There is no such thing as a neutral educational process." Education should be "the practice of freedom" whereby conformity to the "logic of the present system" is abandoned and students are empowered with the knowledge to "transform their world" (34). This approach obliges educators to deploy pedagogical strategies that "foreground the impact of social relations of power," especially when the effect of such relations is to "silence those who are less powerful" (Cowden and Singh 2015, 567).

Structural analyses and critiques of society, government, and even knowledge creation itself are foundational to contemporary conceptualizations of critical theory and pedagogy, although this was not always the case (Davies and Barnett 2015). Structural analyses and critiques of government that highlight the ways dominant groups in society construct(ed) the United States as a white Christian heteropatriarchy enhance students' critical thinking skills about these topics, which research shows is important to the development and perpetuation of multiracial democracy (Costandius et al. 2015; Volman and ten Dam 2015).

In this chapter, I apply lessons from inclusive, anti-racist, and queer pedagogies to American government course design. Specifically, drawing on Fink's (2013) taxonomy of significant learning, I discuss strategies for inclusion of LGBTQ politics in American government course designs by focusing on structural disempowerment of minoritized people in American politics. By deliberately including structural critiques that center LGBTQ politics, instructors can open their classes to full LGBTQ inclusion, enhance students' critical thinking, and provide significant learning experiences. In what follows, I draw on lessons from critical pedagogies and personal experiences to analyze and provide examples of course designs, materials, assignments, and assessments that speak to these suggestions for incorporating LGBTQ politics into American government courses.

LGBTQ Studies in American Politics Courses

Novkov and Gossett (2007, 393) showed that when American government textbooks included discussions of lesbian and gay political experiences, the discussions were limited to civil rights and liberties sections of the texts, and lesbians and gays were almost exclusively framed as "another structurally disempowered group." The study was undertaken at the request of the American Political Science Association (APSA) Committee on the Status of LGBTQ Individuals in the Profession, which advocates on behalf of LGBTQ inclusion in political science, and analyzed the content of introductory American Government and Politics (AmGov) textbooks.

Consistent with later scholars' documentation of intersectional discrimination and disempowerment in the discipline of political science (Ackelsberg 2017), Novkov and Gossett (2007, 393) note that bisexual people are nearly erased while transgender people are "nowhere to be found." Furthermore, all the texts lacked visual representation of LGBTQ people and rarely named LGBTQ people in the photographs that were printed.

More than a decade later, Shawna Brandle (2020) again examined the inclusion of marginalized groups in introductory AmGov textbooks, including Open Educational Resource texts. An index search of eleven textbooks demonstrates traditionally marginalized groups, including women, African Americans, Asian and Pacific Islanders, Latinx, and LGBTQ people, are all underrepresented. Namely, the results suggest that only about one-quarter of the substantive pages in the texts reviewed contain information on traditionally marginalized groups.

Moreover, and consistent with Novkov and Gossett (2007), Brandle (2020, 737) finds discussions of traditionally marginalized groups are "siloed" in sections on civil rights and liberties and are generally only discussed in conjunction with major court cases. Additionally, a content analysis of thirteen AmGov textbooks demonstrates that less than 10 percent of substantive paragraphs in the texts mention traditionally marginalized groups, leading Brandle (2020, 738) to conclude "political science as a discipline does not consistently consider [traditionally marginalized groups] essential to the study of American Government."

Since Novkov and Gossett's and Brandle's analyses reached similar conclusions more than a decade apart, it is apparent that textbook companies and textbook authors are failing to equally include LGBTQ politics in the most widely available AmGov course materials. Paired with our findings about the malleability of the LGBTQ politics cannon in chapter 1 of this volume and observation that "research on issues central to women, people of color, and other minoritized communities has often been ignored" in political science, an important practical question emerges: How can instructors incorporate LGBTQ politics into their AmGov courses?

Call Out LGBTQ Erasure in American Politics

Before discussing course design, it is important to say that one strategy for incorporating LGBTQ politics into American government is to call out its erasure. While this is ultimately an individualized response to a systemic problem that can obscure the root of the problem and foist responsibility for fixing it on marginalized people, the history and politics of LGBTQ visibility shows that when pursued collectively, through group curricular reform efforts, directly confronting LGBTQ erasure in the curriculum can be a successful strategy.

The introduction, conclusion, and chapters by Price and Josephson in this volume all describe the efforts of contemporaneous groups to limit discussions of LGBTQ and anti-racist topics in public schools, colleges, and universities and how schools are, again, the center of political contests over LGBTQ civil equality. Still, many LGBTQ political scientists and their allies may be averse to calling out inequality. The author of chapter 15 in this volume, published under a pseudonym, speaks to the reasons it may not be safe to advocate LGBTQ inclusion, for one. Others may feel that it diminishes the scientific credibility of their work to be seen as advocating LGBTQ inclusion—either actively and visibility through protest or less visibility by incorporating LGBTQ politics into their course designs.

In a symposium on the contributions of LGBTQ politics to the discipline of political science, Gary Mucciaroni (2011, 17) succinctly diffused critiques of LGBTQ politics as "advocacy masquerading as scholarship," saying, "All decisions that we make about what to study are political because they reveal the topics that we consider most legitimate and important to warrant examination. If our decision to study LGBT politics is a political one, so too was our neglect of it for many years."

American politics is fundamentally a struggle over power—as Mucciaroni says, "How democratic regimes cope with the challenges posed by social diversity and how minorities and excluded groups induce the majority to address their claims for recognition, freedom, and equality." Because of this, the study of American politics is also fundamentally the study of queer people and how their political struggles nuance and broaden our understanding of power relationships.

Concerning the queer nature of American political ideals, Hall (2010, 537) notes, "In some respects the long and continuing debate over just what Americanism actually is has characterized the Republic as much as the existence of the [American] creed itself, and its malleability has enabled it to be claimed by forces from across the political spectrum." The understanding of Americanism as malleable complements the most penetrating aspects of queer theory.

At its heart, queer theory challenges the idea that there is any essential or normative notion of what it means to be or perform any "identity" (e.g., American, woman, gay). This is important in political science, and especially in AmGov courses because the institutions, organizations, and individuals that comprise the American governmental system have traditionally only been representative of a privileged elite, those who represent dominant (i.e., constructed as normative) categories of being (e.g., white, cisgender, male, heterosexual).

Knowing this has important consequences for both American government and how professors structure their American government classes. One is the structural disempowerment of non-normative people and identities. Another is the seeming erasure of LGBTQ people from American political history. A third consequence is that AmGov classrooms often replicate these processes and ghettoize minoritized groups to discussions of civil rights or liberties, when they are even discussed (Novkov and Gossett 2007; Brandle 2020).

Understanding the problems associated with incorporating LGBTQ politics into AmGov courses as such suggests two potential avenues of action for AmGov instructors; however, they are not mutually exclusive. First, AmGov courses must be deliberately designed to provoke discussions about structural disempowerment targeting minoritized groups (which necessarily includes discussion of LGBTQ people, but also the intersections of gender, sexuality, race, class, disability, religion, and other axes of oppression). Second, AmGov courses must be deliberately designed to include historical and contemporary examples of LGBTQ political agency, especially examples that "extend the sphere" of political conflict beyond the restrictive frame of liberal civil rights struggles.

Course Design to Engage Structural Disempowerment

Most students of American history, let alone American government, do not know the history of LGBTQ identity construction, nor do they know the ways the United States government facilitated it (Rupp and Freeman 2017; Canaday 2009). The popular narratives that sex(uality) was never a topic of political debate and that LGBTQ people did not exist prior to the twentieth century contributes to the belief (and coverage in American government textbooks) that LGBTQ people and the LGBTQ movement sprang, fully formed, as a civil rights struggle from the Stonewall Inn in the summer of 1969.

The regulation of sexuality and gender and the construction of LGBTQ identity are all linked by structural features of American politics that maintain cis-heterosexism (Canaday 2009). By recognizing these structural features of American government, which permeate all aspects of society and the operation of the American governmental system, AmGov instructors have the opportunity to engage concepts related to structural disempowerment through their course design (e.g., learning objectives, pedagogical approach, materials, and assignments). But what makes for an effective course design when the goal is to include LGBTQ politics? Fink (2013) offers one framework.

Consistent with Freire (2014), Fink (2013) describes "significant learning experiences" as those experiences that alter students' lives. "We want that which students learn to become part of how they think, what they can and want to do, what they believe is true about life, and what they value—and we want it to increase their capability for living life fully and meaningfully" (7).

In the context of AmGov classes, significant learning experiences can be understood as fundamentally altering student perceptions about the systems of power that structure our lives. To achieve significant learning experiences, Fink (2013) proposes a six-part taxonomy for designing college courses that includes cultivating foundational knowledge of a subject, the application of knowledge through practical learning opportunities, integrating course knowledge across aspects of one's life and/or career, introspection and empathy, and perpetuating inquiry beyond coursework.

LGBTQ politics offers a readymade body of knowledge and experience to fit this task in that LGBTQ politics teaches how minoritized groups in American politics "claim dominion over not land but bodies, freedom not from England but from dominant society, and self-determination not for the colonies but for minorities" (Stein 2000, 296–97 quoted in Hill 2010, 561). By harnessing the potential of LGBTQ political studies and incorporating them into AmGov course designs, instructors can "sexualize the founding discourse of the United States" and contextualize the deployment of LGBTQ politics "against the state," all the while empowering students to transform their own understanding of American politics (Stein 2000, 296–97). Some suggestions and examples for instructors to implement the significant learning framework include (re)writing learning objectives, course materials, and evaluating the methods of knowledge creation.

LEARNING OBJECTIVES

When designing a new course (or a new version of a course you already teach), the first thing an instructor must consider are the learning objectives. When crafting learning objectives, Fink (2013) suggests instructors recognize the distinction between foundational knowledge, application, and what the author refers to as the human dimensions of learning, including self-reflection, empathy, and cultivating continual learning. Namely, while foundational knowledge is necessary to convey in any course, it is not enough to provide a significant learning experience. Learning objectives that focus on addressing structural disempowerment in American politics and comport with the significant learning experience framework offer a way for AmGov instructors to assess their courses and move toward inclusive instruction.

In addition to learning objectives that prioritize structural analyses of disempowerment, AmGov instructors who want to incorporate LGBTQ politics into their classes should be prepared to answer two questions. How much are you willing to learn (or already know) about LGBTQ politics? And to what extent are you willing to incorporate LGBTQ politics into your course design? The latter question is more important than the former, in that instructors can learn more about LGBTQ politics (e.g., by reading the other chapters in this volume); however, the extent to which you are willing to include LGBTQ politics in your course design reflects the value you place on equity and inclusivity.

Whitney Ross Manzo (chap. 14, this volume) highlights the fact that inclusive values may not always be something completely controlled by the instructor, noting the "tension between pedagogical best practices related to inclusion and the overall atmosphere in which I teach [i.e., a historically women's college located in a southern community steeped in a traditionalistic political culture]." While Manzo offers suggestions for ameliorating this tension, failure to consider structural inequalities or LGBTQ politics throughout the course design will result in their replication, as Brandle (2020) notes.

Namely, LGBTQ people and their contributions to American politics are usually discussed in the context of civil rights claims by disempowered groups. Affirmative depictions of LGBTQ people as empowered and with political agency generally occur only in the context of social movement organizing (if AmGov courses venture into the realm of social movements) after the 1969 Stonewall Riots and, furthermore, are characterized as another version of liberal democratic rights claiming, instead of organized resistance to state-sponsored violence (see also chaps. 1 and 7, this volume). Inclusion of LGBTQ topics, therefore, is not enough unless the objective is to further silo LGBTQ political topics in civil rights/liberties discussions. Like Elena Gambino and Haley Norris (chap. 13, this volume), I argue that AmGov instructors must also align their learning objectives, materials, and pedagogical approaches with intentional inclusion across all aspects of the AmGov curriculum.

In table 7.1, I offer some suggestions for how to construct learning objectives that focus on structural disempowerment of marginalized groups and learning objectives focused on LGBTQ inclusion. The sample learning objectives focus on American political institutions, which is often a key aspect of AmGov courses. The objectives in the left-hand column of table 7.1 are derived from example syllabi available on the APSA Educate website. I offer suggestions consistent with Fink (2013) in the right-hand column.

Table 7.1. Comparison of Learning Objectives Related to American Political Institutions

Sample Learning Objectives:	Objectives Consistent with Fink (2013):
1. "To provide some of the background information that may help you clarify your own expectations of government."[1]	"Students will reflect on their experience with American politics and how their experience affects their expectations of government."
2. "Identify the three branches of government and both their constitutional and implied powers."[2]	"Students will evaluate how political power in America is wielded by the major governing institutions in order to shape public policy."
3. "Identify informal institutions in the American government (i.e., political parties) and their roles and functions."	"Students will explain how socially constructed categories of difference (e.g., social identities) are used to accrue and deny political power to groups in the United States."
4. "Identify reasons why a political institution may have changed."	"Students will evaluate American majoritarianism; specifically, how majoritarian institutions respond to the concerns of political minorities."
5. "Explain the reasons that specific institutions changed over time."	"Students will (1) research how representation in the U.S. Congress has changed over time, and (2) explain why the Voting Rights Act of 1965 increased the political representation of People of Color in the United States."
Learning Objectives Specific to LGBTQ political inclusion:	
6. "Students will identify major LGBTQ political figures (or organizations) and their contribution to LGBTQ political representation."	
7. "Students will evaluate how law and public policy have defined and regulated gender and sexuality in the United States."	
8. "Students will explore the tensions between assimilation and liberation for minority political existence in Liberal societies."	
9. "Students will reflect on the following question: How can knowledge about inequalities in American government help me in my future educational or career path?"	

1. American Political Science Association, "Intro to American Politics: Syllabus," https://educate.apsanet.org/resource/04-03-2020/syllabus-introduction-to-american-politics.

2. American Political Science Association, "Intro to American Government Syllabus," https://educate.apsanet.org/resource/09-08-2020/introduction-to-american-politics-syllabus-2. Numbered columns 3, 4, and 5 also qtd. from this source.

Recall that significant learning experiences cultivate foundational knowledge of a subject, apply knowledge through practical learning opportunities, integrate course knowledge across aspects of one's life and/or career, induce introspection and empathy, and perpetuate inquiry beyond coursework. The sample learning objectives listed in table 7.1 speak generally about the important aspects of American government that students should understand by the end of the course; however, they generally speak only to foundational knowledge. They do, however, leave open opportunities to intentionally center the experiences of minoritized groups and evaluate the structural features that contribute to disempowerment.

For example, sample objective 3 suggests students will acquire some foundational knowledge, but this is enhanced with introspection and empathy as students not only clinically identify political actors but develop an understanding of the way some actors are afforded or denied power by the objective in column 2. While students will not always organically come to such conclusions, paired with learning objective 1 students are given the opportunity to evaluate and reflect on their own positionality and how they and others are advantaged and/or disadvantaged by the structural features of American government.

Similarly, identifying and explaining the reasons for institutional change are important, but identifying the structural features of American government that contribute to disempowerment and how those features can be changed (as described in objectives 4 and 5 in column 2) give students the opportunity to acquire and apply knowledge.

Learning objectives 6 to 9 apply the same lessons while centering LGBTQ people and/or sexual orientation and gender identity in American politics. In many cases, LGBTQ people fail to appear in AmGov classes because they are an afterthought. Building LGBTQ experiences into the learning objectives will keep instructors accountable for correcting the sins of omission that are rampant in AmGov texts. Similarly, asking students to reflect on why it is important that they learn about marginalization and marginalized groups as part of an AmGov class—and what those lessons can contribute to their future (learning objective 9)—is often not a priority for AmGov instructors. However, much like the quip by the political behavioralists who asked "Why don't Americans participate in politics more?" it is largely because "no one asked" (Verba et al. 1995). If instructors want students to have significant learning experiences that critique structural inequalities with lessons from LGBTQ politics and then understand why it is important, they must first be willing to design such a course and ask their students to participate.

Inclusive Instruction and Critical Pedagogy

Another starting point for instructors who want to (re)design their AmGov classes is to reflect on the following question: What pedagogical approaches are foundational to your course? Pedagogical choices are often reflections of the things we value as instructors, but choices can be limited by the type of class (e.g., introductory vs. advanced), enrollment size, and physical or virtual space the class occupies. Despite these constraints, critical pedagogies, including those derived from queer, anti-racist, multicultural, and decolonial theories, tell us that course designs should help students situate their own experiences within systems of power and evaluate their responsibilities/obligations to the system. These forms of learning have come under increasing scrutiny in recent years, as state legislators seek to ban "controversial" topics and discussions of subjects that make white students "uncomfortable"—which highlights why they are important components of higher education. But how can instructors apply the lessons of critical pedagogies to their AmGov courses? Educational materials and strategies that enable critical instruction and reflection are especially important. In the following, I provide several examples of approachable materials (e.g., texts and other material) and teaching strategies (pedagogical approaches, activities, and assignments) that AmGov instructors should consider adopting.

Course Materials

Most AmGov textbooks follow the pattern outlined by Novkov and Gossett (2007) and Brandle (2020). However, there are texts that apply critical pedagogical perspectives, and instructors may consider curating their own materials. One textbook example is McClain and Tauber's (2021) *American Government in Black and White*. In the text, the authors are deliberate in their approach to structural racism in American politics, and they use the opportunity of an introductory American government textbook to confront the fact that "race and ethnicity are central to American politics." So it is necessary to consider, and center, the experiences of marginalized people because "the United States is not 'one nation . . . indivisible,' but instead, something different to each of us based on our citizenship status, socioeconomic class, religion, age, place of residence, race, ethnicity, gender and many other factors" (McClain and Tauber 2021, xvi).

In discussions of the American founding, not just in sections on civil rights and liberties, the authors provide examples of inclusive pedagogy and critical analysis that recognizes both the founding of the United States and the teaching of American government as structurally unequal endeavors. For example, the authors discuss the violence of European colonialism in the Americas as well as the inattention American government classes pay to the governing traditions and institutions of Native Americans and how they influenced the structures of American government as much as European political theorists like Locke and Rousseau (McClain and Tauber 2021). This kind of inclusivity work and critique is also important to the task of LGBTQ political inclusion in AmGov courses. Beginning with the recognition that Eurocentric Christian conceptions of hetero- and cisnormativity are not the only natural ways of being, nor are they solely representative of the American experience, American government instructors can construct a more inclusive course.

Textbook cost can present an educational barrier, yet Open Educational Resource texts are subject to the same biases as most major textbooks (Brandle 2020). For this reason, when seeking course materials, AmGov instructors can look to other sources that provide structural critiques of American politics while centering the experiences of LGBTQ people. In my own courses, several podcasts have served this purpose. Some podcasts instructors may find useful are *Making Gay History*, *Lovett or Leave It*, *LGBTQ & A*, and *Queer America*.

These external or nontraditional sources, as well as sources beyond AmGov textbooks (e.g., historical texts, biographies, music, videos), are also important because they provide an opportunity to expand course content to include LGBTQ political topics. For example, instructors can highlight LGBTQ members of Congress or the Equality Caucus in discussions of the legislative branch. LGBTQ interest or pressure groups, LGBTQ judges, or cabinet secretaries as well as specific policies from each of these actors/ institutions give students opportunity to flesh out both the functions of government and the structural deficiencies related to sexuality, gender identity, and expression. Other examples for course content include the federal HIV/AIDS response and state same-sex marriage policy, which can be discussed in the context of federalism. LGBTQ voters could be highlighted in the context of political party coalitions. LGBTQ-inclusive policy referenda (e.g., campaigns to repeal local civil rights protections for LGBTQ people) could be discussed within the context of debates over the effectiveness of direct and indirect democracy. The contributions of LGBTQ political theorists and specific notions of how LGBTQ identities implicate "freedom" can contextualize discussions of the founding era as can discussions of social constructivism and the idea that the "state" can/should be an arbiter of identity. These are all specific examples of LGBTQ political agency that can be tied back to the learning objectives in the previous section since they convey foundational knowledge about American politics but also develop provocative questions about power relationships and structural inequality and can induce introspection.

Teaching Practices

In addition to learning materials, AmGov instructors must be prepared to confront structural inequities perpetuated from the governmental system that translate into the AmGov classroom. This necessitates reflection on one's own privileges and teaching practices. Queer pedagogy, for example, highlights the limitations of both the student and the teacher in their capacity to challenge existing knowledge and in the production of new forms of knowledge (Britzman 1995). Using various materials, teaching practices, assignments, and assessments, then, allows for instructors and students alike to be exposed to multiple bodies of knowledge, learn from each other's experiences, and develop new ways of knowledge creation (Bryson and de Castell 1993).

Other chapters in this volume suggest specific assignments that center LGBTQ politics (e.g., chap. 10). Here, I offer two general approaches that fit within the significant learning experience framework and are supported by their own substantial bodies of literature: active learning (Baepler et al. 2016) and critical service learning (Jacoby 2015). As described in the previous section, the topic of LGBTQ exclusion lends itself to discussions of structural inequity. Centering the experiences of LGBTQ people, however, requires more than just inclusion. What other elements are required of inclusive significant learning experiences? I offer two answers that justify the use of both active and service learning strategies. First, both practices allow introspection and help build empathy. Second, they also provide practical learning opportunities through which students can apply course knowledge.

To the first point, in a *Harvard Educational Review* article, Elizabeth Ellsworth (1989) said, "If you can talk to me in ways that show you understand that your knowledge of me, the world, and 'the Right thing to do' will always be partial, interested, and potentially oppressive to others, and if I can do the same, then we can work together on shaping and reshaping alliances for constructing circumstances in which students of difference can thrive." This speaks not only of the need to build empathy but also of the need to help students understand the position of the "other" and teaching the privileged the perspective of the disenfranchised.

Second, a crucial component of critical pedagogy is the understanding that "the capacity of individuals to critically evaluate different truth claims takes place on radically uneven terrain" (Cowden and Singh 2015, 567). This is important because instructors must recognize how students' positionalities affect their perspective. In addition, assessment strategies must account for this variation. Active and service learning strategies speak to both of these needs.

Active learning is a common educational practice. Many instructors may engage active learning techniques without realizing it. Active learning is also increasingly used in political science classes—for example, see the Active Learning in Political Science (ALPS) blog.[1] These strategies generally refer to pedagogical practices that engage students in learning environments intentionally designed to foster connections and apply lessons from course material (see Baepler et al. 2016; Ambrose et al. 2010; Barkley 2010).[2]

Although a review of active learning pedagogy is beyond the scope of this chapter, common strategies include simulation, guided discussions, and team-based or group work. These practices are important to the inclusion of LGBTQ politics in AmGov classes because they are mechanisms by which students can learn about the lived experiences of their peers, build empathy, and apply those shared lessons to American political problems.

For example, one active learning strategy I regularly employ is simulation. Simulations are like games and often require students to take on a role and complete assignments based on the needs/requirements of their character (Lean et al. 2006). Simulations can be short term (a single class) or last an entire semester. For example, in my AmGov course, about 40 percent of a students' final grade is determined by their completion of a semester-long direct democracy simulation. I require students to form direct democracy campaign teams with specific roles assigned (chair, finance officer, marketing, etc.). The object is to study and apply state law related to citizen-sponsored initiatives. These also serve as opportunities to research specific policy problems. Policies can be determined based on contemporary events, but I have previously asked students to work on "campaigns" related to same-sex marriage and/or domestic partnership legalization, sexual orientation– and gender identity–inclusive civil rights laws, and also policies with intersectional implications including incarceration, policing, higher education, and healthcare reform proposals.

If instructors do not have time to build a long-term simulation, single-class active learning projects like "Frankenpapers," structured debates, small group discussion leading, "four corners" activities, or scavenger hunts are all opportunities to reimagine course participation and (re)design assignments that center structural critique and the experiences of marginalized people (see Springer et al. 2001; Baepler et al. 2016). In the end, the type of assignment will be contingent upon specific learning objectives.

Similar to active learning, service learning allows students to identify a need in their local community and develop a strategy to meet it using course concepts. The practice has been criticized because many instructors and students take the position of the "white knight" riding in to save a distressed community; however, critical service learning addresses this concern by emphasizing community partnerships, reciprocal learning opportunities, and personal reflection (Jacoby 2015; Cress et al. 2013). Critical service learning places students in a position to apply course knowledge, build practical skills like teamwork and communication, and to learn from those affected by a particular policy problem or issue in American politics. Students learning about voting rights might partner with local advocacy groups or county election offices to conduct voter registration drives on campus or in the community. Students learning about food insecurity might partner with local farmers, grocery stores, shelters, and so on to establish a food pantry. In each case, particular lessons can be tailored to highlight structural inequities or LGBTQ political concerns.

The key to critical service learning is reflection (Jacoby 2015; Cress et al. 2013). It is not enough to provide opportunities for students to examine or even work to overcome structural inequities; students must also be given the opportunity to reflect on how the work has affected their perspective on American politics. This requires instructors who wish to apply these strategies to also be prepared to (re)design assessment strategies that capture their course learning objectives but are especially sensitive to the significant learning framework's emphasis on empathy. Many universities have service learning offices and/or teaching centers that are equipped with material to help implement active learning strategies. These offices are a good place to start if instructors want to (re)design assignments to take advantage of the significant learning experience framework.

Conclusion

Hetero- and cissexism, prevalent in American society, is often reflected in American government courses that incorporate LGBTQ political themes only within the civil rights silo (if they are incorporated at all). This is demonstrated in two studies conducted more than a decade apart that found AmGov texts and the field of political science, broadly, do "not consistently consider [traditionally marginalized groups] essential to the study of American Government" (Brandle 2020, 738; Novkov and Gossett 2007). In this chapter, I addressed the historical erasure of LGBTQ people and politics from the American political narrative and suggested that educational practices consistent with the significant learning experience framework and lessons from critical pedagogy offer a way for instructors of AmGov classes to include LGBTQ political themes in their classes. Beyond inclusion, I offered suggestions for (re)developing course learning objectives, intentionally selecting course material, and practicing active and/or service learning strategies with varied assessments. This will allow for not only the intentional centering of LGBTQ political themes but an inclusive AmGov class that conveys foundational knowledge and provides opportunities to cooperatively construct and apply knowledge, as well as engage in introspection about the ways American politics structurally disempowers LGBTQ and all marginalized people.

Notes

1. "Active Learning in Political Science," https://activelearningps.com/about/.

2. The journal *Active Learning in Higher Education* also contains peer-reviewed content for instructors interested in active learning strategies. See https://journals.sagepub.com/home/alh.

References

Ackelsberg, Martha. 2017. "The Politics of LGBTQ Politics in APSA: A History (and Its) Lesson(s)." In *LGBTQ Politics: A Critical Reader*, edited by Marla Brettschneider, Susan Burgess, and Christine Keating. New York University Press.

Ambrose, Susan A., Michael W. Bridges, Michele DiPietro, Marsha C. Lovett, and Marie K. Norman. 2010. *How Learning Works: Seven Research-Based Principles for Smart Teaching*. Jossey-Bass.

Baepler, Paul, J. D. Walker, D. Christopher Brooks, Kem Saichaie, and Christina I. Petersen. 2016. *A Guide to Teaching in the Active Learning Classroom: History, Research, and Practice*. Stylus.

Barkley, Elizabeth F. 2010. *Student Engagement Techniques: A Handbook for College Faculty*. Jossey-Bass.

Brandle, Shawna M. 2020. "It's (Not) in the Reading: American Government Textbooks' Limited Representation of Historically Marginalized Groups." *PS: Political Science & Politics* 53 (4): 734–40.

Britzman, Deborah P. 1995. "Is There a Queer Pedagogy? Or, Stop Reading Straight." *Educational Theory* 45 (2): 151–65.

Bryson, Mary, and Suzanne de Castell. 1993. "Queer Pedagogy: Praxis Makes Im/Perfect." *Canadian Journal of Education* 18 (3): 285–305.

Canaday, Margot. 2009. *The Straight State: Sexuality and Citizenship in Twentieth Century America*. Princeton University Press.

Costandius, Elmarie, Margaret Blackie, Brenda Leibowitz et al. 2015. "Stumbling Over the First Hurdle? Exploring Notions of Critical Citizenship." In *The Palgrave Handbook of Critical Thinking in Higher Education*, edited by Martin Davies and Ronald Barnett. Palgrave MacMillan.

Cowden, Stephen, and Gurnam Singh. 2015. "Critical Pedagogy: Critical Thinking as a Social Practice." In Davies and Barnett, *The Palgrave Handbook of Critical Thinking in Higher Education*.

Cress, Christine M., Peter J. Collier, Vicki L. Reitenauer, and Associates. 2013. *Learning Through Serving: A Student Guidebook for Service-Learning and Civic Engagement Across Academic Disciplines and Cultural Communities*. 2nd ed. Stylus.

Davies, Martin, and Ronald Barnett, eds. 2015. *The Palgrave Handbook of Critical Thinking in Higher Education*. Palgrave MacMillan.

Ellsworth, Elizabeth. 1989. "Why Doesn't This Feel Empowering? Working Through the Repressive Myths of Critical Pedagogy." *Harvard Educational Review* 59 (3): 297–324.

Fink, L. Dee. 2013. *Creating Significant Learning Experiences, Revised and Updated: An Integrated Approach to Designing College Courses*. Jossey-Bass.

Freeman, Elizabeth. 2007. "Introduction." *GLQ: A Journal of Lesbian and Gay Studies* 13 (2–3): 159–76.

Freire, Paulo. 2014. *Pedagogy of the Oppressed*. 30th anniversary ed. Translated by Myra Bergman Ramos. Bloomsbury.

Hall, Simon. 2010. "The American Gay Rights Movement and Patriotic Protest." *Journal of the History of Sexuality* 19 (3): 536–62.

Jacoby, Barbara. 2015. *Service-Learning Essentials: Questions, Answers, and Lessons Learned*. Jossey-Bass.

Lean, Jonathan, Jonathan Moizer, Michael Towler, and Caroline Abbey. 2006. "Simulations and Games: Use and Barriers in Higher Education." *Active Learning in Higher Education* 7 (3): 227–42.

Mucciaroni, Gary. 2011. "The Study of LGBT Politics and Its Contributions to Political Science." *PS: Political Science and Politics* 44 (1): 17–21.

McClain, Paula D., and Steven C. Tauber. 2021. *American Government in Black and White*. 5th ed. Oxford University Press.

Novkov, Julie, and Charles Gossett. 2007. "Survey of Textbooks for Teaching Introduction to U.S. Politics: (How) Do They See Us?" *PS: Political Science & Politics* 40 (2): 393–98.

Proctor, Andrew. 2020. "LGBT People as a Relatively Politically Powerless Group." In *Oxford Research Encyclopedia of LGBT Politics and Policy*, edited by Donald P. Haider-Markel. Oxford University Press.

Rupp, Leila J., and Susan K. Freeman, eds. 2017. *Understanding and Teaching U.S. Lesbian, Gay, Bisexual, and Transgender History*. University of Wisconsin Press.

Springer, Leonard, Mary Elizabeth Stanne, and Samuel S. Donovan. 2001. "Effects of Small-Group Learning on Undergraduates in Science, Mathematics, Engineering and Technology: A Meta-Analysis." *Review of Educational Research* 69 (1): 21–51.

Stein, Marc. 2000. *City of Sisterly and Brotherly Loves: Lesbian and Gay Philadelphia, 1945–1972*. University of Chicago Press.

Verba, Sidney, Kay Lehman Schlozman, and Henry Brady. 1995. *Voice and Equality: Civic Voluntarism in American Politics*. Harvard University Press.

Volman, Monique, and Geert ten Dam. 2015. "Critical Thinking for Educated Citizenship." In Davies and Barnett, *The Palgrave Handbook of Critical Thinking in Higher Education*, 593–60. Palgrave MacMillan.

Chapter 8

"Thinking Sex"

Why Every Political Science Major
Should Read Gayle Rubin

C. Heike Schotten

Queer theory isn't usually offered in Political Science departments. If it is offered at the university at all, it is usually taught in Women's/Gender Studies departments or, less frequently, English departments. At my own university, where I teach a 400-level course called Queer Theory & Politics, Political Science majors are often mystified by the very notion of such a class, much less how it might be related to their major, which consists of the more familiar subfields of American politics, international relations, comparative politics, public policy, and, of course, the dreaded political theory graduation requirement. Yet even political theory seems more relevant to students than queer theory. While students may grudgingly acknowledge that Aristotle or Marx are at least peripherally related to the study of politics, they're still not quite sure about a course on "queer stuff." This is all the more true, it seems, in an era of increasing neoliberal austerity and staggering student debt, both of which make a secure financial future increasingly out of reach to students—and thus their interest in seemingly irrelevant subject material increasingly scarce.

Yet neither of these is an argument against teaching queer theory, either in a Political Science department or in the face of financial collapse. Indeed, insistence on queer theory's importance may itself be a kind of resistance—to the neoliberal normalization of the university as job market preparation on the one hand, and the relevance of queer inquiry to economics and economic crisis on the other.[1] In this chapter, I argue that that Gayle Rubin's "Thinking Sex: Notes for a Radical Theory of the Politics of Sexuality"[2] should be required reading for undergraduate political science majors, assigned equally widely and commonly as much more traditional Political Science texts like *The Federalist Papers* in American politics or "The Clash of Civilizations?" in international relations.[3] Indeed, I would go so far as to claim that no Political Science major should be allowed to graduate without having had it assigned in at least one course during their undergraduate career, and this whether queer theory is offered in their department or not.

Rubin's work as a whole, exemplified by this iconic essay though by no means exhausted by it, offers several important lessons, skills, analytic frameworks, and political positionings that to this day remain understudied and underappreciated, not just in Political Science but also in political theory, the subfield of Political Science wherein queer theory might be most comfortably housed. These skills and knowledges are essential to students' development of a critical analysis of not simply of sex/uality but also power and the state, the latter of which are generally presumed to be the subject matter of Political Science but nevertheless too often considered unrelated to sex/uality.[4] This proposal is offered not simply as a means of "including" sex/gender/sexuality in the curriculum of Political Science, then, but also as an attempt at transformation of Political Science from a discipline wherein questions of sex/gender/sexuality get tacked onto its back end, like the embarrassment many political scientists may feel them to be, to one wherein sex/gender/sexuality are considered central to its disciplinary inquiry.

This argument emerges not simply from a commitment to incorporating queer and trans people and knowledges into the study of politics, but also from the urgent need to liberate the Political Science curriculum. While incomplete on its own—no single text could liberate an entire curriculum—the addition of "Thinking Sex" to a Political Science major does significant work not simply to center the history, experiences, and voices of LGBTQ+ people, but also to reorient Political Science away from its default tendency to uphold and reify the status quo as inevitable, natural, normal, and true, whether that status quo be the European nation-state and its institutions, the features and vicissitudes of the international/

global order, or the presumptions of empiricist methodologies. We might consider that the addition of "Thinking Sex" to the curriculum functions not simply as an introduction to queer theory, then, but also as a praxis of queering the curriculum by resisting Political Science's methodological and epistemological normalizations. As Marx might put it, Political Scientists have largely interpreted the world, when the point is to change it.

Changing the world rather than accepting its terms requires making insurgent and liberatory knowledges part and parcel of the Political Science curriculum. This includes interrogating the omissions and gaps in those liberatory knowledges themselves. Crucially missing from "Thinking Sex"[5] (and, all too often, Political Science itself) are the formative ways that white supremacy, empire, and colonization (both "foreign" and "domestic") have molded, constituted, directed, and continue to dominate the very subjects that queer theory (and Political Science) claim to study. Any curricular intervention that overlooks these fails to account for the central political determinants that have constituted the modern world[6] and made not just our respective disciplines but the university itself possible.[7] One consequence, then, of my rather narrow argument in this chapter—that our students should read Gayle Rubin—is that we cannot by any means stop with having our students read Gayle Rubin. Instead, we must allow this modest curricular intervention to inaugurate (as "Thinking Sex" itself has frequently been considered to have done) a broader challenge to institutionalized norms and disciplinary regimes of power/knowledge that proscribe specific people, places, and configurations of power from their purview and/or render them "extra," "critical," or worse, inessential or antithetical to the pursuit of knowledge itself.[8] At various points in this chapter, then, I will indicate via footnotes the places or ways that "Thinking Sex" fails to account for white supremacy, empire, and/or colonization. I do this not to undercut the value of this essay, but rather to demonstrate the necessity of consistent critical interrogation of the production of knowledge from the perspective of liberation, a lesson taught by Rubin in this essay and one with which she would be in full accord.

On the basis of this context and set of caveats, then, I hereby present five reasons why "Thinking Sex" should be required reading for Political Science majors. Among many other things, this essay:

1. challenges students to rethink the meaning of politics and "the political" as a site that necessarily includes sex/uality;

2. makes a compelling argument for the importance of theory and the hollowness of any firm distinction between "theory" and "practice";

3. argues from an unapologetically Left political position that also identifies and names the Right as a political position and force;

4. offers a critique of moralism as extra- or anti-political; and

5. conveys to students something of the meaning of the "queer" in "queer theory," which provides a lesson in both queerness and queer politics.

This last point is especially valuable for those who would never otherwise take (or teach!) a course in queer theory. Assigning "Thinking Sex" in Political Science courses incorporates sex/uality into the curriculum without exceptionalizing queerness or queer theory or sex/uality themselves as somehow different, separate from, more difficult than, or anathema to the "normal" or "straight" Political Science major. As is by now clear, this is an agenda that is as much political as it is pedagogic in aim, and thus worth undertaking in its own right (whether via "Thinking Sex" or some other vehicle).

1. "Sex Is Always Political"

Critical thinking requires the ability to ask foundational questions not simply about the subject matter at hand but also about the very nature and contours of that subject matter, including who determines them and how (whether that be scholars and researchers or the professor and her syllabus). In the case of Political Science, this means not simply teaching students to recognize and understand power's many faces in contemporary life, but also cultivating their ability to ask questions about how power itself has been constructed by the very discipline in which they are majoring. This requires enabling students to learn how to ask what power is, how it has been imagined or theorized across time and geography, and how answers to the question of what power is (of which Political Science is but one) both facilitate certain political and epistemological possibilities and foreclose others.

"Thinking Sex" is essential for this sort of critical thinking endeavor because it is, in its essence, a challenge to the typical Political Science understanding of the political as not primarily concerned with sex and sexuality. Rarely considered the "proper objects"[9] of politics, sex and sexuality are inappropriate not only because they are considered either private or trivial or both, but also because they seem tangential to more explicitly political subjects like regimes, parties, institutions, governance, and public policy. Yet a central insistence of "Thinking Sex" is that "sex is always political" (138). Indeed, even and especially during times of political upheaval, when sex seems remotest from the urgencies of the moment, sex/uality is in fact central and thus worthy of political consideration. The now-famous opening of "Thinking Sex" makes this claim directly:

"The time has come to think about sex. To some, sexuality may seem to be an unimportant topic, a frivolous diversion from the more critical problems of poverty, war, disease, racism, famine, or nuclear annihilation. But it is precisely at times such as these, when we live with the possibility of unthinkable destruction, that people are likely to become dangerously crazy about sexuality" (137).

This introduction functions to introduce Rubin's theorization of moral panics, about which more below in section 4. For now, it is important simply to note that sex/uality is neither trivial nor extraneous to politics, but rather central to it, and especially at heightened moments of political conflict and upheaval when it may seem least relevant.

Second, however, sex and sexuality are also political because "the realm of sexuality also has its own internal politics, inequities, and modes of oppression. As with other aspects of human behavior, the concrete institutional forms of sexuality at any given time and place are products of human activity. They are imbued with conflicts of interest and political maneuvering, both deliberate and incidental. In that sense, sex is always political" (138). One result of US feminist consciousness-raising and activism was the reevaluation of what is sometimes called the public-private distinction. Feminists insisted that so-called "private" matters relegated to the household by liberal politics and theory are, in fact, deeply political matters of power and hierarchy, domination and exploitation.[10] Here we see Rubin extrapolating this basic feminist insight and applying it to sex/uality, arguing that the seemingly most private matters—that is, sex and sexuality—are sites of political determination and contestation.[11] Essentially, Rubin is saying, because sex/uality involves humans and human community, it necessarily involves both social organization and the distribution of power: "[Sexuality] is organized into systems of power, which reward and encourage some individuals and activities, while punishing and suppressing others" (180). This is a clear and important insistence on the innately political character of human activity—an assertion explicitly denied by liberalism, the pervasive (if unspoken and even disavowed) theoretical and methodological frame of most if not all Political Science disciplinary inquiry—as well as an explicit entreaty to include sex/uality in one's understanding of politics and what constitutes the political. In short, "sex is always political" because sex/uality itself is a site of power and its distribution, which require or are co-constitutive of human community and social organization.[12]

2. "The Time Has Come to Think About Sex"

"Thinking Sex" is also an encomium to the importance of theory, both in its argument and in its performance of theory in the essay itself. Indeed, a central claim of "Thinking Sex" is Rubin's admonishment to readers to go forth and make theory about sex/uality.

Of course, it is in some ways ironic to champion "Thinking Sex" as a testament to the importance of theory, given Rubin's sometimes skepticism of the academic production of theory and her worry that, in queer studies, theory is often valued at the expense of empirical investigation.[13] That said, it is difficult to ignore the fact that "thinking" is the first word of this essay's title and that one of its signature entreaties is to begin the project of constructing theory about sex/uality, an entreaty that has come to be received as the inaugural provocation for queer theory. Moreover, Rubin's argument for and demonstration of the importance of theory in this essay have the salutary effect of eroding any hard or fast distinction between "theory" and "praxis," a distinction otherwise firmly entrenched in Political Science.[14] Indeed, Rubin's argument for theory and her performance of it in this essay both persuade on the basis of the same rationale: Theory is intrinsically political in its activity and has inevitably political consequences.

In order to make theory about sex/uality, Rubin argues that major obstacles to this project must be cleared away, obstacles she calls "ideological formations whose grip on sexual thought is so strong that to fail to discuss them is to remain enmeshed within them" (148). The first of these is sexual essentialism, or "the idea that sex is a natural force that exists prior to social life and shapes institutions" (146). This is no small point: Rubin is asserting that naturalizing sex/uality forecloses theoretical consideration and interrogation of it. Put differently, Rubin is articulating a crucial insight of political theory—namely, that the category of "the natural" is fundamentally at odds with the category of "the political." Because any characterization of a thing as "natural" inherently depoliticizes it, our ability to interrogate, critique, or change it is foreclosed: "Sexuality is impervious to political analysis as long as it is primarily conceived as a biological phenomenon or an aspect of individual psychology" (147). Moreover, such essentialism relegates theory to the activity of discovery rather than production. Indeed, if the theorist is beholden to sexual essentialism, her job is to uncover the mysterious yet natural workings of sex/uality, which are somehow given, rather than examine, explain, describe, critique, and construct alternative forms of sex/uality, which are organized and produced via human activity. In other words, if sex/uality is natural, no one could in fact *make* new theory about sex/uality, because it would be somehow given or pre-political.[15] We are thus returned to Rubin's assertion that sex/uality is political at the same time as it becomes clear that theory (whether about sex/uality or otherwise) is itself a necessarily political enterprise.

The other ideological formations that obstruct theorizing about sex/uality—"sex negativity, the fallacy of misplaced scale, the hierarchical valuation of sex acts, the domino theory of sexual peril, and the lack of a concept of benign sexual variation" (148)—and their significance will be discussed in section 4. For now, what I want to underscore is that this most famous part of "Thinking Sex" is also a first-rate exercise in theory, which does not mean something like "hypothetical" or "speculative" but rather analysis and interrogation of the relationship(s) between and among ideas. In this section, Rubin performs theory by examining traditional thought about sex/uality and its parameters, for both what they enable and what they restrict. Rejecting this traditional thought, Rubin shows that if theory about sex/uality is to be made (rather than discovered), it will inevitably be made in certain ways, and that those ways are themselves theoretical and political concerns. Rubin's warning against these ideological formations is an argument about theory that unfolds in the domain of theory and, as such, functions as a performative demonstration of theory and its political and analytic importance. As well, her famous inclusion of charts mapping these ideological formations provides one of the most delightful examples of the ways that theory can also count as evidence—which, in

Political Science, is always reduced to the solely empirical. By contrast, in the domain of theory, evidence can lie in the relationships between and among ideas. Rubin's mapping of her argument regarding sexual theory construction provides a concrete illustration of how theoretical evidence can function *as* evidence, thereby asserting in yet another innovative way the importance of theory for politics and political analysis.

3. "Sex Is a Vector of Oppression"

As already seen, "Thinking Sex" is an essay that demonstrates the interconnected importance of sex/uality, theory, and politics. Above and beyond these formidable achievements, "Thinking Sex" also demonstrates the importance of taking a Left or anti-oppression approach to each of these. Sometimes Rubin uses the term "liberatory" to reference this position; more often she uses "radical" to describe the political theory of sex/uality she is entreating readers to construct, as in the essay's subtitle: "Notes for a Radical Theory of the Politics of Sexuality."

What does "radical" mean in this context? Rubin specifies by saying, "A radical theory of sex must identify, describe, explain, and denounce erotic injustice and sexual oppression" (145). In other words, the political theory of sex/uality Rubin entreats us to construct must be focused on social relations of oppression and exploitation. If sexuality is a system of power that "reward[s] and encourage[s] some individuals and activities, while punishing and suppressing others," theorizing about it requires identifying those rewards and punishments, who gets them, and who does not. It requires identifying "and denouncing" systems of sexual oppression, meaning that a "radical" approach also demands taking a position against domination and oppression.

The pedagogical benefit for Political Science majors here is twofold: first, this understanding of "radical" reveals, if only by way of contrast, how most if not all of the Political Science curriculum is undertaken from a decisively *not* radical position (and is therefore at best silent about and at worst complicit with oppression, rather than in opposition to it). Second, it teaches students how to develop an anti-oppression or Left politics in relationship to sexuality, a position that necessarily goes beyond a (neo)liberal identity politics of diversity and inclusion (more on this in section [5] below). Contrary to popular culture wars mythology, universities are by and large *not* hotbeds of radical Leftism. Even where faculty are more or less progressive in their politics, a standard Political Science curriculum does not, as a matter of course, provide much if any liberatory thinking about power, public policy, the state, or the international order, much less about the politics of sex/uality. Requiring "Thinking Sex" might contribute to changing that—not (simply) in service to creating Leftist students so much as introducing them to broadly different ways of conceiving the world, even those that are antagonistic to what is conventionally presented as normative or even neutral in Political Science.

As with her consideration of theory, Rubin's demand to formulate a radical politics of sex/uality is both an entreaty of "Thinking Sex" and a project it itself tries to realize. Thus, in section 4 Rubin offers a mapping of the "erotic injustice and sexual oppression" current in the US at that time. Central to this task is another virtue of "Thinking Sex": Rubin not only identifies what it means to take a radical or anti-oppression position, but she also names and identifies the Right as a political force in opposition to radical or anti-oppression politics. All this creates a foundation upon which students can draw not simply to (begin to) understand the meaning of categories like "Left" and "Right" but also to identify what they might mean in relation to sex/uality, and thus to identify the erotic injustice and sexual oppression ascendant in their own current moment. Indeed, while much has changed in the forty years since this essay's publication, the continued familiarity and endurance of some of the essential elements of this sexual injustice and oppression are chilling, most of which are attributable to the endurance of those six ideological formations Rubin identifies as obstacles to theorizing and that continue to animate regressive sex law and stigma to this day. Indeed, whether it is the widespread manufactured moral panics around trans kids, trans healthcare, trans women, and trans athletes;[16] the growth of the prison industrial complex, driven not only by the criminalization and hyper-incarceration of Black and brown people but also by the booming industry of "sex offense" crimes;[17] the long game played by the Right to eliminate abortion;[18] or the complicity of all of these with fascism,[19] there are resources in "Thinking Sex" to help students identify these phenomena, understand and analyze their historic and theoretical roots, and provide a political critique of all of them.[20] Indeed, what becomes clear in this essay is that those six ideological formations are, in fact, the theoretical principles or beliefs that underpin Right-wing analyses of sex/uality and that they must be monitored at all times, even or especially in times of political upheaval when sex/uality seems far afield of the political problems at hand because they are, at a minimum, symptoms or harbingers of increasing political repression, even as they are central to that repression.

4. "In Western Culture, Sex Is Taken All Too Seriously"

By teaching us to include sex/uality in the domain of the political, Rubin also challenges us to admit another domain of inquiry into the political: morality.

In the last almost twenty years of teaching Queer Theory & Politics, one of the more astonishing things I have observed is the shift in students' responses to the material, which have changed as quickly as have developments in LGBTQ+ politics. In recent years, I have been particularly struck by students' seeming inability to understand the origins or meaning of homophobia. Homophobia seems so self-evidently stupid to them that they cannot imagine or understand how entire social collectivities might be structured by or through it.

This is evidence of the enormous success of LGBTQ+ political movements in eradicating the shame and stigma of homosexuality specifically.[21] And, of course, it is unoriginal to note that undergraduates tend not to have a strong sense of history or the historicity of ideas, terminology, movements, or events. That said, a singular virtue of "Thinking Sex" is its explanation of the origins of homophobia in Western culture—safely definable, I think, as "Euro-American" culture—specifically in Christianity and its slow, secularized transformation into what today more generally goes unremarked upon as simply "morality."[22] Indeed, those six "ideological formations whose grip on sexual thought is so strong that to fail to discuss them is to remain enmeshed within them" (148) emerge centrally from Christianity—the most important of which Rubin calls "sex negativity," or the idea that sex is "a dangerous, destructive, negative force" (148). Rubin explicitly traces this view to Pauline Christianity, noting, "Such notions have by now acquired a life of their own and no longer depend solely on religion for their perseverance" (148). A "corollary" of sex negativity, she writes, is "the fallacy of misplaced scale," wherein "[s]exual acts are burdened with an excess of significance" (149) not accorded to other human cultural activities like diet or transportation. Their significance, in this case, is related to sex negativity, wherein "[v]irtually all erotic behavior is considered bad unless a specific reason to exempt it has been established. The most acceptable excuses are marriage, reproduction, and love. Sometimes scientific curiosity, aesthetic experience, or a long-term intimate relationship may serve. But the exercise of erotic capacity, intelligence, curiosity, or creativity all require pretexts that are unnecessary for other pleasures, such as the enjoyment of food, fiction, or astronomy" (148). What Rubin is gesturing to here is the moralization of sex/uality, rooted in Christianity, that continues to inform thought and praxis around sex/uality, regardless of whether it has any present-day connection with organized religion or religious texts (hence, I think, part of my students' confusion regarding the origins or "rationality" of homophobia). This moralization leads to what Rubin calls "the domino theory of sexual peril" (150), wherein dabbling in (specific kinds, or really any kind of) sex without a good reason will initiate a downward spiral wherein the dabbler becomes a depraved sexual addict or other unspeakable social derelict. This domino theory is possible because "[m]ost of the discourses on sex, be they religious, psychiatric, popular, or political, delimit a very small portion of human sexual capacity as sanctifiable, safe, healthy, mature, legal, or politically correct. The 'line' distinguishes these from all other erotic behaviors, which are understood to be the work of the devil, dangerous, psychopathological, infantile, or politically reprehensible" (151). The domino theory of sexual peril is empowered by "systems of sexual judgment" that have their roots in Christianity but have since been secularized into psychiatry, psychology, and medicine, among others. Thus, rather than talk about "sin" or "deviance" or "moral depravity," the language is that of "pathology" or "neurosis" or being "socially maladaptive" (149–50).[23] Rubin's point is that their origins are the same and thus contain the seeds of the same six "ideological obstacles" to the construction of a radical political theory of sex/uality.[24]

These "systems of sexual judgment"—be they Christianity, psychiatry, medicine, or importantly, feminism (154, about which more below)—establish "a hierarchical system of sexual value" that ranks sexual acts according to their relative levels of health or virtue or moral rightness. Regardless of the language in which it is couched, however, these hierarchical systems are not at all primarily about morality or health but are rather fundamentally political, and thus entirely about punishment and reward: "Individuals whose behavior stands high in this hierarchy are rewarded with certified mental health, respectability, legality, social and physical mobility, institutional support, and material benefits. As sexual behaviors or occupations fall lower on the scale, the individuals who practice them are subjected to a presumption of mental illness, disreputability, criminality, restricted social and physical mobility, loss of institutional support, economic sanctions, and criminal prosecution" (149). In other words, the point of these hierarchical sexual value systems is to discourage or extinguish the sexual behavior on the lower rungs of the ladder, whether through stigma or material deprivation or violence. They are explicitly political and "function in much the way as do ideological systems of racism, ethnocentrism, and religious chauvinism" (150–51).[25]

The counterpoint to these ideological formations, rooted in Christianity, secularized in modern medicine, and taken up by the Right (and even, at times, regressive segments of the Left), is what Rubin calls a "concept of benign sexual variation," which she argues Western culture fundamentally lacks. As she pithily puts it, "One of the most tenacious ideas about sex is that there is one best way to do it, and that everyone should do it that way" (154). Admiringly referencing the scientific curiosity of Alfred Kinsey, "who approached the study of sex with the same uninhibited curiosity he had previous applied to examining a type of wasp" (155), Rubin encourages those of us interested in taking up the task of producing a radical political theory of sex/uality to surrender a commitment to any notion of "a single ideal sexuality" (154) and instead treat sex the way Kinsey treated insects. As Rubin notes, "Variation is a fundamental property of all life, from the simplest biological organisms to the most complex human social formations. Yet sexuality is supposed to conform to a single standard" (154). The reason for this sexual idealism is, in a nutshell, morality. Whether couched in the language of virtue and vice, health and sickness, bourgeois decadence and the laborers' material reality, or "woman-identified" lesbianism and patriarchal sex-uality, Euro-American culture remains wedded to moralisms about sex/uality, which obscures their fundamentally political nature and deflects interrogation of their hierarchical and oppressive systems of discipline, punishment, and control.[26]

It is not simply that "morality," or the present-day precipitates of Christianity, still govern how sex/uality is theorized, obscuring its political agenda by naturalizing it via discourses of virtue, health, maturity, or normalcy. It is also that this Christian morality provides a repository of affect ripe for mobilization into public furor in the form of moral panics, which subsequently influence lawmaking and public policy. Moral panics are what Rubin calls "the 'political moment' of sex," the moment when political conflicts or disruption get channeled into targeting marginal populations as a distraction or scapegoat by those seeking to profit from political destabilization. They are possible at all in Euro-American culture because of the ideological formations that define our thinking about sex/uality and work to solidify that ideology, in part through rhetorical hegemony and in part by using that hegemony to adopt new and regressive sex laws that maintain sexual hierarchy in place:

> Because sexuality in Western societies is so mystified, the wars over it are often fought at oblique angles, aimed at phony targets, conducted with misplaced passions, and are highly, intensely symbolic. Sexual activities often function as signifiers for personal and social apprehensions to which they have no intrinsic connection. During a moral panic, such fears attach to some unfortunate sexual activity or population. The media become ablaze with indignation, the public behaves like a rabid mob, the police are activated, and the state enacts new laws and regulations. When the furor has passed, some innocent erotic group has been decimated, and the state has extended its power into new areas of erotic behavior. (168)

What makes this frenzy possible is not simply those six ideological formations that define Western thought about sex/uality, but the elevation of them into moral pretexts that characterize sex/uality as "menaces to health and safety, women and children, national security, the family, or civilization itself" (169). This is a key insight that offers Political Science majors enormous critical capacity to analyze assertions otherwise so often taken to be self-evident, not only about the "value" of ostensibly neutral categories like "the family," "national security," or "civilization," but also the cynical deployment of this sort of moralizing to justify everything from repressive sex law and regressive policing to the destruction of publicly funded social goods (e.g., healthcare and public schools) to the seemingly endless expansionism of US imperial warfare.

The identification and analysis of moral panics is in fact a central impetus of "Thinking Sex." While Rubin has since offered extensive discussion of this essay's intellectual origins,[27] in the text itself she explicitly asserts that "Thinking Sex" is offered in an attempt to avert what she then saw as impending moral panics that had her quite worried. Naming the nineteenth-century moral panic over sex work and the mid-twentieth-century moral panics over masturbation, homosexuality, and pedophilia as influential historical precursors, Rubin forecasts the emergence of two new moral panics from her position in the early 1980s: one from the Right, based on its "increasing use of AIDS to incite virulent homophobia," and one from the Left, in "the attacks on sadomasochists by a segment of the feminist movement" (169). It is here that one of many courageous moments in this essay shines forth: Rubin forthrightly argues that she has doubts about the extent to which feminist theory is equal to the task of theorizing a radical politics of sexuality at this moment, and therefore doubts its ability to be a valuable resource to defend vulnerable sexual populations from persecution and oppression. This move, which has been taken up as the theoretical juncture that enabled the field of queer theory to emerge, must also, then, be remembered as the moment Rubin puts her finger on a reactionary segment of the feminist movement as articulating a "conservative sexual morality" (173) anathema to the sexual liberation a radical politics of sexuality would theorize and attempt to achieve.[28] This is the anti-porn, anti-trans, anti-sm[29] segment of the feminist movement "that have condemned virtually every variant of sexual expression as antifeminist" outside of "monogamous lesbianism that occurs within long-term, intimate relationships and does not involve playing with polarized roles" (172). Noting the profound sex negativity, fallacy of misplaced scale, hierarchical system of sexual value, and domino theory of sexual peril that define these sorts of feminist analyses, Rubin reminds us to remain attuned to the material fundaments of sex/uality, its politics, and its political repression:

"A good deal of current feminist literature attributes the oppression of women to graphic representations of sex, prostitution, sex education, sadomasochism, male homosexuality, and transsexualism. Whatever happened to the family, education, child-rearing practices, the media, the state, psychiatry, job discrimination, and unequal pay?" (173).

In short, parts of the feminist movement were no longer allied with a Left or liberatory position regarding sex/uality, but instead (however wittingly or unwittingly) joining forces with the Right. Reflecting on this moment years later, Rubin notes that at the time, "It seemed to me that many feminists had simply assimilated the usual stigmas and common hatreds of certain forms of non-normative sexual practice which they then rearticulated in their own framework."[30] The accuracy of Rubin's surmise here was amply demonstrated by the later alliances between anti-porn feminists and the religious Right in the 1980s,[31] and it is in evidence to this day by anti-trans feminists' alliance with Right-wing Catholic and Evangelical funders to successfully whip up massive moral panics in both the UK and US over the mere existence of trans people.[32]

This important and courageous naming not only helps solidify this essay's useful contribution to an identification and analysis of the meaning of Right and Left as analytic categories and political forces. It also illuminates moral panics as the political scheming they in fact are, making clear that moralizing about sex/uality, moral panics surrounding sex/uality, and even perhaps morality itself are innately conservative, Right-wing, or reactionary ideologies. Rubin notes in the conclusion to "Thinking Sex" that in moments when public debate feels polarized and opposing sides appear increasingly "extreme" or far from one another, there is a liberal tendency to believe that the truth of the matter must lie somewhere in between. This is only true, however, if neither side is already (1) invested in maintaining hierarchy and (2) resourced with the money and power to continue to implement that hierarchy and ensure its continued dominance. In a conflict between Right and Left, then, adequately specified as such (whether that be between Evangelical Christians who want to eliminate abortion and feminists seeking to expand abortion access, or between "radical" feminists seeking to abolish pornography, sex work, sadomasochism, and trans people and [other] feminists seeking to defend these), resolution does not lie in a compromise somewhere between these positions. The reason for this is because the conflict is not between differing but reasonable positions on a controversial issue; rather, the conflict is a contest between oppression and liberation. To presume that advocating oppression is a "reasonable position" not only grants its legitimacy as both an argument and a politics, but also cedes the ground upon which one must stand in order to resist and refute it. As Rubin says, "trying to find a middle course" between such poles "is a bit like saying that the truth about homosexuality lies somewhere between the positions of the Moral Majority and those of the gay movement" (174). Rubin's caution not to fall for this liberal fantasy is a principled commitment to liberation and the defense of sexual freedom and sexual deviants and outlaws, a lesson about both politics and solidarity that students are unlikely to be exposed to in standard Political Science courses, even ones that deal explicitly with social movements. Moreover, her extended critique of liberal tolerance as the compromise position between sexual oppression and sexual liberation is acute and gets at the heart of the condescension and ultimate *in*tolerance that underlies liberal approaches (174–78).[33]

It is ultimately the critique of the Right and Right-wing moralism that leads Rubin to her famous assertion, in the conclusion, that theory about sex/uality must be developed independently of feminist inquiry. In a very historically specific assertion, Rubin argues, "I want to challenge the assumption that feminism is or should be the privileged site of a theory of sexuality. Feminism is the theory of gender oppression. To automatically assume that this makes it the theory of sexual oppression is to fail to distinguish between gender, on the one hand, and erotic desire, on the other" (177–78). Regardless of whether we would accept this distinction today—a question significantly complicated by the historicity of these terms and their usages in different communities across both time and place—what is significant is that, in this call, Rubin asks for the development of a radical theory of the politics of sexuality, explicitly grounded in an understanding and critique of the Right and reactionary tendencies, in feminism but also in thought and politics more generally. The context of this call, which is typically canonized as the invitation and incitation to the field of queer theory, is thus all the more important insofar as it is a reminder that queer theory emerges, in part, from a specific historical entreaty to remain committed to a sexual liberation rooted in material freedom, not moralizing ideology. Indeed, one might venture to argue that queer theory emerges at least in part on the basis of a rejection of morality and moralism per se, at least as they are or have been known in "Western" cultures, that is, as derivatives of Christianity.[34]

5. "I Use the Term 'Pervert' as a Shorthand for All the Stigmatized Sexual Orientations"

Finally, in addition to everything already adduced here, "Thinking Sex" valuably articulates something of the "queer" in queer theory. All students encountering this essay in a Political Science course, then, will learn something about "queer" and queerness in addition to becoming more adept analysts of politics and the politics of sex/uality.

The title of this chapter section is taken from Rubin's own concluding section in the original version of "Thinking Sex" entitled "A Note on Definitions," which is not included in the anthologized republishing of this essay.[35] In the original version, however, Rubin offers an analysis of sex/uality in terms of political positionality rather than identity via fond reference to a varied and diverse collection of people she calls sexual "deviants" or "perverts"[36] who, taken as collectivities, constitute what she calls "erotic minorities" (173) or even sometimes "the sexual rabble" (151). To be sure, this wide net is both a strength and a limitation of this essay's historical value: The inclusion of sex workers is not exactly apposite insofar as sex work is defined by exchanging sexual services for money, rather than any particular sexual inclination or "orientation."[37] Moreover, Rubin's inclusion of trans people has been criticized as a miscategorization of folks who are not best or most adequately characterized in terms of sexuality or as "sexual" deviants per se.[38] Rubin agrees with and has accepted these criticisms with equanimity, noting that her primary interest in including trans people was not to assimilate them inappropriately into the domain of sex/uality, but rather to resist "the nasty vein of anti-transsexual sentiment that had developed within feminism in the 1970s."[39] Moreover, these qualifications are by no means devastating to Rubin's argument overall, which is that those marginalized by systems of sexual (and/or [cis]gender) hierarchy, stigma, devaluation, and violence are a constituency of people defined less by their specific or individual identities (e.g., gay, trans, kinky, polyamorous) than by their marginality in relationship to power. As Heather Love rightly notes,[40] this is the constituency Cathy Cohen argues might best be named by the term "queer": a group of people who are marginal in their proximity to white cis-heteronormative power, rather than unified by a particular social or sexual identity.[41] Rubin notes in her reflections on "Thinking Sex" that this "protoqueerness" is one of the things about which she is most proud.[42] And this is precisely who or what "queer" is often taken to name: a collection of anti-normative sex and gender deviants, rather than specifically gay-, lesbian-, or trans-identified subjects. In "Thinking Sex," one sees the kernel of this emergence and thus the origins of "queer" without having to provide students a comprehensive lesson in the complex historical development and emergence of "queer" and its multiplicity of meanings (or the many debates and contestations over its meanings). This is also, as both Rubin and Cohen insist, an instructive political lesson on the limits of so-called identity politics, which may not necessarily be the best or only basis for a dissident or liberatory politics. Rather, political change may best be accomplished through coalition based on shared goals regarding the material improvement of life and the expansion of freedom for everyone, rather than a shared identity. This is, indeed, Rubin's conclusion in her reflection on the essay's "protoqueerness":

> I wanted to move the discussion of sexual politics beyond single issues and single constituencies, from women and lesbians and gay men to analyses that could incorporate and address with

> more intricacy the cross-identifications and multiple subject positions that most of us occupy. I continue to believe that our best political hopes for the future lie in finding common ground and building coalitions based on mutual respect and appreciation of differences and that the best intellectual work is able to accommodate complexity, treasure nuance, and resist the temptations of dogma and oversimplification.[43]

This sort of coalition politics does not reject identity or its importance or the rootedness of identity politics in liberation (as many liberal and Right-wing critiques of "identity politics" would have it).[44] Instead, it understands the importance of forging collectivity based on shared oppression rather than on the commonalities of identity simply, which fails on its own to realize a project of collective freedom.

The politics of sex/uality are relevant and important subjects for Political Science majors; moreover, this knowledge will be beneficial for the faculty and field practitioners who will teach it, as they may incorporate new knowledge about the theory and politics of sex/uality into their understanding of the discipline. Keeping queer theory as a separate course is still necessary and desirable, not only because queerness and queer theory are subjects worthy of study in their own right, but also because queer theory is an autonomous academic field in which one can gain scholarly expertise. Nonetheless, "Thinking Sex" offers so many crucial lessons about the theory and politics of sex/uality that include, and yet are not reducible to, queer theory alone that it would be a shame to segregate the theory and politics of sex/uality entirely from the Political Science curriculum. Aspirationally, such incorporation will also transform that very curriculum—and discipline!—toward a praxis more compatible with liberation, a liberation that cannot truly be free without the presence, participation, experiences, knowledges, and knowledge production of queer and trans people themselves.

Acknowledgments

I am grateful to lifelong interlocutors, dear friends, and beloved comrades Jude Glaubman and Jason Lydon for, as always, their insightful readings and critical feedback on this chapter, which has been much improved by their comments.

Notes

1. On queer theory, neoliberalism, and economic crisis, see, e.g., the special issue "Queer Studies and the Crises of Capitalism," eds. Jordy Rosenberg and Amy Villarejo, *GLQ: A Journal of Lesbian and Gay Studies* 18, no. 1 (2012); Margot Weiss, "Queer Economic Justice: Desire, Critique, and the Practice of Knowledge," in *Global Justice and Desire: Queering Economy*, eds. Nikita Dhawan, Antke Engle, Christoph Holzhey, and Volker Woltersdorff (Routledge, 2015); Weiss, "Queer Politics in Neoliberal Times: 1970–2010s," *The Routledge History of Queer America*, ed. Don Romesburg (Routledge, 2018). On queer people and capitalism and/or neoliberalism, see, e.g., Roderick Ferguson, *One-Dimensional Queer* (Polity, 2019); Lisa Duggan, *The Twilight of Equality?: Neoliberalism, Cultural Politics, and the Attack on Democracy* (Beacon, 2003); John D'Emilio, "Capitalism and Gay Identity," in *Making Trouble: Essays on Gay History, Politics, and the University* (Routledge, 1992); Amber Hollibaugh and Margot Weiss, "Queer Precarity and the Myth of Gay Affluence," *New Labor Forum* 24, no. 3 (2015): 18–27.

2. I will mostly cite the reprint of this essay in *Deviations: A Gayle Rubin Reader* (Duke University Press, 2011), with page numbers in parentheses in the body of the text.

3. Samuel Huntington's infamous essay is one of the most widely assigned texts in the US undergraduate classroom overall, making it more popular than *Hamlet* and rivaling Plato's *Republic* and Marx and Engels's *Communist Manifesto* in popularity as a syllabus staple (on this ubiquity as well as the broader problems with this essay, see "The Clash of Civilizations in the IR Classroom: A Teaching Roundtable," eds. Andrew Szarejko and Diane Labrosse, H-Diplo ISSF Roundtable XI-6 [November 2019]).

4. To be sure, queer and feminist scholarship in Political Science has proliferated to such an extent that, in principle, it should be impossible at this point to claim that questions of sex, gender, and sexuality are somehow tangential to power or the state. Nonetheless, the mainstream of the discipline—often what is taught in Political Science curricula and core courses—has not incorporated this scholarship to the extent that it has been allowed to challenge or change what constitutes Political Science to begin with, meaning that feminist and queer analyses remain peripheral to the discipline rather than central to it. Thus our syllabi include feminist and queer approaches in the "critical" material in the last weeks of the semester, perhaps alongside other "alternative approaches" like race, class, and (if we're lucky) imperialism, colonization, and indigeneity. This is true professionally as well: In the American Political Science Association, we have separate sections for "Women and Politics" and "Sexuality and Politics," alongside "Race, Ethnicity and Politics" and "Class and Inequality" (sadly, no sections on empire, colonization, or indigeneity just yet). Here too the presumption is that

these "alternative approaches" are separate from the mainstream of Political Science inquiry (even as they are also segregated from one another).

5. Sharon P. Holland, "The 'Beached Whale,'" in the special issue "Rethinking Sex," ed. Heather Love, *GLQ: A Journal of Lesbian and Gay Studies* 17, no. 1 (2011): 89–96; and Holland, *The Erotic Life of Racism* (Duke University Press, 2012).

6. Sylvia Wynter, "Unsettling the Coloniality of Being/Power/Truth/Freedom: Towards the Human, After Man, Its Overrepresentation—An Argument," *CR: The New Centennial Review* 3, no. 3 (Fall 2003): 257–337.

7. Leigh Patel, *No Study Without Struggle: Confronting Settler Colonialism in Higher Education* (Beacon, 2021); Craig Steven Wilder, *Ebony and Ivy: Race, Slavery, and the Troubled History of America's Universities* (Bloomsbury, 2013).

8. C. Heike Schotten, "To Exist Is to Resist: Palestine and the Question of Queer Theory," *Journal of Palestine Studies* 47, no. 3 (Spring): 13–28.

9. On the proper objects of feminist and queer inquiry, both related to and beyond the analysis of these offered in "Thinking Sex," see, among others, Kadji Amin, *Disturbing Attachments: Genet, Modern Pederasty, and Queer History* (Duke University Press, 2017); Judith Butler, "Against Proper Objects," *differences: A Journal of Feminist Cultural Studies* 6, no. 2–3 (Summer–Fall 1994): 1–26; Sharon Holland, "Black (W)holes: A Problem for Feminist Thought," *differences: A Journal of Feminist Cultural Studies* 55 no. 2 (September 2024); Robyn Wiegman, *Object Lessons* (Duke University Press, 2012). On sex/uality as a proper object of critical theory, see Michael Warner's introduction to *Fear of a Queer Planet: Queer Politics and Social Theory*, ed. Michael Warner (University of Minnesota Press, 1993).

10. The classic citations in political theory are Carole Pateman, *The Sexual Contract* (Stanford University Press, 1988) and Susan Moller Okin, *Justice, Gender, and the Family* (Basic Books, 1991); the ubiquity and centrality of this critique across 1970s feminist movements, captured by the well-known feminist slogan "the personal is political," makes attribution of credit to any single activist individual or group both impossible and misleading.

11. This is not to say that feminists in the women's movement did not do this. Consciousness-raising also educated women about the family and household as sites of pervasive rape, sexual assault, and sexual abuse by husbands, brothers, fathers, uncles, and grandfathers, not to mention the maintenance of normative heterofemininity. Rubin's point is an "extrapolation" of this feminist insight to the extent that, as she notes near the end of the essay (about which more below), this feminist consciousness-raising analysis remained within an understanding of gender hierarchy wherein sex/uality was understood as a tool primarily and specifically of women's oppression *as* women, *by* men. One of the central contributions of "Thinking Sex" is considered to be its insistence that sex/uality is a distinct domain of power and oppression, one that is of course related but not reducible to an analysis of women's oppression in the areas of sex/uality and includes far more people under its political and coercive ambit than women

solely (and may include women not solely or simply because they are women, but also, for example, because they are lesbians, kinky, butch, etc.).

12. On sex/uality as a primary site of white supremacy and the manufacture of sex/gender norms, behaviors, and identities as parasitically white (i.e., dependent upon the Black flesh they must disavow in order to constitute themselves precisely as unmarked normative ideals), see, among many others, Evelyn Hammonds, "Black (W)holes and the Geometry of Black Female Sexuality," *differences: A Journal of Feminist Cultural* 6, no. 2–3 1994 (Summer–Fall 1994): 128–45; Saidiya Hartman, *Scenes of Subjection: Terror, Slavery, and Self-Making in Nineteenth-Century America* (Oxford University Press, 1997); C. Riley Snorton, *Black on Both Sides: A Racial History of Trans Identity* (University of Minnesota Press, 2017); Hortense Spillers, "Mama's Baby, Papa's Maybe: An American Grammar Book," *Diacritics* 17, no. 2 (Summer 1987): 64–81.

13. "Sexual Traffic: Interview with Gayle Rubin by Judith Butler," in *Deviations*, 304–07.

14. In challenging theory's academic hegemony in queer studies or its sometimes dismissal of empirical research, Rubin is not claiming theory's irrelevance. Rather, she notes that the "opposition between 'theoretical' and 'empirical' work is a false, or at least, distorted one" and that "the imbalance between conceptual analysis and data analysis needs some redress" in sexuality studies. "In short, I would like to see more 'interrogation' of the contemporary category of 'theory,' and of the relationships between such 'theory' and empirical or descriptive research" ("Sexual Traffic," 305).

15. Donning her anthropologist's cap, Rubin clarifies: "This does not mean the biological capacities are not prerequisites for human sexuality. It does mean that human sexuality is not comprehensible in purely biological terms. Human organisms with human brains are necessary for human cultures, but no examination of the body or its parts can explain the nature and variety of human social systems. The belly's hunger gives no clues as to the complexities of cuisine. The body, the brain, the genitalia, and the capacity for language are all necessary for human sexuality. But they do not determine its content, its experiences, or its institutional forms. Moreover, we never encounter the body unmediated by the meanings that cultures give to it" (146–47).

16. Judith Butler, "Why Is the Idea of Gender Provoking Backlash the World Over?," *The Guardian*, October 23, 2021; Melissa Gira Grant, "'Libs of TikTok' and the Right's Embrace of Anti-LGBTQ Violence," *The New Republic*, September 7, 2022; Heron Greenesmith, "New Anti-Trans Promise: An Ohio State Legislator May Have Leaked a New Set of Anti-Trans 'Principles' Endorsed by Three Major Anti-LGBT Organizations," *Political Research Associates*, February 12, 2021. https://politicalresearch.org/2021/02/12/new-anti-trans-promise.

17. Marie Gottschalk, *Caught: The Prison State and the Lockdown of American Politics* (Princeton University Press, 2016); Erica Meiners and Judith Levine, *The*

Feminist and the Sex Offender: Confronting Sexual Harm, Ending State Violence (Verso, 2020).

18. Political Research Associates, *Playing the Long Game: How the Christian Right Built Capacity to Undo* Roe *State by State*, June 2019.

19. Serena Bassi and Greta LaFleur, "Introduction: TERFs, Gender-Critical Movements, and Postfascist Feminisms," in the special issue "Trans Exclusionary Feminisms and the Global New Right," *TSQ: Transgender Studies Quarterly* 9, no. 3 (August 2022): 311–33.

20. Although Rubin does not name fascism as such in "Thinking Sex," it was clearly on her mind throughout her writing and work in the women's movement; for example, in an earlier essay defending lesbian sadomasochism and fetishism from feminist critique, she argues that "The real danger is that the Right, the religious fanatics, and the Right-controlled state will eat us all alive. It is sad to be having to fight to maintain one's membership in the women's movement when it is so imperative to create broad-based coalitions against fascism" ("The Leather Menace," in *Deviations*, 136). In "Thinking Sex," Rubin presciently documents the emergence of a New Right coalition movement, energized by the success of Anita Bryant's "Save Our Children" campaign to repeal a gay anti-discrimination ordinance in Miami, "to compress the boundaries of acceptable sexual behavior" (143), including within that movement Christian and Evangelical forces (e.g., the Moral Majority) and neoconservatism (143–44). Looking back on "Thinking Sex," Rubin notes it was written in part as a response to "the phenomenal growth of the New Right," which by "the late 1970s" "was mobilizing explicitly and successfully around sexual issues" ("Sexual Traffic," 290).

21. Which is not at all to say that homophobia has been vanquished or that it plays no role in the lives of gay and lesbian people of all ages, who still struggle to live lives free of violence, stigma, shame, and harm. That said, it is astonishing to see, for example, hundreds of Florida high school students walking out of class in protest of the state legislature's proposed bill to ban discussion of gender and sexuality in K–12 schools, popularly known as the "Don't Say Gay" bill, shouting "We say gay!" (*Democracy Now*, March 8, 2022, https://www.democracynow.org/2022/3/8/headlines/we_say_gay_florida_students_walk_out_to_protest_anti_lgbtq_legislation) or, upon a visit from anti-trans state legislator Jeff Younger, University of North Texas students shouting him down by yelling "Fuck these fascists!" (*Dallas Observer*, March 4, 2022, https://www.dallasobserver.com/news/unt-student-protest-of-anti-trans-texas-house-candidate-jeff-younger-attracts-coverage-from-vice-andy-ngo-13530480). Such events were simply unimaginable at the time "Thinking Sex" was written.

22. Cf. Friedrich Nietzsche, *On the Genealogy of Morals: A Polemic*, trans. Walter Kaufmann (Random House, 1967), a diagnosis of the nihilism of European morality, by which Nietzsche centrally means Christianity. Rubin's qualifier "Western" here is welcome, even as it leaves the reader wanting greater clarification as

to what she means by it. Here is one place in Rubin's text to begin constructing a decolonial critique of sexual oppression and a consideration of the ways that Christianity functions as a vehicle of (settler) colonization; see, e.g., Walaa Alqaisiya, "Palestine and the Will to Theorise Decolonial Queering," *Middle East Critique* 29, no. 1 (2020): 87–113; María Lugones, "Heterosexualism and the Colonial/Modern Gender System," *Hypatia* 22, no. 1 (Winter 2007): 186–209; Scott Morgensen, "Theorising Gender, Sexuality and Settler Colonialism: An Introduction," *Settler Colonial Studies* 2, no. 2 (2012): 2–22; and "Settler Homonationalism: Theorizing Settler Colonialism within Queer Modernities," *GLQ* 16, no. 1–2 (2010): 105–31; Mark Rifkin, *When Did Indians Become Straight? Kinship, the History of Sexuality, and Native Sovereignty* (Oxford University Press, 2011); Sunera Thobani, *Contesting Islam, Constructing Race and Sexuality: The Inordinate Desire of the West* (Bloomsbury, 2021); Wynter, "Unsettling."

23. Cf. Michel Foucault, *The History of Sexuality*, vol. 1, *An Introduction*, trans. Robert Hurley (Vintage, 1990), which Rubin acknowledges as a significant resource for "Thinking Sex" ("Sexual Traffic," 291–99).

24. On the ways these systems of sexual judgment—religious, moral, scientific, or otherwise—function as forms of racialization, racial hierarchization, and racial domination and exploitation, see, e.g., Cathy Cohen, "Punks, Bulldaggers, and Welfare Queens: The Radical Potential of Queer Politics?" in *Black Queer Studies: A Critical Anthology*, eds. Mae G. Henderson and E. Patrick Johnson (Duke University Press, 2005); Sander Gilman, "Black Bodies, White Bodies: Toward an Iconography of Female Sexuality in Late-Nineteenth Century Art, Medicine, and Literature," *Critical Inquiry* 12, no. 1 (Autumn 1985): 204–42; Saidiya Hartman, *Wayward Lives, Beautiful Experiments: Intimate Histories of Riotous Black Girls, Troublesome Women, and Queer Radicals* (W. W. Norton, 2019); Siobhan Somerville, *Queering the Color Line: Race and the Invention of Homosexuality in America* (Duke University Press, 2000).

25. Here Rubin uses racism as an analogue for sexual oppression, missing an opportunity to think intersectionally about the ways that white supremacy works in tandem with sexual oppression to limit, punish, criminalize, and eradicate the sexual lives and subjectivities of Black and brown people and/or render Black and brown sexualities and sexual behaviors innately unthinkable, abnormal, perverse, queer, or pathological; see, e.g., Aliyyah I. Abdur-Rahman, *Against the Closet: Black Political Longing and the Erotics of Race* (Duke University Press, 2012); Cohen, "Punks"; bell hooks, *Feminist Theory: From Margin to Center* (South End Press, 1984); Matt Richardson, "No More Secrets, No More Lies: African American History and Compulsory Heterosexuality," *Journal of Women's History* 15, no. 3 (Autumn 2003): 63–76; Spillers, "Mama's Baby."

26. Rubin introduces a contrasting notion of "democratic morality," stating that "A democratic morality should judge sexual acts by the way partners treat one another, the level of mutual consideration, the presence or absence of coercion,

and the quantity and quality of the pleasures they provide. Whether sex acts are gay or straight, coupled or in groups, naked or in underwear, commercial or free, with or without video should not be ethical concerns" (154). While I largely agree with this perspective, I hesitate to call it a morality, or else I would suggest that "morality" means something different when qualified as "democratic." However, I also doubt Rubin hangs much on the use of the term "morality" here, given her slide to "ethical" in the very next sentence and the fact that morality does not seem to be a technical term in the essay. Perhaps it would be simpler to say that a liberatory politics of sexuality is one that is democratic, meaning that it makes judgments about sex/uality based on consent, consideration, and pleasure rather than falsely apolitical notions like virtue, health, or mental fitness.

27. See "Sexual Traffic" and "Blood Under the Bridge: Reflections on 'Thinking Sex'" (also in *Deviations*).

28. On Rubin's attentiveness to fascism within feminism, and fascist feminism more broadly, see Sophie Lewis and Asa Seresin, "Fascist Feminism: A Dialogue," in "Trans Exclusionary Feminisms and the Global New Right," 463–79.

29. In the parlance of the day, "sm" or "S/M" stood for sadomasochism, the second half of larger acronym that was sometimes capitalized and sometimes not: BDSM, or bondage/domination and sadomasochism. Feminist groups like Women Against Pornography conflated pornography with "sm" as similar acts of violence against women and were particularly incensed at the notion that lesbians might practice sm. See Carolyn Bronstein, *Battling Pornography: The American Feminist Antipornography Movement, 1976–1986* (Cambridge University Press, 2011); *Take Back the Night: Women on Pornography*, ed. Laura Lederer (Morrow, 1980); *Coming to Power: Writings & Graphics on Lesbian S/M*, eds. Members of Samois, a lesbian/feminist S/M organization (Alyson, 1987).

30. "Sexual Traffic," 291. In a still-hilarious paragraph of "Thinking Sex," Rubin remarks on the rhetorical commonalities between the speeches of Pope John Paul II and lesbian feminist Julia Penelope (169).

31. Bronstein, *Battling Pornography*.

32. Jacob Breslow, "The Non-Essential Transphobia of Pandemic Disaster Politics," Blog of the London School of Economics and Political Science, May 14, 2020, https://blogs.lse.ac.uk/gender/2020/05/14/the-non-essential-transphobia-of-pandemic-disaster-politics/; Heron Greenesmith, "A Room of Their Own: How Anti-Trans Feminists Are Complicit in Christian Right Anti-Trans Advocacy," *Political Research Associates*, June 14, 2020, https://politicalresearch.org/2020/07/14/room-their-own.

33. Wendy Brown, *Regulating Aversion: Tolerance in the Age of Identity and Empire* (Princeton University Press, 2008).

34. For more on this line of argument, see my "Nietzsche and Emancipatory Politics: Queer Theory as Anti-Morality," *Critical Sociology* 45, no. 2, 213–26.

35. "Thinking Sex," in *Deviations*. For the original essay, see Rubin, "Thinking Sex," in *Pleasure and Danger: Exploring Female Sexuality*, ed. Carole Vance (Routledge and Kegan Paul, 1984).

36. "Note on Definitions." Indeed, despite the almost clinical neutrality in which this note is articulated at the end of the essay, I think it is safe to say that Rubin has a more than objective attachment to the marginal sexual populations whose struggle for justice and liberation she describes in her work.

37. Rubin acknowledges and accounts for this awkward fit in the essay itself; see 157–58.

38. Susan Stryker, *Transgender History: The Roots of Today's Revolution*, 2nd ed. (Seal Press, 2017), 161–62.

39. For Rubin's full response, see "Blood Under the Bridge," 36–37. On the relatively recent emergence of a clear and sharp dividing line between "sexuality" and "gender" and, therefore, between "gay" and "trans," see Kadji Amin, "We Are All Nonbinary: A Brief History of Accidents," *Representations* 158 (2022): 106–19; David Valentine, *Imagining Transgender: An Ethnography of a Category* (Duke University Press, 2007).

40. Heather Love, "Introduction to "Rethinking Sex," 6–7.

41. Cohen, "Punks." The addition of "white" here highlights once again the undertheorization of race and racism in "Thinking Sex."

42. "Blood Under the Bridge," 40.

43. "Blood Under the Bridge," 40. As is clear from Rubin's reflections and work, one can be an adherent of "difference," multiplicity, and complexity without surrendering a commitment to liberation or Left politics.

44. On the rootedness of identity politics in intersectional projects of liberation, see, e.g., Cohen, "Punks"; Keeanga-Yamahtta Taylor, *How We Get Free: Black Feminism and the Combahee River Collective* (Haymarket, 2017). On Right-wing critiques of identity politics and their (non-)relation to either liberation or actual identity politics, see my "Wounded Attachments? Slave Morality, the Left, and the Future of Revolutionary Desire," in *Nietzsche & Critical Theory*, ed. Michael Roberts (Brill, 2020).

Chapter 9

Integrating LGBTQ Issues into Law-Themed Courses

Moving Beyond Marriage and Nondiscrimination

EDWARD F. KAMMERER JR.

Discussion of many specific LGBTQ[1] issues are easy to include in courses on law and the legal system because the cases make clear how LGBTQ identity is central to the interpretation and application of the relevant statutes. When LGBTQ people face legal hurdles because of their LGBTQ identity, the LGBTQ focus is obvious. This is the framework that the LGBTQ movement has relied on heavily when making legal claims for equality (Adler 2018). Equal protection analysis forms the basis for these types of claims. But relying on equal protection focuses LGBTQ legal advocacy on the narrow set of cases where LGBTQ people are discriminated against *because* of their status in the LGBTQ community. This, Adler argues, causes the LGBTQ movement to ignore a multitude of other legal issues that often have a more significant impact on the lives of many in the LGBTQ community, particularly its most marginalized members. Marriage equality, military service, and workplace discrimination are issues that address the concerns of the privileged not the marginalized who often have more pressing concerns (DeFilippis et al. 2017). That is not to say that teaching these issues is not important—it just cannot be the only thing we are teaching. Instead, we must broaden our understanding of

LGBTQ legal issues to include topics beyond marriage equality. We must also move beyond simply focusing on issues that affect LGBTQ people solely because they are LGBTQ people and embrace a broader conception of what role law plays in the lives on all people, including those who happen to be LGBTQ.

The goal of this chapter is to help faculty find ways to integrate a wider range of legal issues into their LGBTQ courses and to integrate LGBTQ issues into their law courses. To do this, I offer a series of doctrinal areas where LGBTQ legal issues are not regularly addressed but could and should be. This includes criminal law (beyond the repeal of sodomy laws), family law (beyond marriage equality), administrative law, healthcare, education, and others. I also offer suggestions for topics to include that center less directly on LGBTQ identity but have some impact on LGBTQ people. But first, I briefly summarize the traditional way of teaching LGBTQ law through a focus on marriage equality and nondiscrimination law.

All of the topics discussed can, and must, address the full breadth of the LGBTQ community. But, because transgender people are currently targeted by wide-ranging legislation across the United States and beyond, it is important to highlight the need to include transgender-specific topics in any course dealing with LGBTQ people or political science more broadly. Transgender legal issues are related to but distinct from those focused more on sexual orientation. But the two areas cannot be truly separated. As shown in chapter 1 of this book, scholars and teachers of LGBTQ politics know this, ranking transgender issues high on a list of topics that are central to LGBTQ politics courses (Kammerer and Cravens). The centrality of transgender concerns to LGBTQ politics faculty highlights the need to ensure an inclusive curriculum, which I attempt to demonstrate in this chapter.

Equal Protection Law: Marriage and Nondiscrimination Legislation

Several of the LGBTQ movement's notable legal successes are grounded in equal protection law. And teaching the cases that led to these victories is common. This framework is most evident in the movement for marriage equality, which became a major issue on the LGBTQ policy agenda in the 1990s. Marriage equality was not on the agenda at any of the major

LGBTQ organizations until private actors filed a lawsuit in Hawaii in the early 1990s (Issenberg 2021). When the LGBTQ couples won a surprising (but brief) victory, the movement saw potential for winning marriage rights in other states. That pushed marriage onto the agenda for the major national organizations. This led to a qualified victory in Vermont, where the state Supreme Court ruled that LGBTQ couples be provided all the rights of marriage but did not mandate extending marriage itself. Same-sex couples were provided equal benefits, just limited to a separate system called civil unions. The next state to address the issue, Massachusetts, also did so through a concerted legal campaign (Bonauto 2005; Kammerer 2016). The movement then spread to other states and eventually the federal courts. It was ultimately resolved by the United States Supreme Court in *Obergefell v. Hodges* in 2015, which brought equal marriage rights to same-sex couples throughout the country. While some states did enact marriage equality through the legislature or by ballot initiative, most states did so through litigation. And the legislative campaigns only took hold after the litigation victories in early states demonstrated that support for same-sex marriage rights was politically tenable.

Nondiscrimination law worked differently. Here, legislation came first. Cities and states took the lead, adopting protections for LGBTQ people in city and state codes. The first city-level sexual orientation–focused nondiscrimination ordinance was enacted in Ann Arbor, Michigan, in 1972 (Pierceson 2022). Other cities followed suit. Some of these laws were more long-lasting than others. Miami-Dade County, Florida, in a notorious example, enacted a law that was swiftly repealed through a ballot measure. That campaign, led by Anita Bryant and her organization Save Our Children, gained significant attention and spurred backlash against gay rights in other cities (Stone 2012). The form that these city- and state-level policies took varied significantly, covering some mix of employment, housing, education, and public accommodations.

Federal statutory law continues, as of 2024, to lag behind. Bills designed to clearly include LGBTQ people under existing federal nondiscrimination law have been introduced in Congress regularly since the 1970s but have never been enacted. Like the various state laws, the proposed federal legislation varied in coverage. The most recent bill, the Equality Act, broadly modifies existing civil rights legislation to protect LGBTQ people in housing, employment, education, and other areas. Given Republican control of the House of Representatives, it is unlikely that this law will pass—leaving the current patchwork of state protections in place.

Some federal protections have been found by courts in existing law. In 2020, the United States Supreme Court interpreted Title VII of the Civil Rights Act's prohibition of sex discrimination in employment as also prohibiting discrimination against LGBTQ people. These cases, *Bostock v. Clayton County* and *R. G. & G. R. Harris Funeral Homes Inc. v. EEOC*, decided the same day, addressed sexual orientation and transgender discrimination, respectively. *Bostock* reasoned that because it is impossible to consider sexual orientation without considering sex, prohibitions on sex discrimination by definition must also prohibit sexual orientation discrimination. *R. G. & G. R. Harris* drew on sex stereotyping cases like *Price Waterhouse v. Hopkins* to hold that discrimination against transgender people was an impermissible form of sex stereotyping and thus prohibited (Pierceson 2022).

The reasoning in the employment law decisions is likely applicable to Title XI's education protections because the statutory language is similar. Title XI prohibits sex discrimination in education and can, and should, be read as broadly as Title VII's prohibition. Shifting executive orders from the Department of Education, however, show how this remains contested (Mezey 2020). This is particularly true when the law is applied to transgender students. The Obama administration offered some protections for transgender students in educational settings. Those policies were rescinded by the Trump administration and then reinstated by the Biden Administration. And this area remains hotly contested. States across the country, for example, have enacted laws targeting transgender students and restricting LGBTQ issues in education. These are being challenged, but their resolution is unclear at this time.

Public accommodations law remains an area of limited protection for LGBTQ people. Federal law prohibiting discrimination in public accommodations does not prohibit sex discrimination. Federal courts interpreting federal statutes will not likely be useful in this area. State and local laws often do cover LGBTQ people, but they do so to varying extents. This leaves a patchwork of protections across the country. And these state policies must comply with the guarantees of free speech and freedom of religion enshrined in the First Amendment. In the 2023 case *303 Creative v. Elenis*, the Supreme Court ruled that nondiscrimination law cannot require a private business to serve LGBTQ customers if doing so would force the business owner to speak a message they object to speaking. It is likely that the Court will continue to limit the ability to protect LGBTQ people under state and local law.

It is also important to remember that any judicial victories that the LGBTQ community has won at the federal level remain far from secure. Justice Thomas has regularly called for the Court to reconsider the line of cases that secured LGBTQ people many of the rights under constitutional law, most recently in his concurrence in the *Dobbs* decision. With the newly emboldened conservative majority, the Supreme Court may finally take Justice Thomas's suggestion and act on it. Statutory guarantees under state law have already begun to fall to various constitutional challenges as the conservative majority reimagines the balance between LGBTQ civil rights law and constitutional protections for anti-LGBTQ beliefs. This underscores the importance of taking a broad approach when teaching LGBTQ legal concepts.

I turn now to areas of law where LGBTQ topics can readily be included, providing some basic suggestions for how best to do that.

Religious Freedom and LGBTQ Rights

The LGBTQ community has had a complicated relationship with the various religious communities in the United States (Ball 2017). Many members of the LGBTQ community are people of faith and have worked hard to make their religious communities more welcoming and supportive environments (Cravens 2018, 2021). At the same time, much of the movement against LGBTQ people has come from conservative religious communities (Stone 2016). The First Amendment's protections for religious freedom embodied in both the Free Exercise and Establishment Clauses have played a role in both advancing and limiting LGBTQ claims for equality. During the Trump administration, the federal government worked hard to ensure that religiously motivated discrimination against LGBTQ people, especially transgender people, would be protected in administration policies (Mezey 2020).

The tension between religious liberty and LGBTQ rights continues as religious adherents continue to seek exemptions from nondiscrimination laws, voicing a mix of free exercise of religion and free speech claims in their lawsuits. Because the Supreme Court has, in recent years, been reassessing much of the doctrine that applies to constitutional protections for religious freedom, these cases have greater chances of success than under prior precedents. This shift spans both the Free Exercise and the Establishment Clauses. The Roberts Court, newly emboldened by its 6–3 conservative majority, has pulled the doctrine in these areas further to the right (Epstein and Posner 2022). These decisions carve out greater and greater protections for religious people, often at the expense of others' rights. One way that shows this involves cases that balance religious freedom against LGBTQ rights.

The Supreme Court has addressed this in a series of cases starting with *Masterpiece Cake Shop v. Colorado Civil Rights Commission*, decided in 2018. That case was decidedly narrowly, allowing the Court to avoid the ultimate issue of how to balance nondiscrimination law, speech, and religion. The Court returned to this issue in both the 2020 and the 2022 terms. The decision in *Fulton v. City of Philadelphia*, from 2021, addressed the authority of city agencies to decline to work with Catholic Social Services on adoption issues due to the charity's refusal to treat same-sex couples equally. The city argued that its nondiscrimination law required it to refuse to contract with service providers who did not adhere to the nondiscrimination law. Catholic Social Services, on the other hand, argued that the city's refusal violated its free exercise rights. The court ruled in favor of Catholic Social Services, setting the stage for future free exercise cases in other contexts.

The cases here all favor religious freedom for those who dissent from recognizing LGBTQ rights. The Court has yet to address a situation where a pro-LGBTQ rights person objects to an anti-LGBTQ law on religious freedom grounds. How the Court would adjudicate an individual's claim that their religion required action in support of LGBTQ rights is unclear. This could arise in the context, for example, of medical care. Courts allows some religious objections to providing medical care contrary to a practitioner's belief. But the reverse claim is untested. As more states ban gender-affirming care for trans youth, it could be possible for a claimant to assert a religious obligation to treat a patient, despite law prohibiting such care. This religious freedom claim would almost certainly not be received as favorably by this Court as recent anti-LGBTQ claims.

From a teaching perspective, this presents an interesting question about the extent of religious freedom protections and which religious adherents are able to make successful claims. Students can be encouraged to wrestle with these competing rights claims and attempt to justify an outcome that reflects both the law, the science, and the values that are inherent in such complicated questions.

Free Speech, Obscenity, and Related Issues

Some of the first legal victories the LGBTQ community secured were in the context of free speech cases (Ball 2017). In these early cases, courts had to assess whether magazines and other material designed for gay and lesbian audiences was obscene and thus unprotected by the Free Speech Clause. The first major case to reach the United States Supreme Court on this issue was *One Inc. v. Olesen* (1958). The Court, in a one-sentence opinion, dismissed the appeal in light of the recent revision to the obscenity standard announced in *Roth v. United States* (1957). A subsequent case, *Manual Enterprises v. Day* (1962), reached the Court a few years later. It was another victory for the LGBTQ movement (Johnson 2021). The government generally argued that discussion of homosexuality, especially the sexuality part, was inherently obscene.

Together, these cases demonstrate the ways that government censorship attempted to silence discussions of sex broadly, but also specifically as applied to the LGBTQ community. From a teaching standpoint, these LGBTQ-focused cases raise important points of discussion around the obscenity standard. Under the Miller Test (announced in the 1970s), obscenity is, in part, determined by contemporary community standards. But which community? Can the LGBTQ community be left to judge its own materials by its own standards or must the views of the general, more heterosexual community be considered? These issues have become relevant again as states enact laws targeting LGBTQ materials in schools and libraries and anti-LGBTQ groups actively work to challenge pro-LGBTQ content (Price 2021, 2024). Obscenity and censorship of LGBTQ material more broadly is likely to remain an important topic for inclusion for the foreseeable future.

The most recent Supreme Court case on this issue, *303 Creative v. Elenis*, was decided in June 2023. In that case, as noted above, the Court was confronted with a conflict between state-level nondiscrimination law and free speech rights. The Court determined that even if state law prohibits businesses from discriminating on the basis of sexual orientation, a business owner cannot be compelled to provide speech-related services for same-sex weddings. This decision departs from traditional understandings of nondiscrimination law and opens the door to a multitude of claims, grounded both in speech and in religion, that may render much of the civil rights laws ineffective at protecting LGBTQ people in society.

Free speech also arose in a series of cases addressing employment issues. LGBTQ people were fired from government jobs in the 1950s and 1960s because they were seen as security risks due to the stigmatized and criminalized nature of homosexuality. In the 1970s and 1980s, as the gay rights movement grew, LGBTQ workers pushed back against this stigmatization. LGBTQ public employees continued to advocate for their rights to equality. But, because of government hostility, that advocacy became grounds for termination. Public school teachers were routinely threatened with termination for being open about their identity—a history we seem to be repeating today. As these teachers challenged their termination, they raised free speech arguments. Courts were not always receptive to these claims. The issues often required balancing protected political advocacy with unprotected discussion of homosexuality. This created challenges for courts in deciding these cases. In one example, the 1985 case *Board of Education of Oklahoma City v. National Gay Task Force*, the Supreme Court was confronted with a law allowing schools to fire teachers for "public homosexual conduct." That term, defined in the relevant statute, included mere advocacy for LGBTQ rights. The Court divided 4–4, leaving these major questions unanswered at that time. The rights of school teachers and other public employees to advocate for LGBTQ equality and for LGBTQ students remains an important topic to consider given the rash of anti-LGBTQ laws being enacted in many states today, most notoriously in Florida's so-called "Don't Say Gay" law.

Several early LGBTQ speech and association cases addressed the rights of students to form organizations like gay-straight alliances. These first started in colleges but eventually included high schools (Ball 2017). In the 1970s, when the courts were first confronted with these cases, same-sex sexual activity was illegal. The organizations were denied official recognition from schools because they were said to be promoting illegal activity. Later, the objections focused on the asserted sexual nature of an LGBTQ student group. This, opponents argued, made the clubs inappropriate for the school setting. Chapter 2 in this volume, by Richard Price, discusses these and other education-related issues in more depth.

Immigration and Asylum Law

Historically, LGBTQ people faced specific barriers when seeking to immigrate to the United States. The Immigration and Nationality Act of 1952 excluded people "afflicted with psychopathic personality" from entering the country. This term was used to exclude LGBTQ individuals, a policy the Supreme Court upheld in *Boutilier v. INS* (1967). *Boutilier* is an interesting case to use to illustrate the complexity in these issues. The petitioner in that case argued that while he had engaged in homosexual activity, he was not a homosexual person—and thus did not meet the criteria for exclusion. This argument shows both the anti-LGBTQ bias in the law and also the difficulty in defining who that law actually excludes. By raising the conduct/identity distinction, the case can illustrate challenges that come with applying laws that target LGBTQ identity rather than specific conduct.

Immigration law also prohibited HIV-positive people from entering the country. These laws were enacted at the height of the AIDS epidemic during the Reagan administration. This exclusion prohibited both immigration and shorter visits, even those on a tourist visa. This, while not predicated specifically on LGBTQ identity, had a significant impact on the community—particularly gay men. Much like the HIV criminalization laws discussed in the section on criminal law, these broad exclusions did not necessarily align with the best science on HIV transmission.

These issues are helpful when teaching the anti-LGBTQ aspects of immigration history. The discriminatory language in the Immigration Act was added to specifically exclude LGBTQ people. This history is often forgotten. Students are likely more familiar with the history of racially discriminatory immigration policies. Policies like the Chinese Exclusion Act and the biases inherent in the quota system are staples of immigration-focused courses. Laws that sought to exclude LGBTQ and HIV-positive people are likely less commonly included. That history should be incorporated more fully into the curriculum, alongside current issues related to visa status and immigration, particularly for LGBTQ couples and their children conceived through surrogacy.

Asylum law provides a more contemporary issue to consider. Under current asylum law, individuals who are members of a "particular social group" are entitled to seek asylum if they have a reasonable fear of persecution based on their group membership. This applies to LGBTQ people seeking asylum in the United States. Courts, however, have struggled with how to apply asylum standards to LGBTQ individuals. From a teaching standpoint, interesting questions arise around proving membership the "particular social group" of the LGBTQ community. What proof can an asylum seeker offer an immigration official to prove their group membership? This can be even more complicated for those coming from cultures that express sexual identity in ways that are less familiar to officials in the United States. If the asylum seeker is successful in proving their identity in the LGBTQ community, they then must demonstrate a reasonable fear of persecution. This too can be challenging, especially for those who appear—in the eyes of immigration officials—less obviously LGBTQ. Courts have consistently struggled with these issues (Morgan 2006; McGuirk 2018; Vogler 2021). Asylum law offers students an opportunity to discuss burdens of proof and what constitutes sufficient evidence to meet the necessary standard. This can be an important supplement to the larger question of LGBTQ asylum and immigration status and relies on legal frameworks outside of the equal protection context.

Criminal Law

LGBTQ people have long been criminalized by the legal system in the United States (Eskridge 2008; Lvovsky 2021; Mogul et al. 2011). Sodomy laws have existed since the colonial times, although the evidence on how widespread they were enforced in the early years is contested. Over time, however, enforcement became routine. This was seen most especially in laws targeting gay men seeking sexual activity and gender nonconforming people, transgender people, and drag queens. These groups were routinely caught up in police raids.

Sodomy remained illegal in every state until the 1960s, when Illinois became the first to remove it from the state criminal code. Other states slowly followed. The issue eventually reached the Supreme Court in the 1986 case *Bowers v. Hardwick*. There the Court upheld sodomy laws that specifically targeted LGBTQ people. The *Bowers* decision was overturned in 2003 in *Lawrence v. Texas*, striking down the country's remaining sodomy laws. This evolution, particularly the Supreme Court's rapid reversal of the *Bowers* decision, is important to include, but these cases are not the only way to draw LGBTQ issues into criminal law courses. The relationship that LGBTQ people have with the criminal justice system is more complicated than a simple discussion of sodomy laws and their repeal.

Police routinely fail to treat LGBTQ people with respect (Mogul et al. 2011; Owen et al. 2018). This stems, in part, from the times when LGBTQ activity was criminalized and heavily policed by vice squads (Lvovsky 2021). But even though sodomy laws were overturned in 2003, Owen et al. (2018) find that LGBTQ people still have more negative perceptions of police than other communities. Negative interactions between trans women and police are so common it has given rise to the term "walking while trans"—akin to the similar "driving while Black" (Carpenter and Marshall 2017). Courses on policing and criminal justice could easily include discussion of these issues alongside discussion of racial bias in policing, particularly as the trans and Black communities are not mutually exclusive. Intersectionality matters. Black trans women face significant bias from the police.

Bias in policing is only the start of negative interactions LGBTQ have with the criminal justice system. Mogul et al. (2011) demonstrate how LGBTQ identity is further weaponized by the legal system to enhance penalties for LGBTQ people charged with crimes. They show how prosecutors reference defendants' sexuality as a way to reduce sympathy, marking LGBTQ defendants as other to help jurors convict them. As recently as 2018, the Supreme Court declined to hear an appeal from a death sentence imposed by a jury grounded in explicit homophobia (Kellner 2020). Because jurors are composed of members of the community, and homophobia remains present in society, the risk of similar sentences grounded in anti-LGBTQ animus rather than a fair evaluation of the evidence will persist. From a teaching perspective, questions about how to ensure that LGBTQ defendants (and victims), get fair trials can be a fruitful avenue for discussion and evaluation of the guarantees of due process.

LGBTQ people also interact with the criminal justice system as crime victims. The bias noted above continues here, even in areas where hate crimes legislation purportedly protects LGBTQ people (Mogul et al. 2011). Research shows that LGBTQ people, particularly trans and nonbinary people, are subject to violence at rates that far exceed their share of the population, and those crimes have significant impacts on LGBTQ people's lives (Flores et al. 2022, 2023). Owen et al. (2018) also found people perceive that police are less fair toward trans people than other members of the LGBTQ community. The failures of the criminal justice system to treat LGBTQ crime victims with respect likely leads to underreporting of crimes. These are all important factors to consider when teaching criminal law's impact on the LGBTQ community.

Society's fear of AIDS, and people living with AIDS, led to laws that criminalized sexual activity for many HIV-positive people (Strub 2017). States across the country enacted laws specifically targeting HIV-positive people who engage in sexual activity without disclosing their status, regardless of the actual risk of HIV infection. Many of these laws have not been updated to reflect changes in medical science. They remain predicated on the science and the risks of the 1980s; they do not take into account the decades of medical advancement, public awareness, and new prevention tools (Price 2017). Price also discusses how regular assault and battery statutes have been used to prosecute HIV-positive people for failing to disclose their status even if the risk of transmission is virtually nonexistent. These HIV criminalization laws, while not directly targeting LGBTQ people, have long been associated with the gay male community and those laws still fall heavily on that community (Novak 2021).

Prisons, too, present important LGBTQ issues for consideration in criminal law courses. Incarcerated transgender people are placed at great risk of violence in prison settings. Sexual assault and prison rape remain serious problems for incarcerated people, and LGBTQ people are routinely targeted at rates significantly higher than heterosexual people (Cahill 2017). Like many of the other issues here, prisons present specific challenges for transgender inmates. Prisons remain sex-segregated, which requires prison officials to determine how to house trans and gender non-conforming individuals. This does not always follow other governmental determinations of sex, like driver's licenses or birth certificates (Currah 2022). This puts trans inmates at increased risk of sexual assault. It also increases the likelihood of administrative punishment from prison officials for failure to adhere to officials' views on appropriately gendered behavior. Class discussion focusing on the ways that prisons create harmful conditions for trans people will enhance students' understanding of prisons and their role in society.

Healthcare Law

Several areas of healthcare law are of particular importance to LGBTQ people. Most crucially is the extent to which law and policy allow trans-gender people to access medically appropriate gender-affirming healthcare. The recent wave of legislation targeting healthcare providers who offer gender-affirming care to young trans individuals shows the importance of covering this area. Some states defer to medical professionals in consultation with parents. Other states have prohibited medically appropriate care, regardless of what parents want and doctors advise. States are even moving to ban this practice for adults. This area of law is currently in flux, but these issues will likely remain important for some time.

Another area to include looks at mental health and efforts to change a patient's sexual orientation or gender identity. Conversion therapy is a discredited practice that attempts to change a patient's sexual orientation or gender identity (APA Task Force on Appropriate Therapeutic Responses to Sexual Orientation 2009). Bans on conversion therapy have been enacted in many states (Lapin 2020). These laws most commonly prohibit the practice for minors. But the extent of this protection varies. Legislation generally applies to providers licensed by the state but not to efforts undertaken by religious leaders (Lapin 2020). First amendment protections, particularly in light of the cases discussed above, likely prevent states from enacting laws that would ban religiously motivated conversion therapy. The extent to which healthcare law can protect people, particularly vulnerable youth, from harmful religious practices is an important concept for students to discuss. This again requires balancing competing values, including parental rights, child safety, and religious freedom. This topic could be compared to other practices where religion and medical care conflict to help students assess how much of these laws are grounded in anti-LGBTQ animus versus sincere religious liberty concerns.

Lastly, it is important to include a discussion of HIV-related laws. While anyone, regardless of sexual orientation or gender identity, can be HIV-positive, laws that rely on HIV status have a disproportionate impact on the LGBTQ community. Until 2023, men who have sex with men were completely barred from donating blood out of fear of HIV transmission. Originally a total, lifetime ban, the policy has become more relaxed. Initially the relaxed policy required a period of celibacy. New rules announced in 2023 now treat men who have sex with men the same as other potential donors (Franklin 2023). But even these policies may still not go far enough. Men who use PrEP, an FDA-approved HIV prevention drug, remain barred despite the incredibly low risks they present. As Novak (2021) notes, laws that criminalize HIV have a negative impact on public health. By perpetuating stigma and discouraging testing, these laws undermine the supposed public health goals of the laws. Whatever legitimacy this policy once had, its continued existence raises important questions for LGBTQ issues in a healthcare law course.

Administrative Law

LGBTQ people encounter the administrative state in a variety of contexts, many of which overlap with other areas of law discussed above. Agencies routinely assess, and classify, people based on sex, gender/gender identity, and sexuality (Canaday 2009; Currah 2022; Murib 2020; Vogler 2021). While not all of these determinations are strictly necessary for government purposes, they still occur regularly (Davis 2017). Determining an individual's gender, or status as a transgender person, remains required for everything from issuing identification, enforcement of criminal laws, placement in prison housing, access to medical care, and more. What documents, reflecting what medical and social information, are necessary for a person to provide in order to administratively change gender markers on government identification? Can a particular person be legally present in certain sex-segregated facilities like bathrooms and locker rooms? What sports teams can someone join? These are all questions that a require an administrative decision determining and classifying individuals' gender and gender identity. Sexual orientation, too, must be administratively determined in certain cases like the asylum petitions discussed above. Making these determinations requires some legally justifiable administrative standards to avoid arbitrary and unequal application of the law. Those standards are contested and hard to define. And, as Currah (2022) notes with respect to sex, they vary from agency to agency. This variation lends itself to important classroom discussion around the purposes of these classifications and the varied evidentiary standards that support them.

In practice, science plays a large role in shaping these standards. But the role of science and administrative expertise in defining and shaping sexual orientation remains an area of conflict. Many LGBTQ people lack the resources necessary to get a "scientific" determination of the identity (Wuest 2019). This can prevent them from accessing facilities and obtaining benefits, and may place them at increased risk from the criminal and administrative law systems. Placing too much faith in science to define and recognize LGBTQ identity limits the ability of administrative law to properly address the needs of the entire LGBTQ community. These concerns are heightened now that the Supreme Court has overturned *Chevron*, placing pro-LGBTQ administrative law at greater risk of being overturned by conservative courts.

Family Law

Family law is an important area to consider when discussing how law and LGBTQ issues intersect. This goes beyond simply talking about marriage as a unit of family formation. Despite the guarantees of marriage equality, legal issues for LGBTQ families persist (Mayo-Adam 2020). Important things to consider here center around adoption and child custody cases. Historically, LGBTQ parents faced significant challenges in seeking to retain custody of their children. Custody disputes regularly emerged when an LGBTQ person came out later in life, after marrying and having children with an opposite sex partner. In states where, at the time, homosexuality remained illegal, this was grounds to show that the LGBTQ parent was unfit to raise children because of their criminality. Even absent that, the commonly used "best interest of the child" standard combined with societal homophobia meant that placement with the LGBTQ parent was rarely in the best interest of the child.

Adoption law followed similar paths. Many states explicitly prohibited same-sex couples from adopting children (Mayo-Adam 2020). These bans lasted well into the 2010s. And, while it is now legally possible for same-sex couples to adopt in all fifty states, other hurdles remain. Many states permit adoption agencies to discriminate against LGBTQ people. Additionally, while international adoption is generally permitted, many countries prohibit same-sex adoption. This leaves LGBTQ couples with fewer options when seeking to adopt children. So, while same-sex couples generally have access to adoption, that access is more limited than straight couples' access. This raises important avenues for discussion in classes on families and family law.

ALTERNATIVE APPROACHES TO TEACHING MARRIAGE EQUALITY AND RELATIONSHIP RECOGNITION

While the main goal of this chapter is to help faculty find ways to include LGBTQ legal issues other than marriage equality into their courses, marriage equality remains an important topic. The Supreme Court extended marriage rights to same-sex couples in *Obergefell v. Hodges*. But, as Justice Thomas makes clear in his concurrence in *Dobbs* (the decision that overturned *Roe v. Wade*), that right may not be fully secure. Faculty will, therefore, likely need to continue to cover marriage equality rights and the legal and political fights that brought marriage equality from a radical idea to a legal reality. There are great resources to teach that traditional approach (e.g., Chauncey 2004; Issenberg 2021; Kaplan 2015; Klarman 2013; Solomon 2014; Witosky and Hansen 2015). Covering that process can be useful for students to understand the role of social movements in legal change. But other approaches can also be incredibly useful in making the discussion of marriage equality more engaging and push students to think about law in new ways. A broader approach to marriage and relationship recognition offers fruitful discussion, particularly for students who have only vague memories (if any) of a time before marriage equality.

One approach is to start with earlier cases on relationship recognition that came before marriage equality. The Courts were forced to address the reality of LGBTQ relationships long before they were ready to embrace the concept of marriage equality. The first case to recognize some rights held by a same-sex couple came out of New York. It addressed the question of whether a surviving partner could take over the lease of a rent-controlled apartment after his partner's death (Ball 2010, 31). Cases like this can help students think about ways to recognize LGBTQ families without necessarily relying solely on the marital framework.

Recognizing LGBTQ families outside of marriage is complicated by the ways that courts determined who counts as a family. The legal system has a narrow conceptualization of what makes a proper, recognizable family, one that only embraces same-sex couples if they closely mimic traditional heterosexual unions (Rosenblum 1994). In questioning victories that relied on same-sex couples' ability to mimic heterosexual relationships, Rosenblum (1994) asks what a truly queer legal victory would look like. He argues that these early cases are "victories" only for the most normative members of the LGBTQ community. He does, however, later argue that cases like *Lawrence v. Texas* and *Goodridge v. Department of Public Health* were better representations of queer victories (Rosenblum 2009). This analysis, however, is less persuasive than his earlier work. Presenting this evolving discussion, though, is an excellent way to encourage critical thinking about the movement toward marriage.

A critical approach to the marriage equality movement is important because marriage equality was not a universal goal of the LGBTQ community or its leading organizations. For some, marriage was not an institution worth joining. Ettlebrick (2004), in a leading example, questions whether marriage can truly be liberatory. There were also conservatives who argued *for* same-sex marriage. This perspective is often lost in the broad way the marriage equality debate is covered. These conservatives argued that marriage would bring those same-sex couples who chose to marry closer to the core social fabric of American life. By embracing marriage, the argument goes, same-sex couples would create more stable families, be less promiscuous, and become better citizens and neighbors. The undercurrent here, of course, that marriage would make LGBTQ people less queer and more normal. This is, of course, the result that many of the anti-marriage voices within the LGBTQ community feared.

New legal issues come from debates around polyamorous and other nontraditional family structures. Somerville, Massachusetts, became the first locality in the United States to recognize multiple partners under city law ("Three's Company, Too" 2022). These benefits are limited, but the official recognition does offer some important symbols of acceptance. Currently, polyamorous relationships receive no recognition at the federal level. Expanding the discussion of marriage equality to recognition of other forms of relationships allows students to examine the logic of providing privileged legal recognition to some family forms, but not others. It also engages with the logical extensions of the marriage equality decisions and the fears raised by the dissents.

Going beyond the usual equality-focused marriage arguments to examine other ways relationships can be recognized helps students realize that these issues are still ongoing rather than something that has been finished.

Other Legal Issues to Consider

In addition to the specific areas of law mentioned above, LGBTQ people also face the same legal issues that other, non-LGBTQ people face. Sometimes, as in the examples discussed in the next two paragraphs, these harms may fall disproportionately on members of the LGBTQ community. But they may not. Since LGBTQ people are everywhere, and law is everywhere, LGBTQ people are relevant throughout the legal curriculum. I highlight two brief examples to show this.

Laws that target unhoused people provide one clear example (Adler 2018). These laws ban sleeping outside, impose hostile architecture designed to make life harder for the unhoused, and limit access to shelter spaces. This year, the Supreme Court upheld the authority of cities to criminally punish people for sleeping outside or in their cars. As Adler notes, LGBTQ people—particularly youth—are disproportionately homeless. As such it is important to consider the impact these laws have on LGBTQ people.

Economic policy similarly hurts many LGBTQ people. Congress has failed to raise the minimum wage for decades. The social safety net has largely been eroded. Employment discrimination historically and currently means that LGBTQ people often work in lower paid, more precarious jobs. Research shows that many LGBTQ people choose to work in less lucrative careers to avoid the discrimination present in other work they could be suited to do (Burn and Martell 2020). Some of these harms could be mitigated through expansive social welfare programs or stronger enforcement of existing laws. But LGBTQ people are not often included in discussions around the economy. Teaching about the laws and policies that shape the economy rarely discuss the ways that these systems harm LGBTQ people specifically.

These two examples demonstrate the importance of approaching teaching in an LGBTQ-inclusive way, using a queer lens to see new areas for discussion and education. Ensuring that LGBTQ people are represented in all discussions about law and its impact on society is essential.

Additional Resources

There are several books to consider when integrating LGBTQ legal issues into existing or newly created law courses. Andersen's (2006) *Out of the Closets Into the Courts* examines the way that the LGBTQ legal movement was created and how it functioned alongside the political movement. As discussed above, Adler's (2018) *Gay Priori* provides a great theoretical foundation and critique of the movement's narrow equal protection focus. William Eskridge's *Gaylaw* (1999) provides a detailed history of LGBTQ legal regulations. The history covered here remains useful, despite the fact that the book is over twenty years old now. Eskridge (2008) also published a detailed history of sodomy laws in the United States that helps contextualize how those laws were drafted and, most importantly, how they were enforced. Carpenter's *Flagrant Conduct* (2012) brings the discussion of sodomy law forward through a detailed account of the *Lawrence v. Texas* case. *Queer (In)justice* (Mogul et al. 2011) explores LGBTQ criminal law across a range of issues and is very accessible for undergraduate students. Carlos A. Ball's *From the Closet to the Courtroom* (2010) explores five key cases in depth, across a range of legal issues. This book is particularly useful because it works to contextualize the cases and provides more details on the people involved. By telling the human story alongside the legal story, Ball's book reminds us that every case involves people who suffered some harm and sought legal protection. It makes the cases and the stakes less abstract. Humanizing the cases helps students relate to the material more than they would with a focus just on the case law.

A number of books discuss the same-sex marriage movement. Some are focused on specific states or cases, for example Iowa (Witosky and Hansen 2015) and California (Boies and Olson 2015). Others take a broader perspective on the movement as a whole (e.g., Chauncey 2004; Frank 2017; Issenberg 2021; Klarman 2013; Pierceson 2014; Solomon 2014). Both Frank's *Awakening* (2017) and Issenberg's *The Engagement* (2021) provide a longer history of the marriage debate in the LGBTQ community. Frank's explores the movement's views on marriage, starting in the 1950s, in addition to the legal and political strategy. There are some concerns with how Frank frames the marriage debate (see Kammerer 2019), but overall the book provides a compelling historical account. Issenberg's incredibly detailed account starts with the Hawaii case in the 1990s and looks at the movement's leaders and their interactions with politicians and the courts.

Many of these books would be easily accessible for undergraduate students. Some may be better suited to graduate students. Others may be more useful for faculty trying to deepen their understanding of these issues.

Conclusion

LGBTQ people have had a long and complicated history with the legal system in the United States. Throughout much of history, same-sex sexual activity was condemned—criminalized, medicalized, stigmatized. But that condemnation, in more recent times, slowly faded. By 2003, the Supreme Court recognized that LGBTQ people had privacy rights protected by the Constitution. Just over a decade later, the Court granted marriage equality. Socially, too, LGBTQ people made significant progress in achieving recognition as a vital part of the American story (Kammerer and Barreto 2022). LGBTQ people's full citizenship and humanity seemed poised for total recognition.

But, as often happens, this progress stalled. And now it has begun to reverse. Backlash against LGBTQ progress is nothing new, even if the root causes of that backlash remain contested (Bishin et al. 2020; Keck

2009). Many of the legal issues that seemed settled are being challenged. Social movements advocate for policy that often becomes law. The relationship between law, policy, and society cannot be overlooked. This new wave of anti-LGBTQ laws underscores the need to teach both the history of LGBTQ law and the issues currently being debated. If we fail to offer our students opportunities to study this complex, contested legal domain, we fail to prepare them to confront the reality that is LGBTQ law and politics in society today.

Note

1. Throughout this chapter, I refer to the movement as the LGBTQ movement unless historical or specific context dictates otherwise. This is an effort to be inclusive and understandable, while also recognizing that any attempt to define and label the widely diverse people that fit under the broad movement umbrella is impossible to do accurately.

References

Adler, Libby. 2018. *Gay Priori*. Duke University Press.
Andersen, Ellen Ann. 2006. *Out of the Closets Into the Courts: Legal Opportunity Structure and Gay Rights Litigation*. University of Michigan Press.
APA Task Force on Appropriate Therapeutic Responses to Sexual Orientation. 2009. "Appropriate Therapeutic Responses to Sexual Orientation." American Psychological Association. http://www.apa.org/pi/lgbc/publications/therapeutic-resp.html.
Ball, Carlos A. 2010. *From the Closet to the Courtroom: Five LGBT Rights Lawsuits That Have Changed Our Nation*. Beacon Press.
Ball, Carlos A. 2017. *The First Amendment and LGBT Equality: A Contentious History*. Harvard University Press.
Bishin, Benjamin G., Thomas J. Hayes, Matthew B. Incantalupo, and Charles Anthony Smith. 2020. "Elite Mobilization: A Theory Explaining Opposition to Gay Rights." *Law & Society Review* 54 (1): 233–64. https://doi.org/10.1111/lasr.12457.
Boies, David, and Theodore B. Olson. 2015. *Redeeming the Dream: Proposition 8 and the Struggle for Marriage Equality*. Plume.
Bonauto, Mary. 2005. "Goodridge in Context." *Harvard Civil Rights: Civil Liberties Law Review* 40 (1): 1–69.

Burn, Ian, and Michael E. Martell. 2020. "The Role of Work Values and Characteristics in the Human Capital Investment of Gays and Lesbians." *Education Economics* 28 (4): 351–69.

Cahill, Sean. 2017. "From 'Don't Drop the Soap' to PREA Standards: Reducing Sexual Victimization of LGBT People in the Juvenile and Criminal Justice Systems." In *LGBTQ Politics: A Critical Reader*, edited by Marla Brettschneider et al., 134–52. New York University Press.

Canaday, Margot. 2009. *The Straight State: Sexuality and Citizenship in Twentieth-Century America*. Princeton University Press.

Carpenter, Dale. 2012. *Flagrant Conduct: The Story of Lawrence v. Texas*. W. W. Norton.

Carpenter, Leonore F., and R. Barrett Marshall. 2017. "Walking While Trans: Profiling of Transgender Women by Law Enforcement, and the Problem of Proof." *William & Mary Journal of Women and the Law* 24 (1): 5–38.

Chauncey, George. 2004. *Why Marriage?* Basic Books.

Cravens, Royal G. 2018. "The Politics of Queer Religion." *Politics and Religion* 11 (3): 576–623. https://doi.org/10.1017/S1755048318000056.

Cravens, Royal G. 2021. "Identity-Affirming Religious Experience and Political Activism among LGBT People." *Journal of Contemporary Religion* 36 (3): 501–24. https://doi.org/10.1080/13537903.2021.1975942.

Currah, Paisley. 2022. *Sex Is as Sex Does: Governing Transgender Identity*. New York University Press.

Davis, Heath Fogg. 2017. *Beyond Trans: Does Gender Matter*. New York University Press.

DeFilippis, Joseph Nicholas, and Ben Anderson-Nathe. 2017. "Embodying Margin to Center: Intersectional Activism Among Queer Liberation Organizations." In Marla Brettschneider et al., *LGBTQ Politics: A Critical Reader*, 110–33.

Epstein, Lee, and Eric A. Posner. 2022. "The Roberts Court and the Transformation of Constitutional Protections for Religion: A Statistical Portrait." *Supreme Court Review* 2021:315. https://doi.org/10.1086/719348.

Eskridge, William N. Jr. 1999. *Gaylaw*. Harvard University Press.

Eskridge, William N. Jr. 2008. *Dishonorable Passions: Sodomy Laws in America 1861–2003*. Viking.

Ettlebrick, Paula. 2004. "Since When Is Marriage a Path to Liberation?" In *Same-Sex Marriage Pro and Con: A Reader*, edited by Andrew Sullivan, 122–28. Vintage Books.

Flores, Andrew R., Rebecca L. Stotzer, Ilan H. Meyer, and Lynn L. Langton. 2022. "Hate Crimes Against LGBT People: National Crime Victimization Survey, 2017–2019." *PLOS ONE* 17 (12): e0279363. https://doi.org/10.1371/journal.pone.0279363.

Flores, Andrew R., Bianca D. M. Wilson, Lynn L. Langton, and Ilan H. Meyer. 2023. "Violent Victimization at the Intersections of Sexual Orientation,

Gender Identity, and Race: National Crime Victimization Survey, 2017–2019."
PLOS ONE 18 (2): e0281641.

Frank, Nathaniel. 2017. *Awakening: How Gays and Lesbians Brought Marriage Equality to America*. Belknap Press.

Franklin, Jonathan. 2023. "More Gay and Bisexual Men Will Now Be Able to Donate Blood Under Finalized FDA Rules." NPR, May 11, sec. Health. https://www.npr.org/2023/05/11/1175622785/fda-blood-donations-gay-bisexual-men.

Issenberg, Sasha. 2021. *The Engagement: America's Quarter-Century Struggle Over Same-Sex Marriage*. Pantheon Books.

Johnson, David K. 2021. *Buying Gay: How Physique Entrepreneurs Sparked a Movement*. Columbia University Press.

Kammerer, Edward F. Jr. 2016. "Judicial Narratives and Same-Sex Marriage: Analysis of the Argument in *Goodridge v. Dept. of Public Health*." *New England Journal of Political Science* 9 (2): 217–52.

Kammerer, Edward F. Jr. 2019. "Review of Awakening: How Gays and Lesbians Brought Marriage Equality to America by Nathaniel Frank." *Law and Politics Book Review* 29 (8): 91–93.

Kammerer, Edward F. Jr., and Amílcar Antonio Barreto. 2022. "American Nationhood in Transition: Sexual Orientation, Race and the Media." *JAm It!: Journal of American Studies in Italy* 6:104–31. https://doi.org/doi.org/10.13135/2612-5641/5980.

Kaplan, Roberta. 2015. *Then Comes Marriage: United States v. Windsor and the Defeat of DOMA*. New York: W. W. Norton.

Keck, Thomas M. 2009. "Beyond Backlash: Assessing the Impact of Judicial Decisions on LGBT Rights." *Law & Society Review* 43 (1): 151–85.

Kellner, Matt. 2020. "Queer* and Unusual: Capital Punishment, LGBTQ+ Identity, and the Constitutional Path Forward." *Tulane Journal of Law & Sexuality* 29:1–24.

Klarman, Michael J. 2013. *From the Closet to the Altar: Courts, Backlash, and the Struggle for Same-Sex Marriage*. Oxford University Press.

Lapin, John J. 2020. "The Legal Status of Conversion Therapy." *Georgetown Journal of Gender and the Law* 22 (1): 251–78.

Lvovsky, Anna. 2021. *Vice Patrol: Cops, Courts, and the Struggle Over Urban Gay Life Before Stonewall*. University of Chicago Press.

Mayo-Adam, Erin. 2020. "LGBTQ Family Law and Policy in the United States." In *Oxford Research Encyclopedia of Politics*, by Erin Mayo-Adam. Oxford University Press. https://doi.org/10.1093/acrefore/9780190228637.013.1216.

McGuirk, Siobhán. 2018. "(In)Credible Subjects: NGOs, Attorneys, and Permissible LGBT Asylum Seeker Identities." *PoLAR: Political and Legal Anthropology Review* 41 (S1): 4–18. https://doi.org/10.1111/plar.12250.

Mezey, Susan Gluck. 2020. *Transgender Rights from Obama to Trump*. Routledge.

Mogul, Joey L., Andrea J. Ritchie, and Kay Whitlock. 2011. *Queer (In)Justice: The Criminalization of LGBT People in the United States*. Beacon Press.

Morgan, Deborah A. 2006. "Not Gay Enough for the Government: Racial and Sexual Stereotypes in Sexual Orientation Asylum Cases." *Law & Sexuality* 15:135–61.

Murib, Zein. 2020. "Administering Biology: How 'Bathroom Bills' Criminalize and Stigmatize Trans and Gender Nonconforming People in Public Space." *Administrative Theory & Praxis* 42 (2): 153–71. https://doi.org/10.1080/10 841806.2019.1659048.

Novak, Andrew. 2021. "Toward a Critical Criminology of HIV Criminalization." *Critical Criminology* 29 (1): 57–73. https://doi.org/10.1007/s10612-021-09557-1.

Owen, Stephen S., Tod W. Burke, April L. Few-Demo, and Jameson Natwick. 2018. "Perceptions of the Police by LGBT Communities." *American Journal of Criminal Justice* 43 (3): 668–93. https://doi.org/10.1007/s12103-017-9420-8.

Pierceson, Jason. 2014. *Same-Sex Marriage in the United States: The Road to the Supreme Court and Beyond*. Updated edition. Rowman and Littlefield.

Pierceson, Jason. 2022. *Before* Bostock*: The Accidental LGBTQ Precedent of* Price Waterhouse v. Hopkins. University of Kansas Press.

Price, J. Ricky. 2017. "The Treatment and Prevention of HIV Bodies: The Contemporary Politics and Science of a Thirty-Year-Old Epidemic." In Marla Brettschneider et al., *LGBTQ Politics: A Critical Reader*, 54–71. New York University Press.

Price, Richard S. 2021. "Navigating a Doctrinal Grey Area: Free Speech, the Right to Read, and Schools." *First Amendment Studies* 55 (2): 79–101.

Price, Richard S. 2024. "Silencing Trans Voices." *Politics, Groups, and Identities*. https://doi.org/10.1080/21565503.2024.2366876.

Rosenblum, Darren. 1994. "Queer Intersectionality and the Failure of Recent Lesbian and Gay 'Victories.'" *Law & Sexuality* 4:83–122.

Rosenblum, Darren. 2009. "Queer Legal Victories: Intersectionality Revisited." In *Queer Mobilizations: LGBT Activists Confront the Law*, edited by Scott Barclay et al., 38–51. New York University.

Solomon, Marc. 2014. *Winning Marriage: The Inside Story of How Same-Sex Couples Took on the Pundits—And Won*. ForeEdge.

Stone, Amy L. 2012. *Gay Rights at the Ballot Box*. University of Minnesota Press.

Stone, Amy L. 2016. "The Impact of Anti-Gay Politics on the LGBTQ Movement." *Sociology Compass* 10 (6): 459–67. https://doi.org/10.1111/soc4.12373.

Strub, Sean. 2017. "HIV: Prosecution or Prevention? HIV Is Not a Crime." In *The War on Sex*, edited by David M. Halperin and Trevor Hoppe, 347–52. Duke University Press.

"Three's Company, Too: The Emergence of Polyamorous Partnership Ordinances." 2022. *Harvard Law Review* 135 (5): 1441–63.

Vogler, Stefan. 2021. *Sorting Sexualities: Expertise and the Politics of Legal Classification*. University of Chicago Press.

Witosky, Tom, and Marc Hansen. 2015. *Equal Before the Law: How Iowa Led Americans to Marriage Equality*. University of Iowa Press.

Wuest, Jo. 2019. "The Scientific Gaze in American Transgender Politics: Contesting the Meanings of Sex, Gender, and Gender Identity in the Bathroom Rights Cases." *Politics & Gender* 15 (2): 336–60. https://doi.org/10.1017/S1743923X18000338.

Chapter 10

Reading Is Fundamental

Pedagogical Strategies for Including SOGIE in Public and Nonprofit Administration Education

Seth J. Meyer, Nicole M. Elias, and Maria J. D'Agostino

With the growing number of anti-LGBTQ+ (lesbian, gay, bisexual, transgender, queer plus) legislation in many states, an expanded knowledge of sexual orientation and gender identity and expression (SOGIE) by students and professionals in the public and nonprofit sector, and a growing LGBTQ+ community, it is no wonder that more public affairs education professors and programs are interested in discussing SOGIE in their classrooms and creating a greater knowledge base through research on SOGIE topics. This is a topic that is not limited to the few professors whose research focuses on SOGIE; instead it is a topic that many would like to include in their teaching but do not have the knowledge to create an inclusive class and syllabus, facilitate discussions around SOGIE, and create classroom activities on SOGIE topics. This chapter provides groundwork on how public administration professors can include SOGIE in teaching and learning, making a more inclusive and welcoming environment to all individuals, and prepare our students to work with diverse sexual orientation and gender communities.

We will focus on a couple of specific classes where SOGIE can be discussed, though this is not an exhaustive list. Instead, it is the beginning of a discussion around how to include SOGIE in all aspects of public administration education. There are many challenges that professors may face teaching about SOGIE. To start, some of the terms, such as heteronormativity and cisnormativity, may be unfamiliar to the students and the professor (Meyer and Elias 2022; Meyer and Millesen 2022). It is important to help students understand the ways that SOGIE is discussed in their community and how this impacts their work (Meyer and Elias 2022), the size and scope of the LGBTQ+ population (Goldberg and Conron 2018), and the local laws (e.g., Swan 2019) as this gives students a perspective of issues impacting the LGBTQ+ community. This is important because as the LGBTQ+ community continues to grow, future public administrators need to better understand how to support all SOGIE groups as clients, consumers, and employees (Larson 2022).

In this chapter, we create guidance for professors to include SOGIE into their classroom. We use the three pillars of gender inclusive pedagogy identified in Elias et al. (2022) to focus on how courses are structured, the content of courses, and the practice of pedagogy. We define structure as the foundational documents and policies of a course that should include gender equitable statements regarding concepts of diversity, inclusion, and representation. Content includes the readings, assignments, and other course materials that should include gender diverse representation of authors and perspectives that have not been historically or widely embraced. Finally, practice entails the interactions and dynamics among class members and instructors that should foster gender equitable and inclusive learning environments. This chapter will explain the importance of gender inclusive pedagogy as well as provide practical recommendations for how to enact a gender inclusive pedagogy.

Though this chapter is focused on public administration, the approaches presented can be used in many fields, such as social work, business, political science, and criminal justice. Politics, human resources, government, and social service delivery are an important part of many curricula. Using this chapter as a starting point, we encourage educators of all disciplines to use this interdisciplinary perspective to better represent SOGIE perspectives in the classroom.

Challenges of Diversity, Equitable, and Inclusive Education

The traditions of public administration scholarship and education are rooted in Eurocentric, patriarchal traditions (Elias and D'Agostino 2019;

Evans and Knepper, 2021). This is evident in theories and research methods that have dominated the field, ranging from assumptions of bureaucratic neutrality (Portillo et al. 2020) to "institutionalization of merit-based hiring in municipal governments," which "exemplifies a rationalized myth diffused throughout the field, and ushered in structural supports for racialized and gendered inequities that have been foundational to the field for more than a century" (Portillo et al. 2020, 521; Elias et al. 2022). Students of public administration are exploring how to provide support and services in an ever-diversifying world and have more of an interest than ever to adopt a gender equitable lens for their future administrative roles (Elias et al. 2022).

In departing from this exclusionary tradition, public affairs education is adopting a focus on diversity, equity, and inclusion (DEI) topics. These DEI efforts include revisiting mission, values and vision statements, holding DEI events, and building a culturally responsive curriculum. Gender and sexual orientation are important components of DEI education (e.g., Meyer and Millesen 2022); however, SOGIE topics remain largely absent from public affairs education in three central ways: how courses are structured, the content of courses, and the practice of pedagogy. Gender and sexual orientation are some of the most rapidly evolving demographic categories today, and as such, public sector professionals need to have the knowledge, skills, abilities to be inclusive and address SOGIE perspectives proactively.

Progression of Gender Equity in Higher Education

Pedagogy in higher education shifted dramatically in the 1970s with the rise of identity politics and the recognition that a neutral approach to teaching did not fit the lived experiences of many students. Freire's (1970) *Pedagogy of the Oppressed* is recognized as the text that began this movement toward a race- and gender-conscious approach to teaching and learning. Since this seminal text, race and ethnicity (Zajda and Freeman 2009; Race and Lander 2014; Hernández 2016; Nelsen 2021), and particularly critical race theory pedagogy, have become central to higher education equity literature (Lynn 1999; Jennings and Lynn 2005; Abrams and Moio 2009; Ledesma and Calderón 2015; Aguilar-Hernández 2020).

Another stream of literature from the Freire tradition is feminist pedagogy, which entails reformation of the relationship between professor and student; empowering students by facilitating participation in a democratic process where at least some power is shared; building community and cooperation within the classroom; encouraging authority in individual's views and knowledge; respective diversity of personal experiences; and challenging traditional views (Weiler 1991; Luke 1996; Webb et al. 2002; Light et al. 2015; Carr 2020). The feminist pedagogy literature is lacking two key components: (1) practical strategies for enacting a gender inclusive pedagogy and (2) accounting for emerging SOGIE categories, particularly for students of nonconforming gender identity or sexual orientation. For instance, adapting the principles of universal learning design and universal instructional design to support LGBTQ+ students have been proposed (Morgan and Houghton 2011; Guðjónsdóttir and Óskarsdóttir 2016; Arendale 2018; Parra-Martínez et al. 2021).

Following is the queer pedagogy movement, which, through the lens of deconstructing heteronormativity and other boundaries, works to expand the way we look at educational practices and research (Nemi Neto 2018; Pennell 2020; Akarcay and Jacobs 2021). From these theoretical traditions, we focus on how inclusive pedagogy seeks to create course designs that are accessible for all the large scope of human diversities (Moriña 2020; Sanger and Gleason 2020). Inclusive pedagogy recognizes and dismisses stereotypes and biases, while fostering consideration and respect for all persons. Examples of inclusive pedagogy include delivering gender-neutral resources (Harbin et al. 2020), lending mindfulness to language and terminology (Akarcay and Jacobs 2021), developing a curriculum that reflects a multicultural society (Arday et al. 2020), and fostering a diverse and accepting atmosphere (Cotán et al. 2021).

Diverse, Equitable, and Inclusive Pedagogy in Public Affairs Education

Scholarship on strengthening inclusive curricula and pedagogy in higher education has grown significantly in recent years (Sleeter 2011; Forlin 2014; Dewsbury and Brame 2019; Hayward et al. 2021). Historically, the concept of inclusive pedagogy was geared primarily toward special needs students in mainstream classrooms (Florian 2008; Florian and Black-Hawkins 2011; Dalton et al. 2019; Livingston-Galloway et al. 2021). However, inclusive education has evolved over the last decade, and an increasingly large body of literature emphasizes the importance of inclusive pedagogy in improving learning outcomes for all students (Spratt and Florian 2015;

Awang-Hashim et al. 2019; Cotán at al. 2021). Moreover, the diversity and inclusiveness framework has been introduced as a guide for integrating cultural competency into public administration classrooms (Blessett et al. 2019; Evans and Knepper 2021). Indeed, cultural competency has been one of the central pedagogical tools in teaching DEI (e.g., Blessett et al. 2019; Rice 2007). It features six interdependent components: (1) address the program's mission, (2) identify core competencies, (3) develop diversity and inclusiveness plans, (4) require faculty and staff training, (5) implement extracurricular and co-curricular activities, and (6) assess students' perception of diversity (Lopez-Littleton and Blessett 2015).

Central to inclusive pedagogy is developing faculty's understanding, participation, and perpetuation of diversity, equity, empathy, and self-awareness (Lewis 2010; Opertti and Brady 2011; Moriña et al. 2015; Drewsbury and Brame 2019). An inclusive curriculum and pedagogy calls for meeting students where they are and understanding that some students experience a higher level of privilege, thus better preparing them for the work before them (Opertti and Brady 2011; Awang-Hashim et al. 2019). Moreover, educators must be cognizant of their own backgrounds and bias, as well as opinion on what they deem "diverse." Everyone must have an understanding that diversity includes, race, gender, socioeconomic status, and accessibility—their personal beliefs influence how well diversity and inclusion is accepted and implemented in the classroom (Wyatt-Nichol and Kwame 2008). With the recent focus of inclusive pedagogy on embracing the DEI of all students, institutions of higher education have the unique ability to challenge normative standards and biases of Eurocentric, male-dominated perspectives that have dominated higher education in the past (Arday et al. 2020; Evans and Knepper 2021).

From the broader focus on inclusive pedagogy, more nuanced approaches to including specific demographics are emerging, such as strategies on how to ensure gender inclusivity for students. Some strategies include introspection on behalf of the instructor to examine personal biases (Ramey 2017; Couillard and Higbee 2018; Dewsbury and Brame 2019); checking in with students to learn preferred names and gender pronouns (Norris and Welch 2020; Ramey 2017; Goldberg et al. 2018) and using inclusive language (Dewsbury and Brame 2019; Sauntson 2018; Paiz 2019); providing diverse examples to supplement coursework (Waitoller and King Thoruis 2016; Black-Hawkins 2017) and being mindful of "low ability" cues (Morgan and Houghton 2011; Moriña 2020); avoiding using students as "token" ambassadors (Quaye and Harper 2007; Ramey 2017);

and mindfulness toward "micro-inequalities" to ensure practice of inclusive classroom behaviors and content (Nemi Neto 2018; Parra-Martínez et al. 2021).

Recommendations for Gender Equitable Pedagogy

Gender Equitable Structure

Gender equitable pedagogy can be strengthened by improving the structure of courses. First, solidifying inclusivity in courses via syllabi; second, implementing flexible policies to meet the needs of students of all genders; third, providing multiple means for students to demonstrate their knowledge and assessments; and fourth, clearly articulating gender inclusivity in the course description and rules of conduct for the class. The literature has identified several barriers that influence the way in which instructors are able to address gender equity, such as lack of administrative support and training (Burke 2017; Black-Hawkins 2017; Staley and Leonardi 2019), social norms and institutional values (Goldberg et al. 2018; Ferfolja and Ullman 2021), cumbersome curricula requirements (Tanner 2013), and having a limited or immensely diverse student population (Wyatt-Nichol and Antwi-Boasiako 2008). Nonetheless, instructors can structure their courses in an inclusive manner by including gender equitable statements regarding concepts like diversity, inclusion, and representation into syllabi, course descriptions, objectives, policies, rules, and codes of ethics, while also expressing a commitment to equitable learning environments—connecting these concepts to public service values can help reinforce their relevance, application, and practicality for Master of Public Administration (MPA) students (Evans and Knepper 2021; Couillard and Higbee 2018). For example, "It is my intent that students from all diverse backgrounds and perspectives be well-served by this course, that students' learning needs be addressed both in and out of class, and that the diversity that the students bring to this class be viewed as a resource, strength and benefit," or "[This classroom] embraces a notion of intellectual community enriched and enhanced by diversity along a number of dimensions, including race, ethnicity and national origins, gender and gender identity, sexuality, class and religion. We are especially committed to increasing the representation of those populations that have been historically excluded from participation in U.S. higher education" (Sheridan Center n.d.).

Further, gender equitable pedagogy can be strengthened through a flexible curriculum design that gives different types of students multiple avenues for learning, interaction, expression, and assessment (Awang-Hashim et al. 2019; Guðjónsdóttir and Óskarsdóttir 2019). For example, instructors can encourage students to collaborate with them to personalize course materials and modify course descriptions and statements, which allows for more diverse perspectives and shifts traditional power dynamics to be more inclusive (Evans and Knepper 2021). Additionally, the course curriculum should incorporate multiple means for students to demonstrate their knowledge by giving them options, alternative forms of assessments—such as self-assessments, instructor/student co-assessment, and ungraded assignments—or the opportunity to request modifications or accommodations to an assessment, which provides better access and means to participate for all students, while also preventing underrepresentation (Couillard and Higbee 2018; Awang-Hashim et al. 2019; Cronin et al. 1999; Evans and Knepper 2021). Moreover, instructors can have students work on collaborative projects, which provide students the opportunity to solve problems together and interact with more diverse perspectives, while also utilizing peer grading to shift traditional power dynamics to be co-created and more inclusive (Awang-Hashim et al. 2019; Evans and Knepper 2021).

Moreover, instructors can use a "gender mainstreaming" approach to the development, design, and evaluation of all course policies and syllabi, with the goal of integrating gender perspectives to promote equality and combat discrimination. For instance, typical course topics in virtually any subject area can be examined through a gendered lens, like how gender impacts various forms of public policy, which gives MPA instructors a great deal of flexibility to integrate gender into a wide variety of topics, depending on scope of the course (Parra-Martínez et al. 2021; Evans and Knepper 2021; Wyatt-Nichol and Antwi-Boasiako 2008). Instructors should also consider setting classroom time for students to ponder and discuss gendered topics or materials during class—for example, increasing "wait time" after posing a question or explicitly requiring students to write out ideas that capture their thoughts (Tanner 2013). Further, by not only encouraging but requiring and actively guiding the participation of all students, instructors can work toward building a more open and diverse conversation (Tanner 2013; Center for the Integration of Teaching, Learning, and Scholarship n.d.). Furthermore, the inclusion of scholarship about women and those with diverse gender identity and expression should be integrated as fully as possible throughout the course and in different forms. For example, this includes integrating gender diversity in assignments, lectures, and class discussions, not just as a single add-on in the syllabus. One method is to make an intentional effort to include gender diverse (assuming gender is known) authors when compiling course material—all of which increases the odds that students will take issues pertaining to gender more seriously (Evans and Knepper 2021; Beaty and Davis 2012; Burnier 2005).

Gender Equitable Content

We offer four major recommendations for gender inclusive content. First, openly addressing and discussing assigned text shortcomings; second, utilizing course readings, materials, and assignments to expose students to different gendered perspectives and identities; third, adopting class materials that positively acknowledge differences in sexuality and gender; and finally, embracing interdisciplinary teaching. Before developing gender inclusive course materials, it is important to openly address and confront the shortcomings that many established texts have. Oftentimes textbooks, course curricula, and other teaching material can reinforce and perpetuate heteronormative worldviews, which can lead to damaging behaviors like bullying, substance abuse, and other destructive behaviors (Paiz 2019; Evans and Knepper 2021). Queer pedagogy, especially in language instruction, should be used to challenge the heteronormative assumptions that many textbooks make—which erase lesbian, gay, bisexual, transgender, queer, intersex, and asexual visibility—by addressing in class what these texts are omitting; including considerations of race, gender, and disability; discussing the social and grammatical meaning of gender in language; and helping students understand "individualities as part of our collectives" (Nemi Neto 2018). For example, instead of avoiding sexist monikers in older texts, use the text as an opportunity to engage in a dialogue about the concerning texts. As instructors carry the responsibility of acknowledging limitations and biases of course materials, they serve to help students interpret and examine the materials through a critical lens (Quaye and Harper 2007; Burke 2017; Guðjónsdóttir and Óskarsdóttir 2019). Having students develop a shared vocabulary around issues of gender, race, age, and cultural difference can also better prepare them for workplace diversity (Norris and Welch 2020).

It is important to consider the perspectives and scholarship of diverse groups being represented when developing course content (Garibay 2015). Course content denotes course readings, assignments, and other materials. One of the first steps in designing a course curriculum involves determining what content to teach, but more consideration should be given to using gender-based materials to examine *all* gendered experiences in the public sector, with an intentional effort to include more gender diverse authors—including gender-based leadership texts, which make strong contributions to an MPA core curriculum (Beaty and Davis 2012; Burnier 2005; Evans and Knepper 2021). Selecting materials that expose students to a variety of viewpoints from "historically marginalized groups," like women, people of color, and queer individuals, can help generate social equity in public administration and public policy (Wyatt-Nichol and Antwi-Boasiako 2008) and tackle the circular pattern of exclusion, where professors tend to select texts they once used as students, which reinforces the "exclusive public administration canon" (Evans and Knepper 2021). Furthermore, using materials that acknowledge gender and sexual differences in a positive manner can improve classroom learning environments by making students feel more empowered and comfortable to express themselves freely as a result of seeing themselves in the course materials—instead of relying solely on texts that reflect heteronormative perspectives, which can make students feel excluded (Nemi Neto 2018; Evans and Knepper 2021). Further, instructors can augment course materials and further increase equity in gender visibility by inviting guest speakers of a different gender and cultural background than themselves (Evans and Knepper 2021).

Inclusivity in pedagogy has many localized aspects. Some issues and challenges will be relevant for certain communities and not others (Awang-Hashim et al. 2019), including course materials that offer perspectives from self-identified nonbinary scholars to flesh out the multitude of viewpoints on a given topic (Abbott 2009; Garibay 2015). For instance, case studies or examples from the field can be used that include the LGBTQ+ communities (New York University n.d.). Moreover, including readings written by and about individuals of all gender identities and expressions—while being explicit about that person's pronouns—allows for students to refer to them correctly during discussions (Barnard Center for Engaged Pedagogy n.d.). Additionally, it is important to recognize and acknowledge the limitations of course readings, class materials, and assignments. Through examining limitations within course materials and issuing gender inclusive assignments, exercises, and engagement (i.e., guest speakers), students are prompted to critique and apply gender equity in course content. Finally, when including authors with nonbinary gender identities, instructors must be mindful to avoid homogenizing, exoticizing, or tokenizing nonbinary experiences (Harbin et al. 2020). Instructors can avoid this by being mindful of the cues and nonverbal messages they send, as students naturally look to their instructors as leaders of the classroom. Faculty and staff may benefit from seeking out development and training opportunities that allow them to become comfortable with managing situations related to gender and pronouns as they arise in the classroom (Danowitz and Tuitt 2011; Dockendorff 2019; Harbin et al. 2020).

Finally, when it comes to assignments, especially ones that include the gathering of data through primary qualitative and quantitative research, inclusive and ethical research practices should be taught to make sure that students are not excluding or miscategorizing gender and sexually diverse populations (Malatino and Stoltzfuz-Brown 2020). Language, instruction, and inclusive vocabulary help in this regard. Further, embracing interdisciplinarity teaching—that is, supplementing existing material with gender studies material—can serve to broaden students' understanding of diverse populations (Barnard Center for Engaged Pedagogy n.d.; Center for the Integration of Teaching, Learning, and Scholarship n.d.).

GENDER EQUITABLE PRACTICE

Facilitating and Moderating Discussions on LGBTQ Issues

Though many professors would like to have discussions around LGBTQ+ issues in public administration classrooms, one thing to consider is how to have these conversations in a way that provides an educational environment to students while also acknowledging that many of these topics and policies impact individuals in the classroom personally. It is important to make sure that the classroom is both a place of intellectual exploration and a safe space for LGBTQ+ individuals. Therefore, here are a few tips on moderating and facilitating discussions around LGBTQ+ issues.

Remember the individual impact of these policies and discussions for LGBTQ+ individuals. Help students understand the individual impact(s) of the policies or procedures that are being discussed and how they may impact LGBTQ+ individuals and communities.

- Never debate someone's humanity. LGBTQ+ people exist and have always existed.

- Do not have bad faith debates. If the laws are created to harm the LGBTQ+ population, acknowledge it.

- Look over questions beforehand to make sure that questions aren't inadvertently or purposefully insulting and questioning an individual's humanity. While it is fine to talk about how to create or craft a certain policy, professors and students should not be asking whether or not individual identities are valid.

- Do not expect individuals who you know are LGBTQ+ to add their personal experiences or to lead/be part of the conversation. They may not feel comfortable talking about their personal, lived experiences and may not be out to the whole class. Respect the privacy and the personal needs of individual students.

- Take questions in advance. This can help you weed out any questions that might be transphobic or harmful to students.

- Allow yourself, as a professor, to not know the answer to certain questions. Across the US, policies are changing constantly and it is hard to stay on top of everything.

This list is not exhaustive, but it can help you think critically while leading discussions on what is important for your classroom both educationally and emotionally. As a professor, having these conversations can be exhausting, and it is important to check in with yourself after these talks. Students may ask hard questions or talk about their own traumas. Allowing yourself, as a facilitator and a professor, to find time to center yourself can help.

The next section presents three classes where SOGIE discussions may come up naturally: human resource management, nonprofit management, and public policy. These are only three suggested classes; indeed, this could be a discussion in any policy class, both in how policies are created and how to implement policies supporting LGBTQ+ individuals and communities (Norman-Major and Becker 2013). A budgeting class can discuss how budgeting may impact different sexual orientations and gender identities differently (e.g., the bureaucratic costs of transitioning).

Providing the room to discuss SOGIE within the classroom allows students to see the ways that public administration impacts vulnerable communities and time to consider how public administration can be used to support equity and inclusion through bureaucratic means. In the following section, we will focus on the content and practice of running these courses through a SOGIE lens.

HUMAN RESOURCE MANAGEMENT

Content

One of the classes that naturally becomes a place to discuss SOGIE is human resource management (HRM). Making sure that policies and procedures within public and nonprofit organizations meet the needs of LGBTQ+ individuals is imperative for students of public administration. Furthermore, students in HRM should be knowledgeable of laws that impact LGBTQ+ employees. Indeed, there is a large corpus of public administration research that can help guide these discussions (e.g., Elias and Colvin 2020; Elias et al. 2018; McCandless and Elias 2021). Including these articles in course readings can help students better understand SOGIE from an HRM perspective.

When discussing SOGIE in the context of HRM, one thing to include is the way gender plays a role in policy. For example, maternity leave assumes that only the mother will take leave after a baby is born. With a growing number of fathers taking leave as well, and a growing number of male same-sex couples having children, using a nongendered policy of parental leave affords more flexibility. This also allows for a discussion in HRM of what policies are in place for the diverse ways families come together, making sure that policies that support adoptive parents may look different from the policies normally in place. Another HRM policy can include having nonbinary options on paperwork (Elias and Colvin 2020) or making it easier for transgender individuals to change their gender within the organization if they decide to transition. When considering healthcare plans, human resource professionals should think about how these plans may be either helpful or harmful to transgender employees. HRM policy is an important way to make sure that your organization is responsive to the growing LGBTQ+ employee population (Larson 2022).

Practice

Professors can start discussions on SOGIE by having students identify policies within nonprofit and government organizations. Allow students to start to dissect how these policies in HRM are gendered, such as maternity leave. When discussing gender, allow students to move beyond a male-female binary, as nonbinary identities are an important part of SOGIE HRM (Elias and Colvin 2020). Outcomes from these conversations can include having nongendered paperwork. Helping students understand how paperwork does not have to be gendered can be one way to build a more inclusive organization. Activities can include creating gender-neutral paperwork and policies. This critical eye can help students think about how to create LGBTQ+ inclusive HRM.

NONPROFIT MANAGEMENT

Content

There is a limited amount of research within the field of nonprofit studies on LGBTQ+ issues (Meyer et al. 2022). Within nonprofits, it is important to consider how LGBTQ+ individuals may interact with your organizations, such as homeless shelters, which tend to be a negative space for LGBTQ+ individuals (Dolamore and Naylor 2018; Trochmann and Millesen 2023). LGBTQ+ communities are vulnerable populations who are in need of culturally competent services (Meyer and Millesen 2022). Importantly, in nonprofit classes, discussions can focus on what it means to provide services to LGBTQ+ individuals and cultural differences that might exist between those in the LGBTQ+ communities and straight communities (Meyer and Millisen 2022).

Practice

Activities can include exploring local and national LGBTQ+ organizations to identify the types of services specifically offered. This will allow students to learn about the unique issues that impact local LGBTQ+ communities. They can also explore how local organizations that are not LGBTQ+ specific can support LGBTQ+ individuals. This creates a conversation about how all nonprofit organizations can make sure they are creating a welcoming environment for LGBTQ+ people.

PUBLIC POLICY

Content

In some states and countries, LGBTQ+ issues are at the center of state and local policy. Indeed, though LGBTQ+ rights have been pushed forward by the US Supreme Court, there are still many laws and rights at the state and local level that both help and hinder the LGBTQ+ community. From an international perspective, an understanding of how nonprofits influence pro- and anti-LGBTQ+ movements is an important part of policy (Velasco 2018).

Discussions around LGBTQ+ rights in public policy should be taken with great care. It is important to remember that we may have students in our class who are LGBTQ+ and therefore may be impacted by these policies, either directly (if it is a local policy) or indirectly. Some debates may, for some students, seem academic, but not for all students. Minority students, especially those who identify as a member of the LGBTQ+ community, may feel that their identity is being debated. The deeply personal nature of this topic means that professors need to be aware of the way students are responding to the discussion. Some students may not even be aware that some of what they say would be offensive. Professors need to help guide the conversation and make sure that students remember that policies impact individuals, including those in the classroom.

Practice

Activities for a policy class can include examining policies that impact LGBTQ+ individuals in your state or community. This can include looking at the various stakeholders, who is supporting (or not supporting) these initiatives, and who is impacted (and how). This 360-degree approach can help students comprehend the life of a policy, from proposal to implementation.

Conclusion and Next Steps

In this chapter, we have provided an introduction into how SOGIE can be included into public administration pedagogy. While LGBTQ+ individuals have experienced more acceptance internationally, there have also been laws being passed that have restricted the LGBTQ+ community and have done substantial harm. As both of the authors are from the United States, this chapter has taken an American perspective. Internationally, there is important work being done in the field of public administration and in related fields to provide support to the LGBTQ+ community, and making students aware of this work can help them understand the place of equity within public administration (Norman-Major 2011). These are only the first steps; as more research becomes available within the field of public administration, there will be more resources for professors to share with students. To help start the conversation, table 10.1 has a list of some articles professors may want to provide to students as readings on

Table 10.1. Readings on Sexual Orientation and Gender Identity and Expression

Author. Year.	Title	Journal	Keywords
Buz, A. M., and T. S. Gaynor. 2022.	"Intersectionality and Social Welfare: Avoidance and Unequal Treatment Among Transgender Women of Color"	*Public Administration Review*	Intersectionality; transgender; social welfare
Davidson, M. 2023.	"Winds of Change: How Street-Level Bureaucrats Actively Represent Minority Clients by Influencing Majority Clients; The Context of LGB Israeli Teachers"	*Public Administration*	Frontline workers; representative bureaucracy
Dolamore, S., and L. A. Naylor. 2018.	"Providing Solutions to LGBT Homeless Youth: Lessons from Baltimore's Youth Empowered Society"	*Public Integrity*	Nonprofit; service delivery; policy

continued on next page

Table 10.1. Continued.

Duam, C. W. 2019.	"Social Equity, Homonormativity, and Equality: An Intersectional Critique of the Administration of Marriage Equality and Opportunities for LGBTQ Social Justice"	*Administrative Theory and Praxis*	Homosexuality; policy
Elias, N. 2020.	"LGBTQ+ Civil Rights: Local Government Efforts in a Volatile Era"	*Public Administration Review*	Local government; LGBTQ+ policy
Elias, N., and R. Colvin. 2020.	"A Third Option: Understanding and Assessing Non-Binary Gender Policies in the United States"	*Administrative Theory and Praxis*	Nonbinary; policy
Elias, N. M., R. L. Johnson, D. Ovando, and J. Ramirez. .2018.	"Improving Transgender Policy for a More Equitable Workplace"	*Journal of Public Management and Social Policy*	Transgender; human resource management
McCandless, S., and N. M. Elias. 2021.	"Beyond Bostock: Implications for LGBTQ+ Theory and Practice"	*Administrative Theory and Praxis*	LGBTQ+; policy
Meyer, S. J. 2023.	"Social Equity and LGBTQ Populations in African Public Administration: A Macro- and Micro-Approach"	*Public Administration Review*	Social equity; front line workers

Meyer, S. J., and J. Benenson. 2023.	"Chai Pride: Using LGBTQIA+ Jewish Identities to Understand Intersectionality in Public Administration"	*Administration and Society*	Intersectionalities
Meyer, S. J., and N. M. Elias. 2022.	"Rainbow Research: Challenges and Recommendations for Sexual Orientation and Gender Identity and Expression (SOGIE) Survey Design"	*VOLUNTAS: International Journal of Voluntary and Nonprofit Organizations*	LGBTQ+; methods
Meyer, S., and J. Millesen. 2022.	"Queer Up Your Work: Adding Sexual Orientation and Gender Identity to Public and Nonprofit Research"	*Journal of Public and Nonprofit Affairs*	LGBTQ+; overview
Norman-Major, K., and C. Becker. 2013.	"Walking the Talk: Do Public Systems Have the Infrastructure Necessary to Implement and Enforce LGBT and Gender Identity Rights?"	*Journal of Public Management and Social Policy*	LGBTQ+; policy
Murib, Z. 2020.	"Administering Biology: How 'Bathroom Bills' Criminalize and Stigmatize Trans and Gender Nonconforming People in Public Space"	*Administrative Theory and Praxis*	Transgender; policy

continued on next page

Table 10.1. Continued.

Naylor, L. A. 2020.	"Counting an Invisible Class of Citizens: The LGBT Population and the US Census"	*Public Integrity*	LGBTQ+; policy
Trochmann, M. B., and J. Millesen. 2023.	"Transforming Power with Pose: Centering Love in State-Sponsored Services for LGBTQ Youth Experiencing Homelessness"	*Administrative Theory and Praxis*	Power; homelessness
Velasco, K. 2018.	"Human Rights INGOs, LGBT INGOs, and LGBT Policy Diffusion, 1991–2015"	*Social Forces*	LGBTQ+; policy; nonprofit; international

SOGIE from LGBTQ+ perspectives. This list is, of course, not exhaustive. Instead, it provides a starting point for professors to think about what readings to assign when discussing the LGBTQ+ community.

For the field of public administration, we hope that there will be more research on the LGBTQ+ community, as this community has been sorely underrepresented in the public administration literature (Larson 2022; Meyer et al. 2022). Furthermore, we encourage more research into how public administration can teach not only about SOGIE but also about other vulnerable populations within all aspects of public administration education (e.g., Guy and McCandless 2020). Through these discussions, we can create a workforce of public administrators who can push forward an agenda of equity, inclusion, and diversity and support all populations.

We hope this chapter creates a conversation on what it means to be LGBTQ+ in public administration and the ways that SOGIE impacts all of our students lives. As LGBTQ+ issues become more prominent in the social milieu, having a space for students to understand the impact of public administration on LGBTQ+ individuals and how bureaucracy can impact LGBTQ+ communities is a way to show students how equity can be achieved through public administration.

References

Abbott, Traci B. 2009. "Teaching Transgender Literature at a Business College." *Race, Gender & Class* 16 (1/2): 152–69.

Abrams, Laura S., and Jené A. Moio. 2009. "Critical Race Theory and the Cultural Competence Dilemma in Social Work Education." *Journal of Social Work Education* 45 (2): 245–61. https://doi.org/10.5175/jswe.2009.200700109.

Aguilar-Hernández, José M. 2020. "Queering Critical Race Pedagogy: Reflections of Disrupting Erasure While Centering Intersectionality." *International Journal of Qualitative Studies in Education* 33 (6): 679–94. https://doi.org/10.1080/09518398.2020.1747660.

Akarcay, L. Alp, and Justin Jacobs. 2021. "Gender- and Sexuality-Inclusive Curriculum in an Intensive Language Program." *SSRN Electronic Journal*. https://doi.org/10.2139/ssrn.3926086.

Arday, Jason, Diania Zoe Belluigi, and Dave Thomas. 2020. "Attempting to Break the Chain: Reimaging Inclusive Pedagogy and Decolonising the Curriculum Within the Academy." *Educational Philosophy and Theory* 53 (3): 298–313. https://doi.org/10.1080/00131857.2020.1773257.

Arendale, David R. 2018. "Introduction to Special Issue on Universal Design for Inclusive Pedagogy and a Future Research Agenda." *Education Sciences* 8 (4): 203. https://doi.org/10.3390/educsci8040203.

Awang-Hashim, Rosna, Amrita Kaur, and Nena P. Valdez. 2019. "Strategizing Inclusivity in Teaching Diverse Learners in Higher Education." *Malaysian Journal of Learning and Instruction* 16 (1): 105–28.

Balakrishnan, Sumitra, and Mallhar Mohapatra. 2022. "Exploring Experiences at Work Beyond the Binary: Identity, Inclusion and Allyship." *IUP Journal of Organizational Behavior* 21 (2).

Barnard Center for Engaged Pedagogy. n.d. "Gender Inclusivity in the Classroom. Barnard College." Accessed January 10, 2022. https://cep.barnard.edu/gender-inclusivity-classroom.

Beaty, LeAnn, and Trenton J. Davis. 2012. "Gender Disparity in Professional City Management: Making the Case for Enhancing Leadership Curriculum." *Journal of Public Affairs Education* 18 (4): 617–32.

Black-Hawkins, Kristine. 2017. "Understanding Inclusive Pedagogy." In *Inclusive Education: Making Sense of Everyday Practice*, edited by Vicky Plows and Ben Whitburn. SensePublishers. https://doi.org/10.1007/978-94-6300-866-2_2.

Blessett, Brandi, Jennifer Dodge, Beverley Edmond et al. 2019. "Social Equity in Public Administration: A Call to Action." *Perspectives on Public Management and Governance* 2 (4): 283–99. https://doi.org/10.1093/ppmgov/gvz016.

Burke, Penny Jane. 2017. "Difference in Higher Education Pedagogies: Gender, Emotion and Shame." *Gender and Education* 29 (4): 430–44. https://doi.org/10.1080/09540253.2017.1308471.

Burnier, DeLysa. 2005. "Public Leaders Are Gendered: Making Gender Visible in Public Affairs Leadership Education." *Journal of Public Affairs Education* 11 (3): 181–92.

Carr, Sadie Suzanne. 2020. *Reviving Rhetoric Through Conversation: Feminist Rhetorical Pedagogies for a Deliberative Democracy.* Master's thesis, University of South Carolina.

Center for the Integration of Teaching, Learning, and Scholarship. n.d. *Gender Inclusive Pedagogy CITLS.* Lafayette College. Accessed October 16, 2021. https://citls.lafayette.edu/gender-identity-in-the-classroom/.

Chetkovich, Carol. 2019. "How Non-Binary Gender Definitions Confound (Already Complex) Thinking About Gender and Public Policy." *Journal of Public Affairs Education* 25 (2): 226–52.

Cotán, Almudena, Arecia Aguirre, Beatriz Morgado, and Noelia Melero. 2021. "Methodological Strategies of Faculty Members: Moving Toward Inclusive Pedagogy in Higher Education." *Sustainability* 13 (6): 3031.

Couillard, Ellyn, and Jeanne Higbee. 2018. "Expanding the Scope of Universal Design: Implications for Gender Identity and Sexual Orientation." *Education Sciences* 8 (3): 147. https://doi.org/10.3390/educsci8030147.

Cronin, Catherine, Maureen Foster, and Elizabeth Lister. 1999. "SET for the Future: Working Towards Inclusive Science, Engineering and Technology Curricula in Higher Education." *Studies in Higher Education* 24 (2): 165–82. https://doi.org/10.1080/03075079912331379868.

Dalton, Elizabeth M., Marcia Lyner-Cleophas, Britt T. Ferguson, and Judith McKenzie. 2019. "Inclusion, Universal Design and Universal Design for Learning in Higher Education: South Africa and the United States." *African Journal of Disability* 8:1–7. https://doi.org/10.4102/ajod.v8i0.519.

Danowitz, Mary Ann, and Frank Tuitt. 2011. "Enacting Inclusivity Through Engaged Pedagogy: A Higher Education Perspective." *Equity & Excellence in Education* 44 (1): 40–56. https://doi.org/10.1080/10665684.2011.539474.

Daum, Courtenay W. 2020. "Social Equity, Homonormativity, and Equality: An Intersectional Critique of the Administration of Marriage Equality and Opportunities for LGBTQ Social Justice." *Administrative Theory & Praxis* 42 (2): 115–32.

Davidovitz, Maayan. 2023. "Winds of Change: How Street-Level Bureaucrats Actively Represent Minority Clients by Influencing Majority Clients: The Context of LGB Israeli Teachers." *Public Administration* 101 (4): 1587–1603. https://doi.org/10.1111/padm.12903.

Dewsbury, Bryan, and Cynthia J. Brame. 2019. "Inclusive Teaching." *CBE: Life Sciences Education* 18 (2): fe2. https://doi.org/10.1187/cbe.19-01-0021.

Dockendorff, Kari J. 2019. *Measuring and Predicting Trans Inclusivity in Higher Education: Understanding the Behavior of Key Institutional Agents.* PhD diss., University of Utah. ProQuest Dissertations Publishing.

Dolamore, Stephanie, and Lorenda A. Naylor. 2018. "Providing Solutions to LGBT Homeless Youth: Lessons from Baltimore's Youth Empowered Society." *Public Integrity* 20 (6): 595–610.

Elias, Nicole M. 2020. "LGBTQ+ Civil Rights: Local Government Efforts in a Volatile Era." *Public Administration Review* 80 (6): 1075–86. https://doi.org/10.1111/puar.13188.

Elias, Nicole M. 2022. "Beyond Binary Treatment of Gender in Public Administration and Policy." In *Handbook on Gender and Public Administration*, edited by Patricia M. Shields and Nicole M. Elias, 103–14. Edward Elgar Publishing.

Elias, Nicole M., and Maria J. D'Agostino. 2019. "Gender Competency in Public Administration Education." *Teaching Public Administration* 37 (2): 218–233. https://doi.org/10.1177/0144739419840766.

Elias, Nicole, Maria D'Agostino, V. Diez, and E. Krause. 2022. *Gender Equitable Pedagogy in Public Affairs Education: Understanding DEI Structure, Content, Practice.* Unpublished manuscript. John Jay Initiative for Equity in the Public Sector.

Elias, Nicole, and Roddrick Colvin. 2020. "A Third Option: Understanding and Assessing Non-Binary Gender Policies in the United States." *Administrative Theory & Praxis* 42 (2): 191–211.

Elias, Nicole M., Rana Lynn Johnson, Danny Ovando, and Julia Ramirez. 2018. "Improving Transgender Policy for a More Equitable Workplace." *Journal of Public Management & Social Policy* 24 (2): 53–81.

Evans, Michelle D., and Hillary J. Knepper. 2021. "Building Inclusive PA Classrooms: The Diversity Inclusion Model." *Teaching Public Administration* 39 (1): 84–106. https://doi.org/10.1177/0144739420937762.

Ferfolja, Tania, and Jacqueline Ullman. 2021. "Inclusive Pedagogies for Transgender and Gender Diverse Children: Parents' Perspectives on the Limits of Discourses of Bullying and Risk in Schools." *Pedagogy, Culture & Society* 29 (5): 793–810. Https://Doi.Org/10.1080/14681366.2021.1912158.

Florian, Lani. 2008. "Inclusion: Special Or Inclusive Education: Future Trends." *British Journal of Special Education* 35 (4): 202–8. https://doi.org/10.1111/j.1467-8578.2008.00402.x.

Florian, Lani, and Kristine Black-Hawkins. 2011. "Exploring Inclusive Pedagogy." *British Educational Research Journal* 37 (5): 813–28. https://doi.org/10.1080/01411926.2010.501096.

Forlin, Christine. 2014. *Teacher Education for Inclusion.* Routledge.

Freire, Paulo. 1970. *Pedagogy of the Oppressed.* Bloomsbury Academic.

Goldberg, Abbie E., Genny Beemyn, and JuliAnna Z. Smith. 2018. "What Is Needed, What Is Valued: Trans Students' Perspectives on Trans-Inclusive Policies and Practices in Higher Education." *Journal of Educational and Psychological Consultation* 29 (1): 27–67. https://doi.org/10.1080/10474412.2018.1480376.

Goldberg, Shoshana K., and Kerith J. Conron. 2018. "Demographic Characteristics of Lesbian, Gay, Bisexual, and Transgender Adults in the United States: Evidence from the 2015–2017 Gallup Daily Tracking Survey." In *The Routledge Handbook of LGBTQIA Administration and Policy*, edited by Wallace Swan, 17–50. Routledge.

Guðjónsdóttir, Hafdís, and Edda Óskarsdóttir. 2016. "Inclusive Education, Pedagogy and Practice." In *Science Education Towards Inclusion*, edited by Silvija Markic and Simone Abels, 7–22. Nova Science Publisher. https://www.academia.edu/download/51587355/inclusive_education__pedagogy_and_practice.pdf.

Guy, Mary E., and Sean A. McCandless, eds. 2020. *Achieving Social Equity: From Problems to Solutions*. Melvin & Leigh.

Harbin, Brielle, Leah Marion Roberts, Roberta Nelson, and Chris Purcell. 2020. "Teaching Beyond the Gender Binary in the University Classroom." Vanderbilt University Center for Teaching. https://cft.vanderbilt.edu/guides-sub-pages/teaching-beyond-the-gender-binary-in-the-university-classroom/.

Hayward, Lorna, Aysha Alawadhi, and Flavia Fretias. 2021. "Listening to Student Voices as a Step toward Strengthening Inclusive and Intercultural Teaching Approaches." *Teaching and Learning Together in Higher Education* 1 (32): 1–9.

Hernández, Ebelia. 2016. "Utilizing Critical Race Theory to Examine Race/Ethnicity, Racism, and Power in Student Development Theory and Research." *Journal of College Student Development* 57 (2): 168–80. https://doi.org/10.1353/csd.2016.0020.

Human Rights Campaign Foundation. n.d. "Workplace Trans Inclusion: Recommended Policies & Practices." HRC Foundation. Accessed January 10, 2022. https://www.thehrcfoundation.org/professional-resources/transgender-inclusion-in-the-workplace-recommended-policies-and-practices.

Jennings, Michael E., and Marvin Lynn. 2005. "The House That Race Built: Critical Pedagogy, African-American Education, and the Re-conceptualization of a Critical Race Pedagogy." *Educational Foundations* 19 (3–4): 15–32.

Larson, Samantha June. 2022. "Actions for Queering American Public Administration." *Administration & Society* 54 (1): 145–63.

Ledesma, Maria C., and Dolores Calderón. 2015. "Critical Race Theory in Education: A Review of Past Literature and a Look to the Future." *Qualitative Inquiry* 21 (3): 206–22. https://doi.org/10.1177/1077800414557825.

Lewis, William T. 2010. "Inclusive Excellence and the Role of Faculty." *Diverse Issues in Higher Education* 27 (5): 20.

Light, Tracy Penny, Jane Nicholas, and Renée Bondy, eds. 2015. *Feminist Pedagogy in Higher Education: Critical Theory and Practice*. Wilfrid Laurier University Press.

Livingston-Galloway, Marcia P., and Andree Robinson-Neal. 2021. "Re-Conceptualizing Inclusive Pedagogy in Practice in Higher Education." *Journal of the Scholarship of Teaching and Learning for Christians in Higher Education* 11 (1): 29–63. https://doi.org/10.31380/sotlched.11.1.29.

Lopez-Littleton, Vanessa, and Brandi Blessett. 2015. "A Framework for Integrating Cultural Competency into the Curriculum of Public Administration Programs." *Journal of Public Affairs Education* 21 (4): 557–74. https://doi.org/10.1080/15236803.2015.12002220.

Luke, Carmen. 1996. "Feminist Pedagogy Theory: Reflections on Power and Authority." *Educational Theory* 46 (3): 283–302. https://doi.org/10.1111/j.1741-5446.1996.00283.x.

Lynn, Marvin. 1999. "Toward a Critical Race Pedagogy." *Urban Education* 33 (5): 606–26. https://doi.org/10.1177/0042085999335004.

Malatino, Hil, and Lars Stoltzfuz-Brown. 2020. *Best Practices for Gender Inclusion in Research.* Pennsylvania State University. https://covidupdates.la.psu.edu/wp-content/uploads/sites/9/Gender-Inclusion-in-Research.pdf.

Mason, Dyana P., Lindsey McDougle, and Jennifer A. Jones. 2019. "Teaching Social Justice in Nonprofit Management Education: A Critical Pedagogy and Practical Strategies." *Administrative Theory & Praxis* 41 (4): 405–23. https://doi.org/10.1080/10841806.2019.1643615.

McCandless, Sean. 2018. "LGBT Homeless Youth and Policing." *Public Integrity* 20 (6): 558–70.

McCandless, Sean, and Nicole M. Elias. 2021. "Beyond Bostock: Implications for LGBTQ+ Theory and Practice." *Administrative Theory & Praxis* 43 (1): 1–15.

Meyer, Seth J. 2023. "Social Equity and LGBTQ Populations in African Public Administration: A Macro-and Micro-Approach." *Public Administration Review* 83 (1): 181–94. https://doi.org/10.1111/puar.13554.

Meyer, Seth J., and Jodi Benenson. 2023. "Chai Pride: Using LGBTQIA+ Jewish Identities to Understand Intersectionality in Public Administration." *Administration & Society* 55 (8): 1623–46. https://doi.org/10.1177/00953997231182998.

Meyer, Seth J., and Nicole M. Elias. 2023. "Rainbow Research: Challenges and Recommendations for Sexual Orientation and Gender Identity and Expression (SOGIE) Survey Design." *VOLUNTAS: International Journal of Voluntary and Nonprofit Organizations* 34 (1): 84–90.

Meyer, Seth J., Elizabeth J. Dale, and Kareem K. M. Willis. 2022 "'Where My Gays At?' The Status of LGBTQ People and Queer Theory in Nonprofit Research." *Nonprofit & Voluntary Sector Quarterly* 51 (3): 566–86.

Meyer, Seth, and Judith L. Millison. 2022. "Queer Up Your Work: Adding Sexual Orientation and Gender Identity to Public and Nonprofit Research." *Journal of Public and Nonprofit Affairs* 8 (1): 145–56.

Morgan, Hannah, and Ann-Marie Houghton. 2011. *Inclusive Curriculum Design in Higher Education: Considerations for Effective Practice Across and Within Subject Areas.* Higher Education Academy. http://s3.eu-west-2.amazonaws.

com/assets.creode.advancehe-document-manager/documents/hea/private/resources/introduction_and_overview_1568037036.pdf.

Moriña, Anabel. 2020. "Faculty Members Who Engage in Inclusive Pedagogy: Methodological and Affective Strategies for Teaching." *Teaching in Higher Education* 27 (3): 371–86. https://doi.org/10.1080/13562517.2020.1724938.

Moriña, Anabel, M. Dolores Cortés-Vega, and Victor M. Molina. 2015. "Faculty Training: An Unavoidable Requirement for Approaching More Inclusive University Classrooms." *Teaching in Higher Education* 20 (8): 795–806. https://doi.org/10.1080/13562517.2015.1085855.

Murib, Zein. 2020. "Administering Biology: How 'Bathroom Bills' Criminalize and Stigmatize Trans and Gender Nonconforming People in Public Space." *Administrative Theory & Praxis* 42 (2): 153–71. https://doi.org/10.1080/10841806.2019.1659048.

Naylor, Lorenda A. 2020. "Counting an Invisible Class of Citizens: The LGBT Population and the US Census." *Public Integrity* 22 (1): 54–72.

Nelsen, Matthew D. 2021. "Cultivating Youth Engagement: Race & the Behavioral Effects of Critical Pedagogy." *Political Behavior* 43 (2): 751–84. https://doi.org/10.1007/s11109-019-09573-6.

Nemi Neto, João. 2018. "Queer Pedagogy: Approaches to Inclusive Teaching." *Policy Futures in Education* 16 (5): 589–604. https://doi.org/10.1177/1478210317751273.

New York University. n.d. "Trans Inclusive Practices in the Classroom." Accessed January 10, 2022. https://www.nyu.edu/life/global-inclusion-and-diversity/learning-and-development/toolkits/trans-inclusive-classrooms.html.

Nisar, Muhammad A. 2018. "Children of a Lesser God: Administrative Burden and Social Equity in Citizen-State Interactions." *Journal of Public Administration Research and Theory* 28 (1): 104–19.

Norman-Major, Kristen. 2011. "Balancing the Four Es: Or Can We Achieve Equity for Social Equity in Public Administration?" *Journal of Public Affairs Education* 17 (2): 233–52.

Norman-Major, Kristen, and Carol Becker. 2013. "Walking the Talk: Do Public Systems Have the Infrastructure Necessary to Implement and Enforce LGBT and Gender Identity Rights?" *Journal of Public Management & Social Policy* 19 (1): 31.

Norris, Marcos, and Andrew Welch. 2020. "Gender Pronoun Use in the University Classroom: A Post-Humanist Perspective." *Transformation in Higher Education* 5:a79. https://doi.org/10.4102/the.v5i0.79.

Opertti, Renato, and Jayne Brady. 2011. "Developing Inclusive Teachers From an Inclusive Curricular Perspective." *Prospects* 41 (3): 459–72. https://doi.org/10.1007/s11125-011-9205-7.

Paiz, Joshua M. 2019. "Queering Practice: LGBTQ+ Diversity and Inclusion in English Language Teaching." *Journal of Language, Identity & Education* 18 (4): 266–75. https://doi.org/10.1080/15348458.2019.1629933.

Parra-Martínez, José, Maria-Elia Gutiérrez-Mozo, and Ana Gilsanz-Díaz. 2021. "Inclusive Higher Education and the Built Environment: A Research and Teaching Agenda for Gender Mainstreaming in Architecture Studies." *Sustainability* 13 (5): 2565. https://doi.org/10.3390/su13052565.

Pennell, Summer Melody. 2020. "Queer Theory/Pedagogy and Social Justice Education." In *Handbook on Promoting Social Justice in Education*, edited by Rosemary Papa, 2291–2311. Springer. https://doi.org/10.1007/978-3-030-14625-2_103.

Portillo, Shannon, Domonic Bearfield, and Nicole Humphrey. 2020. "The Myth of Bureaucratic Neutrality: Institutionalized Inequity in Local Government Hiring." *Review of Public Personnel Administration* 40 (3): 516–31.

Profeta, Paola. 2020. "Gender Equality and Public Policy During COVID-19." *CESifo Economic Studies* 66 (4): 365–75.

Quaye, Stephen John, and Shaun R. Harper. 2007. "Faculty Accountability for Culturally Inclusive Pedagogy and Curricula." *Liberal Education* 93 (3): 32–39. http://files.eric.ed.gov/fulltext/EJ775570.pdf,

Race, Richard, and Vini Lander, eds. 2014. *Advancing Race and Ethnicity in Education*. Palgrave Macmillan. https://doi.org/10.1057/9781137274762.

Ramey, Jessie B. 2017. *Gender Equity in the Classroom and Beyond: 12 Evidence Based Teaching Strategies to Create a Productive and Inclusive Classroom Climate*. Women's Institute at Chatham University. https://my.chatham. edu/documents/documentcenter/12%20Evidence%20Based%20Teaching%20 Strategies%20to%20Create%20Productive%20and%20Inclusive%20Classroom%20Climate%20.pdf.

Rice, Mitchell F. 2007. "Promoting Cultural Competency in Public Administration and Public Service Delivery: Utilizing Self-Assessment Tools and Performance Measures." *Journal of Public Affairs Education* 13 (1): 41–57.

Sanger, Catherine Shea, and Nancy W. Gleason, eds. 2020. *Diversity and Inclusion in Global Higher Education: Lessons from Across Asia*. Palgrave Macmillan. https://doi.org/10.1007/978-981-15-1628-3.

Sauntson, Helen. 2018. "Language, Sexuality and Inclusive Pedagogy." *International Journal of Applied Linguistics* 29 (3): 322–40. https://doi.org/10.1111/ ijal.12239.

Sheridan Center. n.d. *Diversity and Inclusion Syllabus Statements*. https://sheridan.brown.edu/resources/inclusive-anti-racist-teaching/inclusive-teaching/ diversity-and-inclusion-syllabus

Sleeter, Christine E. 2011. "An Agenda to Strengthen Culturally Responsive Pedagogy." *English Teaching: Practice and Critique* 10 (2): 7–23.

Spratt, Jennifer, and Lani Florian. 2015. "Inclusive Pedagogy: From Learning to Action; Supporting Each Individual in the Context of 'Everybody.'" *Teaching and Teacher Education* 49:89–96. https://doi.org/10.1016/j.tate.2015.03.006.

Staley, Sara, and Bethy Leonardi. 2019. "Complicating What We Know: Focusing on Educators' Processes of Becoming Gender and Sexual Diversity

Inclusive." *Theory Into Practice* 58 (1): 29–38. https://doi.org/10.1080/0040 5841.2018.1536916.

Swan, Wallace, ed. 2019. *The Routledge Handbook of LGBTQIA Administration and Policy*. Routledge.

Tanner, Kimberly D. 2013. "Structure Matters: Twenty-One Teaching Strategies to Promote Student Engagement and Cultivate Classroom Equity." *CBE: Life Sciences Education* 12 (3), 322–31. https://doi.org/10.1187/cbe.13-06-0115.

Trochmann, Maren B., and Judith L. Millesen. 2022. "Transforming Power with *Pose*: Centering Love in State-Sponsored Services for LGBTQ Youth Experiencing Homelessness." *Administrative Theory & Praxis* 44 (3); 205–23. https://doi.org/10.1080/10841806.2021.1945375.

Velasco, Kristopher. 2018. "Human Rights INGOs, LGBT INGOs, and LGBT Policy Diffusion, 1991–2015." *Social Forces* 97 (1): 377–404.

Waitoller, Federuci R., and Kathleen A. King Thorius. 2016. "Cross-Pollinating Culturally Sustaining Pedagogy and Universal Design for Learning: Toward an Inclusive Pedagogy That Accounts for Dis/Ability." *Harvard Educational Review* 86 (3): 366–89. https://doi.org/10.17763/1943-5045-86.3.366.

Webb, Lynne M., Myria W. Allen, and Kandi L. Walker. 2002. "Feminist Pedagogy: Identifying Basic Principles." *Academic Exchange Quarterly* 6:67–72.

Weiler, Kathleen. 1991. "Freire and a Feminist Pedagogy of Difference." *Harvard Educational Review* 61 (4): 449–74. https://doi.org/10.17763/haer.61.4.a1022 65jl68rju84.

Wyatt-Nichol, Heather, and Kwame Badu Antwi-Boasiako. 2008. "Diversity Across the Curriculum: Perceptions and Practices." *Journal of Public Affairs Education* 14 (1): 79–90. https://doi.org/10.1080/15236803.2008.12001511.

Zajda, Joseph, and Kassie Freeman, eds. 2009. *Race, Ethnicity and Gender in Education Cross-Cultural Understandings*. Springer. https://doi.org/10.1007/978-1-4020-9739-3.

Chapter 11

Using LGBTQ Politics and Policy to Teach Quantitative Methods

Andrew R. Flores

I was sitting in a coffee shop waiting to meet a fifth-year graduate student who was finishing their doctorate at the University of California at Riverside's political science program. I was admitted to the program, and recruiters thought a chat with someone who did LGBTQ political research would further inspire me to accept the offer. We had a great discussion, and I mentioned how I wanted to further examine research methods—particularly quantitative methods, intersectionality, and queer theory as applied to LGBTQ politics and policy in the United States. He quickly and without hesitation responded, "There's no room in queer theory for quantitative methods." While I had (and have) thoughts on the matter, that interaction implied that I would be a pariah among scholars studying marginalized groups by relying on the "master's tools" (Lorde 2018), and I would be a pariah in political science for doing "me-search" as opposed to research (see Ackelsberg 2017; Ayoub 2022; Novkov and Barclay 2010).

As it turns out, the field of LGBTQ political science is amazingly diverse in methodology, pedagogy, and inquiry such that studying LGBTQ people provides ample fruit for the understanding of power, institutions, public policy, prejudice, and identity (Smith 2011; Tadlock and Taylor 2017; Valelly 2012). As a collection of scholars, we have bridged divides that have harmed the broader discipline for decades (McGovern 2010;

Wilson 2017). Indeed, I fondly recall the father (or daddy) of contemporary LGBTQ political science, Ken Sherrill, amused by the political scientists of LGBTQ politics who collectively overcame these divides, remarking, "We're better." Now, I am a faculty member at a research institution, and I was "voluntold" that I would be teaching the quantitative methods course for the master's in political science program. I took this as an opportunity to among other things show what the LGBTQ case can teach about the promises, limitations, and enduring challenges in quantitative political research.

In the following, I will describe how LGBTQ people, politics, and policy can be effective cases to understand the (mis)application of quantitative methods. I will first describe quantitative data as the product of a data-generating process. Then I will describe the positivist framework in testing falsifiable hypotheses and post-positivist perspectives. A dominant view from positivists is that quantitative data are objective and fixed; whereas post-positivists view data as subjective—interpretations of measures, analyses, and results may be contingent on the researcher—and as highly contingent on time, context, and other social locations. I will then describe how sexual orientation and gender identity provide opportunities to elucidate positivist and post-positivist frameworks in both descriptive and causal inference by relying on examples that I use in the classroom. I then turn to a broader discussion of the social science research endeavor and the pursuit of "truth." Finally, I discuss the student response to the inclusion of sexual- and gender-diverse topics in the classroom.

Quantitative Social Science and the Data-Generating Process

A common framework to think about both qualitative and quantitative data is to carefully consider the *data-generating process*. That is, there is a real though often unobservable set of events (e.g., random variables and the way they are distributed) that result in the observable data points in a dataset. The great thing about this framework is that it is inherently dynamic and fluid—there are interactions among variables that lead to the resultant data. The challenge is that the data-generating process is unknown, which is why social scientists rely on theories that explain some of the variation in their data.

Let me provide an example. In 2012, four states had public votes on marriages for same-sex couples: Maine, Maryland, Minnesota, and

Washington. Three of them granted legal marriage recognition for same-sex couples, while Minnesota had a referendum on banning legal recognition. At the time, the campaigns were the most expensive initiative campaigns (Flores 2019). As can be imagined, voting on marriage rights and the campaigns both for and against those rights can be quite jarring for LGBT people. Prior studies relying on both quantitative and qualitative methods have shown that public referendums can be a source of negative responses such as stress and positive responses such as community efficacy and resiliency (Maisel and Fingerhut 2011; Rostosky et al. 2010; Russell and Richards 2003). However, these prior studies were either retrospective or within a single state that voted on marriage rights. Retrospective studies ask people to associate an event with particular outcomes, but people can be pretty bad at causality! (Did your sports team lose because you forgot to wear your lucky socks?) Only examining a single state also means that all people were in the same campaign environment, and it's hard to show causal relationships if the key causal variables (e.g., the campaigns) do not vary. (If you set an alarm to wake you up at six every morning and you sleep in on some days but not others, then it is highly unlikely that it is the alarm that is causing you to sleep in.) These studies are incredibly informative; while all studies have their limitations, it does require a broader set of assumptions to consider these campaigns as causing these outcomes. But these studies imply a connection between campaigns and the psychological well-being of LGBT people.

Is there a way to possibly think about the data-generating process to help infer that marriage campaigns have some causal association with positive and negative outcomes for LGBT people? That is what I and my co-authors did. First, we relied on a social science theory of the data-generating process. Stigma theory suggests that there are people who have characteristics that are socially less desirable or accepted such that society and government can take actions that harm the stigmatized. At the interpersonal level, this is often expressed as prejudice. Laws, policies, and political campaigns offer opportunities for structural stigma to be expressed. Given this theory and prior studies, we anticipated that the campaigns should be stress-inducing to LGBT people and that there were likely both negative effects from anti-marriage campaigns and positive effects from pro-marriage campaigns. Luckily, we had survey data from the Gallup Organization that interviewed about one thousand people nearly every day throughout the 2012 campaign cycle in a way that is representative of American adults. The survey included an opportunity for interviewees to state that they were members of the LGBT community and also measured stress and emotional well-being. We suspected that part of the data-generating process would be tied to marriage equality campaigns. We acquired a separate dataset that told us which and how often political ads regarding marriage equality were aired in various media markets. What is interesting is that media markets frequently cross state boundaries. Thus, we had a sample of LGBT and non-LGBT people, measures of stress and well-being, and knowledge of how flooded media markets were from either side of the campaign. By analyzing only those who lived in market spillovers (i.e., neighboring states), we eliminated other aspects of the campaign (e.g., canvassers and mailed leaflets). We found that daily levels of stress were higher for LGBT people in more intense campaign environments, that ads favorable to marriage equality were associated with positive emotions, and ads opposed to marriage equality were associated with negative emotions. Those who were not LGBT were not affected by their ad environment. By carefully thinking about theory and the data-generating process, we were able to isolate some relationship between political campaigns on minority rights and their psychological effects on those minorities (Flores et al. 2018).

The previous example also provides insight into how a theory of the data-generating process creates an empirical expectation. This expectation or hypothesis is what we should observe from an analysis of data if a theory is correct. This approach is called a positivist approach to social science research. A theory is developed that leads to a hypothesis that can turn out to be false by analyzing a set of data. We relied on stigma theory and the concept of structural stigma to lead us to the expectation that campaigns can elicit psychological responses among LGBT people.

I will note here that not all scholars agree with the positivist perspective, and there is a post-positivist critique. This is for a few reasons. First, data are seldom value-neutral—what is measured and how it is measured can reflect and reinforce existing societal hierarchies. This means that part of the data-generating process bakes in power and privilege. Second, traditional positivist approaches tend to consider that there is a single, objective "truth" that can be learned from testing empirical expectations from theories and systematic analyses of data. However, any analysis of data requires interpretation, which can be subjective. Many decisions get made when gathering and analyzing data that can be made subjectively. Finally, post-positivists do not fully agree with the idea that there is a singular, objective truth. All science is context-dependent, fluid, and changing such that what is found in one study may strongly deviate from other studies in other contexts. That scientists need to interpret their results means that there could be many subjective realities as opposed to a singular truth.

While these critiques have merit, it further underscores the continued need to conduct rigorous social science research to learn about the world around us. By establishing one fact, we can learn consistency and change, even if current knowledge deviates from the desired narrative of activists. Take public opinion on marriage equality as an example. At one point in time, my integrity was questioned by marriage equality activists because I reported findings that suggested that a certain locality did not have a majority in favor of marriage equality (Flores and Barclay 2013). Such political blowback distinguished in my mind what I do as a social science researcher and what others do as activists. I subsequently published a report documenting statewide opinion change from 1992 to 2016 (Flores and Barclay 2015). At that time, a conservative politician claimed that residents of their state have not changed their minds on marriage equality—something our findings refuted. Thus, post-positivists have something right about how fixed truth is, and political actors can, possibly for their immediate benefit but at the cost of their long-term strategy, reject empirics for their preferred version of reality.

So how does LGBTQ political science facilitate learning quantitative methods? Here, I'll elaborate on two key aspects of inference: descriptive and causal.

Descriptive Inference and Measurement

Speaking of context-dependent research, consider how sexuality and gender can be measured. A primary element of social science research is to describe the world around us. Descriptive inferences bring understanding to populations and can provide rich details and patterns that subsequent scholarship may seek to explain. Yet governments and scholars tend to overlook or not measure sexuality or gender identity/expression. Even when they do, their approach may meet critiques from others (Westbrook and Saperstein 2015).

I will use sex, gender, gender identity, and gender expression as a guiding example of descriptive inference and measurement. Traditional definitions of *sex* tend to be about how a person's sex characteristics or chromosomes fit within male, female, or, at times even if rarely, intersex.

Gender refers to a social understanding of a person as a man, woman, transgender, or nonbinary person. *Gender identity* is how a person self-describes their gender, which may not be the same as the sex they were assigned at birth (i.e., transgender or nonbinary) or is the same (i.e., cisgender). *Gender expression* is an outward way a person behaves or is perceived by others, which may mean that some people may be perceived as transgender even if they are not transgender.

According to a recent consensus study by the National Academies of Sciences, Engineering, and Medicine, the measurement of sex and gender needs to carefully consider what is conceptually desired to be measured and how questions operationalize such concepts (Bates et al. 2022). Often, but not always, research has recommended that measuring the population of people who are transgender is best done by relying on a "two-step" approach. The first step is to ask about a person's assigned sex at birth (e.g., male, female, or intersex). The second step is to ask about a person's current gender identity (e.g., man, woman, transgender, nonbinary, or something else). An alternative approach is to ask people if they identify as transgender (Herman et al. 2022). Either approach tends to result in about 0.3 to 0.7 adults being classified as transgender (Flores et al. 2021; Gates 2011; Herman et al. 2022).

However, not all surveys follow these recommended practices. For political science, the Cooperative Election Survey (CES), one of the largest surveys conducted by adults in the United States about politics, has measured transgender and diverse people in a way that does not follow best practices. The CES asked, "Have you ever undergone any part of a process (including any thought or action) to change your gender or perceived gender from the one you were assigned at birth? This may include steps such as changing the type of clothes you wear, name you are known by or undergoing surgery." This question might encompass a broader conceptualization of transgender people and thus possibly result in a higher proportion of people answering "yes." Indeed, about 1.5 percent of the sample answered this question affirmatively, which doubles the size of transgender adults in the United States. Surely, change the question and the observed data also changes. But what's going on here? Are there suddenly more transgender people? Is it accurate to say that people who responded to this question affirmatively are "transgender"?

I and my co-authors ultimately decided that the best term to describe the people who say "yes" to this question was "transgender and gender diverse" (TGD), meaning that our population under study is different from those who may be classified as transgender under the two-step or self-identification measurement approaches. We learned that the demographic characteristics of people who may be TGD in the CES looked quite similar to the characteristics of transgender people based on the two-step measure (Strode and Flores 2021; Strode et al. 2024).

Importantly, we learned that TGD people in the CES sample were six times more likely than cisgender people to have a problem with their voter registration or identity document (ID) when they attempted to vote. This finding is alarming because it does suggest a systematic violation of voting rights. In the process of publishing these findings, we were fundamentally asked about descriptive inference: Who are the people who say "yes" to this question, and what happens if there is a measurement error? That is, what if some cisgender people are miscategorized as TGD?

How might the data-generating process influence the outcomes we observed? Consider the possibility of a confounding variable that is related to people being more likely to say "yes" to the TGD measure and also encountering problems when attempting to vote. One plausible characteristic could be how familiar people are with political matters. Those with more political knowledge may be more keenly aware of what the TGD question is asking and provide more accurate answers, and they may also be more aware of voting regulations and be less likely to have problems when casting their ballot. If that is the case, then some if not all of the relationships we observe are due to mismeasurement of TGD status.

We decided to take three additional steps to consider this possibility. First, we collected new data from two hundred cisgender and two hundred transgender people, and we asked them the two-step question, the CES question, and an open-ended write-in question about their gender. We found that 93 percent of cisgender people based on the two-step would be cisgender in the CES measure and 6 percent would not. We also found that 96 percent of transgender people based on the two-step would be transgender in the CES measure and 4.5 percent would not. That is a strong relationship and suggests very little measurement error. Second, we relied on statistical simulations that randomly placed some TGD people in the not TGD category and reran our analyses, and we varied what proportion of TGD people would be recategorized. This process allows us to see whether our findings changed if the misclassification was large. Our findings were pretty stable even if we simulated that about 85 percent of TGD people accidentally said they were TGD. Third, we created a variable for political knowledge and assessed the relationship between

TGD status and problems with voting, taking that into account, and our findings remained unchanged.

I elaborate on this example for multiple reasons. It shows the importance of documenting gender identity in survey data to learn about the unique experiences of marginalized people. It appreciates the fluidity of identities and how identities are measured to affect what we infer about groups. And it shows that even with skepticism and fluidity in mind, we can be confident in the conclusions we draw from these data.

Causal Inference and Counterfactuals

I might have cheated a little in that last example because I explained a little bit about how TGD people had more problems while trying to vote. That implies a possible causal relationship: Had a person not been TGD, then they might not have had problems when attempting to vote. That notion of "had conditions been different" is what is known as a *counterfactual*. What is observed in our day-to-day lives are facts; they are occurrences that happened. We can imagine what the world would look like had an occurrence not happened (e.g., What if my alarm did not go off this morning?), but we can never observe it. This is what is known as the *fundamental problem of causal inference*—we can only observe what happened (the factual) not what did not happen (the counterfactual).

How then can causal effects be observed? One way is known as experimentation. Collect data on a bunch of people and randomly assign some of them to get treatment and others to get control. The virtue of random assignment is that people cannot self-select their preferences. This means that any background characteristics and differences among a set of individuals do not matter to their assignment. After people receive their treatment or not, then we can compare the average differences between the groups. Those differences are attributable to the only difference, on average, between these two groups—that is what the treatment intervention did.

What is the relevance of this for LGBTQ people and LGBTQ politics? There are several examples. For example, Broockman and Kalla (2016) performed a field experiment—an experiment that happens in the real world as opposed to in a laboratory—where canvassers knocked on people's doors in a city in Florida. The canvassers either engaged in a conversation about transgender people and transgender rights or something else (i.e., the control condition). Before these conversations, members of these households were recruited to take part in a series of surveys that contained numerous political questions. Unbeknownst to the people who answered their doors was that their opinions on these surveys would provide the data needed to see if attitudes changed as a result of these conversations and if attitudes remained changed over a longer period. Broockman and Kalla (2016) learned that transphobic attitudes were reduced and that change persisted for months. This is an incredibly helpful study to identify strategies for reaching people and giving them a perspective that can reposition their own opinions (see also Kalla and Broockman 2023). Another interesting experiment tested whether presenting gay people in a socially respectable way increased support for gay rights compared to a less respectable way (Jones 2022). Many social movements have had to grapple with how to make their appeals for social justice to the broader society, and it is generally assumed that doing so requires that advocates make their appeals relying on dominant norms, values, and presentation. Jones (2022) found that such respectable appeals did not differ much from other appeals, so perhaps prioritizing respectability is not doing much in persuading the general public.

Experiments can also help understand within-group politics. For example, some commentators on the recent rise in anti-transgender legislation have expressed a concern that focusing on a vulnerable subgroup within the LGBTQ community might create greater intracommunity disagreements. That is, some LGBTQ people might think the focus on transgender rights is hurting the overall movement. However, some theories suggest that when groups face threats they can close ranks and become more supportive of the group, including its most vulnerable members. I and my co-investigators experimented on about 1,200 LGBTQ people, and we randomly assigned them to read an article that said the religious conservative movement was making fundraising gains by focusing on antigay rights or anti-transgender rights or being in a control group. We wondered if emphasizing the transgender component might change what people thought should be a priority of the LGBTQ movement.

We learned that by emphasizing transgender rights LGBTQ respondents increased their prioritization of ensuring transgender youth have access to medically necessary care (i.e., transition-related medical care). This suggests that as opposed to sowing divisions among LGBTQ people, the recent uptick in anti-transgender legislation might be motivating LGBTQ people more generally to shore up the importance of transgender rights. As has been common in the history of LGBTQ activism, real threats to the rights of LGBTQ people tend to bring this incredibly diverse group together. We have even greater support for this inference because LGBTQ people who felt they were less connected to the LGBTQ community were the ones who were *more affected* by the emphasis on anti-transgender politics (see figure 11.1). This is because those that are connected to the LGBTQ community were already more likely to say transgender rights were a top priority, while those less connected tended to rank trans-gender rights lower. It is among this latter group where threats seem to shift priorities. So much can be learned from a single well-designed experiment!

I elaborate on these examples because they are ways I introduce central concepts in quantitative methods to my students. LGBTQ people and politics provide an excellent pedagogical tool to explain the complexities of descriptive and causal inference.

Figure 11.1. Difference between the treatment group and control group on the priority of protecting transgender youth's access to medically necessary care by community connectedness. Positive values indicate a higher priority; zero indicates no difference from the control group; 95 percent confidence intervals are represented by dashed lines. *Source*: Created by the author.

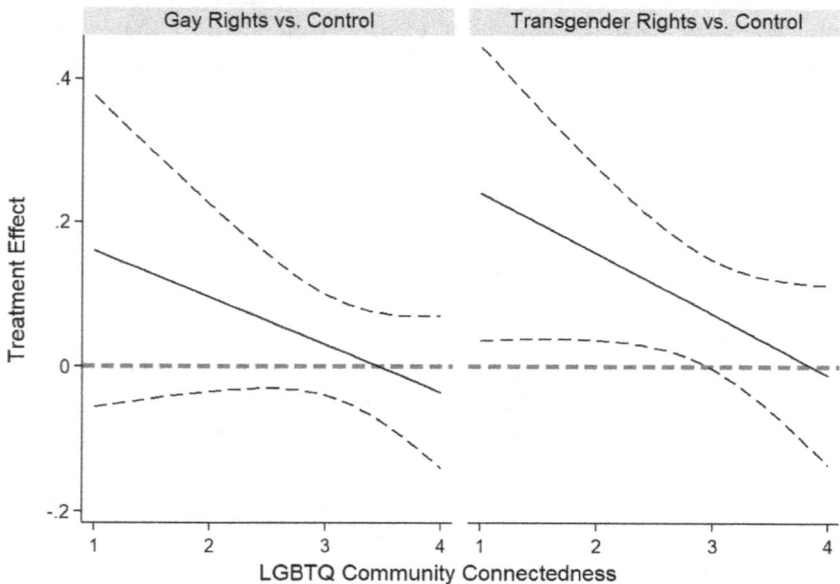

Knowledge as "Fixed" Versus Knowledge as Fluid

Some perspectives of the scientific endeavor are to observe and find truth. That is, there is an objective, knowable, and observable fixed value parameter, and statistics facilitate inferring what that parameter is. This concept, while helpful in differentiating "sample statistics" from "population parameters" (or $\hat{\beta}$ from β), might also make it seem like there are fixed truths. However, a central lesson in statistics is that population parameters are never observable and that all scientists have are sample statistics, which are *estimates* with *uncertainty*. That uncertainty is what is fun for me! It implies less of a singular truth but more of a variety of possible truths. It is this fluidity that I think can offer a queerer lens through which statistics could be understood. Further, some statistical perspectives inherently incorporate this fluidity by considering someone's prior expectations, what they observe or experience, and then how that observation or experience updates their prior expectation with new knowledge. In that sense, truth is not fixed but a constant process of updating based on experience. That is the sort of journey I think many, if not all, people are engaging in.

Another way to consider this is the fluidity of the language around LGBTQ identities and what that means for learning about LGBTQ people. Prior to Stonewall, activists tended to prefer the term "homophile" to describe themselves because "homosexual" was too medicalized and emphasized sex. Following Stonewall, "gay" was a broadly used term and "lesbian" also emerged. What might be learned from studies is quite contingent on language. As language changes, how concepts are measured must also change. Additionally, prior thoughts regarding LGBTQ people might also change. For instance, millennials and older generations who identify as LGBTQ tend to more often use monosexual labels (i.e., gay or lesbian) than Generation Z and younger generations. Among the younger generations, bisexual and pansexual among many other categories are more prominent. How might that change both how data are collected and what is learned? This is exciting!

Note that this change of labels is not isolated to LGBTQ people. This fluidity can be found in categories that some people once thought were fixed. For example, race and whiteness. Throughout American history, who is white and nonwhite has changed significantly. Even today, some Latinos, even if they are great-grandchildren of immigrants, consider themselves white. These changes also reflect how the construction of identities and categories are fundamentally political (Omi and Winant 2014).

Fluidity means that the scientific endeavor needs to keep going.

The Student Response

Of course, centering marginalized populations in courses not about those groups often entails the occasional criticism that the class focused "too much" on LGBTQ people. The overall response, however, is a need for more. Students want to sit with the notion of queerness in research even when I must move the conversation forward. It sparks curiosity. It makes them think carefully about assumptions, concepts, and frameworks, and they benefit from a critical and analytical perspective when consuming and designing research.

For example, I often assign Joanna Wuest's research on the scientific gaze and challenges produced with the "born this way" argument for rights claims (Wuest 2023). Alongside that, I assign policy reports about the characteristics of individuals who identify as transgender (Herman et al. 2022). I subsequently ask whether I engaged in the scientific gaze with these population estimates. Students ultimately respond, "Well, the numbers *can* change." While that response might be influenced by the fact that I am in the room, students clearly see the benefit of LGBTQ population data while also resisting the notion that these numbers are fixed.

Since queerness cuts across cultures, it is also a tractable topic for both domestic and international students. Because of the diversity of scholarship and methods contained within LGBTQ politics and policy, I can also introduce other studies that approach a similar question by relying on a completely different method. This way, students can appreciate whether and when quantitative methods may be a useful approach and when qualitative methods may also be useful if not better.

Conclusion

LGBTQ political science has value in it. It further carries benefits to the broader discipline and to students learning the traditions and methods of political science as a field of inquiry. In this chapter, I have outlined some examples of how quantitative methods can benefit by appreciating the complexity of sexuality and gender. Majorities of students, particularly sexual- and gender-diverse students, want these topics in the classroom. They want a faculty member who can speak to the complexity of numbers and the data-generating process. The moment those of us who rely on quantitative methods acknowledge such complexities, we can see, communicate, and understand what these tools can do and their inherent limitations in quantification.

I will conclude with one final observation—and this is likely me on a soapbox. Many criticisms about quantitative social science (surely not all) are from individuals who never revisited quantitative methods after their required sequence in graduate school. I believe that complex theories and frameworks such as feminist or queer theory have not found much of a home in quantitative social science because scholars in these traditions think quantification is too simple to capture a complex, multilevel process and that quantitative scholars follow popular fads that can often lead to asking less complex questions. I respond to the former concern by saying that this is because their view of quantitative methods tends to end at linear regression, and there can be more complex models to capture more complex theories with intuitive research designs. I respond to the latter that there are incredibly well-developed areas of theory because they are effective theoretical frameworks, but it is a different skill set than causal identification. The tools are there—the field needs scholars willing and ready to think carefully about theory and method that cuts across what can be siloed ways of knowing.

References

Ackelsberg, Martha. 2017. "The Politics of LGBTQ Politics in APSA: A History (and Its) Lesson(s)." In, *LGBTQ Politics: A Critical Reader*, edited by Marla Brettschneider, Susan Burgess, and Christine Keating. New York University Press.

Ayoub, Phillip M. 2022. "Not That Niche: Making Room for the Study of LGBTIQ People in Political Science." *European Journal of Politics and Gender* 5 (2): 154–72.

Bates, Nancy, Marshall Chin, and Tara Becker, eds. 2022. *Measuring Sex, Gender Identity, and Sexual Orientation*. National Academies Press.

Broockman, David, and Joshua Kalla. 2016. "Durably Reducing Transphobia: A Field Experiment on Door-to-Door Canvassing." *Science* 352 (6282): 220–24.

Flores, Andrew R. 2019. "Persuasion and Ballot Initiatives: How Persuasive Were the Televised Campaign Ads on Same-Sex Marriage?" *Politics, Groups, and Identities* 7 (1): 177–93.

Flores, Andrew R., and Scott Barclay. 2013. *Public Support for Marriage for Same-Sex Couples by State*. Williams Institute.

Flores, Andrew R., and Scott Barclay. 2015. *Trends in Public Support for Marriage for Same-Sex Couples by State: 2004–2014*. Williams Institute.

Flores, Andrew R., Mark L. Hatzenbuehler, and Gary J. Gates. 2018. "Identifying Psychological Responses of Stigmatized Groups to Referendums." *Proceedings of the National Academy of Sciences of the United States of America* 115 (15): 3816–21.

Flores, Andrew R., Ilan H. Meyer, Lynn Langton, and Jody L. Herman. 2021. "Gender Identity Disparities in Criminal Victimization: National Crime Victimization Survey, 2017–2018." *American Journal of Public Health* 111 (4): 726–29.

Gates, Gary J. 2011. *How Many People Are Lesbian, Gay, Bisexual, and Transgender?* Williams Institute.

Herman, Jody L., Andrew R. Flores, and Katherine O'Neill. 2022. *How Many Adults and Youth Identify as Transgender in the United States?* Williams Institute.

Jones, Philip Edward. 2022. "Respectability Politics and Straight Support for LGB Rights." *Political Research Quarterly* 75 (4): 935–49.

Kalla, Joshua L., and David E. Broockman. 2023. "Which Narrative Strategies Durably Reduce Prejudice? Evidence from Field and Survey Experiments Supporting the Efficacy of Perspective-Getting." *American Journal of Political Science* 67 (1): 185–204.

Lorde, Audre. 2018. *The Master's Tools Will Never Dismantle the Master's House.* Penguin.

Maisel, Natalya C., and Adam W. Fingerhut. 2011. "California's Ban on Same-Sex Marriage: The Campaign and Its Effects on Gay, Lesbian, and Bisexual Individuals." *Journal of Social Issues* 67 (2): 242–63.

McGovern, Patrick J. 2010. "Perestroika in Political Science: Past, Present, and Future." *PS: Political Science and Politics* 43 (4): 725–27.

Novkov, Julie, and Scott Barclay. 2010. "Lesbians, Gays, Bisexuals, and the Transgendered in Political Science: Report on a Discipline-Wide Survey." *PS: Political Science and Politics* 43 (1): 95–106.

Omi, Michael, and Howard Winant. 2014. *Racial Formation in the United States.* 3rd ed. Routledge.

Rostosky, Sharon Scales, Ellen D. B. Riggle, Sharon G. Horne, F. Nicholas Denton, and Julia Darnell Huellemeier. 2010. "Lesbian, Gay, Bisexual Individuals' Psychological Reactions to Amendments Denying Access to Civil Marriage." *American Journal of Orthopsychiatry* 80 (3): 302–10.

Russell, Glenda M., and Jeffrey A. Richards. 2003. "Stressor and Resilience Factors for Lesbians, Gay Men, and Bisexuals Confronting Antigay Politics." *American Journal of Community Psychology* 31:313–28.

Smith, Charles Anthony. 2011. "Gay, Straight, or Questioning? Sexuality and Political Science." *PS: Political Science and Politics* 44 (1): 35–38.

Strode, Dakota, and Andrew R. Flores. 2021. "Voter Registration Rats and Traits by Sexual Orientation and Gender Expression." *Public Opinion Quarterly* 85 (3): 913–28.

Strode, Dakota, Tenaya Storm, and Andrew R. Flores. 2024. "Transgender and Gender Diverse People Disproportionately Reports Problem While Trying to Vote Compared to Cisgender People." *Journal of Politics*. https://doi. org/10.1086/732978.

Tadlock, Barry L., and Jami K. Taylor. 2017. "Where Has the Field Gone? An Investigation of LGBTQ Political Science Research." In Brettschneider et al., *LGBTQ Politics: A Critical Reader*.

Valelly, Richard M. 2012. "LGBT Politics and American Political Development." *Annual Review of Political Science* 15:313–32.

Westbrook, Laurel, and Aliya Saperstein. 2015. "New Categories Are Not Enough: Rethinking the Measurement of Sex and Gender in Social Surveys." *Gender and Society* 29 (4): 534–60.

Wilson, Angelia R. 2017. "Our Stories." In Brettschneider et al., *LGBTQ Politics: A Critical Reader*.

Wuest, Joanna. 2023. *Born This Way: Science, Citizenship, and Inequality in the American LGBTQ+ Movement*. University of Chicago Press.

Part 3

Pedagogical Issues in Teaching LGBTQ Politics

Part 3 of *Teaching LGBTQ Politics* includes chapters on the theory and practice of teaching LGBTQ issues in a diversity of environments. While the prior sections cover how to structure courses, part 3 examines the practice of learning about the LGBTQ community in different teaching contexts and in ways that meet the full panoply of student needs. In particular, the chapters in part 3 pay special attention to the standpoint of students and the strategies teachers can adopt when addressing LGBTQ issues in the classroom. This includes how to incorporate LGBTQ activism on campus in the classroom, how to address the rejection of identity and representational politics when teaching queer theory, how to incorporate LGBTQ politics at a historically women's college, how to mentor new scholars conducting research in anti-LGBTQ environments, and how to use libraries to expand the potential of an LGBTQ politics curriculum. Each chapter tackles one of these pedagogical issues in the teaching of LGBTQ politics, and in doing so helps prepare teachers and students for LGBTQ politics instruction in a variety of environments, including those that are hostile to LGBTQ people.

The final part of this book opens with a chapter by Anthony Perez, Jamie Putnam, Fi Whalen, and Zein Murib entitled "Beyond Binaries: Bridging Theory and Praxis in the Classroom." Perez, Putnam, and Whalen were Zein Murib's students who formed an organization called The Positive to address the needs of transgender and gender nonconforming (TGNC) students at Fordham University. The chapter focuses in on an interview with the students, who used their coursework to help drive an activist movement on campus that achieved important victories for TGNC students, including all-gender restrooms and the adoption of a chosen name and pronoun policy. Murib frames the interview with a discussion of the pedagogical lessons instructors can learn from student activism and the teaching approaches that best shape student's burgeoning activist needs in return.

Chapter 13, "Teaching like a Dyke: A Pedagogy for Unresolved Authority in the Queer Classroom" by Elena Gambino and Haley Norris, continues the activist thread from the prior chapter by examining how instructors can use queer theory to destabilize identity and representational politics in the classroom. Gambino and Norris examine how the queer theory tradition of "subjectless critique," which argues for the relinquishment of authority, can be negotiated in a classroom environment where out instructors are required to speak as experts, arbiters, and norm-setters. Their chapter argues for "teaching like a dyke"—a way of role-modeling embodied responsibility in the classroom and encouraging students to world-build beyond accepted identity and political norms.

Following up on the limits of identity, chapter 14 by Whitney Ross Manzo, entitled "Including LGBTQ Politics at a Historically Women's College," addresses various pedagogical issues associated with teaching LGBTQ politics in another limiting environment—a historically women's college. Because women's colleges are identity-based institutions, they are by definition exclusive, particularly those in the South, where Whitney Ross Manzo teaches. Manzo delineates an array of strategies for teaching inclusively in an exclusive context. Some of the strategies discussed include clearly defining course terms, modeling inclusivity, tracing the development of civil rights over time and across different minority communities, and encouraging debate by having students role-model real-world characters.

Chapter 15, "Teaching Queer Scholars to Plan and Conduct Fieldwork in Hostile Environments," published under a pseudonym, further tackles LGBTQ issues in exclusive environments by examining how to conduct fieldwork in countries where the government outlaws LGBTQ identity. This chapter is particularly important given the lack of training in how to conduct fieldwork in political science graduate programs generally, let alone in this specific context. This chapter considers ethical dilemmas associated with conducting fieldwork in hostile environments and strategies new scholars might adopt in order to navigate this complexity.

The final chapter in part 3, Daryl J. Barker's "Using Library Instruction to Teach LGBTQ Politics," takes a different approach to pedagogical issues in the classroom by urging instructors to utilize librarians when building an LGBTQ-inclusive curriculum. The chapter opens with an anecdote—an example of a class on LGBTQ issues that failed to address student needs because the curriculum had become dated. This is a common problem in LGBTQ studies, where language and identity adapt and change rapidly. Baker illuminates how, by turning to librarians, instructors can adopt learner-centered curricula that better adapt to the fact that LGBTQ identity and community are fluid and never stable. Baker's chapter helps conclude part 3 on a more positive note following the prior chapters, which focus on teaching in hostile and exclusive environments.

Taken together, the chapters in part 3 address LGBTQ issues across a spectrum of LGBTQ experiences and contexts. This includes activism in environments that are more amenable to change (like Fordham University, which changed LGBTQ policies following student activism) to those that are not (like the more exclusive environment of a historically women's college or a country hostile to LGBTQ people). Given the array of contexts addressed, part 3 is sure to be especially useful to those who seek to advance LGBTQ inclusivity in the classroom regardless of the political context.

Chapter 12

Beyond Binaries

Bridging Theory and Praxis in the Classroom

ANTHONY PEREZ, JAMIE PUTNAM, FI WHALEN,
AND ZEIN MURIB

Although many lesbian, gay, bisexual, transgender, and/or queer (LGBTQ) students arrive at college campuses having already come out to family and friends, there are a significant number who use their coursework and activities both on and off campus to negotiate these identities during their time as students (Wilson 2020). Indeed, for many, being free to experiment away from family and established social networks is one the primary reasons to go away from home for an undergraduate degree. This chapter focuses on how college educators can use curriculum and classroom interactions to support LGBTQ students, particularly with respect to how exploring the rich history of transgender, queer, gay, lesbian, and bisexual activism can inform students on tactics and goals for political and social organizing on their college campuses and beyond. These lessons are especially pressing in the current climate of anti-LGBTQ discourse and policy developments.

One of the main factors that shapes college life for LGBTQ students is the degree of acceptance they perceive on campus. In recent studies, students who identify as lesbian, gay, or bisexual report generally positive feelings about their college experiences when reflecting on fitting in; however, the same is not true for transgender and gender nonconforming students, many of whom graduate or leave their undergraduate institutions with relatively more negative perceptions of their time in school (Rankin et al. 2010). There are a variety of reasons for this discrepancy. Those who are out as lesbian, gay, or bisexual before starting college confront a second coming out if and when they identity as transgender or gender nonconforming (TGNC hereafter) during their time in school (Wilson 2020). For these students, a welcoming campus climate is especially important. A 2019 study, for example, found that TGNC students who report relatively less welcome campus environments also are more likely say they are depressed and/or anxious and engage in risky behaviors, such as binge drinking and unprotected sex (Hood et al. 2019, 799). Additionally, a lack of opportunities to access restroom facilities, such as gender-neutral or any-gender restrooms, and failure to adopt gender-affirming housing policies is a significant predictor of declining mental health among TGNC students, including suicidal ideation. These effects endure even after controlling for experiences with bullying (Price-Feeney et al. 2021).

A growing body of research on higher education pedagogy and administration underscores the importance of mitigating these negative outcomes for TGNC students by designating all-gender restrooms, updating housing policies to allow students to select into gender segregated housing that will be comfortable for them, sharing and using pronouns, chosen name policies, and inclusive curriculum (Hood et al. 2019; Stegmeir 2018; Woodford 2018). Although public and private secular schools have gradually begun to adopt these policies, progress on these fronts has been slow at private and religious institutions, creating additional obstacles for TGNC students, faculty, and staff at those schools to overcome (Etengoff 2021). The recent politicization of transgender students stands to aggravate these trends as more attention is devoted to the question of where TGNC people belong in institutions and spaces that are historically segregated by sex assigned at birth, which include sports, restrooms, and most college dormitories.

In this view, courses that engage the history of transgender, queer, lesbian, gay, and bisexual activism do more than familiarize students with LGBTQ history and queer theory; they are opportunities to introduce students to material on how to mobilize on their college campuses to agitate for the changes they want and need to see in order to ensure their well-being. These tools are useful long after students have graduated and moved onto careers and lives as members of the polity, where LGBTQ people too often confront quotidian forms of marginalization and even violence.

This chapter builds on these insights from the scholarship on LGBTQ history and pedagogy in two ways. First, it offers an instructive overview on how to teach a course on LGBTQ political history and activism by drawing on courses taught by Zein Murib at Fordham University over the span of seven years. Next, it pivots to foreground the perspective of three former students who were involved in applying the lessons learned in these courses to their on-campus activism between 2017 and 2020 with the goal of establishing all-gender restrooms. We have chosen to present this interview as a complete transcript, which mirrors the way early lesbian and gay publications presented interviews of activists to foster a sense of intimacy by inviting readers to consider their own answers to questions (Murib 2023, 46–48). In this way, the chapter emulates the ultimate goal of teaching LGBTQ political history: finding ways to apply lessons from the past to contemporary political and social problems.

Structuring Courses to Foster Student Activism

On November 9, 2016, I arrived at my Gender and Sexuality Class completely unprepared to address students' questions about how a virulently anti-immigrant, anti-woman, anti-LGBTQ candidate could be elected to office. I recall printing out thirty-six copies of Audre Lorde's 1981 essay "The Uses of Anger" and inviting students to read it, reflect, and share their thoughts. What became immediately apparent to me during our conversation was that these students came of political age during the Obama administration; the 2016 presidential election was the first in which many of them were eligible to vote. The election of Trump to office represented a seismic shift for them on par with the first presidential election I had participated in, on November 7, 2000, when I went to sleep assured that Al Gore would continue Bill Clinton's policy agenda, only to wake up the following day to news of Florida's "hanging chads." In retrospect, the 2000 election foreshadowed the questions students raised that day in our class: What is the electoral college, why do people support candidates who foster frightening discourse against minorities and women, and, perhaps most importantly, what do we do now? These questions serve as the backdrop against which I developed a set of courses designed to cultivate student knowledge about legacies of activism and how to apply it to their own lives as members of the polity.

I developed three courses to introduce students to theories of activism and approaches to politics. In 2017, I offered a course titled American

Social Movements, in which I defined grassroots political mobilizations as efforts to disrupt the status quo. After 2016, I've also regularly taught Gender and Sexuality in US Politics as well as an annual seminar titled The Political History of Sex and Sexuality that might be more aptly referred to as a course on transgender politics. Across each of these courses, my focus has been to accomplish three goals: (1) present intersectionality as an analytic framework for understanding political, economic, and social problems; (2) challenge students to approach institutions, laws, and policies as outgrowths of dominant ideologies, such as white supremacy, capitalism, patriarchy, citizenship, ableism, and Christian normativity; and (3) view what gets glossed as "identity politics" with distrust, replacing it with analyses that focus on how power shapes what comes to be known about groups and to what effect. I will use Gender and Sexuality in US Politics as a case study for how I work toward these goals in my teaching in the remainder of this chapter.

Intersectionality as an Analytic Framework

The first step is to lay a strong theoretical foundation in intersectionality. This objective has always been a cornerstone of my teaching, but has become even more important in the recent political climate and the weaponization of "critical race theory" by conservatives and the far-right. I view providing students an opportunity to engage with the texts that introduced intersectionality to the academic lexicon as a way to combat these efforts.

To that end, we begin with Kimberlé Williams Crenshaw's (1989) "Demarginalizing the Intersection of Race and Sex: A Black Feminist Critique of Antidiscrimination Doctrine, Feminist Theory and Antiracist Politics." I start the discussion by asking students to analyze each of the metaphors Crenshaw introduces in the article: the intersection and the basement. This focus emphasizes that intersectionality is not an additive framework in which harm accumulates, rendering some more vulnerable than others, but rather a structural critique that analyzes the ways that institutions and ideologies interact to shape experiences of vulnerability and precarity. For example, Crenshaw's intersection metaphor underscores the normative effects of harm experienced at the intersection of ideologies such as heteronormativity and white supremacy by asking the reader to consider if a person hit by cars approaching from two angles creates more injury than if they had been hit by one car, or ideology. The answer is plainly no: It is impossible to qualify (or quantify) degrees of harm for those who are made precarious by dominant ideologies that are mutually reinforcing.

Crenshaw's tools for intersectional analysis and critiques of liberal legalism are cemented when students read Lisa Marie Cacho's (2014) essay "The Presumption of White Innocence." That article compares the criminal punishment system's treatment of two Florida "stand your ground" cases: George Zimmerman and Marissa Alexander. Cacho's analysis highlights the differences in how the law is applied to Zimmerman, who claimed self-defense against a Black boy—Trayvon Martin—to justify murdering him, and Alexander, a Black woman who fired a gun to scare away her abusive Black husband. That Zimmerman was acquitted and Alexander received a prison sentence illustrates in stark terms how whiteness holds a monopoly on victimhood that requires scripting threat onto Blackness. The overarching point by the end of this unit is that intersectionality is not something located in any individual person, but rather a structural critique. These lessons direct attention away from inclusion and reform and shed light instead on the ways that laws, institutions, and ideologies interact to shape experiences of harm, injury, and death for many at the expense of a dominant few.

Underscoring the Effects of Dominant Ideologies

Once students have a grasp on intersectionality, we turn to asking questions about who benefits from rights claims. This is often a challenge as it contradicts one of the main tenets of liberalism: that pursuing rights is the preferred way to address the political interests of marginalized groups. In contrast, Wendy Brown's (2000) "Suffering Rights as Paradoxes" directs students' attention to how the exercise of rights by some groups almost always entails the denial of rights for others. After walking students through multiple examples that range from the right to private property to gun rights to illustrate the differential effect of rights that vary with respect to a person's location in relation to the exercise of those rights, I ask students to consider the failure of rights in their own lives. The instances shared by students are usually shaped by what is happening in the broader social and political context, with students most recently using Brown's framework to understand the paradox of anti-vaccine discourse in the context of the COVID-19 pandemic. Those claiming a right to be free of vaccine mandates do so at the expense of the broader public in a variety of ways: by creating the conditions for ever-more variants to develop, by overwhelming hospitals, and by accumulating medical expenses that in many cases will be shouldered by tax payers (Amin and Cox 2021).

Drawing on intersectionality in this discussion points students to critique liberalism and the attention to what scholars refer to as "rights talk." Key to these lessons is questioning who comprises aggrieved groups and against whom those groups are defined. In other words, what does it mean to say that the "women's movement" seeks equality with men? What does it mean to claim rights as women, and which women are elevated when these strategies are deployed? bell hook's (1987) essay "Feminism: A Movement to End Sexist Oppression" addresses these questions, explaining that these strategies define white, able-bodied, and educated non-transgender men as the baseline for the equality sought by (white) women, leaving all other groups out of the equation. Students come away from this reading understanding that feminism is not a movement for equality, but rather an analytic framework and associated political praxis that aims to end sexist oppression, broadly defined as inequalities that are shaped by patriarchy, white supremacy, and heteronormativity.

Against Identity Politics and Toward Mobilization

I round these lessons out in the remainder of the class with readings that draw attention the normative implications of these theories. For example, Heath Fogg Davis's (2018) "Why the 'Transgender' Bathroom Controversy Should Make Us Rethink Sex-Segregated Public Bathrooms" underscores how physical structures—such as sex-segregated restrooms and sex-segregated sports—create conditions for excluding those who do not neatly fit into raced and sexed binaries from public space. They do this by rendering all those outside of binary gender as illegible and therefore excludable from restrooms and, in the latest iteration, youth athletics.

Riki Ann Wilchins's 1997 book chapter "Why Identity Politics Really, Really Sucks," further highlights who gets left of out mobilizations organized around identity. Wilchins urges readers to consider how power operates in the creation of identities such as woman and transgender, both of which require defining who does *not* belong within the boundaries of those identities. Instead of identity, Wichins argues that "our movement shifts its foundations from identity to one of functions of oppression. Coalitions form around particular issues, and then dissolve. Identity becomes the result of contesting those oppressions, rather than a precondition for involvement. In other words, identity becomes an effect of political activism instead of a cause. It is temporary and fluid, rather than fixed" (Wichins 1997, 86). Students can better imagine how to mobilize political aims to address root causes of oppression, and thus benefit as many groups as possible, by moving away from an identity-based framing. This, in turn, invites an understanding of social and political problems as products of oppressive ideologies, such as white supremacy and heteronormativity, that are mediated through the sex-segregated structures and spaces identified by Davis.

These perspectives are rounded out by Paisley Currah's (2022) book *Sex Is as Sex Does*. Currah analyzes several case studies of when states use "sex" as an amorphous concept to realize different goals that often map onto state strategies to maximize profits. These include the smooth transfer of property (and maintenance of heterosexual relationships) via inheritance and marriage laws. Currah's analysis consequently moves the conversation about sex and gender away from how to define each term—a question that has vexed feminist and gender theorists—to what sex in particular does for the state. This analytic sensibility points students toward developing critical understandings of state power, institutions, laws, and policies.

Foregrounding radical political goals that target systems of oppression and strive to avoid reformist measures were embraced by a group of student activists who took my classes between 2017 and 2020. In the transcript that follows, three former students—Anthony Perez, Jamie Putnam, and Fi Whalen—speak passionately about ensuring that the newly established single-occupancy restrooms at Fordham were not "gender neutral," which would retrench binary gender by creating a third space, but rather "all-gender" spaces, following Wichins's recommendation to leave access fluid and free-floating.

In 2017, they formed an organization called The Positive to draw attention to issues affecting transgender and gender nonconforming students on campus, including the lack of all-gender bathrooms, using sex assigned at birth in housing and guest policies and the inability to update pronouns and chosen names on official academic records. In 2019, after two years of mobilization, The Positive won victories that included the addition of all-gender restrooms on campus and the adoption of a chosen name and pronoun policy. In 2020, the university acquired academic records technology to allow students to update their chosen names on official university documents. Although the students were successful, these victories were hard won.

In the following transcript, the students discuss the social and political landscape of Fordham and New York City, how they drew on insights from coursework to formulate their approaches, tactics for mobilizing other students, obstacles they overcame, and their takes on the factors that ultimately tipped the scales in their favor. The conversation concludes with their reflections on best practices for students and faculty at other institutions.

Interview

Zein Murib (ZM): Thank you so much for making the time to meet with me and discuss your work with The Positive. I'm really excited for this conversation! Before we begin, I want to share with you that it's been nice to be back on campus and see students taking advantage of the single-occupancy all-gender restrooms that you all helped to establish. Whenever I am waiting in line to use one, I see just about every queer student at Fordham and I think about all the work you put into establishing those spaces. I wanted to share that because I think it's easy to lose sight of the meaningfulness of all the work you did.

To begin, I'd love it if you could tell me a little about the context of your activism at Fordham, both at the university and New York City.

Anthony Perez (AP): 2017–2019 is when we were active as The Positive.

Jamie Putnam (JP): And organizing was also happening on campus before then. I first started working on getting all-gender restroom signage to increase bathroom access in 2014, with a trans student who was a senior and had been working on the issue before I arrived at Fordham. My freshman fall I encountered anti-LGBTQ policies (and frankly, people) that disturbed me. I remember that some students would go to the Starbucks down the block in between classes to use the bathroom, so bathrooms specifically were creating a barrier to education for trans students. The organizing picked up again in 2017, I think in the context of both more trans and queer students finding each other and talking about their shared challenges, and in the context of the federal policies and hate being broadcast by national media after the 2016 election.

AP: At Fordham, the issues were bathrooms, housing, and chosen names. For example, when I arrived, housing was sex-segregated; I took it upon myself to have a conversation with the residential director about my housing situation, as a trans student. However, because there were no explicit policies regarding housing for trans students, I was forced to live with females despite identifying and presenting as male. The other issue related to housing was the guest policy because students are only allowed to host students of the "same sex." This was problematic in the sense that it forced trans individuals to out themselves in a public setting in order to get a guest pass. For example, because Fordham had my sex listed as female, I was only allowed to get guest passes for people whose legal sex was listed as female. As such, every time I would request a guest pass, I would have to explain to the RA [resident advisor] on duty that I was trans, Fordham has me listed as female, and that I could receive this pass. This essentially forced me, and other trans students, to repeatedly out ourselves to strangers in a public setting.

Fi Whalen (FW): I think one factor was the passage of the New York City law that required all public single-occupancy restrooms to be designated as gender neutral that went into effect in 2017. We took that as an opportunity to push for all-gender restrooms on campus. The administration claimed that since they are a private university, they do not need to comply with New York City law, but we did some digging and the university receives city money, meaning they would have to comply with city laws. When we brought this to their attention, we received only provisional signage on the single-occupancy restrooms. An A4 paper slipped into a plastic folder was taped to the bathroom door saying something along the lines of "this bathroom can be used by all members of the Fordham community. Please be sure to lock the door." Gender was not mentioned on the temporary signage at all. It felt as though there was an effort by the university, at every turn, to avoid recognizing that there were transgender students on campus at all.

JP: We were looking for any form of tangible acknowledgment that there are transgender community members on campus who are valued, and I think that Trump's anti-trans rhetoric and the New York City law passing created a window for us to act and highlight the importance of recognizing the needs of trans students. I called the New York City Commission on Human Rights to get some information and was directed to the only trans person there. We had a laugh about the circumstances of us being put together, and they told me about a meeting that was happening at Hunter College to make similar pushes there, and that's how I was able to network with other students in New York City.

ZM: I know that one of the resources you took advantage of throughout your mobilization was the broader context of New York City and students at other schools. How did developments at other universities help to put pressure on the administration? Both New York City and other Jesuit institutions?

AP: What was interesting is that when we started doing research, we were able to see that Fordham was significantly behind the curve compared to other Jesuit institutions.

JP: Yes, that was shocking, especially because Fordham would use papal rhetoric to justify their actions, but there were other big universities, such as University of San Francisco and Georgetown, that had and have trans-friendly housing policies and widely accessible single-occupancy bathrooms.[1]

AP: Yeah, learning that gave me hope and made me feel like what we were asking for wasn't crazy or unachievable.

FW: It's an interesting tension, too, because Fordham brands itself as the Jesuit university of New York City, and learning how far behind they were compared to other Jesuit institutions like Georgetown just motivated us even more. They had this rhetoric in the context of the Trump administration of being a campus located in a sanctuary city where all students were welcome, but in the end their actions didn't match up. All they seemed to care about was appeasing their conservative Catholic board members and donors because that's where their money came from.

EP: The hypocrisy was enraging.

ZM: How did coursework and other things you encountered during your time as students help you to develop your tactics and political demands?

JP: I think your history of social movements class and your gender and sexuality in politics class helped me think through how to organize effectively and made me aware of some of my blind spots. I enjoyed reading Riki Ann Wilchins's (1997) "Read My Lips" and shared excerpts at a couple meetings. I'd also taken Dr. Christina Greer's urban politics class where we'd studied issues of public transit access and presented proposals to make specific subway stations more accessible, which I think formed how I approached some campus issues.

JP: We would also just make a point of talking to students to learn about their experiences in classes: which professors were asking for and respecting people's names and pronouns, and which ones weren't. That helped us to identify departments that might be open to us approaching them.

FW: Yeah, I think those conversations made it easy to accomplish more simple things like the chosen name policy.[2] The Modern Languages department was a logical choice because we knew that they were excited about language. I was connected to that department as a French major and it was in my Francophone classes where I learned about anticolonial political and artistic movements in places like Haiti, Lebanon, and Algeria. That began my own political education process and led to me connecting with other student activists on campus.

FW: I also remember an article that I think you gave me—Finn Enke's (2016) "Stick Figures and Little Bits"—about exploring the fun and possibility of language and gender play in the classroom, and I used that as a way to frame the way we talked about pronouns and chosen names to faculty departments. A lot of getting the chosen name and pronoun policy enacted was relationship building with department chairs. I'd go to meetings to introduce the policy and then stay to answer questions. In many cases, I was successful because I was able to argue that there were ways to integrate teaching about pronouns into their curriculum in relevant ways—like in the Modern Languages and English departments. But I also think needing to do it that way was kind of bullshit. There shouldn't need to be some greater educational reason to justify having people addressed correctly.

AP: We targeted faculty and not administration because the administration was deliberately slow—they seemed more concerned with stalling than seriously addressing any issues we raised. Considering that the need for chosen name and pronoun policies was so immediate, it only made sense to go through the academic departments because they don't need institutional or administrative approval to implement these policies in the classroom. Essentially, departments turned out to be more useful for students because they were faster and it made the policies easier to implement.

ZM: Did you encounter any obstacles that surprised you?

AP: The hardest thing was seeing how difficult it was for the administration to recognize that trans students were even there. It was clear that the policies were made without considering the existence of trans folks. But it was especially hurtful to sit in a meeting with administrators and tell them how these policies negatively affected my and many others' experiences at Fordham, for them to consistently disregard these experiences and make no changes at all. In fact, it wasn't until they were threatened by a lawsuit that they took any action on gender-neutral bathroom signage, and even then, getting the explicit all-gender wording—the actual acknowledgment of our existence—was our biggest fight. It's kind of wild to think about.

FW: It's smart for them to deny the existence of trans students because then you don't have to make a policy—you don't have to do anything at all. It culminates in feeling like you don't belong here and then you begin to wonder if you do really exist. At least I did sometimes. You get that feeling from the twin tools of bureaucracy and silence. It really was an effective strategy on their part.

ZM: That's something that I want to highlight—what you're talking about is epistemic erasure through university policies.

JP: They also never connected students and always denied that there were others at Fordham who were facing similar obstacles. I remember there was a first-year student who was made to feel isolated and alone, and that her request to live with other women would be denied.[3] Fordham just played out the clock. So one of the most important things we could do was make a display of critical mass to show that we were, in fact, there and that TGNC students weren't alone in the challenges they faced. We became visible enough that students in the social work program and in the law school were reaching out to us, both to offer help and to ask for help. They reserved rooms for us so we had a safe on-campus space to meet. This created a coalition of people who were also impacted by the silence around and lack of single-occupancy bathrooms. We were contacted by many students who weren't trans as well, who were new parents, for example, and didn't have anywhere to pump.

AP: I think another thing that made it hard for the administration to ignore us was when we opened up the meetings and started getting more people involved. The administration can use the strategy of running down the clock because they assume that a class of students leaves every year. When we started getting more first- and second-year students involved, I think they started to realize that the problem wouldn't go away.

ZM: I remember that was a deliberate strategy on your part—to build institutional memory and develop other student activists. It should also be noted that Fordham was particularly inhospitable to student action as it's consistently rated one of the worst campuses for free speech.[4]

FW: It's frustrating because it wasn't our job to make policy for them. We were there to go to school.

ZM: What got you over the finish line? What advice would you offer other students doing similar mobilizing?

JP: Look beyond your own community and campus. It helped to see what students on other campuses were doing. Also, I don't know how to say this quite right, but find a way to not be afraid. I think for me this came in the form of meeting, organizing, protesting with my peers. That helped, especially when we would organize events on campus that Public Safety offices showed up to, all of whom are retired NYPD [New York Police Department] and honestly, I found that intimidating. There was something about the university wanting us to think we were alone and having to know for ourselves that we weren't. I didn't come out until after I graduated, even though I was in New York City, because I didn't feel safe or comfortable on campus. But because I was working on these issues on campus, I was able to talk to my employers about restroom access and pronouns while I was a student.

FW: Yeah, I'd say that the most important thing to do is to meet people. It was nice, Zein, to hear you open the meeting by talking about the line of queer students waiting to use the single-occupancy restrooms on campus because I'd say that when I graduated I didn't know if we had been successful? I mean, sure, we got these bathrooms, but we didn't succeed in destroying gender on campus [group laughs]. We didn't get rid of sex-segregated spaces and policy. It was more incremental. So my advice would be to remember that you don't know how it's going to play out in the long run. It might surprise you. I also think being involved in that work helped me in my life after undergrad. I worked at Trader Joe's and I was able to talk about finding ways to get the right names and pronouns on name tags for employees. Nothing that was part of my formal education at Fordham prepared me for that, but the people in this room did.

AP: The same is true for me as well. I worked as a case worker briefly, and the skills I developed with The Positive helped me to form groups, run meetings, and find ways to bring people together. I also believe that the most impactful thing about organizing around these issues was the relationships I made along the way. Think about it, after college you have three things: the knowledge you learned, the friendships you made, and student debt. Don't undervalue those relationships—they will last far beyond the current issues you are tackling.

JP: Yes, find your allies. Find the decision makers. We spent a lot of time having conversations with people who were on our side but couldn't really do anything to help us get changes made. We also faced many walls with administrators who were opposed to us, and worked to convince them before realizing that they also weren't the ultimate decision makers. We became more successful as we became more strategic, and more practical about what would make the most difference tangibly in the lives of students immediately, like educating faculty members. Part of developing that strategy was educating ourselves as well. We brought an organizer from Sylvia Rivera Law Project to facilitate a large workshop on effective activism, which both educated and mobilized students.[5] Finally, be sure to celebrate your wins. There's now a page on the university website about housing policy and a map of all-gender restrooms on campus.

Conclusion

This chapter opened with questions students asked about political participation after Donald Trump's 2016 presidential election and a description of the courses developed to address their interest in activism to contest the status quo. We hope that pairing the conversation among the student activists and Zein's reflections on course design conveys that the process of bridging theory in the classroom and campus activism can be recursive: Faculty plan courses with certain learning goals in mind, students adapt what they learn to inform their political work, and in so doing, engage in their own form of queer world-building that shapes pedagogy moving forward. This is illustrated most persuasively by Anthony, Jamie, and Fi's comments about the communities and networks they built during their time as students, which ultimately created conditions for kinship and accountability that endure beyond the four years on campus.

In spring 2024, these questions about political participation and campus activism have once again come front and center as students across the country formed Palestine solidarity encampments and called for their colleges and universities to divest from weapons manufacturing (Nam 2024). These protests were met with administrative censure; in many cases, university presidents invited police to break up encampments and arrest students (Otterman 2024). This fostered a new set of policies designed to stifle protest of any kind. These include most notably the University of California system-wide ban on encampments of any sort and a prohibition on wearing face masks designed to mitigate the spread of COVID-19, which critics claim are used to obscure the faces of those participating in crime (Nowell and Anguiano 2024). These adaptations mimic historic and contemporary efforts by governments to stifle protest and chill speech, such as requiring protesters to obtain permits to demonstrate after the student uprisings of the 1960s (McCarthy and McPhail 1997) and increased penalties for protesters who engage in disruptive actions, such as blocking traffic or destruction of monuments that took place during the Black Lives Matter uprisings in 2020 (Quinton 2021).

These new and ongoing developments underscore the urgency of looking to histories of LGBTQ protest actions for lessons on how to approach campus activism moving forward. The rich history of disruption and rebuttal of the status quo—often against all odds—offers some instructive examples on how to balance the power of protest with legal consequences. Our hope is that this chapter provides some ideas for how to make those connections salient and useful to students moving forward.

Notes

1. For policies at USF, see https://myusf.usfca.edu/cultural-centers/gender-sexuality-center/gender-non-conforming-student-resources. For policies at Georgetown University, see https://lgbtq.georgetown.edu/resources/transatgu/.

2. The policy at Fordham reads as follows: Chosen Name Policy: Political science faculty will be sensitive to students whose legal name differs from a chosen name. They will address the student by their preferred name and pronoun. It is recommended that instead of calling roll, faculty ask students to provide their name (either aloud or in writing with a name tent or other method). Similar to the Office of Disability Services Policy, political science faculty must inform students of the Chosen Name/Pronoun Policy on syllabi day.

3. In 2018, a Fordham Student, Aria Lozano, transferred to Barnard University after confronting opposition to her appeal to share dormitory space with other women. She wrote this letter describing her experience for the school newspaper, *The Observer*: https://fordhamobserver.com/34568/opinions/the-transphobia-of-fordhams-dorm-policies/.

4. For more on Fordham's ranking as one of the least hospitable university campuses for free speech, see https://www.thefire.org/10-worst-colleges-for-free-speech-2021/.

5. Sasha Alexander, with the Sylvia Rivera Law Project, facilitated two student activism trainings with Fordham students. More information about Alexander and the organization can be found here: https://srlp.org.

References

Brown, Wendy. 2000. "Suffering the Paradoxes of Rights." In *Left Legalism/Left Critique*, edited by Wendy Brown and Janet Halley. Duke University Press.

Cacho, Lisa Marie. 2014. "The Presumption of White Innocence." *American Quarterly* 66 (4): 1085–90.

Crenshaw, Kimberlé. 1989. "Demarginalizing the Intersection of Race and Sex: A Black Feminist Critique of Antidiscrimination Doctrine, Feminist Theory and Antiracist Politics." University of Chicago Legal Forum, 139–67.

Currah, Paisley. 2022. *Sex Is as Sex Does*. New York University Press.

Davis, Heath Fogg. 2018. "Why the 'Transgender' Bathroom Controversy Should Make Us Rethink Sex-Segregated Public Bathrooms." *Politics, Groups, and Identities* 6 (2): 199–216.

Enke, A. Finn. 2016. "13. Stick Figures and Little Bits: Toward a Nonbinary Pedagogy." In *Trans Studies: The Challenge to Hetero/Homo Normativities*, edited by Yolanda Martínez-San Miguel and Sarah Tobias. Rutgers University Press. https://doi.org/10.36019/9780813576435-015.

Etengoff, Chana. 2021. "Praying for Inclusion: Gay Men's Experiences on Religious College Campuses." *Journal of College Student Psychotherapy* 35 (4): 345–76. https://doi.org/10.1080/87568225.2020.1739584.

Hood, Logan, Devon Sherrell, Carla A. Pfeffer, and Emily S. Mann. 2019. "LGBTQ College Students' Experiences with University Health Services: An Exploratory Study." *Journal of Homosexuality* 66 (6): 797–814. https://doi.org/10.1080/00918369.2018.1484234.

hooks, bell. 1984. "Feminism: A Movement to End Sexist Oppression." In *Feminist Theory: From Margin to Center*. South End Press.

Lorde, Audre. 1981. "The Uses of Anger." *Women's Studies Quarterly* 9 (3): 7–10.

McCarthy, John D., and Clark McPhail. 1997. "The Institutionalization of Protest in the United States." In *The Social Movement Society: Contentious Politics for a New Century*, edited by David S. Meyer and Sidney Tarrow. Rowman and Littlefield.

Murib, Zein. 2023. *Terms of Exclusion: Rightful Citizenship Claims and the Construction of LGBT Political Identity*. Oxford University Press.

Nam, Rafael. 2024. "Top Companies Are on Students' Divest List. But Does It Really Work?" NPR, April 30. https://www.npr.org/2024/04/30/1248088063/divest-divestment-university-college-protesters-campus-israel-gaza-invasion.

Nowell, Cecilia, and Dani Aguiano. 2024. "University of California Bans Encampments and Face Masks." *The Guardian*, August 19. https://www.theguardian.com/us-news/article/2024/aug/19/university-california-gaza-protests-encampment-face-mask-bans.

Otterman, Sharon. 2024. "Columbia Said It Had 'No Choice' But to Call the Police." *New York Times*, May 1. https://www.nytimes.com/2024/05/01/nyregion/columbia-university-protests-arrests.html.

Price-Feeney, Myeshia, Amy E. Green, and Samuel H. Dorison. 2021. "Impact of Bathroom Discrimination on Mental Health Among Transgender and Nonbinary Youth." *Journal of Adolescent Health* 68 (6): 1142–47. https://doi.org/10.1016/j.jadohealth.2020.11.001.

Quinton, Sophie. 2021. "Eight States Enact Anti-Protest Laws." *Stateline*, June 21. https://stateline.org/2021/06/21/eight-states-enact-anti-protest-laws/.

Rankin, Sam, Tim Cowan, James Morton, Patrick Stoakes, Equality Network, and Scottish Transgender Alliance. 2010. "Public Bodies and the Public Sector Duties Relating to Transsexual and Transgender People: Report of Findings and Case Studies." Equality and Human Rights Commission.

Stegmeir, Mary. 2018. "Escaping Stigma: School Support for LGBTQ Students." *Journal of College Admission*, 38–43.

Wilchins, Riki Anne. 1997. *Read My Lips: Sexual Subversion and the End of Gender.* Firebrand Books.

Wilson, Jo D. 2020. "They're Crying in the All-Gender Bathroom: Navigating Belonging in Higher Education While First Generation and Nonbinary." *Vermont Connection* 41 (17): 136–41.

Woodford, Michael R., Alex Kulick, Jason C. Garvey, Brandy R. Sinco, and Jun Sung Hong. "LGBTQ Policies and Resources on Campus and the Experiences and Psychological Well-Being of Sexual Minority College Students: Advancing Research on Structural Inclusion." *Psychology of Sexual Orientation and Gender Diversity* 5, no. 4 (December 2018): 445–56. https://doi.org/10.1037/sgd0000289.

Chapter 13

Teaching like a Dyke

A Pedagogy for Unresolved Authority in the Queer Classroom

ELENA GAMBINO AND HALEY NORRIS

In their iconic essay "Sex in Public," Lauren Berlant and Michael Warner set out a bold new agenda for queer analysis. Rejecting a politics seeking merely "to destigmatize those average intimacies . . . for persons of the same sex" or "to certify as properly private the personal lives of gays and lesbians" (2005, 203), Berlant and Warner claim for queer theory a more transformative objective: a form of "queer world building" that invites "changed possibilities of identity, intelligibility, publics, culture, and sex that appear when the heterosexual couple is no longer the referent or privileged example of sexual culture" (187). In other words, for these authors, thinking and acting queerly not only shows how "obnoxiously cramped" (197) sexual culture has become, but also hints at the possibility of a world in which unexpected political and sexual intimacies can be put to use to "[elaborate] a public world of belonging and transformation" (199).

In this essay, we take up the questions that inspired Berlant and Warner's analysis anew, asking how queer politics and theory—a set of analytical and political tools that we argue is distinct from both mainstream politics and political science as well as a politics of LGBTQ+ representation—changes our relationship to the "public" of the classroom. What kinds of queer counter-intimacies are possible in the classroom, and how

279

do they both overlap with and diverge from other kinds of mainstream intimacies? How can instructors cultivate these counter-intimacies in ways that promote queer world-building while also attending to the real political challenges, hierarchies, and unresolved authorities that inhere in these worlds?

On the one hand, we argue, the paradigmatic debates raised by queer theory are essential for drawing political science students into these questions; more than almost any other framework in our discipline, queer theory raises serious questions about students' core assumptions about politics. On the other hand, we also suggest that some of queer theory's political and conceptual shortcomings are thrown into relief in the classroom, and that the field has tended to neglect key areas of insight that offer different, often unexpected, ways of cultivating a queer world. In what follows, then, we have three aims: first, to explore the distinctive political promises that queer theory makes to students of politics; second, to identify some limitations of queer theory's grandest aims in the context of the classroom; and third, to suggest an alternative pedagogical approach to inviting students to negotiate key questions about what it means to engage in queer world-building. In our view, the reflections on queer theory that we offer in this chapter can and should be applied to the ways that studying theory more broadly authorizes instructors and students alike in the "public sphere" of the classroom.

In the first section, we explore the idea of subjectless critique that sits at the center of queer theory, arguing that this paradigm casts queer theory as a politics of *refusal* rather than a politics of *representation*. By this, we mean that queer theory poses serious critiques of frames that take the presence (or non-presence) of LGBTQ+ individuals in formal politics as an end in itself. Instead, queer theory teaches students of politics that inclusion in such institutions can be put to deeply homophobic and heterosexist ends, and it invites us to think about what queer world-building might look like. Put differently, queer theory asks how we might build new institutions at both local and global levels toward the end of a radical democratic project that does not take the presence of a stable subject (e.g., "LGBTQ individuals") as its end. We argue that this question, along with the various answers that queer theorists have suggested, is an important lesson to both political scientists generally and queer scholars and students in the discipline specifically. Below, then, we first unpack some of the ways we have tried to invite students to think along queer theory's "subjectless" lines.

As important as queer theory has been for those insistent upon keeping open the possibility of queer world-building practices like the ones Berlant and Warner describe, however, we argue that it presents unique challenges for instructors; namely, in locating "the queer" as a political metaphor for unsettling fixed identities across all normative contexts, queer critique can also have the effect of persuading queer students that they must exemplify both refusal and world-building at every moment of their everyday, ordinary lives. As a consequence, we argue, such formulations can enable instructors and students alike to sidestep questions of unresolved authority both in the world and in the classroom. For example, as we explore below, students tend to enter conversations about politics in terms of "good" (queer) politics and "bad" (mainstream) politics. In the second section of this essay, then, we explore how this tendency of queer theory has manifested in our experiences in the classroom. We find that students often digest the lessons by taking on a "paranoid" stance, in which they approach all political examples—including past queer ones as well as at-hand dynamics in the classroom—for evidence of hidden conservatism and latent oppression. We argue that one of the biggest challenges of teaching queer politics is therefore helping students to move away from this defensive or paranoid position and inviting them to commit more generously to the lessons of collective and collaborative world-building.

Taken together, we conclude that teaching queer theory effectively requires instructors and students alike to remain attentive to the embodied relationships of power and authority that structure the "public" of the classroom. When we can model what world-building looks like in the classroom, we find, we can more effectively demonstrate how queer politics requires both attention to the subtle, subterranean workings of power and a generous, reparative, and collaboratively world-building approach that does not stop at sniffing out "bad" actors and "problematic" ideas. We call this dual strategy "teaching like a dyke." Rather than teach from a "subjectless" queer position, we advocate for teaching like a dyke, a practice we describe as beginning from our own (and our students') embodied presence in the classroom in order to both identify subterranean relationships of power and cultivate new intimacies, vocabularies, and relationships with one another.

Ultimately, we argue that teaching like a dyke offers an important mode of materiality and embodiment in a queer classroom: A dyke pedagogy is one that emphasizes trust-building and responsibility-taking for the concrete locations from which each of us enters. Calling attention to the ways that we—and our students—embody different forms of authority, teaching like a dyke reminds us to pay close attention to the bodies, desires, fears, and attachments we bring into the shared space of the classroom as we work toward new forms of queer counter-intimacy. Throughout, we draw from our personal experiences to suggest three pedagogical tactics for teaching like a dyke: standing in and standing for, the politics of location, and the phenomenology of race.

Subjectless Queers in the Classroom

Queer theory is not a representational discipline. In fact, for many of its advocates, a "queer" analytic demands that scholars and activists attend to the impossibility of representation, both in language and in politics, in any kind of settled way. Put differently, queer theorists argue that while it is sometimes "necessary to assert political demands through recourse to identity categories" (Butler 1993, 19) like "LGBTQ+," these acts of political representation are always risky in the sense that they threaten to exclude or overdetermine the scope of political struggle against more unexpected or unsettling possibilities. When we attempt to name the subjects to be represented by queer theory, questions about who is included in that name almost immediately follow: As the ever-growing list of identities included in LGBTQIA+ suggests (and as a growing list of critics of queer theory from Black, postcolonial, and Native studies attest), it is nearly impossible to represent all queer people in a single, stable category.

Queer theory thus begins with this conundrum, suggesting that representation is not (and should not be) the goal of a properly queer politics. Teresa de Lauretis (1991), who coined the term "queer theory," for example, argues that it is at its core an "effort to avoid all of these fine distinctions in our discursive protocols . . . to both transgress and transcend them" (v). "Queers," in the idiom of queer theory, are not a group to be represented but rather embody a "critical stance," an ethical imperative to *un*settle seemingly settled political positions. Far from representing a coherent group of specific individuals, queerness in queer theory is a shorthand for what Judith Butler has called a "self-critical dimension within activism, a persistent reminder to take the time to consider the exclusionary force of one of activism's most treasured contemporary premises" (Butler 1993, 19).

In short, queer theory's political claims are decidedly rooted in "a firm understanding of queer as a political metaphor without a fixed referent" (Eng et al. 2005, 1). The refusal to settle on any one representation of queerness as its object of study "disallows any positing of a proper subject *of* or object *for* the field," and instead demands critical attention to "a wide field of normalization . . . through which certain subjects are rendered 'normal' and 'natural' through the production of 'perverse' and 'pathological' others" (Eng et al. 2005, 3). In other words, these scholars argue that queer theory must remain a "subjectless" endeavor capable of turning its attention to how sexualities are implicated in political processes as wide-ranging as state formation, political economy, the geopolitics of war and terror, colonial legacies, and racial violence. As a framework for understanding politics, "subjectless" critique thus refuses the notion of LGBTQ+ individuals as legible, rights-bearing subjects.

In staking its central claims in subjectlessness, queer theory directly challenges some of the most basic assumptions about political science research and—more importantly—the assumed political good of achieving representational equity in political institutions, academic discourses, syllabi, or classrooms. From its earliest articulations, queer theory's advocates have strongly resisted the desire to practice a straightforward "LGBTQ politics," in which achieving descriptive or substantive representation for a distinct, definable, and coherent category of individuals is a normative goal. In fact, for scholars like Eng and Puar, the representational aims of LGBTQ+ politics actually undermine the "queerer," more democratic, dimensions of politics to which queer theory aspires. As Eng and Puar put it, attempts to include or represent queer people in existing institutions often leads to unintended consequences including the ongoing oppression of racially minoritized queer people, the reproduction of empire, and the valorization of white, middle class, Western values:

> The politics of subjectless critique today demands an explicit acknowledgement of how . . . queer studies has often presumed an ever-expanding sphere of identifiable subjects laying claim to liberal rights, recognition, normalization, and inclusion. The decriminalization of sodomy, the ability to serve openly in the military, same-sex marriage, issues of bathroom access—the continuing expansion of LGBTQ+ is predicated on a signifying chain of identity as analogy and the awarding of legal rights

and entitlements through a politics of incremental recognition. . . . It is not designed to address intersectional identities and group injury nor is it capable of redressing material inequalities such as the maldistribution of life chances and the ethical conditions by which life might be livable. (Eng and Puar 2020, 5–6)

For Eng and Puar, to free queer theory from such unintended consequences is to subject an ever-expanding and unpredictable schedule of locations, bodies, and histories to the scrutiny of queer critique. Subjectless critique is, as they argue, an agenda of *refusal:* to be queer is to refuse to be domesticated by framing one's aims in terms of mainstream politics.

Because it forms the basic premise of queer critique, the theoretical framework of subjectless critique is a central feature of queer theory syllabi, and moving students away from a politics that pursues representation is a key pedagogical task of any queer theory course. As instructors, we have both constructed our syllabi around the idea that queer politics is not just about what queer people do in formal institutions—how they vote, how they act as legislators and representatives, and how they claim and wield rights—but about inviting students to see queerness as a lens to interrogate some of the unintended "normalizing" consequences of mainstream institutions.

When we teach about the history of US gay liberation as a social movement that emerged in the late 1960s and exploded onto the political scene at the Stonewall Inn in June 1969, for example, we take great care to make clear to students that, first, these actions were the result of considerable coalition-building among a range of poor, Black and brown, gay, lesbian, and trans people who had been organizing against bar raids, state censorship, and economic oppression. Just as importantly, however, our syllabi are constructed in ways that make clear that contemporary celebrations of pride (typically scheduled on or near the anniversary of the Stonewall uprising) can obscure the political meanings of this event as much as they commemorate them. To the extent that such narratives focus on the increasing visibility of queer people and the extension of formal rights such as the right to privacy or the right to marry, they can paradoxically occlude the ways that this visibility also reproduces the assumed whiteness, monogamy, and Western nuclear family orientation of queer people and remarginalizes queer subjects (like those who started the Stonewall uprising) who do not fit this narrative. Further, such narratives have been deployed in justifying ongoing warfare in the Middle East and beyond—for example, in hawkish narratives about the oppression of queer people in Gaza that legitimize state violence. In this example—likely familiar to most scholars and instructors working in LGBTQ and queer political science—we aim to employ the concept of "subjectlessness" explored above to help students to see how even ostensibly progressive aims can have the unintended consequences of remarginalizing and excluding the very queer subjects whose political efforts are at the center of our history.

Yet subjectless critique is not without its own complications and limits. Indeed, our experience with teaching queer theory suggests that students sometimes digest the lessons we describe above in ways that encourage what we will call a "paranoid" stance; that is, one in which they focus on distinguishing "good" queer politics from "bad" ones at the expense of a more capacious conception of queer world-building. Because one of the lessons of queer theory is its focus on the unintended consequences of exclusion and marginalization, we have found that students tend to approach most texts and historical examples in our class suspiciously, searching for hidden oppressions and subterranean exclusions rather than for points of connection and coalition-building across differences.

Extending the example we began to unpack above, we see the "paranoid" effects of subjectless critique as a tactic that students use to evade being seen as "bad" queer subjects. To the extent that subjectless critique invites students to ask who is excluded from and marginalized by narratives of mainstream representation, inclusion, and visibility, we have seen students shy away from taking ownership of their own embeddedness in these very dynamics as they seek instead to embrace the idea that they can exemplify subjectlessness in their own personal choices, political actions, and intellectual evaluations. Most often, we have found, this occurs when students attempt to signal their affinity with "good" queer politics by disavowing historical figures or texts that they associated with "bad" effects—for example white feminists, assimilationists, TERFs, or homonationalists. We unpack this dynamic at length in the sections that follow; for now, though, we want to suggest that this dynamic produces a specific kind of problem for the classroom we hope to create, whereby the desire to call out "bad" politics overtakes what we understand to be the more capacious, queerer desire to engage in world-building.

What's more, subjectless critique is an abstraction of an abstraction: It is a framework that one can only begin to comprehend by thinking about the metaphor of queerness cumulatively, across time and space, in overlapping archives and epistemologies, and against all sorts of changing normative regimes. What is lost in this move toward subjectless critique as the exemplary expression of queer world-building is the way that each of us appears *as subjects*—ones marked by materialities of race, class, and colony—in irreducibly embodied ways.

Dykes in the Classroom

In our view, the tension between the need for a subjectless critique capable of unsettling the unintended consequences of mainstream "progress," on the one hand, and the ways that this approach invites its students to take on a paranoid posture, on the other, is the central question in contemporary queer theory. Moreover, we suggest that the challenges this tension raises are especially salient in the queer theory classroom, where we believe it is crucial to emphasize the goal of world-building in the context of our students' different embodied realities and positions. In the classroom, our—and our students'—embodied presence structures our students' every encounter with the theoretical and political substance of queer theory. Though we share queer theory's desire to embrace transgressive refusal, we have found that teaching these ideas is especially difficult because students do not enter the classroom primed to relinquish their own—or our—embodied positions, and these positions can become easily entangled with students' desire to identify clear delineations between "good" and "bad" queer positions. As queer instructors ourselves, our whiteness and pedagogical authority in the classroom permeate how students digest what we are teaching. Just as in sex and in everyday politics, pedagogy in the queer theory classroom requires a careful engagement in the bodies, attachments, desires, fears, and fantasies with which participants enter, and this simple fact militates against a "subjectless" approach in several ways.

For example, as we argued previously, teaching about an event like Stonewall from a queer theory perspective requires that we emphasize the role that privileged, white queers have played in occluding the diversity of the uprising's participants, on the one hand, and replicating an exclusionary "progress" narrative that downplays the ongoing harms to queer people in poor, Black and brown, and trans communities globally, on the other. As we suggested earlier, students tend to interpret this lesson to mean that white queers are inherently suspect unless they engage in a performative disavowal of their own mainstream aspirations. This response manifests strongly in specific kinds of classroom dynamics. As white instructors at one of the nation's most racially and economically diverse state universities, we have found not only that students react to our own racial and pedagogical authority by expecting us to model the kind of performative disavowals they imagine to be the only response to queer theory, but that they approach texts by white authors, particularly in the past, with knee-jerk suspicion and very often preemptively reject them on the grounds of their presumed weaknesses.

While these kinds of knee-jerk rejections of "progress" narratives may be important moments in our students' learning, we nonetheless argue that they stop short of the kind of queer world-building to which we think the best queer theory and politics aspires. First, such responses can put students of color and trans students in the awkward and untenable position of being rendered as both exemplars and spokespersons of "good" queer politics. Second, they can alienate students who are not ready to let go of their attachments to mainstream inclusion, whether because of their own privilege or because of a broader attachment to the narrative that mainstream recognition is and will be a driver of political change. And third, paranoid responses to queer theory can drive students of all identities and positions to hear *only* the lesson that politics is exclusionary, harmful, and normalizing, rather than invite them to practice the kind of queer world-building toward new institutional and intimate futures that we see as a central component of queer theory and politics. In each case, we argue, the paranoid response robs students of a deeper engagement with queer ideas and practices that our syllabi and pedagogy aims to instill.

Responding to these challenges does not mean ignoring the fact that mainstream politics can and does exclude, marginalize, and normalize—indeed, to do so would be to confirm students' suspicions. Instead, we advocate for a kind of pedagogical world-building that we will call "teaching like a dyke," since it is inspired by lesbian feminist sexual and political identities during the late 1980s. We argue that this pedagogical technique takes seriously this alternative genealogy of sexual politics to revisit a set of questions around *embodied sexual ethics* that animated lesbian feminist theory in the 1980s. In what follows, we seek to understand how the space of the queer theory classroom—a space, like the bedroom, marked as much by unresolved histories of authority, hierarchy, and harm as by transgressive pleasure and play—invites a similar turn toward embodied ethical questions. In contrast to a subjectless pedagogy that would emphasize a radical refusal of hierarchies and boundaries in

the name of transgression, the dyke pedagogy we advocate instead emphasizes acknowledging and taking responsibility for those hierarchies and
their persistence in the classroom. If the classroom, like the bedroom, is
a space of complex and overlapping hierarchies, desires, attachments, and
fantasies, then a dyke pedagogy emphasizes a "politics of location" (Rich
1995b) that situates each of us *within* those relationships and encourages
us to work through them, together, toward new futures.

In embracing our presence as dykes in the classroom, we call attention to the ways that we appear to students within structures of power
and authority—the specific raced/gendered/classed histories we represent
with our clothing and hair, our racial identities, our professional areas of
expertise, and our relationship(s) to the discipline, to the university, and
to the world(s) our students inhabit. We invite the recognition of our
"outness" in these ways by students not because they enable us to make
abstract claims about our own transgressive refusal or our performative
embrace of "good" queer politics, but because they enable us to model
what it means to engage intimately and ethically with others, to be simultaneously structured by overlapping regimes of power, and to refuse the
university's nexus of power/knowledge even as we interrogate our own
lingering attachments to these structures.

To teach like a dyke is to embrace the unsettled questions of sexual ethics that were powerfully articulated by lesbian feminists but are
often ignored or left out of queer theory pedagogies and politics. Indeed,
lesbian feminists, unlike queer theorists, placed considerable emphasis
on practices of speaking *as* a lesbian; coming out was understood by
these activist-writers as a way to enter into the shared political project
of redefining reality from a point of view traditionally marginalized. As
Adrienne Rich writes, for example, lesbian feminists saw coming out as
a highly symbolic political act that "means refusing to let others do your
thinking, talking, and naming for you; it means learning to respect and
use your own brains and instincts; hence, grappling with hard work"
(1995a, 233). For Rich, "in its deepest, most inclusive form," coming out
at as a lesbian was to partake in "an inevitable processes by which women
will claim our primary and central vision in shaping the future" (226).
In this sense, lesbian feminists tended to view the act of speaking "as"
a lesbian "as an ethics, a methodology, a more complex way of thinking
about, thus more responsibly acting upon, the conditions of human life."
Coming out, as Rich continues, "is a question of the community we are
reaching for in our work and on which we can draw; whom we envision

and our hearers, our co-creators, our challengers; who will urge us to take our work further, more seriously, than we had dared; on whose work we can build" (214).

We argue in what follows that this practice of "coming out" as claiming relationships to others is a powerful way of thinking about pedagogy in the queer theory classroom. Whereas subjectless critique invites students and instructors to disavow their positionality, we see the practice of teaching like a dyke as one that invites students to develop a shared grammar for articulating, working through, and undoing the unresolved—yet deeply embodied—forms of authority that inevitably structure the classroom. In what follows, we describe this pedagogical practice in a series of reflections on our intimate, ethical encounters with students in the classroom.

Closets and Coalitions

In this section, we want to present some of the practices we have incorporated in our classrooms in order to model what it looks like to teach like a dyke and to move students beyond their paranoid responses to the lessons of queer theory. Throughout this section, we want to emphasize how our classroom habits and conversations are integrated with some of the queer theory readings we teach. We approach our conversations about all of these readings—from social science classics like Ken Plummer's *Telling Sexual Stories* to queer theorizing in the humanities like Eve Sedwick's *Epistemology of the Closet* and more contemporary queer theories like Eng and Puar's "Introduction: Left of Queer" from the idea that we *embody* the politics elaborated by these texts as much as we *interpret* them.

One of the first steps we take in the classroom is to come out with and for our students, and to make explicit the various locations from which and to which both we and the students are coming out. For us, coming out occurs from the first moments of student introductions, meeting new students, and beginning a course. In this section, we explore how a lesbian feminist understanding of coming out as coalition-building enables the instructor to perform the ambivalence of role-modeling—a practice we call "standing in and standing for"—as the first step of teaching like a dyke.

The specter of the closet has haunted queer theorists since the beginning. In an analysis of coming out stories, Ken Plummer (1996) identifies the reliance on the hero-narrative by both the person coming out and the audience. Most people, he argues, understand stories about sexuality best when they are presented as a struggle against the internal homophobe and the external homophobic society. The queer, in these stories, overcomes an enemy that is inside and out: It is only through valiant efforts at self-acceptance and expression that they are able to articulate their non-normative sexual orientation. Following Plummer, we might argue that we risk turning ourselves into a feel-good spectacle for our students when we come out. This is all the more true if we do not investigate the politics of coming out narratives—and the representational claims they enact—in our classroom. Simply being out, while indeed important and dangerous for many, stops the discussion before it can even be started. Rather than inviting students into a queer space, it can create a new type of relationship: the instructor as the brave hero and the students as our celebrators. From the jump, the practice of calling into question what it means to be out (both in politics and in the classroom) gets students thinking about the stakes of visibility and a range of unintended consequences that might be at play within a seemingly progressive story.

Queer theorists tend to be wary of relying on coming out as a political strategy precisely because of this trope. Because queer theory is interested in coming out as a metaphor for the ways that power maintains divisions between private/public and deviant/normal, casting the queer as a heroic actor can obscure the way that power functions endlessly to reclaim the deviant and repurpose it as "normal." Eve Sedgwick's work has largely shaped this line of investigation in queer studies. Sedgwick argues that the closet functions as the primary way of knowing for Western culture. In this setup, the homosexual is the discursive object that gives away the existence of the closet—mostly when we come out of it. The homosexual is an object to be controlled since upholding the secret is the best way to maintain the borders of what is public (heterosexual). Sedgwick points out that by identifying homosexuals as a particular class of person through the metaphor of the closet, heterosexuality remained "preserved and essential." Other foundational queer texts echo Sedgwick on this point. Though Sedgwick's text can be abstract and inaccessible to many students at first, we have found that grounding this central insight in the larger context of what it means for each of us to be out in the classroom points students toward the political and pedagogical priorities we elaborated previously.

This context frames our own embodied presence in the classroom. However, as we mentioned above, it can also cause students who approach queer politics from a paranoid position to demand that we perform "good" queer politics at the expense of some of the subtleties of authority and power that we seek to empower students to grasp. To that end, then, we turn to lesbian feminism and teaching like a dyke as a way to anchor our pedagogy. Lesbian feminism, we argue, sees coming out as a moment of coalition-building through the acknowledgment of material *and* discursive realities of being a lesbian. This framework is especially important for understanding how coming out as dykes might promote world-building—and not just suspicion and critique—in the queer theory classroom.

Take, for example, Biddy Martin's exploration of lesbian autobiographies in *The Lesbian and Gay Studies Reader* (1993), in which Martin reads lesbian autobiographies as "explicitly committed to the political importance of just such reading strategies for the creation of identity, community, and political solidarity" (278). This is a far cry from queer theory's perspective on what coming out looks like and the limitations of representational, identity-based politics. To come out as a dyke is to "render suspect" the very nature of the category itself. Martin suggests that identifying as a lesbian becomes a stilted, nonproductive practice when we allow it to stand as our entire identity. She emphasizes the importance of coming out as a process of naming and exploring our differences. To come out as a dyke, then, is about a process of naming a community, practice, and political orientation to which we are accountable rather than a discrete identity; it is about *standing in* for that community's expectations and aspirations and *standing for* its shared commitments. As Martin puts it, when we understand coming out in these terms,

> lesbianism ceases to be an identity with predictable contents, to constitute a total political and self-identification, and yet it figures no less centrally for that shift. It remains a position from which to speak, to organize, to act politically, but it ceases to be the exclusive and continuous ground of identity or politics. Indeed, it works to unsettle rather than to consolidate the boundaries around identity, not to dissolve them altogether but to open them to the fluidities and heterogeneities that make their renegotiation possible. (Martin 1993, 289)

Here, Martin's analysis of lesbian writers points toward the action-oriented capacities of standing in for and standing as "a dyke." Lesbianism is, here, a place of dynamic political resistance and existence. Coming out as a lesbian is thus, for us, a move toward world-building politics that queer theorists insist upon. In this way, coming out as dykes can enact what Sedgwick (2002) calls "reparative performances." If our desire to uncover the horrors of exclusion in mainstream politics can lead us to emphasize shocking truths over a practice of building a better world, coming out can be a pivotal invitation to reflect on our shared experiences of coming out with and for one another in the classroom.

Understanding coming out as a moment of creating a shared space of collaboration and action changes everyday classroom practices in concrete ways, and this is how we define the concept of standing in and standing for. Instead of coming out to claim an identity as static, we come out to role model what it looks like to engage in reflexive and community-oriented learning. Consider, for example, the ritualized ways that classrooms out transgender students and teachers through the sharing of pronouns. When this process is done without further discussion of what is at stake for transgender students or instructors in the university spaces, it does not meet the threshold of radical politics from a queer or lesbian perspective. Instead, the practice of outing trans people through pronouns can echo what Malatino (2015) calls the "guest-inclusion" model of teaching trans-gender studies, in which we introduce trans topics in a queer classroom only to highlight the discrimination faced by transgender people in our cisnormative society. Teaching like a dyke, like our practices of reflecting on the meaning of coming out from and into the various locations in our classrooms, would instead invite students to consider both how seemingly progressive narratives of visibility and naming can harm trans students and how we might navigate these problems as a community of differently situated and embodied individuals.

Highlighting the violences faced by marginalized people around the world is only the first step in teaching like a dyke. It is up to us as instructors to teach our students what to do with the information. I (Haley) often turn to a quote from Sedgwick's essay, "What do we know, that we didn't know before?," to guide subsequent discussions in my classroom: "To read from a reparative position is to surrender the knowing, anxious paranoid determination that no horror, however apparently unthinkable, shall ever come to the reader *as new*; to a reparatively positioned reader, it can seem realistic and necessary to experience surprise" (2002, 146). Rather than expecting the students to solve the world's problems with their heroic identities or their ability to discern "good" from "bad" politics, I (Haley) emphasize the agency they have in their relations with friends and other community members. What actions are available to them now that they have this critical framework? How can they use "coming out" as a community-building tool rather than simply flagging their identity categories? Sedgwick states that the power of reparative reading is our ability to recognize, through affective responses of surprise and horror, that the "past, in turn, could have happened differently than it did" (2002, 146). For Sedgwick, this realization frees us to imagine a better future instead of remaining locked in the truths of a paranoid reading in which every category, system, and moment is inevitably, if unintentionally, harmful.

In other words, we are re-creating our subjectivity *through* reparative acts including coming out, which sometimes requires us to claim the authoritative position of the visible dyke (Phelan 1997; Lauretis 1991). It is impossible, in the framework we propose, to come out as a dyke and remain isolated and solitary. Drawing on this tradition of coming out in lesbian feminism as a way of claiming and cultivating new practices of world-building, we argue that this point also invites queer theorists to consider other contexts in which claiming an identity and audience similarly contests familiar political narratives, especially those that seem to reify binaries about "good" and "bad" identities and positions.

Malatino, for instance, argues for an alternative approach to teaching trans studies that focuses on "gender as process, craft, and becoming" by drawing connections between transgender and cisgender experiences. This mirrors Sedgwick's call for reparative strategies in which the past is no longer seen as an inevitable description of the future. Like Martin, Malatino turns to the radical potential of autobiographies to teach the processes of "institutional exclusion, the trouble with the medicalization of gender, the experience of being marked for social death, or the technoscientific developments that have shaped the contemporary terrain of gender transition" (2015, 398). When the instructor stands for a group or identity, they are able to mobilize the power of autobiography without relying on students to do so themselves. This can help manage tensions in the classroom by displacing critique from the students' bodies to the body of the instructor.

Another dimension of "standing in" in a dyke pedagogy is one where the instructor engages their authority to serve as the object of critique for students. This can look like multiple things: inviting student critiques of the syllabus and being open about one's pedagogical choices and goals, spending a day midsemester reflecting on how conversations around sensitive topics have unfolded, and inviting both informal and anonymous feedback through the use of "Dear Prof" letters. By standing in as an object of critique in ways that invite reparative feedback and modeling what it looks like to engage in reparative world-building, teaching like a dyke thus takes pressure off queer of color or trans students to be visible and allows discussion of what those identities mean, or could mean, by using the instructor as the point of reference. At the same time, these strategies challenge the knee-jerk rejection of representative (white, privileged) identities and mobilizes the practice of coming out as a pedagogical strategy.

Residue and Remainder: Teaching Queer Theory as a Response to Embodied Authority

So far, we have argued that queer theory's unique commitments challenge the central assumptions of political science—namely, the concept of "representation" as a normative good—by insisting that its students see how power coalesces around complex, intersectional identities in unexpected ways. In the queer theory classroom, understanding how and why scholars have turned away from representational politics is undoubtedly a crucial pedagogical goal. And yet the "critical stance" that queer theorists adopt in order to track the movements of power—a stance we follow Halberstam, Eng, and Muñoz in naming "subjectless critique"—can paradoxically invite students to focus so exclusively on the abstract, cumulative effects of power that they allow their own embodied entanglements in power to fall away from view. As we argued above, the desire to leave behind the forms of unresolved authority that structure our appearance in the classroom is the desire to sidestep the messier questions of world-building in favor of a paranoid approach that seeks to disavow "bad" politics and to instead enter into a space of transgressive freedom.

To us, teaching like a dyke means cultivating this desire for transgressive freedom *even as* we encourage students to remain attentive to the ways in which the classroom, like the bedroom, remains marked as much by unresolved histories of authority and harm as by transgressive freedom. One effective way of teaching this idea, we have argued, is to play with and call attention to our own "outness" as a practice of standing in and standing for. In experimenting with our outness in the classroom, we have found that such conversations highlight unresolved authority that go to the heart of queer theory's analysis of power. Below, we elaborate on two more examples of how we push students to recognize these questions by staging a conversation between key texts of queer theory and the practices of embodiment and location we explored in the section above.

ELENA'S STRATEGY: POLITICS OF LOCATION

Instead of presenting queer theory's subjectless critique as a methodological improvement on feminist, intersectional, or lesbian feminist ideas, my (Elena's) class is designed to emphasize subjectless critique *as* a deeply embodied strategy emergent from a specific set of historical and political conditions. In addition to playing with my own embodied outness as a pedagogical tool, I also stress the deeply embodied and contextual nature of the texts we read.

One of the first pieces we read in my feminist and queer theory class, for instance, is the classic interview between Gayle Rubin and Judith Butler (1994) entitled "Sexual Traffic," where Rubin describes the contexts of her two iconic pieces, "Traffic in Women" and "Thinking Sex." There's an interesting tension in the interview. On the one hand, the whole premise of the conversation, as Butler frames it, is Rubin's singular position in relation to feminism and queer theory: "Some people" she says, "say that you set the methodology for feminist theory, then the methodology for lesbian and gay studies." Butler's own piece in the same volume, "Against Proper Objects," argues for a view of feminism capacious enough to see queer theory as a generative interlocutor rather than a traitorous critic, and her line of questioning clearly reflects her desire for Rubin to make this case against a more rigid "division of labor" in which feminism and queer theory tackle the distinct and "non-contradictory" objects of gender and sexuality, respectively.

But what's interesting about the piece, and the reason I have my students read it alongside Rubin's iconic essays, is that Rubin systematically avoids answering the questions about queer theory as a *methodology* that Butler raises. Rubin continually moves to local sites of conflict to situate her essays: She describes an effort to unionize local sex workers in Ann Arbor, an effort to disrupt an uptick in policing of local cruising sites including a truck stop near the University of Michigan, a deeply embodied debate with Marxists over gender in the 1960s, and then a different but still deeply embodied debate with psychoanalytic feminism and anti-pornography feminists in the 1980s. She writes, for instance,

> I suppose the most basic differences [between the essays] were that, theoretically, I felt that feminism dealt inadequately with sexual practice, particularly diverse sexual conduct; and practically, the political situation was changing. "Thinking Sex" came from the late 1970s, when the New Right was beginning to be ascendant in U.S. politics, and when stigmatized sexual practices were drawing a lot of repressive attention. Nineteen seventy-seven was the year of Anita Bryant and the campaign to repeal the Dade County gay-rights ordinance. . . . This period was when Richard Viguerie's direct-mail fund-raising operation was underwriting a new era of radical right-wing political organizing. By 1980 Reagan was in office. This shifted the status, safety, and legal positions of homosexuality, sex work, sexually explicit media, and many other forms of sexual practice. (280)

I cite this passage at length because in my class we linger on this point for almost an entire session. The interview performs, in concrete terms, exactly the tension we sketched out previously, but it also invites students to see how queer theory has always been about repair and world-building as much as it has been about the critique of unintended consequences. Readers of Rubin's work are constantly tempted to turn what were deeply contextual, *political* questions about embodied vulnerabilities and expressions of power into methodological maxims about the "proper objects" of feminism and queer theory; this temptation to abstract away from the concrete questions of embodiment are what we have argued lead to a paranoid stance and the desire to only encounter "good" queer politics. Yet on the other hand, Rubin constantly reminds us that this cumulative methodological approach does not excuse us from engaging in local, intimate questions about the forms of unresolved authority that emerge even in the most seemingly liberatory spaces.

When I teach this text, I ask students to consider the contexts that they believe structure their normative commitments. Like Rubin, I suggest, our analysis of unintended consequences can help guide our evaluation of different political strategies and tactics, but it should also lead us into conversations about how best to (re)build a world in which new intimacies and attachments can flourish.

Another way to frame the questions that Rubin raises is to think alongside lesbian feminists about how greater attention to the "politics of location," to borrow another phrase from Adrienne Rich, tracks the shifting, intersectional effects of power in ways that both overlap and diverge from queer theory's subjectless critique. Against the temptation to abstract away from her own entanglements in power by claiming the methodological rightness of her own feminism or queerness, Rich argues that a fuller grappling with how power structures our creative and intellectual life would require us to

> "[recognize] our location, having to name the ground we're coming from, the conditions we have taken for granted. . . . It was in the writings but also the actions and speeches and sermons of Black United States citizens that I began to experience the meaning of my whiteness as a point of location for which I needed to take responsibility. It was in reading poems by contemporary Cuban women that I began to experience the meaning of North America as a location which had also shaped my ways of seeing and my ideas of who and what was important, a location for which I was also responsible. I traveled then to Nicaragua, where . . . I could physically feel the weight of the United States of North America, its military forces, its vast appropriations of money, its mass media, at my back; I could feel what it means, dissident or not, to be part of that raised boot of power, the cold shadow we cast everywhere to the south. (1995b, 219–20)

To have worked through one's location in as-yet unresolved structures of power *even while* working to cultivate spaces of reciprocity, freedom, and pleasure is the ethical and political work of lesbian feminism and of coming out as and teaching like a dyke. That these twin tasks require us to linger in the ambivalent fact that there is no "right" way to subvert power—that the projects of anti-subordination and liberation are always more complex than the hero-frames that some coming out narratives promote—is, ultimately, the very impulse behind the turn to subjectless critique in the first place. This story emphasizes the importance of coming out as a role-modeling practice that is active, reflexive, and student-oriented.

HALEY'S STRATEGY: PHENOMENOLOGY OF RACE

One piece that has been invaluable to my (Haley's) teaching as a white dyke is "Phenomenology of Whiteness" by Sara Ahmed (2007). Phenomenology is a methodology for studying bodies, space, and experience and is therefore a key tool in our queer theory syllabi for thinking about the questions we have raised here. One key point of Ahmed's approach to phenomenology is that our experiences and actions are shaped by the spaces we are in—spaces limit bodies. To look at teaching through a phenomenological lens brings to the center the experience of teaching and learning. How does it feel to be taught? How do our histories of experiences come to bear on our teaching? What types of actions become impossible when we allow those histories to remain unseen? Ahmed specifically defines whiteness as being an unnoticed, ongoing history (2007, 149–59). The pedagogical strategy that I specify in this section is focused on making that history transparent to students in order to further their own learning and world-building capacities.

To begin, Ahmed argues that white bodies enter a space and immediately feel "at home," the privilege of whiteness is insulating and also exclusionary. In the following story I show how grappling with these lessons reveals my own missteps in teaching two critical pieces: Crenshaw's groundbreaking work on the concept of intersectionality and Puar's attempt to retheorize intersectionality using assemblage theory (Puar 2012; Crenshaw 1989). I propose that instructors learn to bring those problematic teaching histories into future classrooms, share openly how a specific lesson has gone wrong in the past, and invite students to reflect on those failures.

In this instance, my whiteness created a barrier toward the full expression and learning of my students of color. As a white instructor, my presence is received as one of undeniable authority, even on issues of race. We must remember the broader social context that our students operate in, and that means we must create more space for their stories than for our own. If I had adopted more readily the ethics we discuss in "teaching like a dyke," I could have generated a much better discussion—one in which the class could have imagined alternative modes of studying and articulating race, rather than the antagonistic debate that I created out of my desire to be "right" about intersectionality.

Because my course aimed to introduce students to the major debates within women's and gender studies (WGS), I assigned Jasbir Puar's (2012) critique of the intersectional paradigm during the weeks on intersectionality. I had read the piece several times during my graduate school career, and as someone trained in a women and politics program, I felt defensive of her critiques of Crenshaw and intersectionality. I felt that her article was punishing Crenshaw for mistakes and problems that other, mainly white, scholars had made in their deployment of intersectionality. I split my students into two groups: Half were to read Puar and the other half to read Crenshaw. During the class session they would be partnered up and have to teach the other student the main point of the article. As I gave my free-form lecture that day, I mentioned offhand that I didn't like Puar's interpretation of Crenshaw's work. I went as far as to say the piece was anti-Black because it was dismissive of a framework developed to center Black women in political, social, and cultural analyses.

To my surprise, and shame, all of my students returned to class that week and parroted my critiques. Not a single one of them claimed to enjoy the piece. I was shocked and disturbed. I felt that I had botched the teaching of this piece—one that makes important critiques and introduces a new dimension to the role of intersectionality in feminist studies—and that I had inadvertently engaged in precisely the "bad" politics my students were on the lookout for. Even worse, Puar is a faculty member at Rutgers' WGS department. This meant I was sending students into the program who had an established distrust of her and her work. How, and why, did this happen?

I had made a monumental error in assuming that my students saw me the way I saw myself, as someone still learning what it meant to be a feminist, queer educator. This is not the case. Standing behind a podium week after week, giving assignment extensions, handing out grades, and so on had all turned me into the authority in our classroom. While I may hold the position that queer feminism disavows disciplinary pedagogies, my students hadn't gotten the memo. When they had finished teaching their peers and we had regrouped as a class to clarify the key concepts, I made a point to stress that "my opinion doesn't have to be your opinion. I have my reasons for feeling this way toward the article, but I do not expect, or want, you to feel the exact same way." My students were confused. Permission to disagree? Permission to dismiss the instructor's statements? From this experience I learned that I cannot give up authority. It exists in my body and words, even if I do not want it to. How might I have reframed this experience around the possibility of world-building rather than as a mere misuse of my pedagogical authority?

I had relied heavily on the work of Black feminists to defend my own anti-assemblage position. The works of Cooper and Alexander-Floyd, in particular, guided my desire to be "right" (Cooper 2016; Alexander-Floyd 2012). At the time, I could not appreciate fully that these pieces were directed at a different audience—not a white dyke teaching the introductory course. As Nash and Pinto described, I allowed my fear of being a white feminist and my own discomfort to dictate the flow of discussion. At the podium I sought to demonstrate the ways that I allowed Black feminists to discipline me, rather than engaging in the work and creating space for my students to do so as well.

Nash and Pinto (2021) have articulated the punishing function of Third World feminisms, arguing that white feminists position themselves in a place of punished victimhood in order to express shame that comes from messing up on issues of race, a space that disables accountability through our desire to be punished into the right answer or perspective. Relying on Third World feminists to tell us how we are "wrong" is not sufficient in developing an anti-racist teaching strategy and indeed can lead to a shutdown of ideas and dialogue from students of color. When a white person leads discussions on racism—especially as an out queer person in the context of a queer theory course—we are positioned as authority figures in multiple overlapping ways. The classroom authority held by the instructor mimics the broader social authority held by white people that is frequently used to shut down criticisms from people of color against whiteness. If I cannot facilitate an open discussion of key texts, then how will I provide a productive space for my students to build a better future?

I couldn't change the outcome in that story, and taking responsibility means changing the way I taught that piece moving forward. Each time I teach the concept of intersectionality and assign Puar's work, I now present this problematic teaching history to my students so that we can reflect on what it means to hold authority over knowledge. I title this strategy "phenomenology of race," following Ahmed (2006, 2017) to emphasize how histories of teaching are carried by our bodies into the classroom. We suggest that instructors make those problematic teaching histories known to their students to emphasize how racial power dynamics influence teaching, learning, and the classroom space. Opening up about my mistakes allowed students to engage directly with my teaching style and practices—offering up their own views of what it means to learn and what is worth learning. Being out as a dyke in this instance went beyond simply outing myself, but instead relied on the strategic deployment of authority that was articulated in the strategy of "standing in, standing for."

Performing responsibility in this way is not available to everyone, particularly instructors who are already perceived by their students as lacking the authority to hold their role. In those moments, sharing histories of misteaching may backfire. However, the problem in those cases is not the same as what I describe above—my story illustrates not only what happens when we misuse authority that we hold, but how we might move forward from the recognition of these shortcomings toward a queerer, more capacious form of future oriented world-building.

Conclusion: Teaching like a Dyke

There is power in naming our identities and articulating the history of our subjectivities. We do not yet exist in a subjectless world, or one where easy choices between "good" and "bad" politics exist. Though queer theory offers important avenues for research, analysis, and teaching, we must remain grounded in our bodies all the while. We have further specified three strategies. First, we have argued that a dyke pedagogy relies on *standing in and standing for*, a strategy in which our outness allows us to become both an object of our student's critique and advocates and role-models for the type of embodied, responsible politics we view as central to queer world-building. By acknowledging that we *stand in* for certain forms of authority in the classroom, we *stand for* our students' engagement in—and critique of—the structures and systems that sustain our interactions. Second, we have argued that such a practice requires a *politics of location:* Rather than framing queer politics through the seeming freedom of subjectless critiques, we emphasize that all texts—like bodies—come from a particular location, with particular histories, attachments, and assumptions for which we as readers are responsible. Finally, teaching like a dyke begins from a phenomenological approach to our own racial, gendered, and sexed appearance in the classroom, meaning that we emphasize how it *feels*—and feels differently for each of us—to encounter texts, ideas, and other individuals in spaces that are structured by the unresolved hierarchies of racism, patriarchy, homophobia, and transphobia. We conceptualize it as a community-oriented and caring pedagogy because that is what our students need and that is the only way to build better futures for all the queers. More than that, our arguments in this chapter invite every political scientist to reflect on the ways we mobilize authority to the detriment of political imagination.

Teaching like a dyke isn't always possible or even desirable. We know that our authority in the classroom is the result of our race and our more masculine presentations. The type of intimacy, possible for us, is not always available to other instructors—particularly cis or trans women, femme queers, and people of color. The ability to play with authority in the ways that we have described is risky for those who already have to fight for respect and dignity from students. In cases where authority is denied by students we must determine if reparation is possible and desirable. Yet as we discussed, it is impossible and ill-advised to pretend that the subject-less critique disembodies us—even as we encourage imaginative politics in our students, we must attend to the material realities that come with being instructors in increasingly neoliberal institutions.

In sum, we believe that queer perspectives and queer politics are vitally important for our students because they highlight questions that would be ignored or overlooked in a political science classroom. Queer theory illuminates the pitfalls of a "rights and representation" approach to politics, but it is not feasible to remain wholly subjectless as we teach these ideas. Rather, we encourage instructors to use experiences of embod-iment and/or marginality to build coalitions with their students. What this means to us is teaching like a dyke, but its lessons—that pedagogy is something one must practice for and with students, that it is irreducibly embodied, that pleasure and play often come with the risk of harm—are in themselves important political lessons for students.

References

Ahmed, Sara. 2007. "A Phenomenology of Whiteness." *Feminist Theory* 8 (2): 149–68.

Ahmed, Sara. 2017. *Living a Feminist Life*. Duke University Press.

Alexander-Floyd, Nikol G. 2012. "Disappearing Acts: Reclaiming Intersectionality in the Social Sciences in a Post-Black Feminist Era." *Feminist Formations* 24 (1): 1–25.

Berlant, Lauren, and Michael Warner. 2005. "Sex in Public." In *Publics and Coun-terpublics*. Zone Books.

Butler, Judith. 1990. *Gender Trouble: Feminism and the Subversion of Identity*. Routledge.

Butler, Judith. 1993. "Critically Queer." *GLQ: A Journal of Lesbian and Gay Studies* 1 (1): 17–32.

Butler, Judith. 1994. "Against Proper Objects." *differences* 6 (2–3): 1–26.

Cooper, Brittney. 2016. "Intersectionality." In *The Oxford Handbook of Feminist The-ory*, edited by Lisa Disch and Mary Hawkesworth. Oxford University Press.

Crenshaw, Kimberlé Williams. 1989. "Demarginalizing the Intersection of Race and Sex: A Black Feminist Critique of Antidiscrimination Doctrine, Feminist

Theory, and Antiracist Politics." *University of Chicago Legal Forum* 1989 (1): 139–67.

Eng, David L., Judith Halberstam, and José Esteban Muñoz. 2005. "What's Queer About Queer Studies Now?" *Social Text* 23 (3–4): 1–17.

Eng, David L., and Jasbir K. Puar. 2020. "Introduction: Left of Queer." *Social Text* 38 (4): 1–24.

Hames-García, Michael, and Ernesto Javier Martínez, eds. 2011. *Gay Latino Studies: A Critical Reader*. Duke University Press.

Lauretis, Teresa de. 1991. "Queer Theory: Lesbian and Gay Sexualities An Introduction." *Differences* 3 (2): i–xviii.

Malatino, Hilary. 2015. "Pedagogies of Becoming." *TSQ: Transgender Studies Quarterly* 2 (3): 395–410.

Martin, Biddy. 1993. "Lesbian Identity and Autobiographical Differences[s]." In *The Lesbian and Gay Studies Reader*, edited by Henry Abelove, Michèle Aina Barale, and David M. Halperin. Routledge.

Nash, Jennifer C. 2019. *Black Feminism Reimagined: After Intersectionality*. Duke University Press.

Nash, Jennifer C., and Samantha Pinto. 2021. "A New Genealogy of 'Intelligent Rage,' or Other Ways to Think About White Women in Feminism." *Signs: Journal of Women in Culture and Society* 46 (4): 883–910.

Phelan, Shane. 1997. "The Shape of Queer: Assimilation and Articulation." *Women & Politics* 18 (2): 55–73.

Plummer, Ken. 1996. "Intimate Citizenship and the Culture of Sexual Story Telling." In *Sexual Cultures*, edited by Jeffrey Weeks and Janet Holland. Explorations in Sociology. Palgrave Macmillan.

Puar, Jasbir K. 2012. " 'I Would Rather Be a Cyborg Than a Goddess': Becoming-Intersectional in Assemblage Theory." *PhiloSOPHIA* 2 (1): 49–66.

Rich, Adrienne. 1995a. "Claiming an Education." In *On Lies, Secrets, and Silence: Selected Prose 1966–1978*. Norton. Originally published in 1979.

Rich, Adrienne. 1995b. "Notes Toward a Politics of Location." In *Blood, Bread, and Poetry: Selected Prose 1979–1985*. Norton. Originally published in 1986.

Rubin, Gayle, and Judith Butler. 1994. "Sexual Traffic." *Differences* 6 (2–3): 62–99.

Sedgwick, Eve Kosofsky. 2002. *Touching Feeling: Affect, Pedagogy, Performativity*. Series Q. Duke University Press.

Sedgwick, Eve Kosofsky. 2008. *Epistemology of the Closet*. Updated with a new preface. A Centennial Book. University of California Press.

Sedgwick, Eve Kosofsky, and Adam Frank. 2003. *Touching Feeling: Affect, Pedagogy, Performativity*. Series Q. Duke University Press.

Warner, Michael. 1991. "Fear of a Queer Planet: Queer Politics and Social Theory." *Social Text* 29:3–17.

Chapter 14

Including LGBTQ Politics at a Historically Women's College

Given advances in technology and transportation, the world is smaller than it has ever been. This brings many different cultures, behaviors, and attitudes into contact with each other, both within the United States and globally. Therefore, it is vital that instructors employ inclusive and multicultural pedagogies in order to prepare their students for citizenship in an increasingly diverse society (Gay 2003). However, much more has been published about how to be properly multicultural in the K–12 classroom than there has been in higher education atmospheres, which is why this volume is so needed. As Camicia (2016) argues, a curriculum dedicated to educating future democratic citizens must be inclusive of the concerns of all of those citizens, not just some of them. This is especially true in political science classrooms, which most directly engage with civic engagement and education.

However, not all political science classrooms are the same. Differences include size of the class, which influences how many students can talk; size of the institution, which influences how many different political science classes can be offered; and region of the country, which influences the student population's overall political attitudes. For example, the historically women's college at which I work has small class sizes, so student participation in class discussion is regularly encouraged and expected.

It is also a relatively small institution, so the majority of our political science classes are broad introductions rather than having a specialized focus. Lastly, the college is located in the South, in which traditionalistic, conservative political views tend to dominate (Elazar 1972).

As a result of these characteristics, there exists a tension between pedagogical best practices related to inclusive, multicultural teaching and the overall atmosphere in which I teach. I work hard to ensure that my classroom environment is welcoming to all students, and it is my sincerest desire that every student who walks through the door feels empowered and included, especially those who occupy marginalized statuses. However, many of the students in my classes are unused to hearing diverse points of view and sometimes even use outdated terminology to refer to their classmates. I do not believe that they mean harm; I believe that, in many cases, they simply aren't educated in these aspects. Therefore, it is incumbent upon me to narrow that educational gap. This chapter begins by explaining the challenges involved with inclusion in a historically exclusive climate. Then, I discuss the two steps I take each semester to overcome these challenges: first, laying an inclusive foundation that underpins the overall class atmosphere, and second, using class activities to broaden the perspectives of all of my students.

The Challenges of Being Inclusive at a Historically Women's College

When I was in fifth grade, I was sent home from school because I was wearing an "inappropriate" shirt. On the front, it read "Weaker sex?" and on the back, it read "Your serve, big boy." I had bought it as a warning to anyone who wanted to challenge me in tennis, but all the boys in my class were giggling that a "dirty" word was on my shirt, so I was sent to the office for "disrupting the school atmosphere." As I waited for my mother to come pick me up, I gave the entire front office of my elementary school a lecture on the extreme injustice of punishing me because the silly boys in my class could not behave themselves. When my mom arrived and was informed as to why I was being sent home, she rolled her eyes, but she never let me wear that shirt to school again. Full of righteous indignation, I changed into the shirt after school every day for a week. I finally stopped after my brother said, "Yes, Whitney, we get it! You're a giant feminist! Can you wear a shirt that doesn't smell, though?"

I share this story as an illustration of my early and consistent commitment to justice and equality. I spent the rest of my adolescence being "the feminist girl," the one who could always be trusted to write her class papers on abortion or the pay gap. Fast-forwarding to my undergraduate career, I majored in political science so that I could go to law school and fight for civil rights. I ended up getting a PhD instead, but I was warned early on in graduate school that studying gender or racial and ethnic politics was too niche, and that if I ever wanted an actual job I needed to study something with a broader appeal. As a first-generation student, I had no idea whether that was true or not, so I trusted my advisers and focused on electoral law and direct democracy instead. I was able to squeeze just a little bit of those "niche" topics into my dissertation, though: One of the chapters was devoted to analyzing the impacts of referenda whose topics involved a minority population (e.g., Black, Latino, and LGBTQ Americans) on public perception of the targeted minority group.

The joke ended up on my naysaying advisers anyway, because I landed my actual job at a historically women's college where I was strongly encouraged to shift my research agenda to gender politics. Being "the feminist girl" that I am, I very enthusiastically agreed. However, I began noticing that my students were hesitant to call themselves feminists. If you don't believe in gender equality and empowerment, I thought, why in the world would you go to a historically women's college? It eventually dawned on me that, in my excitement to teach women like me, I had made a big assumption that my students would, in fact, be women like me. This was a faulty assumption for a few reasons. First, women are not a monolith. Women hold political views across the entire ideological spectrum, and each woman has different intersectional identities that interact differently in different social contexts, influencing those ideological views (McCall 2005). For example, Cassese and Barnes (2019) found that white women hold political views distinct from nonwhite women, and these distinct views are strongly correlated with sexist views. Even among white women, though, there were distinctions based on class and educational attainment. This demonstrates that I cannot and should not have expected a solidarity based simply on shared gender.

Second, our college is located in the South, and most of our students come from rural areas within the South. This is a region with a long history of racial and ethnic discrimination, as well as fairly conservative attitudes related to gender relations (Rice and Coates 1995). Elazar (1972) argued that the South, and in particular North Carolina, is a primarily traditionalistic political culture that values the status quo and distrusts too much government meddling in the family and society. Politics and society in this political culture are hierarchical, just like their conception of the ideal household: men (usually wealthy and white) at the head, women and children (and anyone not white or wealthy) following behind. While Elazar's results were based on a study of the states in the early 1900s, Morgan and Watson (1991) updated his findings by adding religious affiliation data and found that the South should still be considered a distinctly traditionalistic political culture because of the intensity of religious attachment in the region, particularly to Evangelical Protestant religions.

This leads me to the third reason I could have expected an atmosphere less friendly to feminism than I hoped, which is that our college was affiliated with the Baptist State Convention of North Carolina until 1997. This means that a majority of our alumnae could be assumed to be Baptist, or at least to agree with Baptist ideals, and many of our current students are daughters or nieces of these alumnae. This is important for understanding the mindset of our students, because Baptist ideals encourage female submission (North Carolina Baptists n.d.). Furthermore, the institution of the church is ideal for encouraging consensus of political views among its membership, and there is evidence that a church's overall political outlook is more influential in its members' political views than their individual worldview (Wald et al. 1988). Therefore, it is important for me to remember that many of my students grew up hearing from conservative and/or traditional attitudes regularly, and deviation from them can feel like a betrayal of their religion.

At the same time, I have noticed that students' religious concerns about feminism and including LGBTQ politics in class have decreased in the years I have been teaching. This is likely related to the fact that my students are increasingly members of Gen Z, which is a generation apart from the others on both LGBTQ identification and religiosity. As *NBC News* reported in June 2021, almost one in five members of Gen Z does not identify as straight and 4 percent identify as transgender, gender nonconforming, gender fluid, or nonbinary (Moreau 2021). Additionally, over one-third of Gen Z considers themselves unaffiliated with a religion (Cox 2022). This combination of increased diversity and decreased religiosity has almost certainly impacted how open some of my students are now to feminism and inclusive education, but there is still a strong and sizable number of Evangelical Protestants on our campus, and this group tends to disfavor same-sex marriage and other LGBTQ legislation (Marr 2015).

Why is all of this context important? Because understanding the traditional and conservative attitude that pervades the historically women's college at which I work is essential for understanding why obvious opportunities for inclusion become controversial or ignored altogether. For example, a few years ago, the adoption of a campus-wide diversity, equity, and inclusion (DEI) statement proved extremely contentious despite general campus support among faculty, staff, and students for the existence of such a statement. The sticking point? Whether a statement that professes inclusion of all identities would announce to the world that we were going to become a co-ed institution. Similarly, references to our students who do not necessarily always identify as women are usually shut down fairly quickly by the administration. This is because, again, they do not want a whiff of an appearance that we might be leaving our women's college status in the past. The college did end up ratifying the campus-wide DEI statement, and it explicitly mentions inclusion of all sexes and gender identities, which is a positive step forward. At the same time, though, the statement also explicitly states that all inclusion must occur "in alignment with our core values and our mission as a women's college." This is a problem because it means that those students who do not primarily identify as women become invisible on our campus and may not receive the support they need.

The issue becomes magnified in the classroom when LGBTQ issues arise during the course of class discussion. Because a majority of my students identify as women and come from the rural South, they can be unused to talking sensitively and inclusively about LGBTQ people and political issues involving the LGBTQ community. And because those students who do identify as LGBTQ often feel excluded on our campus, they can be reluctant to speak up in class. Therefore, there exists a gap between the welcoming, multicultural, and inclusive atmosphere I would like to foster in my classroom and my students' expectations for class discussion and behavior, as well as their knowledge of LGBTQ issues. As their instructor, it is up to me to narrow this gap.

Step One: An Inclusive Classroom Foundation

Much has been written about the importance of establishing an engaging student environment in the classroom from the very first day of the semester. Nilson (2003) advocates getting started right away with activities that will be important throughout the semester, like discussion and writing, while Hermann and Foster (2008) encourage use of a reciprocal interview activity that will introduce students to the instructor and vice versa. McGinley and Jones (2014) demonstrated that students feel more interested and engaged in a course from the first day when the instructor shows caring toward their students. Therefore, how a professor conducts the first day of class can have an immediate and lasting impact on the classroom atmosphere for the remainder of the semester.

Nonetheless, students may have different expectations for the first day of class. Some students may still be undecided about which classes to take and need to weigh them against each other (Henslee et al. 2006). They may want to ask the instructor questions about what the course content will be rather than answer questions designed for everyone to get to know one another (Robinson 2019). Therefore, professors should think carefully about how to balance their desire to start the semester in a positive, engaging manner with the students' desire to learn the practicalities of the course in order to determine if it fits with their overall degree plan and career goals.

I argue that the second day in a political science classroom is the most crucial class period. At this time, the students who are present are likely the ones that will remain in the course. It is also generally expected that this day will be the first to seriously address the course material, so students come more prepared to participate than they might on the first day, which can be a bit overwhelming, particularly for students new to the college classroom. However, before I dive into the material—no matter what topic it is—I begin with a discussion of how to learn about politics and government. This is because our subject matter examines the hottest controversies of the day. We study power and how it is used by individuals, institutions, and systems. This means that political science classrooms are often on the front lines of the "culture wars," from discussing the Equal Rights Amendment and the Vietnam War in the 1970s to violent video games and AIDS in the 1990s to critical race theory today (Hartman 2015). Students often enter our classrooms spoiling for a fight, or at the very least expecting to watch one. Of course, the study of political science is much more than the day's headlines, but during the first week of class our students don't know that yet. Therefore, it is vitally important that political science professors set a strong foundation for the class from the second day, not only to dispel the myth that a political science class is an undergraduate version of the old TV show *Crossfire* but also to demonstrate how to discuss controversial topics in a sensitive, civil manner.

The first way I do this is by directly acknowledging the elephant in the room: This is a political science class, and we will talk about all the things your mother told you were impolite to discuss with others. Then, I ask students to tell me a little about how they have seen others discuss politics. Was it mean-spirited? Was it thoughtful? Did it seem like a genuine exchange of ideas, with demonstration of listening and consideration, or more like the comments section of a social media post, with straw man arguments and trolls? A vast majority of the time, students relate that their experience with politics, though usually minimal, mostly consists of the latter. This presents an opportunity to have a conversation about good classroom discussion practices, which can be explicitly tied to good democratic discourse later in life (Flynn 2009).

I present students with a document titled "General Discussion Guidelines," which was created by the Center for Teaching and Learning at Columbia University and can be found in figure 14.1. This is used as a guide to begin a conversation about how we would like our classroom discussions to proceed. The students may decide to adopt that document as is, or they may wish to add or subtract something. For example, in my Introduction to American Government class one fall, the students wanted to add to the third guideline (what is shared in the circle, stays in the circle) that no conversations should ever be recorded, lest someone's comments be taken out of context. Also, I always say that I reserve the right to briefly suspend the thirteenth guideline (commit to learning, not debating) when it is time to hold in-class debates over proposed policies as part of our course assignments (discussed further in this chapter). Beginning with an example document speeds the conversation up, to be sure, but it also shows students the kinds of things that are important to consider when having scholarly discussions. I ask for their input as to additions, substitutions, or subtractions so that they feel ownership of their learning experience and a personal responsibility to follow its rules (Lemieux 2010).

This classroom discussion foundation is complemented by an outline of terms and their definitions that I know or suspect may come up in class over the course of the semester. In the past, I admit that I did not spend time on this, but as I became more familiar with the student body at my institution and recognized that many of my students had fallen into the same faulty assumption that I had regarding the gender identity of students at our college, I realized that it was important to begin this way in order to start us all on the same page. Additionally, many of the courses I teach concern explicit discussion of different races, ethnicities, sexual

Figure 14.1. General Discussion Guidelines from the Center for Teaching and Learning at Columbia University.

Handout 1
General Discussion Guidelines

General guidelines

- Allow everyone the chance to speak.
- Do not interrupt or engage in private conversations while others are speaking.
- What is shared in the discussion circle, stays in the discussion circle. Keep confidential any personal information that comes up in the conversation.

As you listen to other participants...

- Listen carefully and respectfully, without interrupting.
- Be aware that tone and body language are powerful communicators. Show respectful listening by facing and looking at the speaker, making eye contact, staying quiet, nodding, etc.

When it is your turn to speak...

- Share briefly from your own experiences.
- Use "I" statements to state your views.
- Build on others' comments. Acknowledge them, even if you disagree.
- Be careful not to generalize about people and/or experiences.

Speaking up...

- If you think something is missing from the conversation, do not wait for someone else to say it; say it yourself.
- If you find another's statement to be problematic, do speak up.
- Try not to silence yourself out of concern for what others will think about what you say.

When interacting with other participants...

- Commit to learning, not debating.
- Challenge or criticize ideas, not individuals.
- Avoid blame, speculation, and inflammatory language.
- Be careful about putting other participants on the spot. Do not demand that others speak for a group that you perceive them to represent.

Adapted from
- Guidelines for Planning and Facilitating Discussions on Controversial Topics. Center for Research on Teaching and Learning, University of Michigan. Online at http://bit.ly/21dIJW9.
- Establishing Ground Rules. Center for Teaching Excellence, Cornell University. Online at http://bit.ly/1p1Rwt4.
- Talking Circles, First Nation Pedagogy. Online at http://bit.ly/1KI8jeA.

COLUMBIA | CTL
Center for Teaching and Learning

ctl.columbia.edu • ColumbiaCTL@columbia.edu • 212-854-1692

orientations, and gender identities, and some of these identities have had pejorative names associated with them. In my naiveté, I considered these pejorative names historical, but I quickly discovered that some parts of the country (particularly rural areas) continued to use these terms. Often, the students had heard them growing up and were unaware that the term was considered negative or offensive.

As a result, I began the practice of sharing resources in our learning management system (LMS) that students could turn to for help with proper terminology. It has become a normal part of setting up my LMS, like setting up the gradebook or including a syllabus, and I show students where the resources are located on the first day of class as I'm going over the syllabus and how to use the LMS. I do this in every class now, whether we will definitely use the terms in class or not, and always on the first day, because I believe it is important information for all students to have, even if they end up dropping my class. One resource is a glossary that the Human Rights Campaign created that helpfully outlines several terms related to the LGBTQ community. Another is a guide to inclusive language published by the Department of Diversity Initiatives at the University of South Carolina–Aiken. This resource is nice because it covers terms for many underrepresented groups in American society, as well as examples of how to use them and how not to use them. Finally, I include a link to a discussion of race and ethnicity from the United States Census Bureau. This is good for showing students how the US government might refer to different races and ethnicities in official communications, and I like that the website includes the bureau's research on how and why it landed on the terms it did. All of these resources can be found in the references section of this chapter.

Part of the conversation around proper terminology involves a discussion of pronouns. It is more common these days to see and hear people explicitly discussing their pronouns, but for much of my teaching career this did not happen. I learned to invite students to share their pronouns with me after a mortifying incident in which I referred to a student using a different pronoun than they actually used. It is always an invitation, and not a requirement, so that students who are uncomfortable sharing are not singled out (Haimson and Airton 2019). I also share my own pronouns so that the practice is normalized and signals to everyone in the room that proper recognition of the pronouns that have been shared is important to me. I even tell the story about using the wrong pronoun, so I can show students that I am learning too. My hope is that being open about my own ever-evolving education helps them understand that we are all learners, and mistakes sometimes occur. However, as long as we are all committed to listening to and including each other, mistakes can be opportunities to grow rather than evidence we do not belong (Bennett 2020).

Step 2: Inclusive Class Activities

After the class foundation is set, we then move into the course material, whatever it is. My college is a teaching-intensive institution, which means I carry a higher teaching load and have become a sort of jack of all trades—I have taught everything from Introduction to American Government to Terrorism and Counterterrorism to an honors course on the Civil Rights Movement. At the same time, there are only three political scientists in our department, so we cannot offer many classes that are more specialized. This means that several important subfields within political science like judicial politics, race and ethnicity politics, LGBTQ politics, political psychology, and others must be incorporated into the broader classes. Because one of my areas of interest is law and civil rights, this is the angle through which I incorporate activities that introduce LGBTQ political issues to my students.

Below I outline two examples of class activities that I have used in multiple classes. Both are rooted in active learning, or a constructivist model of instruction. This is because active learning fully involves the student in creation of knowledge, and students who co-create knowledge are more likely to retain it (Falance 2007). Additionally, research has shown that active learning activities help students learn better communication skills with those unlike them and promotes more open-mindedness (Shaaruddin and Mohamad 2017). These outcomes align well with my goals of inclusive and multicultural education, which is why I began designing active learning activities for my courses.

ROLE-PLAY

In my sophomore-level law and society class, we hold debates over current topics (this is when I suspend that thirteenth discussion guideline). However, instead of students offering up their own position on a given topic, I randomly assign them roles to play: real-life people who hold different positions on that topic. For example, one of the debates involves whether the Selective Service System should be opened up to all Americans, and not just those who were designated male at birth. On the pro side, I have Dr. Ellen Haring, a retired Army colonel and senior fellow at Women in International Security who has published extensively on opening up the draft; Harry Crouch of the National Coalition for Men, who has filed lawsuits challenging the discriminatory nature of the draft; and Chris Christie, who spoke in favor of opening up the draft during the Republican primary debates in 2016. On the against side, I have Jude Eden, a retired Marine Corps sergeant who speaks regularly on cable television against opening up the draft to women; Phyllis Schlafly, the conservative commentator who helped stop the passage of the Equal Rights Amendment due at least in part to arguments about women being drafted; and Ted Cruz, who spoke against opening up the draft at the same primary debate in which Christie spoke.

To complete the assignment, students must first write a short research paper on their character and their views on the topic at hand. Then students must perform as their character in an in-class debate. Each side briefly presents their main points, and then they are permitted to question each other on their respective positions, and students in the audience are also permitted to ask questions. The debates can become quite humorous as students work to act as their character; my very favorite performance would have to be the student who came to class in a black robe, a white wig, and a giant white mustache to play former Supreme Court Justice Oliver Wendell Holmes in a debate about whether the US Constitution should be considered a living document. At the same time, students are learning about the diversity of political views in the United States, both by playing a character and by watching other debates. I try my best to make sure each debate has characters that, while they may end up on the same side of an argument, have different reasons as to why they believe what they do. So in the Selective Service example, there is a character who believes the draft should be opened up because women can do anything a man can do and another character who believes the draft should be opened up because limiting it to only those assigned male at birth is discriminatory.

Students playing these characters do not have to worry about whether they will be made fun of by others for their opinions, because they are play-acting the opinions of others, which helps everyone feel less self-conscious and allows us to develop knowledge together (Barkley et al. 2014). Role-play has also been found beneficial in the development of communication skills (Nestel and Tierney 2007). Finally, role-play allows students to put themselves in the shoes of those who might be entirely unlike them, which hopefully increases their empathy and understanding (Douglas and Coburn 2009). I do not expect students' core political values to change as a result of this assignment, but I do hope that, in the future, they consider the lives of those unlike them when thinking about the implications of various public policies, particularly those in marginalized communities who have less of a voice in a majoritarian political system.

While I have received generally positive feedback from students about this assignment, there have been some challenges. The biggest has been what to do when, on in-class debate day, a student fails to show up. This harms their individual grade, of course, but it also throws off the debate because now one side has fewer characters. This can make it seem like the other side has a stronger argument just because they have more points they can make. In these situations, I have jumped in to play the missing character, but that can be difficult if it has been a while since I studied the person (I sincerely hope my former students have forgotten the time I tried to play Cesare Beccaria in a debate about capital punishment). This assignment has also been a challenge for students who dislike the character they have been assigned. For example, I had a very liberal student who was randomly assigned to play Robert Nozick in a debate about social justice. She found it very hard to put herself in his shoes and convincingly make an argument that social justice was an inappropriate ideal because it necessarily involved government redistribution and defend it from the opposing side's debaters who argued that social justice was important for achieving legal and social equality. We have kept in touch since that semester, and she has told me that the debate experience in my class taught her a lot about how to build a strong argument, but in the moment she didn't like me very much for forcing her to take a position she was intensely against.

SIMULATION

There is similar active learning in my civil rights law class. In this course, students are introduced to civil rights via the passage of the Fourteenth Amendment and the earliest civil rights case law, like the *Slaughterhouse Cases* (1873). We progress through the biggest cases related to race and ethnicity law, and then we shift into talking about civil rights related to gender case law. The final third of the course covers the development of LGBTQ law out of gender law, and then we close with oral argument of a "fake" Supreme Court case centered on LGBTQ issues. Our case is always inspired by a current real-life controversy; for example, in spring of 2021, our fake case was based on *R. G. and G. R. Harris Funeral Homes v. EEOC* (2020), which was about whether Title VII of the Civil Rights Act of 1964 prevented discrimination against transgender people. In spring of 2018 we had two fake cases: one based on *Masterpiece Cakeshop v. Colorado Civil Rights Commission* (2018), which was about whether a business owner can refuse to serve LGBTQ customers if it contradicts his religious beliefs, and one based on *Pavan v. Smith* (2017), which concerned whether same-sex couples could both be listed as parents on a birth certificate. Overall, the course is structured so that students hopefully understand that modern frontiers in civil rights, such as whether adoption agencies that discriminate against same-sex couples could constitutionally receive taxpayer dollars, are versions of older fights against discrimination between races and genders.

The aim of the final project is for students to demonstrate their understanding of civil rights law by engaging in oral argument related to the most current civil rights controversies. Some students play lawyers representing the two sides of the case, and they must write a six-page legal brief outlining their legal arguments and then deliver those arguments in class. Other students play judges, and they must ask questions of the lawyers during the in-class trial and then write a six-page opinion explaining their ruling on the constitutional question. I ask students to emphasize the connections between race and ethnicity law, gender law, and LGBTQ law by basing their arguments and/or opinions on precedent, and I require that students use precedent from all three areas (so they cannot only use LGBTQ-related precedent). The students are permitted to gain inspiration from real-life judges and lawyers, but ideally they are delivering their own argument or opinion based on what they have learned about the development of civil rights over time in the United States. Across the years I have taught this class, roughly two-thirds of our cases ended up decided differently than how real-life courts settled the question. This is why this particular assignment is better characterized as a simulation, rather than role-play; in role-play scenarios like the debates in my law and society class, the students are taking on an established character, while in simulations, students act as independent thinkers who make their own decisions (Dorn 1989).

This is a useful activity because it allows students to demonstrate their learning in a fun, engaging way compared to the regular term paper. There is a written element to the assignment, of course, but students, especially those who play the lawyer role, are also developing their public speaking skills (Kammerer 2018). All students have to think quickly on their feet in order to ask and answer relevant legal questions. It is also useful for showing students a little taste of what law school is like. Most of the students who enroll in the course are political science majors who are considering law school, and it is beneficial for them to experience a bit of the stress of law school to make sure they really want to invest the time, money, and effort law school requires. Additionally, legal simulations like this have been demonstrated to help students perform well in law school (Crosby 2018).

All of these positive skills outcomes help engage even the most conservative, religious students, who might otherwise check out due to their preexisting skepticism toward LGBTQ issues. I have found it helpful to allow students to choose their role (lawyer or judge), as well as which case they work on if we have more than one, in order to help students feel a little more comfortable with the assignment. It is also important to remind students before the oral argument begins about the foundation of our class—our discussion guidelines and proper terminology—so there are hopefully no incidents related to exclusion or insensitivity. One downside to this assignment is that the procedures of the trial itself are fairly distinct from actual legal proceedings; as Asal and Blake (2006) have noted, simulations are easier for students to understand when the professor is emphasizing either content or process, but not both. In my case, I am emphasizing the content.

Conclusion

At a historically women's college like mine, the inclusion of LGBTQ politics can be difficult due to the administration's desire to avoid controversy and many students' relative lack of knowledge about and/or sensitivity toward LGBTQ people and the LGBTQ community. Therefore, I have implemented a few practices in my classes in order to broaden my students' understanding while remaining responsive to the differences among them regarding LGBTQ political issues. The first step is to establish a strong classroom foundation from the second day of class that emphasizes inclusive discussion and proper terminology, and the second step is to use experiential class activities that introduce students to LGBTQ politics and help them develop empathy and understanding toward members of the LGBTQ community.

Overall, my personal feeling is that my classroom is more welcoming and inclusive today than it has ever been in my decade-long teaching career. In order to help my class become better for my students, I had to immerse myself in higher education pedagogy and learn how to become better on these issues myself. Of course, I had to complete this professional development on my own time, and it would have been better if there had been more professional development related to teaching and inclusion during my graduate education (Manzo and Mitchell 2018). According to my students, as measured via student evaluations of teaching, my classroom is generally a welcoming place where they feel comfortable sharing their opinion. They also overwhelmingly approve of my active learning activities, which corroborates the sense I have during those activities in class that students are more engaged and interested. Therefore, while including LGBTQ politics at my institution has been a bit of a bumpy ride, it has improved both my teaching and my students' learning, which are the primary goals of every educator.

References

Asal, Victor, and Elizabeth L. Blake. 2006. "Creating Simulations for Political Science Education." *Journal of Political Science Education* 2 (1): 1–18.

Barkley, Elizabeth F., Claire Howell Major, and K. Patricia Cross. 2014. *Collaborative Learning Techniques*. 2nd ed. Jossey-Bass.

Bennett, Jessica. 2020. "How to Overcome Imposter Syndrome." *New York Times*, June 11. https://www.nytimes.com/guides/working-womans-handbook/overcome-impostor-syndrome.

Camicia, Steven. 2016. *Critical Democratic Education and LGBTQ-Inclusive Curriculum*. Routledge.

Cassese, Erin C., and Tiffany D. Barnes. 2019. "Reconciling Sexism and Women's Support for Republican Candidates: A Look at Gender, Class, and Whiteness in the 2012 and 2016 Presidential Races." *Political Behavior* 41:677–700.

Columbia University Center for Teaching and Learning. n.d. "Learning Through Discussion."

Accessed March 26, 2022. https://ctl.columbia.edu/resources-and-technology/resources/learning-through-discussion/.

Cox, Daniel A. 2022. "Generation Z and the Future of Faith in America." Survey Center on

American Life, March 24. https://www.americansurveycenter.org/research/generation-z-future-of-faith/.

Crosby, Teresa Nesbitt. 2018. "To the Head of the Class: Quantifying the Relationship Between Participation in Undergraduate Mock Trial Programs and Student Performance in Law School." *St. John's Law Review* 92 (4): 797–832.

Department of Diversity Initiatives, University of South Carolina Aiken. n.d. "Inclusive Language Guide." Accessed March 24, 2022. https://www.usca.edu/diversity-initiatives/training-resources/guide-to-inclusive-language/inclusive-language-guide/file.

Dorn, Dean S. 1989. "Simulation Games: One More Tool on the Pedagogical Shelf." *Teaching Sociology* 17 (1): 1–18.

Douglas, Kathy, and Claire Coburn. 2009. "Students Designing Role-Plays: Building Empathy in Law Students?" *Legal Education Review* 61:55–63.

Elazar, Daniel J. 1972. *American Federalism: A View from the States.* Crowell.

Falance, Theresa. 2007. "Constructivism." In *Models and Strategies for Training Design*, edited by K. L. Medsker and K. A. Holdsworth. University of Michigan Press.

Flynn, Nora K. 2009. "Toward Democratic Discourse: Scaffolding Student-Led Discussions in the Social Studies." *Teachers College Record* 111 (8): 2021–53.

Gay, Geneva. 2003. "The Importance of Multicultural Education." ACSD, December 1, 2003. https://www.ascd.org/el/articles/the-importance-of-multicultural-education.

Haimson, Oliver L., and Lee Airton. 2019. "Making Space for Them, Her, Him, and 'Prefer Not to Disclose' in Group Settings: Why Pronoun-Sharing Is Important but Must Remain Optional." *Medium*, June 4. https://medium.com/national-center-for-institutional-diversity/making-space-for-them-her-him-and-prefer-not-to-disclose-in-group-settings-why-1deb8c3d6b86.

Hartman, Andrew. 2015. *A War for the Soul of America: A History of the Culture Wars.* University of Chicago Press.

Henslee, Amber M., Danny R. Burgess, and William Buskist. 2006. "Student Preferences for First Day of Class Activities." *Teaching of Psychology* 33 (3): 189–91.

Hermann, Anthony D., and David A. Foster. 2008. "Fostering Approachability and Classroom Participation During the First Day of Class." *Active Learning in Higher Education* 9 (2): 139–51.

Human Rights Campaign. n.d. "Glossary of Terms." Accessed March 24, 2022. https://www.hrc.org/resources/glossary-of-terms.

Kammerer, Edward F. 2018. "Undergraduate Moot Court: Student Expectations and Perspectives." *PS: Political Science & Politics* 51 (1): 190–93.

Lemieux, Catherine M. 2010. "Learning Contracts in the Classroom: Tools for Empowerment and Accountability." *Social Work Education* 20 (2): 263–76.

Manzo, Whitney Ross, and Kristina M. W. Mitchell. 2018. "We Need to Rethink Training for Ph.Ds." *Inside Higher Ed*, September 11. https://www.inside-highered.com/advice/2018/09/11/academic-training-phds-needs-focus-more-teaching-opinion.

Marr, Elisha. 2015. "The Contact Hypothesis and Millennial Evangelical Protestants' Attitudes Toward Same-Sex Families." *Michigan Family Review* 19 (1): 1–25.

McCall, Leslie. 2005. "The Complexity of Intersectionality." *Signs: Journal of Women in Culture and Society* 30 (3): 1771–1800.

McGinley, Jared J., and Brett D. Jones. 2014. "A Brief Instructional Intervention to Increase Students' Motivation on the First Day of Class." *Teaching of Psychology* 41 (2): 158–62.

Moreau, Julie. 2021. "Nearly 1 in 5 Young Adults Say They're Not Straight, Global Survey Finds." *NBC News*, June 9. https://www.nbcnews.com/feature/nbc-out/nearly-1-5-young-adults-say-they-re-not-straight-n1270003.

Morgan, David R., and Sheilah S. Watson. 1991. "Political Culture, Political System Characteristics, and Public Policies Among the American States." *Publius* 21 (2): 31–48.

Nestel, Debra, and Tanya Tierney. 2007. "Role-Play for Medical Students Learning About Communication: Guidelines for Maximizing Benefits." *BMC Medical Education* 7 (3). https://doi.org/10.1186/1472-6920-7-3.

Nilson, L. B. 2003. *Teaching at Its Best*. Anker.

North Carolina Baptists. n.d. "Beliefs: About Us." Accessed March 24, 2022. https://ncbaptist.org/beliefs/.

Rice, Tom W., and Diane L. Coates. 1995. "Gender Role Attitudes in the United States." *Gender & Society* 9 (6): 744–56.

Robinson, Des. 2019. "Engaging Students on the First Day of Class: Student-Generated Questions Promote Positive Course Expectations." *Scholarship of Teaching and Learning in Psychology* 5 (3): 183–88.

Shaaruddin, Jamila, and Maslawati Mohamad. 2017. "Identifying the Effectiveness of Active Learning Strategies and Benefits in Curriculum." *Creative Education* 8 (14): 2312–24.

United States Census Bureau. 2022. "About the Topic of Race." Last modified March 1, 2022. https://www.census.gov/topics/population/race/about.html.

Wald, Kenneth D., Dennis E. Owen, and Samuel S. Hill Jr. 1988. "Churches as Political Communities." *American Political Science Review* 82 (2): 531–48.

Chapter 15

Teaching Queer Scholars to Plan and Conduct Fieldwork in Hostile Environments

CAMPBELL M. STEVENS

The Approach

As the authors in this volume make clear, Queer perspectives have long contributed to science and learning, both as researchers and as subjects of inquiry.[1] Nine interviews and my own experience is insufficient to cover the breadth of Queer identities, but the semi-structured interview method revealed common themes, which this chapter will explore. I have purposefully organized the interviewees list to identify pairs with complementary fieldwork experiences or research interests, namely Nicholas and Philip, Sadie and Ethan, and Alex and me. These pairs were helpful in identifying themes and providing a means to compare experiences in similar fieldwork contexts. Undoubtedly, more work is needed to excavate fieldwork realities for trans and lesbian scholars, notably absent here,[3] but this chapter is still able to identify major topics and themes for consideration in assisting Queer scholars in their research design and fieldwork experience.

Selecting Field Sites

The initial decision on a field site is a humbling but critical one for Queer scholars. I use the word humbling because as political scientists we are often interested in questions relating to power imbalances or poor institutional design. As such, our work is increasingly interested in addressing Eurocentrism, both in field site selection and theoretical underpinnings. Yet if a Queer scholar selects field sites that offer the greatest legal protections for Queer people, the available field sites would skew toward Eurocentrism. Nevertheless, Latin America should not be forgotten as a world region with significant progress on LGBT rights an social acceptance (Angelo and Bocci 2021). Some societies may not offer as many legal protections but can offer broader social acceptance, like Thailand and the Philippines (Poushter and Kent 2020; Flores 2021). Similarly, at the subnational level, municipalities or other subnational units may offer far more protections for Queer persons than others, such as in nondiscrimination statutes in city law within the US.[4] On the whole, it is true that much of the world may not be an ideal place for a Queer scholar to simply "show up somewhere and watch for politics," as a glib colleague once described fieldwork. Yet Queer scholars can conduct research in a vast array of field sites and circumstances with the proper methods and research design, even if the environment is not as amenable as one would hope.

None of the scholars interviewed for this chapter selected their fieldwork site with their Queer identity as a primary frame for making the decision. Instead, the scholars selected their field sites based off their research question, their methodological background, and their cultural familiarity. The last factor was relevant for a number of scholars, myself included, as prior in-country experiences had informed whether it was possible to conduct research in a given society. Particularly for Philip, Cameron, and Morgan, this prior experience was critical to ensuring that they would be able to gain the trust and access to the Queer populations of interest to their research. Indeed, they selectively revealed their Queer identity to gain the trust of interlocutors in their respective field sites, which was made all the easier due to their cultural fluency. Overall, previously cultivated linguistic skills and prior fieldwork experiences were fundamental in establishing their selected field site for the respective research question rather than a Queer identity.

For Morgan, however, prior fieldwork experiences had informed their decision regarding field site location, because they had experienced considerable racism in other field sites. Initially, they had sought to conduct research on racial attitudes in globally significant urban centers in Eurasia, but they found that their Blackness was a point of friction and suspicion for those with whom they interviewed. Their study participants were defensive and Morgan felt that it was not worth pursuing the research if it only led to a resistance they had experienced consistently in the United States. Thus, Morgan's primary frame for determining their field site was vis-à-vis a racial positionality and not their Queer identity. After their disappointing experiences in cosmopolitan urban centers, they participated in a foreign language program in a society where they found a new interest in conceptions of gender, rather than race, and they found a much more fruitful field site for their ethnographic work. As such, Morgan's experience echoes the importance of predissertation fieldwork and linguistic training to all the scholars interviewed because it was more effective in defining the bounds of a given research project than their Queer identities, particularly in the midst of progressing through their graduate programs.

Determining Method

By extension, the choice of method is a difficult one, as a researcher must balance multiple demands, from claims on causality and quality of data to budget constraints. In my fieldwork, I have utilized semi-structured, elite-level interviews with a set of publicly identifiable officials and then use snowball sampling to expand my participant pool. This method has worked very well, as cooperative and informative participants usually referred me to similarly engaging colleagues, increasing the efficiency of my fieldwork. Undoubtedly, being a white male was crucial to the efficacy of this method, as was my comfort in adjusting to Russian norms regarding masculine behavior as I perceived them. Nevertheless, the occasional referral has placed me in a deeply uncomfortable situation, and one either has to prepare for such situations or be willing to forego the data. In my field site, in-person meetings are usually easier to arrange and carry out, but technology is offering exciting new possibilities.

Researchers can use encrypted end-to-end communications affordably and easily with potential participants, by comparison to previous pay-by-the-minute digital interfaces. WhatsApp, Zoom, and other platforms offer the capacity to conduct interviews with a high degree of confidence in the security of the interaction, and encrypted end-to-end interviews via Zoom were how I conducted the interviews for this chapter. Some world regions have their preferred apps, like Telegram in Russia, and a researcher should work diligently to ensure their quality for their own safety as well as that of their research participants. Furthermore, the use of such apps must be balanced against the chances for government surveillance, a continual possibility when working in Russian society, for example. Gaining access to potential study participants still presents an issue, and digital interactions may not yield the social trust and extended social networks that an in-person interview and connection may offer. Yet these tools can rapidly expand the opportunities for fieldwork if leveraged correctly, particularly if paired with shorter research visits.

There is also an increasing number of firms and research groups able to offer fieldwork data collection on behalf of a researcher. These services are often expensive, but they may make a difference in reliable data collecting for those living in a dangerous situation with suboptimal data collection. This is a situation where a Queer researcher may be able to find a larger overarching field project to temporarily collect their data, whether an omnibus survey or working with another scholar to add a few prompts to a focus group session. Being completely in charge of data collection has its advantages, but in the face of possible harm or considerable social obstacles, such alternatives may present a Queer researcher with the data necessary to push a project toward completion.

Of the scholars interviewed, all save for Simon self-identified as primarily qualitative methodologists, particularly in their use of ethnographic methods and semi-structured interviews. All scholars interviewed rated their graduate training in qualitative methods lacking, which may be surprising given that Morgan and Philip are anthropologists and Alex is a sociologist.[5] Ethan utilized a variety of methodologies in his dissertation project, opting for months of participant observation in a local nonprofit to gain trust in the low-income neighborhood in which his study population lived then training and supervising a team of enumerators to administer a survey during subsequent fieldwork trips. Philip incorporates a wide range of interactions, both in-person and digital, in his work investigating Queer expression and Queer community in urban India. Collectively, the methodological approaches of the scholars interviewed highlights that Queer identity need not be an insurmountable barrier to participating in fieldwork. Participant observation, ethnographic embeddedness, and semi-structured interviews can carry tolls associated with opting out of disclosure, as discussed earlier. Nevertheless, these scholars have conducted highly interpersonal research methods with the knowledge of their field sites and respective cultural contexts, showing that Queer identities do not automatically preclude any particular methodology at the onset.

Ethics for Participants and Interlocutors

Given the focus on human subject training to consider the ethics of our study participants, it is clear that there ought to be limits to our work. If a given project is interested in Queer human subjects in a marginalized societal position, considerable efforts must be made to ensure the research can be completed with minimal risk to the participant. In particular, the test should not be whether a Queer study participant is at similar risk of harm as a non-Queer study participant, because that test could be very difficult to perceive. Instead, it should be about general harm and risk, and many projects need to consider either less than ideal methods or abandonment, as the expanse of science should not come at the expense of pain and hardship.

Working with Queer populations, Philip, Cameron, and Morgan all engage in thoughtful, patient, and measured interactions with their study participants. Working in the MENA region, Cameron's Queer study participants are at considerable risk of harm from their state and society writ large. As such, Cameron attends Queer activist meetings only, taking cues from the community itself as to the safest means of meeting. Similarly, Morgan does not conduct one-on-one interviews outside of Queer spaces, such as rotating gay bar nights or Queer group meetings, because doing so would expose that individual unnecessarily. Morgan also refuses to participate directly in any public demonstrations and protests, even when the motivating issue has been close to their work; Morgan has recognized that their interlocutors would likely prioritize Morgan's safety as part of the ethics of hospitality, which Morgan believes is an unnecessary risk to her interlocutors. Philip's field site in urban India has a more readily accessible Queer population, but he still engages with the Queer community in the spaces in which they comfortably express Queer identities. Unfortunately, all three recalled instances in which another researcher sought to access their entrusted social networks haphazardly, failing to recognize the work of properly reducing the risk of harm to Queer study participants. Cameron and Morgan acknowledge the element of luck, patience, and earnestness necessary to gain the trust of Queer interlocutors, but in turn, these Queer interlocutors and study participants offer the meaningful insights necessary for their research.

Beyond Queer participants, a concern that is difficult to comprehend without limited fieldwork prior to a large project is whether certain methodologies put study participants at risk due to association with the researcher.

To explain by way of an example, my dissertation fieldwork was profoundly impacted by the Russian annexation of Crimea and supporting separatists in the Donbass. Suddenly, my nationality as an American became a liability and additional care was necessary to ensure that I did not put my interview subjects or their organizations at risk. As the conflict intensified, I decided that the risk was too great for nonprofits, then regionally funded organizations, until I was limiting myself to federally connected organizations and individuals. Those federally connected individuals had greater clarity regarding whether it was safe for them to participate in my study than individuals and groups with less direct contact with federal authorities. In this example, my Queerness was not the facet of my identity that posed the greatest risk to study participants, but it speaks to issues we may not prepare for, particularly in situations where rumor regarding our research spreads and potentially harms future participants. In such cases, Queer researchers may experience fewer reserves of patience, hospitality, or understanding, and it is simply a part of how fieldwork does not go as planned.

By extension, there are also issues with maintaining close relationships with interlocutors, who often are gatekeepers to their social networks but also to legitimacy for a researcher. In the case of my fieldwork in Russia, I was fortunate to receive support from a regional research institute that subsequently opened doors to area universities. This network of scholars was phenomenal, the scholars were exceptionally well trained, and many of them were more liberal in their personal views, which has also been Alex's experience in his fieldwork in Russia. This did not mean that he and I agreed on all the perspectives when we would discuss professional or personal topics with these colleagues. Instead, our colleagues' liberal perspective came with the capacity to agree to disagree, an acceptance of difference rather than conformity. Officials or academics in more senior positions, who were trained in a more rigid and hierarchical Soviet model, have a far greater tendency to be less accommodating. Nevertheless, Alex and I were able to access academic networks that offered accepting and collegial relationships in support of our research, despite shifting attitudes in Russian society away from Queer acceptance.

The Investigator's Physical Well-Being

Exposure to physical harm can be mitigated by selecting appropriate field sites, using ethical methodologies, and working with trustworthy interlocutors. Queer scholars simply face additional factors in identifying safe practices for fieldwork, but all fieldwork requires considering the safety of transportation, location, and other risks. Ethan and Sadie in particular sought out best practices to ensure physical safety in the field, as their research sites dealt with legacies and current practices of political violence. For both, the paramount importance of safety overpowered other considerations, such as the immediate consequences to their mental and emotional health. Their Queer identities did not factor into their evaluation of their safety, because the possibility of harm was pervasive in their respective field sites. Sadie did, however, have to increasingly deal with being a female scholar because it caused interlocutors to treat her differently, suggesting certain opportunities for research were beyond her ability to carry out safely. Pushing against these social barriers became a frustration in her work, but they speak to some of the power we bring into the field as scholars, because our safety is considered separately from those whom we study.

Cameron's experience with maintaining his safety while conducting research on Queer activism in the MENA region requires that we acknowledge the differences in risk based on nationality. Unlike the other interviewees, Cameron's citizenship is with a state in the MENA region, and this fundamentally alters the threat of arrest or harassment while conducting fieldwork on Queer activism in a range of MENA societies. The threat of violence against himself and his study participants limits the MENA states in which he is willing to conduct fieldwork, but he cannot rely on the protection and advocacy of his embassy if he is arrested, unlike his Western colleagues. This became clear to Cameron once when he was observing a Queer activist meeting in the MENA region and he left the event with the participants at its conclusion. Suddenly, Cameron was walking through the streets with activists who behaved and dressed in an expression of Queer defiance, drawing attention to themselves at a time in which he is trying to limit his profile. For Cameron, walking through the heavily policed streets as part of a Queer group was exhilarating, yet he suddenly panicked that their Queer visibility would not escape the intrusive gaze of the police. In subsequent discussions with Western colleagues, Cameron faced resistance to his reaction as they did not appreciate the precarity of not having a passport that could offer leverage against police harassment. The lack of professional acknowledgment for the barriers his research faces is an indication that greater training in qualitative methodologies and their risks is needed not only in graduate school programs but also in professional circles.

Sadie, Claire, and Morgan face a different risk profile in the field as women, and each have found ways to mitigate the dangers. They

Table 15.1. Descriptions of Interviewees

Pseudonym	Basic Demographics	Fieldwork Experience
Simon	Gay cis man	Sub-Saharan Africa
Morgan	Pansexual nonbinary person	Eurasia
Claire	Bisexual cis woman	Central America
Cameron	Gay cis man	MENA
Nicholas	Gay cis man	Rural India
Philip	Queer cis man	Urban India
Sadie	Bisexual cis woman	Mexico
Ethan	Gay cis man	South America
Alex	Gay cis man	Russian Federation
Myself (author)	Gay cis man	Russian Federation

have used their identity as women to their advantage to gain access to greater protections in specific moments of precarity but still having to fight against attempts to infantilize them. For Claire, much of her early work was conducted while she was in a heterosexual relationship, which allowed her to bring her male partner along to mitigate the chauvinism and machismo in her field sites. Similarly, Sadie and Morgan disclosed their heteronormative relationships to ensure that they were not perceived as the promiscuous single foreign female or a similar trope. For Morgan, however, their partner is trans male, and so the concerns relating to physical safety are not completely assuaged. Regarding her recent fieldwork, Claire's current life partner is female and she has not joined her on research trips. This largely reflects Claire's fieldwork shifting to be of multiple trips of shorter duration, but there is also the concern for how their relationship will be perceived. It should be stated, however, that all three have conducted considerable fieldwork without their partners. It is simply worth noting that at different points in time, their heteronormative partner offered additional support and occasional social leeway.

Queer Intimacy in the Field

Sex and intimate relationships in fieldwork is not a new consideration for research ethics, and the interviewees' experiences ranged from maintaining their committed relationships to dating in the field to a policy of celibacy. For example, Alex conducted his dissertation fieldwork in the Russian Federation prior to its current political salience, which gave him the ability use online dating openly, through which he met his boyfriends. Throughout subsequent fieldwork, Alex felt comfortable disclosing his homosexual relationships to trusted colleagues and never felt that he obscured his Queer identity. He does recognize, however, that the degree of that expression and openness certainly depended on the respective social circumstance, just like in his everyday life, but he sought to control the disclosure of his relationships to manage those social dynamics. I conducted fieldwork in the same city years later, and the threat of harassment for Queer persons was much higher. My partner did not join me for fieldwork, and upon the end of our relationship, I did not attempt to date and adopted a policy of celibacy out of concern for my safety (Balmforth 2013). The differences in our experiences reflect not only the shifting sociopolitical realities for Queer people in Russia but also the differing personal capacities and confidence in navigating Queer life in Russia.

Others sought to create protective distances in their fieldwork to provide a space for intimacy and self-expression. Nicholas has his primary research site in rural India, and he noted that the social conservatism of his field site was protective—sexuality was taboo. This provided him considerable social protection in his field site as a cisgender white gay man, but he found the need to occasionally stay in an apartment in a nearby city every few weeks to enjoy the comforts of a city, as well as the possibility for intimacy. Similarly, Ethan did not pursue any intimate relationships in the low-income neighborhood in which he was embedded, but he was able to date by traveling to upper-income neighborhoods in his research site. The social barriers between the two neighborhoods were powerful and ensured that he could avoid any issues in his embedded fieldwork, in which physical safety was a paramount daily concern.

Where it was available, Queer spaces also provided opportunities for interviewees to revel in their Queer identity, which was an act of intimacy in its own right. Even as Philip conducted fieldwork in Queer spaces in urban India, he often felt the need to enjoy those same spaces outside of research, just as he would in his everyday life. While this came at the expense of observational data, the boon to mental health was a worthwhile investment. Similarly, Ethan, Alex, and Morgan sought out Queer spaces in their field sites as safe places in which to socialize with their partners, as well as spaces for joy. Access to an established Queer space is not guaranteed at all field sites, but half of interviewees noted that seeking out spaces, even in places far from their primary field site, was a worth the effort in hindsight given the mental health benefits.

"Field Closeting"—Nevermore?

As a final consideration, Queer researchers must deal with the practice of "field closeting,"[6] and they must do so in an entirely selfish manner. Unlike some other gatekept characteristics, Queer identities can often be seen as optional. Whether "flamboyant behavior" or "provocative dress," there can be a casual reflex by others to suggest simply "toning it down." Field closeting captures a range of strategies to alter one's appearance and behavior to better fit established social norms in a given field site, and many researchers engaged in fieldwork modify their behaviors to reduce social friction. Women quite frequently encounter situations in which they consider altering their dress or behavior, though men also experience the pressure of adhering to social norms.

For certain Queer individuals, these genuflections to societal expectations can amount to personal harm. Embracing a Queer identity can be a lifesaving act, and compromising on such personal breakthroughs should not be taken lightly. In my fieldwork, I engage in what I perceive to be substantial field closeting, but, as stated previously, my status as a cisgender white man has typically given me social leeway for remaining behaviors that do not conform perfectly to social standards. My privileged position also means that I face fewer instances in which my decision to field closet wears on my mental and emotional health. I have been afforded respect in professional situations, given all the courtesies of being a male guest. Access to such social graces make my field closeting a much more tolerable experience for me personally. Queer researchers should not dismiss out of hand how serious the toll can be of field closeting.

In discussing these dynamics with interviewees, Philip and Alex pushed back on field closeting as a novel process. Both wished to ensure that fieldwork and "being in the field" were not exoticized from everyday life outside fieldwork, particularly in considering behaviors related to closeting. While not engaging directly, the perspectives reflect the continual process of navigating a Queer identity in everyday life as explored by Sedgwick, which necessitates "new calculations, new draughts, and requisitions of secrecy or disclosure" (Sedgwick 2008, 68). Their critique is notable, because as scholars we must avoid pejorative or condescending understandings of our field sites. I acknowledge their critique to state that scholars may face different costs and strains of closeting while in the field than in their everyday life, and those differences are meaningful and difficult. They should be acknowledged and considered in research design, but we should also ensure that the difficulties in the field are not unfairly amplified to diminish the field site in the eyes of the researcher.

Concluding Suggestions

The sheer amount of interview data and range of experiences of the scholars participating in this project make it difficult to offer universal suggestions for Queer fieldwork. What follows is not meant to be comprehensive and definitive, but it is based in a single foundational premise: Queer scholars should engage in research design that is cognizant of their Queer realities. Across all the interviewees, there was not a universal experience or reflection on fieldwork, and the range of methods and field sites reflects this diversity. As Queer junior scholars and graduate students design their projects, they should not be dismissive of safety concerns and known personal tolls in fieldwork simply to achieve an external research gold standard. A life of scholarship is a marathon, and the spectrum of Queer realities requires unique approaches to ensure fieldwork does not traumatize or derail a future career.

While none of those interviewed selected their field site(s) with their Queer identity as a paramount lens for that decision making, each have adjusted fieldwork methods and research design in subtle and notable ways vis-à-vis their Queer identities to ensure that access to the field and quality of research is maximized. All interviewees agreed that predissertation fieldwork was vital to their research design decision making and identifying appropriate fieldwork sites for their research question. While funding can be scarce for such work, making the investment in time and energy to secure such funding proved pivotal for several interviewees. A second overarching finding was that over half of respondents would not pursue a second project in line with their dissertation's research design. For those unwilling to do so, the dissertation was the longest and most straining stint of fieldwork in their career, and their lives and careers have developed such that attempting another project of that scale and intensity is either untenable or undesired. I raise this point to emphasize that how a research career begins does not dictate its overall course, and young

Queer scholars should be empowered to pursue a project's research design with the research question in mind, cognizant that method, duration, and field site are all subject to change at their discretion.

On this note of methodological flexibility, utilizing subnational variation and using multiple research trips within a given study period could be a way to mitigate harm for a Queer researcher. Given the variation in Queer acceptance and protections globally and domestically, a researcher can utilize these variations to their advantage, if the payoff for research is deemed sufficient. For example, a research question may be applicable in two country cases, but one of the cases does not provide legal protections for Queer people and has worrisome political rhetoric. Rather than feeling compelled to do work in both countries, it is possible to design a comparative fieldwork project within the less problematic case, and the more hostile location can be handled as a shadow case within the project. In addition, rather than attempting to stay for months on end, shorter research trips could be considered in order to minimize risks. Often in fieldwork, our research designs do not materialize and we are forced to improvise, which leads to a consistent preference for longer-term fieldwork. Repeated trips can offer a researcher multiple chances to improvise as needed, but these shorter trips may drastically mitigate the risks for a Queer researcher than staying in a hostile environment without pause. These are not solutions that can ameliorate the problem in its entirety, nor can they remove additional transportation costs, but they could be the difference for data collection and a successful research project.

For those seeking to conduct research on Queer populations or movements, a key piece of advice from the interviewees is to be patient and follow the lead of your study participants. Cameron and Morgan were approached by other researchers who demanded access to their networks at their field site, and this brazen request was made without deference to the lives of their Queer study participants. Accessing Queer spaces and populations in hostile environments requires time and significant trust, and Cameron and Morgan had to wait and slowly gain trust to the various spaces that exist in their field sites. While a junior scholar may be rushed on predissertation fieldwork or struggling to gain access on their own, inquiring with fellow researchers to learn best practices is a much more useful pathway for gaining trust, as well as demonstrating the appropriate concern for the Queer populations of study. Relatedly, Cameron, Morgan, and Philip spoke about adopting the practices of Queer populations in your research site, as they are the trusted methods for safety and privacy in that environment. For example, taking a Queer study participant out of a trusted space in which initial contact was made to conduct a one-on-one interview in a different public space can unnecessarily expose that participant to potential harm. Instead, work with the potential study participant to determine what is most comfortable and safest rather than assuming a best practice that is divorced from local practices.

Unfortunately for this chapter, I was not able to interview a trans scholar directly, but Morgan was able to shed light on how they conduct research while traveling with their trans husband, who fortunately has a deep cultural knowledge of their field site. Undoubtedly, a primary concern for trans scholars is whether they have access to healthcare in a given field site, particularly for maintaining consistent access to hormonal therapies. In Morgan's case, traveling to remote rural areas was not a realistic option for her husband, due to the open-pit restroom facilities and unreliable transportation, which would have unnecessarily exposed her husband to potentially uncomfortable or unsafe conditions. While these are unfortunate limits, they nevertheless demonstrate that trans researchers can conduct research safely in a range of societies, but careful consideration is required to ensure the safety of the researcher (Compton et al. 2018; Robinson 2022).

Overall, this chapter cannot definitively identify every obstacle to Queer scholars or provide solutions to each of those problems. We must continue to improve transparency in how we conduct fieldwork, and Queer experiences are vital for improving our practices across the social sciences. Doing so successfully will require that those scholars who enjoy social privileges in their respective fieldwork context recognize the lack of social privileges for scholars belonging to marginalized populations in their field site. This entails not only validating fieldwork methods that fall short of gold standard practices but also advocating for and defending the work of colleagues who may experience a wider array of obstacles to their preferred research design. Queer scholars have long conducted field-work, and we will continue to do so. By celebrating and recognizing such research, we can recognize the contributions of Queer scholars and better support a more diverse and rich scholarly community for future cohorts.

Editors' Note

This chapter is published under a pseudonym to protect the author's anonymity and future research agenda. The reasons for this decision should be clear to those reading the chapter. The editors have confirmed the author's identity and expertise. The author has published related work under the same name; see Campbell M. Stevens. 2024. "Field Closeting: Navigating Fieldwork as a Queer Scholar." *PS: Political Science & Politics* 57 (2): 302–5.

Notes

1. I use the term "Queer" to indicate a broad range of identities, though I recognize potential issues in doing so (Orne 2017). When I refer to my personal experiences or those of my interviewees in this chapter, I make clear reference to the respective identity, but I will use "Queer" to be inclusive of identities and realities faced by interviewees in their range of field sites that may not fit into a broader Western perception of LGBTQ-related identities. Furthermore, I capitalize "Queer" in response to dialogue with my interviewees, who preferred its use to elevate the importance of Queer communities in a time of considerable political hostility.

2. The Defense of Marriage Act (DOMA) was a federal law signed in 1993 that limited federal recognition of marriage to unions of a man and a woman in the United States, as well as providing states the capacity to define marriage as they saw fit. Eventually, thirty-one states passed DOMA-related legislation, as well as twenty-nine state constitutions amended to limit access to marriage. The Supreme Court case *Obergefell v. Hodges* in 2015 ruled these statutes as unconstitutional, which has been reinforced by the 2022 Respect for Marriage Act at the federal level. Nevertheless, many of the state-level DOMA-related laws and amendments have not been officially repealed.

3. For those seeking such perspectives, see Browne and Nash 2010; Compton et al. 2018; Robinson 2022.

4. For the discipline, the 2012 American Political Science Association Annual Meeting in New Orleans, Louisiana, was a notable reflection point on these issues. Louisiana's formerly discriminatory state constitution led to a widespread boycott, since Queer members would not enjoy access to full rights in Louisiana, despite New Orleans' acceptance of Queer persons. For additional information (see Glenn 2008; Jaschik 2012).

5. I had hoped that I would get an account of superior methodological training by purposefully seeking an interdisciplinary group of scholars. Unfortunately, all those interviewed had to pursue additional training in qualitative methodologies outside of their graduate programs or rely on their fieldwork experience to determine appropriate qualitative approaches. Greater methodological training is needed throughout the social sciences, at least according to the scholars interviewed for this chapter.

6. For a further exploration of this concept, see Stevens 2024.

References

Ahram, Ariel I., and J. Paul Goode. 2016. "Researching Authoritarianism in the Discipline of Democracy: Authoritarianism in the Discipline of Democracy." *Social Science Quarterly* 97 (4): 834–49.

Aldrich, Daniel P. 2009. "The 800-Pound Gaijin in the Room: Strategies and Tactics for Conducting Fieldwork in Japan and Abroad." *PS: Political Science & Politics* 42 (02): 299–303.

Angelo, Paul J., and Dominic Bocci. 2021. "The Changing Landscape of Global LGBTQ+ Rights." Council on Foreign Relations, January 29. https://www.cfr.org/article/changing-landscape-global-lgbtq-rights.

Balmforth, Tom. 2013. "In Russia, Violent Videos Show a Startling New Form of Gay Bullying." *Atlantic*, August 2. https://www.theatlantic.com/international/archive/2013/08/in-russia-violent-videos-show-a-startling-new-form-of-gay-bullying/278294/.

Browne, Kath, and Catherine J. Nash, eds. 2010. *Queer Methods and Methodologies: Intersecting Queer Theories and Social Science Research.* Ashgate.

Calvey, David. 2008. "The Art and Politics of Covert Research: Doing 'Situated Ethics' in the Field." *Sociology* 42 (5): 905–18.

Chacko, Elizabeth. 2004. "Positionality and Praxis: Fieldwork Experiences in Rural India." *Singapore Journal of Tropical Geography* 25 (1): 51–63.

Chambers, Joseph. 2020. "When Fieldwork Falls Apart: Navigating Disruption from Political Turmoil in Research." *Area* 52 (2): 437–44.

Compton, D'Lane R., Tey Meadow, and Kristen Schilt, eds. 2018. *Other, Please Specify: Queer Methods in Sociology.* University of California Press.

Driscoll, Jesse. 2021. *Doing Global Fieldwork: A Social Scientist's Guide to Mixed-Methods Research Far from Home.* Columbia University Press.

Essig, Laurie. 1999. *Queer in Russia: A Story of Sex, Self, and the Other.* Duke University Press.

Flores, Andrew R. 2021. "Social Acceptance of LGBTI People in 175 Countries and Locations, 1981 to 2020." Williams Institute. https://williamsinstitute.law.ucla.edu/wp-content/uploads/Global-Acceptance-Index-LGBTI-Nov-2021.pdf.

Fujii, Lee Ann. 2012. "Research Ethics 101: Dilemmas and Responsibilities." *PS: Political Science & Politics* 45 (04): 717–23.

Glasius, Marlies, Meta de Lange, Jos Bartman et al. 2018. *Research, Ethics and Risk in the Authoritarian Field.* Springer International.

Glenn, David. 2008. "Lesbian and Gay Advocates Object to New Orleans Site for Political-Science Conference." *Chronicle of Higher Education*, May 30. https://www.chronicle.com/article/lesbian-and-gay-advocates-object-to-new-orleans-site-for-political-science-conference/.

Healey, Dan. 2018. *Russian Homophobia from Stalin to Sochi.* Bloomsbury.

Hellawell, David. 2006. "Inside–Out: Analysis of the Insider–Outsider Concept as a Heuristic Device to Develop Reflexivity in Students Doing Qualitative Research." *Teaching in Higher Education* 11 (4): 483–94.

Jacobs, Alan M., Tim Büthe, Ana Arjona et al. 2021. "The Qualitative Transparency Deliberations: Insights and Implications." *Perspectives on Politics* 19 (1): 171–208.

Jaschik, Scott. 2012. "To Boycott or Not?" *Inside Higher Ed*, August 27. https://www.insidehighered.com/news/2012/08/27/political-science-meeting-faces-boycott-over-gay-rights.

Johnson, Janet Elise. 2009. "Unwilling Participant Observation Among Russian Siloviki and the Good-Enough Field Researcher." *PS: Political Science & Politics* 42 (02): 321–24.

Kapiszewski, Diana, Lauren M. Maclean, and Benjamin L. Read. 2015. *Field Research in Political Science: Practices and Principles*. Cambridge University Press.

Khazov-Cassia, Sergei, and Carl Schreck. 2019. "'Something Inside Me Died': An Ethnic Chechen Says He Was Tortured in Antigay 'Purge.'" Radio Free Europe/Radio Liberty, October 11, sec. Russia. https://www.rferl.org/a/chechnya-gays-purges/30211574.html.

Kondakov, Alexander Sasha. 2022. *Violent Affections: Queer Sexuality, Techniques of Power, and Law in Russia*. UCL Press.

Marks, Zoe. 2020. "Cooking Soup and Killing Chickens: Navigating Gender and Food-as-Fieldwork in West Africa." In *Stories from the Field: A Guide to Navigating Fieldwork in Political Science*, edited by Peter Krause and Ora Szekely. Columbia University Press.

Newsome, Akasemi. 2014. "Knowing When to Scale Back: Addressing Questions of Research Scope in the Field." *PS: Political Science & Politics* 47 (02): 410–13.

Orne, Jason. 2017. *Boystown: Sex & Community in Chicago*. University of Chicago Press.

Ortbals, Candice D., and Meg E. Rincker. 2009a. "Embodied Researchers: Gendered Bodies, Research Activity, and Pregnancy in the Field." *PS: Political Science & Politics* 42 (02): 315–19.

Ortbals, Candice D., and Meg E. Rincker. 2009b. "Fieldwork, Identities, and Intersectionality: Negotiating Gender, Race, Class, Religion, Nationality, and Age in the Research Field Abroad: Editors' Introduction." *PS: Political Science & Politics* 42 (02): 287–90.

Poushter, Jacob, and Nicholas Kent. 2020. "The Global Divide on Homosexuality Persists." Pew Research Center's Global Attitudes Project (blog), June 25. https://www.pewresearch.org/global/2020/06/25/global-divide-on-homosexuality-persists/.

Robinson, Brandon Andrew. 2022. "Non-Binary Embodiment, Queer Knowledge Production, and Disrupting the Cisnormative Field: Notes from a Trans Ethnographer." *Journal of Men's Studies* 30 (3): 425–45.

Sauer, Pjotr. 2022. "Russia Passes Law Banning 'LGBT Propaganda' Among Adults." *The Guardian*, November 24, sec. World News. https://www.theguardian. com/world/2022/nov/24/russia-passes-law-banning-lgbt-propaganda-adults.

Scoggins, Suzanne E. 2014. "Navigating Fieldwork as an Outsider: Observations from Interviewing Police Officers in China." *PS: Political Science & Politics* 47 (02): 394–97.

Sedgwick, Eve Kosofsky. 2008. *Epistemology of the Closet*. Updated. University of California Press.

Seidman, Steven. 1998. "Are We All in the Closet? Notes Towards a Sociological and Cultural Turn in Queer Theory." *European Journal of Cultural Studies* 1 (2): 177–92.

Sirnate, Vasundhara. 2014. "Positionality, Personal Insecurity, and Female Empathy in Security Studies Research." *PS: Political Science & Politics* 47 (02): 398–401.

Stevens, Campbell M. 2024. "Field Closeting: Navigating Fieldwork as a Queer Scholar." *PS: Political Science & Politics* 57 (2): 302–5.

Tewksbury, Richard, and Patricia Gagné. 1997. "Assumed and Presumed Identities: Problems of Self-Presentation in Field Research." *Sociological Spectrum* 17:127–55.

Chapter 16

Using Library Instruction to Teach LGBTQ Politics

Daryl J. Barker

The chapters in this volume show how instructors tasked with teaching LGBTQ politics can do so in a meaningful way. This premise is based on a fundamental belief that learners and instructors benefit from a culture that engages in collaborative learning styles. Recently, as a graduate student instructor for a first-year seminar, an interdisciplinary year-long learning experience for incoming students, I encountered a situation that I think clearly highlights the pitfalls of failing to explore collaborative methods in instruction. The course focused on concepts of sex and gender, and implicitly sexuality; much of the material that was selected, however, elevated positions that reinforced normative values and presented harmful information about gender and sexual minorities. As a result, I spent a large portion of our weekly discussion sections unpacking and addressing the experience of harm my students encountered through readings and lectures. Instead of fostering a learning environment that encouraged my students to ask questions, grow, and thrive academically, we were engaged in a persistent exercise of damage control. A librarian, empowered to provide additional materials from a more LGBTQ-inclusive perspective, could have collaborated with the faculty in my course if given the opportunity. This could have been an opening for providing materials from a variety of perspectives that better reflect the current consensus among leading scholars in the fields under study. Instead, without the assistance of a librarian, the course relied on a dated syllabus, and the course was ultimately discontinued. The most frustrating part of this story is that a librarian was assigned to assist with the course, we just did not have the framework for meaningful collaboration that allowed them to contribute to course materials, course planning, and pedagogy.

This chapter specifically addresses the role librarians play in collaborating with professors and instructors to effectively teach LGBTQ political science. Ultimately, the librarian's role is to help instructors teach and gain access to materials that will enrich the learner's experience. For students, the library can be part of what Jane Martin (1976) termed *hidden curriculum*, and the same is true for professors. Martin thinks through what the curriculum teaches learners in a superstructural way. She explores what values are being taught, what is being reinforced by what is taught, and how these are being internalized by those engaged in educational practice.

In this chapter, I will explore some more mainstream and recognized tools that are available and explore some resources that have not historically been represented in the teaching of LGBTQ politics but that offer new points of entry for scholarly consideration. Martin (1976, 142) cautions against the arguments concerning the inevitability of harmful hidden curricula, saying, "There is always a possibility that we will end up with a better [curriculum]." The project of this chapter is to participate in the possibility of finding a better curriculum for instructors teaching queer politics in collaboration with librarians.

Underlying each of the pedagogical approaches that will be discussed in this chapter are three core principles that form the foundation upon which the collaborative efforts of librarians and professors can be most successful. The three principles are, first, *learner-centered pedagogy*, a philosophy of teaching/instruction with a humanistic approach that places learners at the center of any educational effort with instructors as facilitators who build a curriculum by considering inquiry-based learning from the learner's perspective (Klipfel and Cook 2017). Second, *critically engaged pedagogy*, which bell hooks articulates as a method of instruction that recognizes the lived experiences and values of students' preexisting knowledge in educational settings and connects learning to those experiences. For instructors, hooks (2014) encourages being vulnerable in sharing their own experiences as a starting point for being present with learners. Third, *intersectionality*, which calls on scholars to recognize systemic oppression as a factor in every interaction and to work toward equitable frameworks for the future and, among other features, encourages an approach that engages both inquiry and praxis (Collins and Sirma Bilge 2020). These principles have many volumes written about them, so I will not attempt to recreate the breadth of that work here. Each of the works referenced above are good primers to understand the theory behind these principles. With this core forming the bases for the work of teaching LGBTQ politics, collaborations can emerge as a transformative practice of learning with a focus on usable pedagogical techniques for application.

This chapter will be structured to provide a clear scaffolded framework for how professors can engage with librarians to do the work of teaching LGBTQ politics. The first section will provide an overview of types of collaborations that librarians often engage in to provide a clear sense of the mechanics for collaboration. The next section will interrogate how to address the complicated concepts of queer subjects as they appear in library and archival research. It will also look critically at problems of naming conventions and offer some solutions for how librarians can help shape assignments toward inclusive topics of inquiry for a variety of fields of study across political science subdisciplines. The last section will address possibilities for continuing to work outside of traditional sources available in college and university libraries. In each of these sections, instructors should consider what resources and approaches they select carefully, incorporating principles of learner-centered, critically engaged, and intersectional frameworks to think about constructing pedagogical approaches for the teaching of LGBTQ politics in collaboration with the library.

A Note About Library Anxiety

Walking into the library in my first few weeks of college I observed that students who were clearly much younger than me all seemed to have a purpose, knew where to go and what to do, and knew how to use the library. I was a nontraditional student, having returned to college seven years after finishing high school. I came from a field where I rapidly approached middle management and was seen as a subject matter expert in my field by peers. In the college library, I was lost. I was experiencing firsthand what Dr. Scott Lee (2011) calls *library anxiety*. I was lucky enough to observe my own mother return to school after a first career (and having me) and watched her complete an undergraduate and a master's degree. I knew I could ask her when I had questions or didn't know where to look to find the answers on my own. The truth is, I was incredibly lucky to have her as a resource in my educational experience. Not everyone is so lucky.

As a result, much of my work stems from a desire to demystify some of these processes for those who do not have a similar person available to them. The truth of my perception from those early days in the college library is also a bit flawed. Just because people *appeared* to know what they were doing, does not necessarily mean they did. In this chapter, you will find examples of what the UCLA Center for the Advancement of Teaching describes as transparency in teaching and learning.[1] This is another method by which we can reduce barriers to entry for learners as we demonstrate that the research process is iterative, valuing expertise while also valuing personal experiences and growth at the same time. Transparency also has the added bonus of helping students feel less anxious as they learn how to navigate the resources available to them in the library. Students, instructors, and librarians each bring something different to the table that we can use in collaborative instruction efforts. Doing research in the library can be a daunting undertaking, especially when dealing with topics of gender, sex, or sexual identity, which may be particularly sensitive for LGBTQ individuals. This, in turn, can lead to library anxiety. The techniques that follow will help address library anxiety and help instructors and librarians collaborate to the improve learner's experience and expose them to LGBTQ politics.

Collaborating with Librarians

The Association of College and Research Libraries (ACRL) adopted the *Framework for Information Literacy* in 2016,[2] creating a set of concepts to guide college and university library instruction goals for information literacy. They define information literacy as "the set of integrated abilities encompassing the reflective discovery of information, the understanding of how information is produced and valued, and the use of information in creating new knowledge and participating ethically in communities of learning." This framework drives modes of library instruction today, informing how librarians approach working with instructors and students. The framework also provides a set of common core philosophies that can be helpful in communicating meaningful learning standards and objectives when working with a professor on a specific lesson plan.

In order to best collaborate with a librarian, it is important to understand what different modes of instruction are in the librarian's tool kit in order to assist faculty. These instructional tools include access to resources, one-shot librarian instruction, synchronous and asynchronous library workshops, and embedded models. Resources in this context can mean several things, including physical/digital materials (books, ebooks, media, primary materials, secondary periodicals, etc.), library/librarian-produced materials (how-to videos, worksheets, workshops, research assistance sessions, etc.) or vendor-provided materials (data visualization software and text analysis tools or hardware). Each of these tools offers a different set of strengths and weaknesses that should be considered when evaluating what will best serve any particular class or learning goal.

STAND-ALONE RESOURCES

Librarians spend a great deal of time and energy maintaining easily accessible and readily available resources that any patron can access freely. This can include things like library or research guides, reading lists, and information literacy handouts, all of which exist as stand-alone documents that students can pick up outside of a specific workshop or class and are easily transferable between learning environments. Including these resources in a syllabus, including them in an online learning environment, or leaving physical copies available for students to pick up in a classroom are easy ways to encourage students to utilize the myriad of instructional tools available in the library. This particular mode of literacy instruction offers the added benefit of being relatively easy to implement by any course instructor. A newly arriving visiting or adjunct professor might not have a close relationship with the political science liaison librarian but can easily look up these resources offered by the library on their website. Additionally, this method encourages students to be in the driver's seat for seeking out relevant resources themselves.

Presenting this as the first step in a series of engagements (scaffolding) using an intersectional lens can become part of a more learner-centered approach. This includes offering materials in multiple formats for learners with different learning styles. In this context, intersectional framing could include highlighting queer materials from the Global South or highlighting the voices of gender nonconforming folks of color, making an explicit effort to consider axes of power and oppression that intersect with queer identity. This can become an even more effective tool if an instructor connects with the subject librarian to create class- or subject-specific resources like research guides or handouts.

This process has the added benefit of starting to form a collaborative relationship between the subject liaison librarian and the instructor for more involved instructional opportunities in the future. By engaging the subject librarian in this conversation, the instructor and librarian can work together to think about the kinds of queer resources that they can acquire. This can be done through collection development and through finding open-source materials that include or focus on queer political subjects. A national organization for student affairs developed a working group in 2021 called the Coalition for Sexuality and Gender Identities who put together a list of the current publications focused on queerness from a variety of disciplines. This is a good place to start a conversation about making additions to the collection development strategy to include more queer materials.[3]

For stand-alone materials, the instructor and librarian could develop a handout that highlights the available collections, databases, or journals that focus on queer political subjects or offer lists of search terms that include historical as well as contemporary naming conventions. Jennifer Snow at the Yale University Library produced a library guide that includes a tab with all of the relevant Library of Congress (LoC)[4] subject headings on queer topics, displaying those in current use that are explicitly queer, and the LoC itself now offers a LGBTQ research guide to using the library.[5] A tool like this will allow students to more effectively navigate the highly structured library searches that rely on LoC subject headings, which can be very different from using a natural language search (like Google) on the internet.

As academics ourselves, we all know the pitfalls of this mode too. We've all been handed a twenty-plus page syllabus on day one of a course to pick it back up only once or twice during the term. A single paragraph in a document, like one directing students to read about available materials in the library, is not likely to garner much attention, especially in today's highly attention-competitive digital environments. This mode of collaboration is also lacking in the creative collaborative elements that offer possibilities for engaging students in the material more deeply. Keeping in mind these underlying principles, this method would not pass muster as either learner-centered or critically engaged if offered in isolation. Letting students know that library assistance is offered with large print materials for visually impaired students, having handouts available in multiple formats and languages, or including resources that are more representative of all students who might use them are all ways that this could be implemented in a more meaningful way.

ONE-SHOT INSTRUCTION

One-shots are the bread and butter of most instructional librarians. If you have ever worked with a librarian to teach in the past, this is most likely the mode of instruction that you encountered, and it is also the most balanced approach in terms of time commitments and learning outcomes for instructors, librarians, and learners. This mode of instruction occurs when an instructor reaches out to the library or a specific librarian to conduct a one-time visit to class in order to achieve one specific learning objective. Buchanan and McDonough's book *The One-Shot Librarian Instruction*, 3rd ed., offers numerous insights into the multiple styles, approaches, and environments that can be termed "one-shot" instruction. They caution, though, that there is no silver bullet; specific instructors and librarians will have to be thoughtful and communicative about the goals and methods of a particular one-shot instruction to be successful (Buchanan and McDonough, 2021, 5). Buchannan and McDonough's work reflects on the importance of having source material that is both relevant and engaging, which when done correctly can also provide perspectives that engage with power and oppression in the political sphere while also allowing the learner to take the lead in exploring the meaning derived from the sources.

As Buchanan and McDonough describe, being thoughtful about the types of source material that will most benefit students in a given class is a good starting point. Highlighting data sources the library has available for a political science research methods course is a good example of pairing relevant source material to the course subject material. Several organizations look specifically at data on queer folks that provide relevant source materials for engaging students in conversations on queer politics. Librarian Diana King at the UCLA library produced a library guide highlighting LGBTQ studies materials, where she provides a range of data sources that focus on queerness.[6] This guide includes some well-known sources like the Pew Research Center,[7] as well as others like the Movement Advancement Project, which maps LGBTQ populations, providing insights about queer populations across the US.[8]

Alternatively, if a professor has already provided datasets, focusing on datasets may not be the most useful tool for those students to learn in a one-shot session. Instead, highlighting interdisciplinary critiques of data may add to students' existing scaffolded knowledge while also offering a chance for students to engage with other material that may be more relevant or meaningful to their personal experience. Modeling for students a specific critical search technique, then allowing them time in the one-shot to practice the skill themselves, can create a sense of efficacy and demonstrate the collaborative nature of searching. Scholarship in digital humanities offers a useful framework for engaging here. In digital humanities it is common not only to analyze what the data present tell us but also to looks for gaps in the data; what data are not present and where data have null values may point to ways we can demonstrate who is seen or not seen in our data sets and what their presence (or lack of presence) says about the power dynamics represented by the data we are working with (Trouillot 2015). One data researcher, Charlie Whittington (2018), describes the invisibility of queer people in widely collected data, like the annual American Community Survey, in terms of the government's lack of ability to even recognize when specific problems face queer folks and queer communities. This has historically been a problem, but as Whittington notes, it is still a common issue across many fields and can skew or render queer identities invisible in data.

Focusing on small group learning activities is a good way to allow students to engage with peers in a process of experiential learning, and posing problems for them to solve can engage students in learning exercises that have been recognized going back to John Dewey. Problem solving also has the added benefit of recentering the learner's own experiences; even if the instructor or librarian has a specific solution in mind, there is still likely more than one way to solve a problem in the context of literacy instruction. This will allow students to use their existing strengths and knowledge to build another tool in their kit to creatively solve a problem. Group problem solving has the potential to encourage students to engage each other in sharing meaningful experiences that are different from each other as well, reinforcing our principle of critically engaged pedagogy through a practice of structured learning environments that both encourage students to feel safe sharing their lived experiences of a political issue and allow students to hear how these topics have affected their peers.

Discussion and demonstration are powerful tools for an instructor in any setting to engage students in the material. In the context of library instruction, it will also help us show rather than tell about the concept of knowledge and information being engaged through interpersonal connection. Being able to think and write about ideas in the abstract is a useful skill, but in the context of scholarship, being able to discuss ideas with peers offers the opportunity to make students part of the knowledge production process. Librarians will often make errors in their demonstration searches so that students can see that even librarians make mistakes or do not find exactly what they are looking for on the first try. This is important for many reasons, but especially if it encourages students to participate even after making similar steps in their own research and thereby reducing library anxiety. Being able to talk about it is also a tool to help all learners engage with each other to overcome the barriers they encounter in their research, to seek out assistance if needed, and to be creative in answering their own questions long after a one-shot instruction is over.

Now we have explored some of the key aspects of the one-shot that can make it more effective. But the obvious shortcoming is in the name—there is only one shot! This can make it challenging to fit all of the relevant information, learning objectives, or available resources into the session, especially if trying to keep stick to one class session meeting, which for undergraduate courses can be as short as one hour. There is also limited direct one-on-one or small group engagement between learner and an instructor or librarian, engagement that can help students be comfortable seeking assistance in the library. In a one-shot for an introductory course, even if the class is broken down into smaller groups, there is not likely to be more than one or two librarians and maybe one to three student assistants (if any) in a given session, meaning there will be very limited direct contact.

On the more positive side though, it is possible to model multiple search methods, engage with a variety of resource types, conduct inquiry-based learning, focus on student experiences, and engage with materials using critical framings. The form also allows for opportunities to engage in scaffolding for learning, providing one part of the tool in the session and the knowledge to employ other parts individually or in groups. It also offers a relatively low barrier to entry for trying out creative educational tools. Students can enter not knowing about a skill, be exposed, apply personal knowledge, and build a tool in the space of one session. This is particularly relevant with emerging data-driven visualization (e.g., Tableau) or geolocation software (QGIS), which do a lot of the heavy lifting without students needing to know the ins and outs of computer coding. In short, the one-shot can be a space of creative, collaborative problem solving at every level of the process.

LIBRARY WORKSHOPS

After reading about the ways that one-shot instruction sessions can be used to engage students in material specific to a learning goal, it may seem counterintuitive to move to a less responsive, more structured approach in the form of library workshops. Library workshops are often regularly scheduled events in academic libraries that focus on development of a particular skill. These differ in kind from one-shot instruction sessions because they are not generally tailored to a specific curriculum. These sessions however have a couple of benefits that make them a very useful tool for instructors to be aware of. Regularly scheduled skills workshops are common services offered by instruction librarians at colleges and universities. These usually will cover introductory concepts to information literacy—things like developing a research question, using a database, searching for materials in the catalog, citation and managing sources, or writing an annotated bibliography. All of these skills are essential to a process at any level of education for which students need to conduct research. Because workshops are usually regularly scheduled, students can pursue them at their own pace, making them learner-centered.

Instructors can incentivize students to attend by offering extra credit or providing corresponding in-class assignments that will be completed in the workshops. Furthermore, the fact that these workshops are independent of a particular class means that students that need or want a refresher can reattend to make sure they understand the material fully or get additional practice in a given skill set. This also means that students will be going to the library on their own, which any librarian will appreciate, providing opportunities for students to form relationships with the librarians and library staff. Again, while this is definitely no silver bullet, as part of a broader scaffolded learning environment the library workshop can serve a clear and meaningful purpose in building information literacy skills in a learner-centered way. While these sessions may not address a specific LGBTQ political science–related skill building, general efficacy in the skills offered through library workshops can serve as a good buttress to an LGBTQ-related curriculum. If learners are already proficient in using a library database or navigating data sets, they can then turn these skills to the study of LGBTQ political questions.

EMBEDDED LIBRARIANS

Working with an embedded librarian is the form of library instruction with the highest barrier to entry but can also have the highest impact. Embedded librarianship refers to the teaching of course with a librarian as a co-instructor or assigned to the course. This means the professor and the librarian will have to engage in developing the curriculum well in advance and decide who will be responsible for what instructional materials and milestones. This is a pretty uncommon practice, but it does provide opportunities for extended learning environments to develop in concert with unique resources at a given institution's library. For example, the California State University–Monterey Bay (CSUMB) special collections hosts an archive of two queer magazines, a gay men's periodical from the 1960s[9] and a lesbian feminist magazine from the 1970s.[10] One could imagine a course built around using these unique sources that prominently feature local landmarks and political actors. This would encourage students to engage with community partners to learn about how these areas have changed or stayed the same and integrate those narratives into a geographical model using GIS. This example illustrates one way to think about engagement between students, the library, professors, and the local community to form creative learning communities. The true strength of this approach from an information literacy perspective is the way in which it creates proximity to the learning environment in an ongoing way. Students, faculty, and librarians engaging on a regular basis allows for formation of community in a way that is much harder to achieve in a one-shot session.

The example case of the CSUMB is just one example of a way to meaningfully engage queer primary source material. Similar archives, in addition to CSUMB's Digital Commons, provide access to digital materials that could inspire similar projects. The national queer archive in Canada (ArQuives) provides free online access to a wide range of materials that could be used to similar effect. One example could be to use a collection from the ArQuives called In Defence of Queers,[11] which highlights letters to the editors of tabloid newspapers from the '60s and '70s and intersects with many of the political questions around queer liberation, including subjects of privacy, legal recognition, and questions of competing interests between religious organizations and queer people, all issues that are still live debates today. Let's now take a look at some other primary source material that is available to use in instruction.

The Ephemera of Queer Life

Artifacts left by queer people themselves are some of the best sources of queer politics. The ONE Archive at the University of Southern California began when the founder of one of the first gay mass-market publications collected all of the papers of the Mattachine Society, an early self-described homophile organization that advocated for gay rights.[12] The José Sarria Foundation is home to a collection of artifacts from the estate of Sarria, a queer iconic leader in San Francisco who ran for office nearly twenty years before Harvey Milk.[13] Numerous oral histories of the activist generation who fought a politics of indifference to their suffering during the AIDS epidemic offer numerous primary sources for exploration, whether it is through the National AIDS Memorial[14] or from the ACT UP Oral History Project.[15] There are countless other local communities and groups doing work like this, including Boston's History Project,[16] San Francisco's GLBT Historical Society,[17] and New York's LGBT Historical Sites project.[18] Each of these examples are source materials that show the breadth of what queer politics is. Each offers unique perspectives on the political history of queerness, and as educators these sources offer pedagogical tools to engage students in the history of queer politics. These community-based archives often do not have the institutional support of larger organizations or funders but provide real-world and personal encounters for many of the major political, social, and historical moments that are generation-defining, offering alternative ways to bring learners into key political moments. This work is made accessible through collaboration between instructors who use the materials and librarians who manage the collections; additionally, opportunities to create specific library or research guides makes these materials available to students in a centralized location and allows learners to encounter similar journals, collections, and resources alongside of the materials they were seeking originally.

Queer Subjects

Much of the scholarship on queerness and in the queer theory canon wrestles with the concept of what it means to be queer and whether queerness exists in a way that can be understood in the context of formal analysis. Stated another way, Is queerness definable? If so, how is it defined? In this section, I will approach these questions in three layers. The top layer will look at how to frame searches in the context of navigating library resources on queer subjects, the middle layer will look at how professors can encourage the queering of research questions through challenging ideas of what we consider to be queer, and the final layer will explore several examples of how to approach learning about queer subjects in the context of specific political science disciplines. This list is not meant to be exhaustive; queerness often exists in opposition to categorical solutions, and as such particular subjectivities are best explored in specific and local contexts, not in broad gestures. With this in mind, the following sections are set out as one possible scope for approaching these questions, one possible starting point for academic inquiry into the realm of queer politics.

BUILDING GENERAL PROFICIENCY

In the first instance, being proficient at using the library's various resources will be invaluable in conducting subject-specific research. Thinking back to our underlying principle of learner-centered design, exposing students to a library workshop about searching for articles, books, and other materials both in the physical library and in the digital catalog will serve a key skill building part of the scaffolded learning experience toward being able to effectively research queer subjects in the political science field. Introductions to the various databases and source materials available in the library will help students understand how to explore more fully in their research topics and questions. Building this efficacy can also bolster the two other underlying principles by encouraging students to recognize the value of the knowledge they bring into any search and by focusing demonstrations and learning opportunities on cases that highlight the experience and counternarratives of marginalized voices.

THE POLITICS OF NAMING

The politics of naming is central to the identities of queer subjects. The politics of naming refers to the contested nature of how queer individuals and communities identify and recognize themselves, which often differs from how they are referred to by mainstream, dominant, or hegemonic institutional actors. This poses a problem for instructors, librarians, and learners, who are often members of different generations and have a wide range of cultural and social references for naming conventions when referring to queer topics or subjects. What is considered acceptable, or not acceptable, when thinking about how we name queer subjects is also often contested. This section explores these complexities to help make sense of, use, and challenge the naming conventions in scholarly contexts. Who decides what and how something is named is not now, nor has it ever been, a neutral choice in the context of queerness (Berman 1993). Foucault (2012) famously penned "the sodomite had been an aberration; the homosexual was now a species." Foucault goes on to explain at length the phenomena of medicalization and observational control employed by the rapid expansion of monitoring and naming the various deviant sexualities in the *History of Sexuality*. The emergence of the LGBTQ+ moniker places multiple gender and sexual minorities in proximity to each other, and it changes, expands, and contracts on the salient political identities being discussed (Murib 2017, 2023).

For instance, one might be interested in the marriage rights campaign that primarily comes out of the gay and lesbian communities seeking recognition, while academic scholarship on bisexuality may be interested in finding the political impact of a phenomena like bi-erasure. We might also see how trans communities organize in response to current movements to regulate the availability of gender-affirming care, recognition, and access in medicine or education for transgender youth. The changing nomenclature of queer titles offers a clear example on the problem of naming conventions when thinking about how to search for queer subjects or topics in a database.

LGBT emerged as a meaningful group identity relatively recently, in the 1980s.[19] During this same period, queer literature began to emerge from activist movements around the AIDS epidemic and as a field of study from feminist and critical traditions. The tension between these two conceptualizations is a problem of naming—one compounded by the fact that queer as a gender identity is adopted into the acronym as LGBTQ. Assimilationists tend to reject the adoption of the Q in LGBTQ because of its association with the term "queer" as a slur in early twentieth-century parlance. This question is relatively a minor one for a term that could be used to identify materials in the context of doing political research (the single character difference between LGBT and LGBTQ), but it illustrates how unstable the framing of "LGBT" as a construct is as it grows to include intersex, asexual, agender, questioning, and pansexual identities, among others. What is included under the umbrella of queerness grows. It is also important to keep in mind that these categories, which appear distinct and meaningfully identifiable today, have not always been the preferred terms in common (or even uncommon) use; the language in use today would not be how individuals would have described themselves historically.

This evolution of terminology makes searching for subjects on those topics relatively difficult. Let's look at one example: *gay liberation.* In the 1960s the Gay Liberation Front (GLF) emerged as a radical leftist queer political activist movement that was opposed to the politics of respectability espoused by the existing homophile movement. In the past, groups organizing for gay rights would dress in suits, ties, and dresses and march in an orderly manner, carrying signs with slogans telling onlookers how much like straight people they were. Then the GLF flipped that dynamic on its head. Inspired by the work of the Black Power movement in the 1960s, the GLF sought to be themselves publicly and unapologetically. Fast-forward to today, and it's hard to imagine an inclusive discourse centered on the idea of "gay liberation," as gay is seen as a relatively limited framing for understanding queerness. In the space of just a couple of decades, gay liberation moves from nonexistent to radical politics to outdated for lack of inclusivity. Add to this the complexities of cataloging conventions that are not moving at the same speed as the language around these movements, and we can see how the problem of queer subject searches multiplies. Is it meaningful to describe a fifteenth-century European monarch who sleeps with individuals of the same sex or gender as gay? Would queer be more appropriate? Does their self-identification matter for how we might understand them today? The distinction between behavior and identity becomes important in understanding these individuals. John D'Emilio (1993) argues that gay identity is a product of capitalism, and as such, to refer to historical instances of homosexual people as having a gay identity is not appropriate. I introduce these questions here in order to point out the limitations of the catalog naming conventions writ large and to use this as a jumping off point to say that being creative with search terms and techniques will allow exploration.

Consider a search like *lesbian politician*, which might yield a certain number of results. This terminology is in relatively common usage today. The use of creative follow-up searches may use phrases that are not as common but will still successfully uncover same-sex-loving female political figures. The Rainbow Roundtable, the American Library Association's professional organization for LGBTQ people and subjects, produced a list of controlled vocabularies for use in a variety of settings that can also be useful in this context.[20] This collection of thesauruses, classification schema, bibliographies, and encyclopedias is a great source for better understanding how librarians think about and classify LGBTQ+ subjects. Tools like the Rainbow Roundtable's controlled vocabularies can be included in research and library guides to help navigate starting points for database searches and inquiries in systems that utilize the LoC's subject heading classification scheme. Emily Drabinski's (2013) influential work "Queering the Catalog" reframed the question from being one of purely a cataloging question, highlighting the importance of adapting the language used in library catalogs, to being one of library engagement. Drabinski (2013, 96) articulates queer theory as follows: "Rather than taking these identities as stable and fixed, queer theory sees these identities as shifting and contextual." She goes on to say that the resulting problem for queer subjects in catalogs is not the particularities of a given label, but rather the perceived permanence of those labels. The idea that one can find the right label for a queer subject, in Drabinski's framework, is the real culprit here. As such, when thinking about the questions we ask students to investigate in a study of LGBTQ political science, any instructor must recognize that they are aiming toward an unfixed target. What is perceived to be in LGBTQ+ or queer political spheres today will necessarily be different than those of the past, as well as varied by discipline, locale, and time. From this perspective, thinking about queer politics as a practice of decentering permanence and fixedness, and a move toward more inclusivity, emerges as one key facet of engaging students in the study of the subject.

EXPLORING SUBDISCIPLINES

In the following section I will explore some conceptual approaches to collaborating in various subdisciplines of political science. This is not meant to be prescriptive, but rather to demonstrate some possible approaches to tailoring collaborative efforts between instructors and librarians with some more discipline-specific examples. Ultimately, the scholarship of the instructor, and the experience of the librarian engaged in any particular collaborative effort, should be the skill set driving those sessions, as using your expertise will be a much more holistic approach than simply implementing a lesson plan produced in the abstract.

Political Theory

The *Stanford Encyclopedia of Philosophy* describes ancient political philosophy as "reflections on the origin of political institutions, the concepts used to interpret and organize political life such as justice and equality, the relation between the aims of ethics and the nature of politics, and the relative merits of different constitutional arrangements or regimes."[21] For our purposes here, this will serve well as a definition for political theory.

Shane Phelan's (1997) edited volume *Playing with Fire* was one of the first books to articulate queer theory in the context of being a queer political movement. One possible form of collaboration could begin by exploring the various mainstream political ideas that the queer theorists in this volume engage with. The instructors and librarian could work together to make the range of topics covered in this volume accessible in the form of a course-specific library guide or through a one-shot instruction session from a librarian, covering how to access and conduct bibliographic research based on this volume. Instructors could break the class into smaller groups and assign each group a chapter to engage with and produce a creative work based on their findings. This makes a relatively dense theoretical text more accessible to individual learners, as they are focusing on one part of the text. Asking students to be creative in their synthesis of an analysis opens space for critical thinking and engagement and allows them to use personally relevant relationships in the telling of their own stories relating to the subject matter.

Comparative Politics

Peter Mair (1998) describes comparative politics in terms of being simultaneously about a particular subject, countries other than the researcher's own, and a methodology, the comparison of varied systems across countries.

As a specialization or discipline in the field of political science, comparative study does appear to lend itself easily to a queering of research questions.

In class recently, I explored the classification and relative lack of state recognition of male sex workers in the Republic of Ireland and Northern Ireland (Maginn and Ellison 2014). Introducing a study of how this compares with the treatment of male sex work in other countries could offer insight into how the categories are understood and socially constructed in a way that destabilizes any essentialist arguments about them. For instance, an exploration of the gendered language around "protecting women" would ostensibly not include regulation of male sex workers under its guise and would seem to highlight how the category of male sex worker is a queer category.

In this context, who is offered services by the state, who is targeted by state violence and regulation, and who is perceived to be in need of protection all emerge as possible veins of inquiry, and comparisons between states may uncover new ways of understanding their political norms. This could also lead to a set of data-driven analyses that allow students to either find evidence of queer representation in the data or find and spotlight gaps in the data. They could explore what the political implications of such an omission would be by comparing national data sets where some do include this information with others that do not. This also offers an opportunity to speak with a librarian about gaining access to a variety of source materials in this area.

Americanists, National Politics, and Local Politics

These three categories could each likely find their homes in completely independent sections, and indeed scholars in these areas cover vastly different aspects of political science. For our purposes here, though, this area of American politics looks at the nuts and bolts of politics at various levels—whether that is a study of voting, nonvoting political behavior, public policy, or any other political experience specific to the US, another nation, or some subunit of the nation. Han and Heldman (2017) explore the nature of gendered politics in the US, and they use the opportunity to elevate queer issues as well. They explore a range of topics, from openly queer candidates to the effects of national policies like Title IX (gender nondiscrimination) on queer people and more. This book demonstrates the multiple entry points available to discussing and researching queer subjects as people, policies, projects, and social movements and not just the label of LGBTQ, which can be adopted in a political science context.

One example that may offer clear insight to a possible mode of engagement is the Social Justice Sexuality Project, which collects national data on queer BIPOC individuals, providing points of entry for working with data from a wide range of communities across the country. This could also include working with resources provided by the National Center for Transgender Equality to create course materials in collaboration with the locally available resources at the instructor's university library.

Legal Theory/Law and Society

Today, law and legal theory are recognized as a ground for political discourse, and the American Political Science Association hosts a permanent section where these ideas are debated. Since the preeminence of rights-based frameworks in the 1960s civil rights movement, the space has now also become home to a variety of legal debates on queerness as well. Martha Fineman explores the relationship between feminist and queer legal theories in a research paper published as a series at Emory University.[22] This exploration illustrates one way to engage with queer legal subjects in a new and innovative way. She positions the papers as a sort of discursive call-and-response, with each section representing viewpoints with contrasting positions that are responsive to each other and to the more mainstream legal narratives being produced in other law review journals. The particular beauty of this form, though, is that it offers insight into a way to engage students in the law, which can be daunting to undergraduates, and with each other. Let's take Introduction to Constitutional Law, a common undergraduate political science course, as an example. Students could be encouraged to explore the legal frameworks and how they affect queer subjects through the lens of constitutional legal challenges, highlighting major Supreme Court cases, This could open the door to the politics of the Court itself.

Again, to stress the point, this list is by no means exhaustive; there are assuredly other disciplines in the field of political science and countless ways to approach teaching each of them. In one of his final published works, Paulo Freire (1998, 78), the Brazilian patron of critical pedagogy, wrote, "Regardless of the fundamental nature of the subject area, its importance does not reside in isolated subject matter but in the manner in which it is learned by the students and incorporated in their practice. To teach subjects is something more serious and complex than to merely teach facts about them." As Freire articulates in this work, so too can the instructor and librarian think about the nature of teaching queer politics. Teaching the subject of queer politics means teaching about the practice and exercise of those politics and engaging learners critically and meaningfully in the methods by which they are taught, as much if not more than materials being taught.

In the next section, I highlight some nontraditional sources that are available to students in many library settings that may open pathways to queer source material.

Finding Relevant Data

As previously mentioned, part of the issue with collecting data on queerness and queer subjects is their almost essential quality of challenging categorization. One recent example of an attempt at quantification is the Gender Sex and Sexual Orientation computer ontology,[23] which is essentially a dictionary and thesaurus for computers to use to introduce queer subjects into their data, providing a set of definitions and related terms for topics that would be relevant to understanding these terms (Kronk and Dexheimer 2020). While this particular ontology may not be the best source for a political theorist, it is one of the most comprehensive data treatments of queerness that exists. This ontology was published in 2019 and was the first of its kind to be used in the biomedical space. No comparable set exists for computers dealing with things like textual analysis. There is an emergent discourse on the possibilities for similar ontologies like those described by Benjamin Haber (2016) as not being a queer methodology but rather a queer practice of playing with methods outside of their accepted form, something akin to what Halberstam's (2011) aptly named book calls the *queer art of failure*. In this regard, using existing data sets from more mainstream organizations (e.g., Williams Institute or RAND) that produce data on LGBTQ people in innovative ways can be one way to queer the research process, and by example teach about queer politics as questions emerge from the data.

Conclusion

Teaching LGBTQ and queer politics presents some unique challenges for engaging students and can be difficult to access for many of the reasons described. This chapter set out to offer a framework for collaboration between instructors, librarians, and students in order to make the teaching of queer politics more accessible. I began by exploring some underlying principles that can inform the teaching of this subject. Considering how to make materials accessible and relevant, to share expertise of instructors and librarians with students while also recognizing the experiences and values that students come into the classroom with, is a good starting point for engaging in any queer political project. Next, I explored some tools that librarians can bring into instructional settings when working with instructors to build a learner-centered approach and critically engaged assignments for learning about queer politics. Next, I examined some innovative ways of finding meaningful source material in library catalogs that otherwise mask queer subjects. In this section, I also explored how to introduce themes from specific political science disciplines and subdisciplines into the collaborative teaching environment. Lastly, I addressed some important considerations when approaching queer research topics today—how library anxiety might prevent students from seeking assistance, how to incorporate emerging fields of analysis predicated on new methodologies of queer understanding, and how to tap into the real-world artifacts left by queer people and political actors. From beginning to end I have sought to describe clearly and concisely each of these topics. By explaining some of the tools available to librarians I hope to make them available to instructors and students. Ultimately, the instruction librarian's mission is to support, enhance, and build on the work being done by instructors and students and to provide a means by which we can all engage in learning together.

Notes

1. UCLA Resources for Remote Learning & Teaching," EPIC Program, UCLA, last modified October 12, 2020, https://epic.ucla.edu/ucla-campus-resources-and-support-for-transition-to-remote-learning-and-teaching/.

2. ACRL, *Framework for Information Literacy for Higher Education*, 2021, https://www.ala.org/acrl/standards/ilframework.

3. ACPA, "LGBTQ Peer Review Scholarly Journals," College Student Educators International, last modified June 23, 2021, https://myacpa.org/lgbtq-peer-review-scholarly-journals/.

4. Jennifer Snow, "Yale University Library Research Guides: LGBTQI: Research Guide: LGBTQ Subject Headings," Yale University Library Research Guides at Yale University, last modified March 21, 2019, https://guides.library.yale.edu/c.php?g=295883&p=1972812.

5. Library of Congress, "Research Guides: LGBTQIA+ Studies: A Resource Guide: Introduction," Research Guides at Library of Congress, last modified April 10, 2020, https://guides.loc.gov/lgbtq-studies/.

6. Diana King, "Research Guides: Lesbian, Gay, Bisexual, Transgender, and Queer (LGBTQ) Studies: Data & Statistics," Research Guides at UCLA Library, last modified May 24, 2022, https://guides.library.ucla.edu/lgbt/statistics.

7. Pew Research Center, *A Survey of LGBT Americans: Attitudes, Experiences and Values in Changing Times*, Washington, DC, 2013, https://assets.pewresearch.org/wp-content/uploads/sites/3/2013/06/SDT_LGBT-Americans_06-2013.pdf.

8. "LGBT Populations," Movement Advancement Project, accessed May 31, 2022, https://www.lgbtmap.org/equality-maps/lgbt_populations.

9. "The Paper," Monterey County LGBTQ History, California State University, Monterey Bay, Digital Commons @ CSUMB, accessed August 31, 2021, https://digitalcommons.csumb.edu/thepaper/.

10. Demeter newspapers and ephemera, MS-003. California State University, Monterey Bay Archives and Special Collections.

11. ArQuives, "In Defence of Queers," LGBTQ+ Tabloid, ArQuives Digital Exhibitions, accessed May 31, 2022, https://digitalexhibitions.arquives.ca/exhibits/show/tabloids/defence.

12. "History," ONE Archives Foundation: Independent, Community-Partner of ONE Archives at the USC Libraries, last modified June 16, 2021, https://www.onearchives.org/about/history/.

13. Jose Sarria Foundation, last modified July 15, 2021, https://josesarria.org/.

14. "Surviving Voices," Home, last modified August 31, 2021, https://www.aidsmemorial.org/surviving-voices.

15. ACTUP Oral History Project, accessed September 1, 2021, https://www.actuporalhistory.org/.

16. The History Project, accessed May 31, 2022, https://historyproject.org/.

17. GLBT Historical Society, accessed May 31, 2022, https://www.glbthistory.org/.

18. NYC LGBT Historic Sites Project, accessed May 31, 2022, https://www.nyclgbtsites.org/.

19. *Acronyms, Initialisms & Abbreviations Dictionary*, 1985, vol. 1, part 1. Gale Research. Factsheet five, issues 32–36, Mike Gunderloy, 1989. See also Zein Murib's chapter in *LGBTQ Politics: A Critical Reader*.

20. Jessica Colbert and Matt Johnson, *GLBT Controlled Vocabularies and Classification Schemes* (American Library Association: Rainbow Roundtable, 2017).

21. "Ancient Political Philosophy (Stanford Encyclopedia of Philosophy)," *Stanford Encyclopedia of Philosophy*, last revised March 22, 2023, https://plato.stanford.edu/entries/ancient-political/.

22. Marth A. Fineman, "Introduction: Feminist and Queer Legal Theory," *Feminist and Queer Legal Theory*, 2016, xx, https://doi.org/10.4324/9781315582207-4.

23. For our purposes here, an ontology can be understood as the framework, or street map, used by a computer to label and define various categories used in the computer system.

References

Abelove, Henry, Michèle A. Barale, David M. Halperin, and John D'Emilio. 1993. "Capitalism and Gay Identity." In *The Lesbian and Gay Studies Reader*. Routledge.

Berman, Sanford 1993. *Prejudices and Antipathies: A Tract on the LC Subject Heads Concerning People*. McFarland.

Buchanan, Heidi E., and Beth A. McDonough. 2021. *The One-Shot Library Instruction Survival Guide*. 3rd ed. ALA Editions.

Colbert, Jessica, and Matt Johnson. 2017. *GLBT Controlled Vocabularies and Classification Schemes*. American Library Association: Rainbow Roundtable.

Collins, Patricia H., and Sirma Bilge. 2020. *Intersectionality*. John Wiley & Sons.

D'Emilio, John. 1993. "Capitalism and Gay Identity." In *The Lesbian and Gay Studies Reader*, edited by Henry Abelove, Michèle Aina Barale, and David M. Halperin. Routledge.

Drabinski, Emily. 2013. "Queering the Catalog: Queer Theory and the Politics of Correction." *Library Quarterly* 83 (2): 94–111. https://doi.org/10.1086/669547.

Fineman, Marth A. 2016. "Introduction: Feminist and Queer Legal Theory." *Feminist and Queer Legal Theory*, 15–20. https://doi.org/10.4324/9781315582207-4.

Foucault, Michel. 2012. *The History of Sexuality: An Introduction*. Vintage.

Foucault, Michel. 2005. *The Order of Things*. Routledge.

Freire, Paulo. 1998. *Politics and Education*. UCLA Latin American Center.

Haber, Benjamin. 2016. "The Queer Ontology of Digital Method." *WSQ: Women's Studies Quarterly* 44 (3–4): 150–69. https://doi.org/10.1353/wsq.2016.0040.

Halberstam, Judith. 2011. *The Queer Art of Failure*. Duke University Press.

Han, Lori C., and Caroline Heldman. 2017. *Women, Power, and Politics: The Fight for Gender Equality in the United States*. Oxford University Press.

hooks, bell. 2014. *Teaching To Transgress*. Routledge.

"José Sarria." Legacy Project Chicago. Accessed September 1, 2021. https://legacyprojectchicago.org/person/jose-sarria.

Klipfel, Kevin M., and Dani B. Cook. 2017. *Learner-Centered Pedagogy: Principles and Practice*. American Library Association.

Kronk, Clair A., and Judith W. Dexheimer. 2020. "Development of the Gender, Sex, and Sexual Orientation Ontology: Evaluation and Workflow." *Journal of the American Medical Informatics Association* 27 (7): 1110–15. https://doi.org/10.1093/jamia/ocaa061.

Lee, Scott. 2011. "An Exploratory Case Study of Library Anxiety and Basic Skills English Students in a California Community College District." PhD diss., University of California Los Angeles.

Maginn, Paul J., and Graham Ellison. 2014. "Male Sex Work in the Irish Republic and Northern Ireland." In *Male Sex Work and Society*, edited by Victor Minichiello and John Scott. Columbia University Press.

Mair, Peter. 1998. "Comparative Politics: An Overview." In *A New Handbook of Political Science*, edited by Robert E. Goodin. Oxford University Press on Demand.

Martin, Jane R. 1976. "What Should We Do with a Hidden Curriculum When We Find One?" *Curriculum Inquiry* 6 (2): 135. https://doi.org/10.2307/1179759.

Murib, Zein. 2017. "Rethinking GLBT as a Political Category." In *LGBTQ Politics: A Critical Reader*, edited by Marla Brettschneider, Susan Burgess, and Christine Keating. New York University Press.

Murib, Zein. 2023. *Terms of Exclusion*. Oxford University Press.

Onwuegbuzie, Anthony J., Qun G. Jiao, Sharon Bostick, and Annette Butcher. 2005. "Library Anxiety: Theory, Research and Applications." *Library Management* 26 (8/9): 544–45. https://doi.org/10.1108/01435120510631945.

Phelan, Shane. 2020. *Playing with Fire: Queer Politics, Queer Theories*. Routledge.

Trouillot, Michel-Rolph. 2015. *Silencing the Past: Power and the Production of History*. Beacon Press.

"Unerased: Mic's Database of Trans Lives Lost to Homicide in the US." Last modified December 7, 2016. https://unerased.mic.com/.

Whittington, Charlie. 2018. "Invisible in Data: The Lack of LGBTQ Data Collection." *Georgetown Public Policy Review*. https://gppreview.com/2018/07/17/invisible-data-lack-lgbtq-data-collection/.

Afterword

In Search of Queer Liberation

DOROTHEE BENZ

> But I who am bound by my mirror
> as well as my bed
> see causes in color
> as well as sex
> and sit here wondering
> which me will survive
> all these liberations.
>
> —Audre Lorde, "Who Said It Was Simple"

In 2019, on the fiftieth anniversary of the Stonewall Riots, a long-simmering rift in LGBTQ+ politics broke into the open. For the first time, there was an organized alternative to the official Pride March in New York City. Fed up not just with corporate sponsorship from companies like Wells Fargo but also with the fact that corporate sponsors now get to march at the front of the parade, organizers of the Queer Liberation March had had enough. "Their march stands for corporate pride and the status quo. Ours stands for change," Reclaim Pride's Bill Dobbs told *The New York Times*, "You can't talk about economic justice when you have Fortune 500 companies marching in your parade" (Kilgannon 2019).[1]

Along with a vocal opposition within queer communities, there is by now a rich body of literature that critically assesses the state of LGBTQ+ politics in the twenty-first century and offers trenchant analyses of the interrelated failures of LGBTQ+ organizations to advance the interests of the majority of queer people and to challenge the dominant contours of US politics. Many of these accounts interrogate one or more dimensions of the problem—such as the racism, classism, or sexism of mainstream LGBTQ+ politics; the embrace of patriarchal institutions like marriage, monogamy, and what Lisa Duggan (2003) has termed "homonormativity"; the limits of constitutional politics and the liberal construction of equality; or the dominance of nonprofits—but stop short of suggesting that our entire model of queer-centered politics needs to be scrapped. Surprisingly, white supremacy and racial capitalism do not occupy a central place in most of these critiques, even as they generally acknowledge the racist impacts of mainstream LGBTQ+ politics.

How do we teach the history of LGBTQ+ politics and talk about its current condition without replicating the exclusions and biases that have led to this state of affairs? In answering that question, we must first acknowledge that our higher education institutions are of course shaped by the same distorting forces: white supremacy, patriarchy, liberal individualism, hetero/homonormativity and respectability politics, and above all, racial capitalism. We need to recognize how these forces are constitutive of our universities, our departments, our standards, our curricula, and our selves. If we are going to transcend the limits of LGBTQ+ politics as it is constructed today, we need to also critically interrogate the politics of the university. This has never been more crucial than in our current era of right-wing backlash, when the attacks on education and queer existence are so intensely intertwined. The narrow lens of mainstream LGBTQ+ politics is of no help in this task, precisely because it is embedded in the same structures that created the current crisis.

It is my contention that the "single-issue" model of queer politics, even when covered in a coat of intersectional paint, is, as a practical matter, irredeemably flawed and incompatible with a comprehensive politics of liberation. It may be theoretically imaginable to build a queer politics centering a radically transgressive ethic that destabilizes and contests social hierarchies of race, class, sexuality, gender, and deviance, but three-quarters of a century of actual experience has brought us to a place where that is no longer possible. The question for those of us who are unwilling to settle for a little bit of liberation—as if that weren't an oxymoron—is, Where do we look instead? Luckily, queer-inclusive radical analysis and transformative politics are alive and well in the work of Black and other women of color. Moreover, there is a half century of rich, intersectional work that provides both a theoretical and a political framework to coherently structure a genuinely liberatory LGBTQ+ politics as part of a larger project of liberation.

If we are unwilling to settle for liberation lite in our queer politics, then we will also be unwilling to settle for it in how we teach our students, inside and outside the classroom. This means rethinking the single-issue approach to our LGBTQ+ politics courses. Here, too, Black feminism provides a way forward, a firm foundation from which to unpack our inherited politics and recenter marginalized queer communities and their concerns. There is plenty in our history to draw on, from pioneers like Marsha P. Johnson and Sylvia Rivera to the revolutionary vision of the Combahee River Collective to the contemporary work of organizations like Southerners on New Ground.

What follows is, first, an overview of the various problematic dimensions of contemporary LGBTQ+ politics and a brief sketch of an alternative approach to construction a liberatory politics that benefits all queer people. From this unpacking and repacking I then draw some implications for the teaching of LGBTQ+ politics. And finally, I offer a few words about the importance of such a broad approach to queer politics in contesting the right-wing assault on US education, academic freedom, and inclusive politics.

But first, a word situating myself in this project. While I have a PhD in political science and briefly taught American Government 101, I write this chapter not primarily as a scholar but as a practitioner. I have been involved in some form or another of LGBTQ+ politics since I was the co-chair of the Harvard Gay and Lesbian Students Association in 1984. I have been a contributing writer at *Learning for Justice*, the educational magazine and web hub of the Southern Poverty Law Center, a role in which I research and write about K–12 education, particularly in the Deep South. I also write from a specific social location—as a white middle-class cisgender butch lesbian—informed (sometimes deformed) and shaped by a particular constellation of social relations. At the same time, I "exceed these relations," as Chris Dixon (2014, 3) puts it, and aspire to a radical analysis and politics committed to the liberation of all oppressed people. I reject the idea that there is or can be such a thing as a non-normative politics; all politics embody values and all politics create boundaries of inclusion/exclusion and legitimation/delegitimation. The question is always, What values, whose norms, and who exactly is included?

How Did We Get Here?

In its foundational statement of purpose in 1969, the Gay Liberation Front declared, "Complete sexual liberation for all people cannot come about unless existing social institutions are abolished" and called for "new social forms and relations," explicitly including "uninhibited sexuality" (D'Emilio 1983, 234). The critique of existing institutions took central aim at the nuclear family, which Martin Duberman (2018, xvii), notes was "vigorously condemned . . . as nothing more than a detention center for women and children." Monogamy similarly came in for derision as "unnatural" (Duberman 2018, xii). The Gay Liberation Front's rejection of the status quo also extended to condemnation of "imperialist Amerika," and the organization actively mobilized for protests against the Vietnam War (D'Emilio 1983). A time traveler from 1969 would thus have been flabbergasted if not horrified to land at the 1993 gay and lesbian march on Washington, which was focused on demands for gay marriage and the right of gay people to join the military. Though I had lived through the intervening years, I was more than a little taken aback myself. By 2015, when the Supreme Court gave its blessing to same-sex marriage, "marriage equality" so dominated LGBTQ+ politics that virtually no other issue of concern to queer people got any airtime.

This historical trajectory and transformation has been described and analyzed by numerous scholars and writers over the last two decades. I want to review and synthesize a representative sample of this work by way of laying bare both the causes and the consequences of this political makeover.

At the heart of the gay liberationist impulse in the post-Stonewall moment was the embrace of sexual *difference* and the recognition that what makes us different as gay people offers insight into overlapping systems of oppression beyond homophobia.[2] Most immediately, homophobia is intimately connected to sexism, misogyny, and patriarchal control. The policing of gender roles assigned to female and male bodies includes retaliation for violations of expected norms of both femininity/masculinity and sexual object choice. In decoupling the link between sex and sexual object choice, gay liberationists opened up a door to rejecting additional heteronormative assumptions. They embraced subcultural values that shunned monogamy, traditional family structures, and the automatic linking of emotional and sexual connection. The highlighting of differences—as opposed to sameness, the hallmark of homonormativity—created a certain capacity for critical re/assessment of social norms more broadly. The cultural milieu of the late 1960s played a significant role in this ability and *desire* to upend social relations; without the example and inspiration of the Black protest movements, second-wave feminism, and the antiwar movement—movements in which many of the gay liberationists were active—Stonewall would not have happened.

Accounts like Duberman's *Has the Gay Movement Failed?* (2018) and Michael Warner's *The Trouble with Normal* (1999) center the homonormatization of LGBTQ+ politics as the primary way to understand the transformation of what once was a fundamentally oppositional, liberative politics into the assimilationist politics of the current era. *The Trouble with Normal* was published in 1999, but its analysis of the mainstreaming of LGBTQ+ politics holds up well in the 2020s. Warner (1999, 24–25) takes "the official gay movement" to task for being "enthralled with respectability." Specifically his lament is that instead of leaning into sexual difference, combating stigma by dignifying what is stigmatized and expanding the reach of dignification from there to embrace and reclaim other stigmatized acts and people, LGBTQ+ organizations have opted (now for decades already) to "normalize" gay people. That normalization takes place by severing the sexual acts that define us as queer from the identity of gay/lesbian/queer. For Warner, the stigmatization of gay identity derives from the stigmatization of gay sex, and thus "to have a politics of one without the other is to doom oneself to incoherence and weakness. It is to challenge the stigma on identity but only by reinforcing the shame of sex" (31). Warner recognizes that this respectability politics excludes all kinds of non-normative sexual behavior beyond monogamous vanilla (gay) sex, including group sex, public sex, commercial sex, and sadomasochism or S/M. Thus the fight for gay liberation is narrowed to a fight for liberation for *some* gay people, not all. Moreover, though Warner does not focus on this, those who are excluded are disproportionately multiply oppressed. In particular, economically marginalized people are far more likely to engage in commercial sex. For some, public sex is also driven by economic necessity. Economic discrimination in the US always also inherently involves racial bias, since the country is so thoroughly shaped by racial capitalism.

Speaking of racial bias, Warner does not extend his analysis to nongay people whose sexual behavior, and through it, identity, is also stigmatized—that is, heterosexuals who would benefit from an expanded project of dignifying stigmatized sexuality—but Cathy Cohen (1997) makes exactly this point when she points out that heteronormativity is coded not only with homophobia but also with racism, patriarchy, and class exploitation. "The stigmatization and demonization of single mothers, teen mothers, and, primarily, poor women of color dependent on state assistance" rests on the exclusion of "non-normative sexual behavior and family structures" as surely as the non-normative categories that Warner includes (455, 456). More on this later.

The key nugget in Warner's analysis is the articulation that people who prided themselves on their difference and who reclaimed a despised identity were thereby able to recognize inherited norms as "false morality" (Warner 1999, 36). The further away from an oppositional identity that LGBTQ+ politics moved, therefore, the less able it became to challenge dominant norms.

Duberman similarly centers the flight from deviance into respectability in his analysis of the problem with the contemporary LGBTQ+ mainstream, though his emphasis is less on the necessity of reembracing sexuality and sexual difference per se and more on the cumulative consequences of this trend. The pinnacle of this normalization is of course the quest for same-sex marriage, which Duberman (2018, 163) says "positions the movement squarely withing the framework of a Normal Rockwell painting." His account takes note that the successes of LGBTQ+ politics have been possible precisely because our politics have not challenged any of the core institutional arrangements in the US but rather have functioned to "*bolster* the current system of social control and domination that distributes large rewards to the relative few." Moreover, our politics "*don't* raise the tough questions of who is left out of the prosperity mill and why" (108). Duberman is clear that "who is left out" is people of color, economically disadvantaged people, gender nonconforming people, sex workers, and queer youth, but his account is mainly descriptive rather than analytical in probing the mechanisms that drove the homonormalization of queer politics.

In *Gay Priori*, Libby Adler (2018) traces the role of rights discourse in shaping the tamed and normalized nature of dominant LGBTQ+ politics. She maintains that "a crucial factor in explaining the priorities of the mainstream LGBT law reform movement," priorities that she, like others, criticizes for their significant exclusions, "is the power of LGBT rights discourse" (3). Adler contends that by emphasizing discourses of equality, the inherited mainstay of civil rights politics and litigation, "we stifle our own imaginations" (4). By swimming in the waters of formal legal equality, litigators and activists focused on LGBTQ+ rights fail to envision or enact a reform agenda that would address the needs of a majority of queer people and particularly the most marginalized members of our communities. Redistributive politics, in particular, are excluded by this equal rights discourse.

Adler's account dovetails with Warner's and Duberman's in noting that LGBTQ+ litigation organizations focus on respectable homonormative "archetypes, such as the civic-minded lesbian soccer mom." While Warner traces this development to the shedding of any sexual radicalism of LGBTQ+ groups, Adler explains it in relationship to the imperatives of litigation: "Gay rights advocates carefully select plaintiffs for high-profile courtroom battles, while outside the courtroom they make deft use of public relations campaigns" (11).

As someone whose job it was to deftly design and deploy public relations campaigns in support of high-profile LGBTQ+ civil rights litigation, I want to supplement this observation with some comments from my experience.[3] It is absolutely true that LGBTQ+ litigation is part and parcel of queer respectability politics, and from a law reform perspective it's nearly impossible to do it otherwise—which of course is a primary reason to decenter litigation strategies in the LGBTQ+ movement. Plaintiffs are carefully selected to isolate the claim at stake in a case. So, for instance, a challenge to employment discrimination wants to ensure that neither defendants nor judges can reasonably claim a plaintiff was fired for reasons other than their sexual orientation or gender identity; this means a white plaintiff is preferable to a Black one, and it means that a flamboyantly gay or polyamorous or drug-using or—you get the idea—plaintiff is out of the question. Thus, as so many have pointed out, a victory in such a case theoretically protects all LGBTQ+ people but in reality mostly protects homonormative white queers who have the means to sue for discrimination.

Adler's choice to analyze this state of affairs through a discursive lens is in some ways a curious one. For sure, the imperatives of civil rights litigation contribute to the generation of archetypes and shape contemporary LGBTQ+ identities. Among other things, they reinforce the coding of LGBTQ+ as white, which, needless to say, is a major problem. But the construction of both constitutional and statutory law in the US is inextricable from the liberal individualism that undergirds the capitalist state. A polyamorous drug-using plaintiff is impossible for civil rights litigation, but so is a claim, for instance, that housing discrimination violates a right to shelter. US constitutional law rules out claims to positive rights, notably fundamental economic rights (like the right to shelter), and precludes any intersectional analysis. These are all material consequences of our liberal constitutional order. A shift from an equal rights focus to distributive justice, which Adler calls for, is right on, but the nondiscursive constraints to making it possible are considerable.

All this brings us to the central role of capitalism in shaping the LGBTQ+ movement. It's impossible to understand either the formation of LGBTQ+ identities or the trajectory of LGBTQ+ politics without taking account of the decisive role of capitalism in shaping our economic, social, and political relations. Lesbian, gay, bisexual, transgender, and queer identities are, like race and gender, social constructs and they have emerged in the context of the capitalist social transformations of the last two hundred years. The decline of the family as an economic unit of production and the rise of wage labor during the industrial revolution set in motion a series of social changes that paved the way for both a pathologized understanding and a self-understanding of sexual identity as homosexual. This history has been well documented by writers from Michel Foucault to Peter Drucker; John D'Emilio's 1983 essay "Capitalism and Gay Identity" is a classic on his subject and Stephen Valocchi's book *Capitalisms and Gay Identities* pays tribute to D'Emilio in its title and brings the story into the twenty-first century.

Particularly relevant here is that the modern (post-Stonewall) gay rights movement burst onto the scene at precisely the moment when the postwar welfare state (such as it was in the US) came under the sustained assault we now name as neoliberalism. Gay politics came of age in the era of TINA—Margaret Thatcher's famous declaration "there is no alternative" to neoliberal capitalism. It had to contend, therefore, not only with the political economy of "competition, inequality, market 'discipline,' public austerity, and 'law and order,'" but also the sweeping ideological claim that "there is no alternative" (Duggan 2003, x). Talk about stifling our own imaginations. In this environment, gay organizations evolved in ways similar to other "identity politics" groups. Duggan notes these "balkanized" groups "appeared out of the field of disintegrating social movements. Single-group or single-issue organizations dedicated to lobbying, litigation, legislation, or public and media education had existed earlier *as only one part* of larger, shaping social movements . . . large portions of the organized efforts of social movements succumbed to liberalism's paltry promise—engage the language and institutional games of established liberal contests and achieve equality." Whereby, as we have already seen, "equality" here means "equality disarticulated from material life and class politics, to be won by definable 'minority' groups, one at a time" (Duggan 2003, xviii).

One distinctive feature of the US during this half century of neo-liberalism is the dominance of the nonprofit sector, and as Myrl Beam (2018, 7) has argued, "This expansion of the nonprofit system—and its pernicious effect on queer politics—is an important, and undertheorized, engine of the so-called homonormative turn in queer politics." In 1965 there were three thousand 501(c)(3) organizations in the US; in 2018, there were more than 1.5 million (7). The saturation of civil society with nonprofits functions as a brake on movement toward radical change in multiple ways, two of which are particularly germane in the case of the LGBTQ+ nonprofit space. The first of these is the massive influence of wealthy donors, and the second is the tendency toward single-issue politics; these two characteristics are mutually constitutive. Wealthy donors are overwhelmingly white and cisgender, and only slightly less overwhelmingly male. Their cumulative economic, racial, and gender privileges mean that intersectional issues that are central to less privileged queer folx—for instance, affordable housing or police brutality—simply aren't high on their agenda. Both Beam and Valocchi offer multiple examples of organizations that had to shut their doors after they dared focus on issues that queer elites weren't sufficiently interested in. In the case of Empire State Pride Agenda (ESPA) in New York State, donors simply moved on after the state legalized same-sex marriage, despite the fact one of ESPA's longtime priorities, expanding the state's anti-discrimination statute to include gender identity, was left unrealized (Valocchi 2020, 146).

I want to add an example from my nonprofit executive days, one that I feel encapsulates the absurdity and moral bankruptcy of LGBTQ+ single-issue politics. In May 2017, President Obama commuted whistleblower Chelsea Manning's sentence. It was suggested to me, as the head of the communications department where I was working, that we should do a social media post thanking her for her work as a transgender rights activist. I pointed out that Manning's bigger contribution to US democracy, not to mention the reason she had been tortured, convicted, and imprisoned in the first place, was that she had exposed US war crimes. It was inexcusably distorting of reality to leave out all mention of her whistleblowing, I argued. I drafted a post that avoided the term "US war crimes" (this wasn't my first nonprofit industrial complex rodeo) and read,

> Chelsea Manning has been released from military prison!
> Chelsea is a patriot, a courageous woman, a whistleblower who sacrificed to expose government wrongdoing and a pioneer for trans rights. Her conditions of confinement were barbaric and unconstitutional, and she helped pave the way for other incarcerated transgender people by fighting for her right to health care. She's just one of countless trans people in prison who are denied care, protection and dignity. We must never stop fighting to right these abhorrent wrongs.
> Chelsea Manning is a hero so many times over.
> Welcome home, Chelsea.

After editing by the head of the organization, the text came back:

> Chelsea Manning has been released from military prison!
> Chelsea is a courageous woman, who was motivated by conscience to become a whistleblower and then became a pioneer for trans rights. Her conditions of confinement were barbaric and unconstitutional, and she helped pave the way for other incarcerated transgender people by fighting for her right to health care. She's just one of countless trans people in prison who are denied care, protection and dignity. We must never stop fighting to right these abhorrent wrongs. Chelsea Manning will always be an inspiration in this fight.
> Welcome home, Chelsea.

Yet even this was not enough in the end. Within hours of publishing, we were ordered to delete the post because of a call from an irate donor who was upset that we were condoning Manning's actions. Not only were any criticisms of "imperialist Amerika" long forgotten, but as an organization we were willing to crop out of existence the very reason Manning became a pioneer for transgender prisoners' rights in the first place.

"The nonprofit structure is fundamentally antithetical to a multi-issue, anticapitalist politics," says Beam (2018, 199). Single-issue politics inevitably reinscribe other systems of oppression into their logic. If we insist on lifting one dimension of social inequality up for redress while leaving the others in place, we become part of the structure that keeps those other systems in place. There is no way around this. If I only care that Chelsea Manning is a trans activist, then I abandon any challenge to the US imperialism that led to the Iraq invasion and the murder of Iraqi civilians. If I only care about reclaiming non-normative sex as central to our movement and not about police brutality, then Black gay men who like to fuck in the Ramble will continue to be unsafe no matter the outcome of that effort. If I care only about marriage equality and not voting rights, then I have nothing to say about the Supreme Court's gutting of the Voting Rights Act in *Shelby County* on the day before the victory in *Windsor*. "Single-issue" thus quickly equals *white*, and Black queers who might want to vote or avoid police violence as well as get married are on their own. Without an intersectional analysis and an abandonment of single-issue politics, gay/lesbian/bi/trans/queer/intersex/gender-nonconforming/asexual/ demisexual and any other of the wonderful diversifications of our queer self-understandings will remain coded as white.

Countless—literally countless—LGBTQ+ activists, writers, organizers, scholars, and nonprofit staff people of color have been pointing this out for at least half a century. "Race drops out of the LGBT political and policy agenda again and again," says Urvashi Vaid (2012, 15) in her *second* book to address this problem, *Irresistible Revolution*: "The definition of 'gay,' 'lesbian,' 'bisexual,' or 'transgender' that the mainstream LGBT movement operates from, the definition of who it represents that it holds in its mind when it speaks of the community, is unconsciously (and at times consciously) limited to white LGBT people. . . . How else can one explain the LGBT movement's silence on issues that have a clear and disproportionate impact on LGBT people of color?" Cohen (1997) notes that the rise of queer politics in the 1990s—as a deliberate rejoinder to LGBT assimilationist politics—had some early promise for manifesting a more radical analysis but fell into the same trap of single-issue politics. Queer activists had "begun to prioritize sexuality as the primary frame through which they pursue their politics," and in using a "single perspective of consciousness" to "organize their politics," they necessarily ended up rejecting the relevance of how multiple, intersecting systems of power shape the lives of queer people (Cohen 1997, 440). Thus queer politics ultimately gave us a "reconstruction of a binary divide between heterosexuals and queers," flattening the actual contours of oppressive power out of existence (447). In the end, all we did was add Q to the acronym.

Capitalism drives the nonprofitization of LGBTQ+ politics and, partially through that, the dominance of single-issue politics with its inevitable replication of other dimensions of oppression, including most obviously racism. But the role of racism in shaping our politics and distorting our priorities is more profound than this statement allows. There is nothing, absolutely nothing, in the US that is untouched by the inextricably intertwined systems of white supremacy and capitalism named by Cedric Robinson as *racial capitalism*. Racial capitalism created the wealth of the nation on the backs of Black slaves and channeled it exclusively to white people. It also birthed racism as we know it, enforced through countless restrictions from Black Codes to Jim Crow to mass incarceration. It distorted US policy in every conceivable way; it is the reason our labor law is shaped the way it is, the reason home ownership among Black USians is drastically lower than among whites, and the reason we don't have national healthcare. It is also at the root of the intractable educational inequality in the US. Genocide of native peoples paved the way for territorial expansion and expulsion. The Indian Removal Act of 1830 was our first deportation law, followed by a long lineage of other racist immigration laws, from the Chinese Exclusion Act in 1882 and the National Origins Act of 1924 to the 1996 Illegal Immigration Reform and Immigration Responsibility Act and the Muslim ban and asylum bans of recent years.

We cannot understand the whiteness of nonprofit donors or executives without examining the role of racial capitalism. We cannot understand the targeting of transgender people of color by police or the ongoing lethal violence against trans women of color without racial capitalism. We cannot understand the restrictions of transgender healthcare without looking at the role of racial capitalism in our for-profit healthcare system. And we cannot make sense of the epidemic of homelessness among queer youth of color without examining the role of racial capitalism in producing housing insecurity.

White supremacy and racial capitalism are constitutive of the circumstances of *all* queer people—most obviously queer people of color, but the distortions of healthcare and housing policy, for instance, harm us all, as does the massive militarized police presence in our cities, which necessarily diverts resources from human needs. Moreover, the structurally racist dimensions of our education system help ensure the continued replication of other structural disadvantages. An LGBTQ+ politics that does not confront racial capitalism not only does not serve the needs of a majority of queer people; it also leaves the driving force of inequality and injustice in the US completely unchallenged. There is no liberation without the liberation of Black, Indigenous, and other people of color.

Liberation or Accommodation?

If we want an LGBTQ+ movement that is fighting for the liberation of *all* queer people, then, as the foregoing analysis makes clear, we need a movement that challenges hetero- and homonormativity; fights for meaningful social, economic, and political equality; reverses the one-dollar-one-vote mechanism of setting priorities; and recognizes the centrality of ending white supremacy for the possibility of liberation. But there are LGBTQ+ people who are actively opposed to some or even most of this agenda, and in particular, there are LGBTQ+ people who are opposed to it for reasons of self-interest. Is it actually possible to construct a queer politics that truly represents the interest of all LGBTQ+ people? Or, as Drucker (2014, 394) put it, "Defining the potential of queer anti-capitalism in an expansive way puts in question the idea that there can ever again be 'a' gay movement, a sort of 'big tent' including the whole LGBT spectrum from left to right."

By way of arguing that the answer is no, we cannot actually construct a queer politics that both prioritizes queer identity and offers a program of liberation for all, I want to draw attention to an intra-LGBTQ+ conflict that multiple scholars have written about, the Take Back Boystown campaign in Chicago in 2011 (see Beam 2018; Stodolka 2017). Boystown is an upscale, white area that is considered a gay neighborhood and is home to Chicago's LGBTQ+ community center, Center on Halsted. Alongside its economically and racially privileged residents, Boystown is also a hangout for poor, often homeless, often gender nonconforming queer youth of color. In 2011, following years of complaints about "loitering" youth and using two violent incidents as a pretext, business and property owners started a Facebook group called Take Back Boystown. The group, though little more than a place to spew racist objections to the young people who were "invading" "their" neighborhood, reflected an ongoing material reality in which wealthy white gays worked with police to criminalize queer youth of color, and the "community" center enacted successive restrictive policies to keep the youth out of the center's building as much as possible.

How do we understand the Take Back Boystown campaign? The first thing to note about it is the pervasive, racist hostility from white residents toward young people with whom they could have—but did not—identify as sibling LGBTQ+ people. The role of overt racism here is important and so is the racist coding of LGBTQ+ as white. Center on Halsted, for instance, was really only for *some* members of the community, members who were overwhelmingly white. Differing class interests are the other obvious factor at play here. "The antagonism that business, bar, and property owners express toward 'loitering' youth can be understood to some extent," says Jason Stodolka (2017, 421), "as self-interest, as these community members seek to protect the investments they have made." In the class conflict between youth and property owners, the latter chose class as well as race solidarity over queer solidarity. Third, and very importantly, are the features of racial capitalism that produced the entire scene in the first place: the for-profit housing market that creates housing insecurity and exacerbates poverty, racialized homelessness, and gentrification, and the reliance on state violence and criminalization in order to protect property "rights."

Lastly, I think it is critical to recognize that the gap in terms of power and privilege between the youth and the property owners in this situation is wider than that between these youth and other homeless people of color. Indeed, it's arguable that these young queer people have more in common with economically struggling cis-het people, housed and unhoused, white and nonwhite, than the slice of wealthy white LGBTQ+ property owners of Boystown.

What does this mean for the construction of a radical, liberative queer politics? Cohen (1997, 438) offers a way forward that I find appealing: "I envision a politics where one's relation to power, and not some homogenized identity, is privileged in determining one's political comrades," she says. Her approach is worth quoting at some length:

> I am suggesting that the process of movement-building be rooted not in our shared history or identity, but in our shared marginal relationship to dominant power which normalizes, legitimizes, and privileges.
>
> We must, therefore, start our political work from the recognition that multiple systems of oppression are in operation and that these systems use institutionalized categories and identities to regulate and socialize. We must also understand that power and access to dominant resources are distributed across the boundaries of "het" and "queer" that we construct. (Cohen 1997, 458)

This is the end of LGBTQ+ politics as we have come to define it over recent decades; it is not a politics that seeks to orient itself around a single pole. And yet, it *is* a politics that challenges homophobia and transphobia along with hetero- and homonormativity, racism, classism, and sexism. By being rooted in intersectional analysis, it is a politics that can address the needs of queer people across the spectrum of our experiences and social locations—whether those needs are housing security, protection from police violence, access to healthcare, or protection from discrimination at work.

Equally importantly, it is a politics that exists in the real world. Not at the big national LGBTQ+ nonprofits, our community centers, or at most of the small service-oriented organizations at the local level.[4] Instead, the places where this politics mainly lives are BIPOC-led movements and organizations that are not specifically LGBTQ+ groups. The Movement for Black Lives' visionary platform, for instance, contains as robust an analysis and set of demands for queer justice as you will find at any LGBTQ+ organization, along with a comprehensive political program and 360-degree analysis of the obstacles to liberation in the United States.[5] Southerners on New Ground and Black Visions Collective are two of the better known organizations whose radical vision ranges from abolition to queer liberation, but there are many more. I'll mention just three, ones I have personal experience with through my work: BLM at School, Communities United for Police Reform, and South Bronx Mutual Aid.

Cohen's suggestion to organize radical politics intersectionally, around "relation to power," is part of a long lineage of Black feminism. "The major systems of oppression are interlocking," the Combahee River Collective declared in its famous 1977 statement. "The synthesis of these oppressions creates the conditions of our lives . . . we see Black feminism as the logical political movement to combat the manifold and simultaneous oppression that all women of color face." Then, as now, Black feminists understood the necessity of fighting heterosexism and capitalism alongside racism and sexism because the connections between these systems were obvious to them through their own experiences. "We might use our position at the bottom . . . to make a clear leap into revolutionary action. If Black women were free, it would mean that everyone else would have to be free since our freedom would necessitate the destruction of all the systems of oppression."[6]

This principle, using relation to power as a guiding framework for a liberation politics, has some concrete consequences. It means "building a political analysis and political strategies around the most marginal in our society," Cohen (1997, 460) emphasizes. Addressing the implied

LGBTQ+ audience of her article, she adds, "some of whom look like us, many of whom do not. Most often, this will mean rooting our struggle in, and addressing the needs of, communities of color." By this point in this chapter, this last statement is mostly obvious, but I want to pause on it for a moment and consider it honestly in the context of LGBTQ+ politics. As currently stands, visible LGBTQ+ politics is coded as white, is articulated through organizations in which positions of decision making are overwhelmingly occupied by white people, and centers around an agenda that does not include issues most germane to people of color. To construct a queer politics around our "shared marginal relationship to dominant power" is virtually a 180-degree shift.

White queer people have a choice to make: Do we (continue to) identify with and give our energy and time to the nonprofitized white LGBTQ+ organizations, whose work inevitably reinforces race, class, and other inequalities, or do we look to multi-issue, multiracial efforts led by Black, Indigenous, and other people of color for leadership of a movement toward liberation for all oppressed people, including LGBTQ+ people? For property owners in Boystown as well as garden-variety middle-class queers like this author, the question is, Can we deprioritize our class, race, and homonormative privilege in favor of a solidaristic politics of liberation that exceeds our social locations?

What Do We Tell the Kids?

If we pursue a queer politics organized around a "shared marginal relationship to dominant power," an approach that is a radical departure from mainstream LGBTQ+ politics, then we also need to rethink how we teach LGBTQ+ politics. Bringing the same Black feminist methodology to our classrooms, we can, for instance, look at the Stonewall Riots through a lens of race, class, and gender analysis, asking about the multiply oppressed identities of the Stonewall's patrons and the role of both the bar's owners and the police in reinforcing their marginality and vulnerability. We can center the work of lesbian women of color, putting, for instance, *This Bridge Called My Back* or *Sister Outsider* on our syllabi, two groundbreaking texts that refused the demands of single-issue movements to prioritize one or another part of the authors' identities. Or, more recently, Patrisse Cullors and asha bandele's *When They Call You a Terrorist* or Alicia Garza's *The Purpose of Power*. We can use our classes to unravel the juggernaut of marriage equality, investigating how this issue came to eclipse everything else on the official queer agenda and teaching racial capitalism through that exploration. We can explain how and why LGBTQ+ has been coded as white and invite our students to imagine how this coding might be undone.

Efforts like these broaden the understanding of what queer politics is and can be. This is an important correction to the distorted LGBTQ+ politics we've inherited, but it is also an urgently needed critical perspective that helps us understand our current political moment and build a broad-based resistance to the attacks on both US education and queer people.

Just a few years ago, there was a certain celebratory, almost giddy note in mainstream LGBTQ+ politics. The cover of the Linda Hirshman's (2013) *Victory: The Triumphant Gay Revolution* promises a story of "How a Despised Minority Pushed Back, Beat Death, Found Love, and Changed America for Everyone." In 2017, Gary Mucciaroni declared that "full legal equality for all LGBTQ Americans . . . is virtually inevitable."

Of course, the "gay revolution" was very much a bourgeois revolution, but even the most privileged LGBTQ+ communities have been rattled by the backlash of the post-*Obergefell* years. Legislative attacks against transgender people are happening at the rate of hundreds of bills a year, with dozens enacted into law, and trans youth are especially in the crosshairs, with their right to healthcare and public space under assault. So-called religious exemptions allowing businesses to circumvent anti-discrimination laws have the Supreme Court's blessing, and the overturning of *Roe v. Wade* makes clear that a radically right-wing court is willing to toss precedents that the resurgent white Christian nationalists don't like out the window. Florida's "Don't Say Gay" law and others like it make it illegal for educators to even mention the existence of LGBTQ people, and librarians are facing felony convictions if they're caught with the wrong books on their shelves.

Simultaneously, bills banning the teaching of "critical race theory," "divisive ideas," or anything "woke" have swept across the country. Under whatever guise, what is targeted is anything that suggests that structural racism exists in the contemporary US or any curriculum that teaches the legacy of chattel slavery accurately. The attacks on education have taken primary aim at K–12, but higher education is also in the crosshairs. From educational gag orders that prohibit the teaching of certain concepts to policies that ban diversity, equity, and inclusion (DEI) programs, the right is coming for what it sees as a bastion of liberal indoctrination (LaFrance 2024; Mangan 2024; PEN America 2023).

All of these attacks are about reasserting white male patriarchal power and authority, and they are part of a profoundly dangerous, ascendant proto-fascist politics in the United States. But the LGBTQ+ mainstream is spectacularly ill-equipped to respond to this threat. Siloed in single-issue organizations, they file lawsuits state by state, issue press releases condemning the latest attacks or celebrating the reprieve of court injunctions, but none of it contributes to an intersectional analysis of this political moment and none of it galvanizes a broad movement from below or builds the political power to effectively confront the right. Thus, paradoxically, the triumphal LGBTQ+ politics that seemed to give us a seat at the table as a domesticated—homonormatized—nonthreatening addition to capitalist-compatible politics turns out to be a less than stable foundation now that a resurgent right is escalating its attacks.

Educators have a critical role to play in counteracting this political weakness of LGBTQ+ organizations. An intersectional analysis of the current situation and a commitment to a multi-issue, multiracial politics of resistance is not going to come from Big Gay. But it can come from your LGBTQ+ politics course and your campus queer rights caucus. It is more important than ever to teach queer politics—to *say gay* in the classroom, to name this history, even, in fact especially, where and when it is dangerous to do so. Teaching politics *is* politics. And a liberative queer politics, inside as well as outside the classroom, has everything to offer in this perilous moment.

Notes

1. The 2023 sponsors of corporate Pride included Mastercard, Hilton, Skyy Vodka, Northwell Health, Target, Estée Lauder, and Delta. Find a full list here: https://www.nycpride.org/pride-partners/partners.

2. A word about language. I am trying not to be anachronistic in my vocabulary choices for earlier eras. Hence "gay" for the '60s and '70s in particular. For recent decades, I use "LGBTQ+" and "queer" interchangeably, though I am aware that while for some (like me) "queer" is a collective noun that encompasses all of the other letters of the acronym, for others it is meant to signal a differentiation from LGBT respectability. Both uses of the term are common today, but for clarity's sake, I needed to pick one to be consistent here. I also want to note that I am using "queer" to be inclusive of "trans," which is also something that varies within contemporary descriptions.

3. I served as the communications director at the Center for Constitutional Rights from 2012 to 2017, and as Lambda Legal's chief communications officer from 2017 to 2019.

4. Exceptions include the Sylvia Rivera Law Project, the Audre Lorde Project, and the Kentucky Fairness Campaign.

5. Movement for Black Lives, https://m4bl.org/policy-platforms/.

6. Combahee River Collective, 1977, "Combahee River Collective Statement," archived on Black Past, https://www.blackpast.org/african-american-history/combahee-river-collective-statement-1977/. It is also worth noting that this statement was written within the larger global context of the Vietnam War and the African revolutionary fights for independence, both of which shaped the Combahee River Collective's work and speak to a broader conception of intersectionality beyond US politics that is often erased.

References

Adam, Barry. 1987. *The Rise of a Gay and Lesbian Movement*. Twayne Publishers.

Adler, Libby. 2018. *Gay Priori*. Duke University Press.

Beam, Myrl. 2018. *Gay, Inc.: The Nonprofitization of Queer Politics*. University of Minnesota Press.

Benz, Dorothee. 1995. "It's in the Jeans." In *Out in All Directions: The Almanac of Gay and Lesbian America*, edited by Lynn Witt, Sherry Thomas, and Eric Marcus. Warner Books.

Benz, Dorothee. 2019. "Swiss Cheese Civil Rights." *Medium*, October 7.

Benz, Dorothee. 2023. "A Refuge for LGBTQ+ Young People." *Learning for Justice* 4 (Spring): 29–33.

Benz, Dorothee. 2023. "Building a Just Future." *Learning for Justice* 5 (Fall).

Bérubé, Allan. 1990. *Coming Out Under Fire*. Plume.

Bronski, Michael. 2011. *A Queer History of the United States*. Beacon Press.

Center for Constitutional Rights. 2012. *Stop and Frisk: The Human Impact*. Center for Constitutional Rights.

Chauncey, George. 1994. *Gay New York: Gender, Urban Culture, and the Making of the Gay Male World 1890-1940*. Basic Books.

Cohen, Cathy. 1997. "Punks, Bulldaggers, and Welfare Queens: The Radical Potential of Queer Politics?" *GLQ: A Journal of Lesbian and Gay Studies* 3 (4): 437–65.

Cohen, Cathy. 1999. "What Is This Movement Doing to My Politics?" *Social Text*, 111–18.

Crass, Chris. 2013. *Toward Collective Liberation: Anti-Racist Organizing, Feminist Praxis, and Movement Building Strategy*. PM Press.

D'Emilio, John. 1983. *Sexual Politics, Sexual Communities: The Making of a Homo-sexual Minority in the United States, 1940–1970.* University of Chicago Press.

D'Emilio, John. 1983. "Capitalism and Gay Identity." In *Powers of Desire: The Politics of Sexuality,* edited by Ann Snitow, Christine Stansell, and Sharon Tompson. Monthly Review Press.

DeFilippis, Joseph Nicholas, and Ben Anderson-Nathe. 2017. "Embodying Margin to Center: Intersectional Activism Among Queer Liberation Organizations." In *LGBTQ Politics. A Critical Reader,* edited by Marla Brettschneider, Susan Burgess, and Christine Keating. New York University Press.

Dixon, Chris. 2014. *Another Politics: Talking Across Today's Transformative Move-ments.* University of California Press.

Drucker, Peter. 2014. *Warped: Gay Normality and Queer Anticapitalism.* Haymarket Books.

Duberman, Martin. 1993. *Stonewall.* Dutton.

Duberman, Martin. 2018. *Has the Gay Movement Failed?* University of California Press.

Duggan, Lisa. 2003. *The Twilight of Equality? Neoliberalism, Cultural Politics, and the Attack on Democracy.* Beacon Press.

Eaklor, Vicki. 2008. *Queer America: A People's GLBT History of the United States.* New Press.

Franke, Katherine. 2015. *Wedlocked: The Perils of Marriage Equality.* New York University Press.

Garza, Alicia. 2020. *The Purpose of Power. How We Come Together When We Fall Apart.* One World.

Gore, Dayo Folayan, Tamara Jones, and Joo-Hyun Kang. 2001. "Organizing at the Intersections: A Roundtable Discussion of Police Brutality Through the Lens of Race, Class, and Sexual Identities." In *Zero Tolerance: Quality of Life and the New Police Brutality in New York City,* edited by Andrea McArdle and T. Erzen. New York University Press.

Havey, Nicholas. 2021. " 'I Can't Be Racist, I'm Gay': Exploring Queer White Men's Views on Race and Racism." *Journal Committed to Social Change on Race and Ethnicity* 7 (2): 137–72.

Hirshman, Linda. 2013. *Victory: The Triumphant Gay Revolution.* Harper Perennial.

INCITE! Women of Color Against Violence, eds. 2007. *The Revolution Will Not Be Funded.* South End Press.

Kaba, Mariame, and Andre J. Ritchie. 2022. *No More Police. A Case for Abolition.* New Press.

Kennedy, Elizabeth Lapovsky, and Madeline D. Davis. 1993. *Boots of Leather, Slippers of Gold.* Routledge.

Khan-Cullors, Patrisse, and Asha Bandele. 2017. *When They Call You a Terrorist: A Black Lives Matter Memoir.* St. Martin's Press.

Kilgannon, Corey. 2019. "'Clash of Values': Why a Boycott Is Brewing Over Pride Celebrations." *New York Times*, June 20. https://www.nytimes.com/2019/06/20/nyregion/nyc-pride-march.html.

LaFrance, Samantha. 2024. "Six Dangerous Bills That Would Censor Speech on Campuses Across the Country." PEN America, February 7. https://pen.org/six-dangerous-bills-that-would-censor-speech-on-campuses-across-the-country/.

Lorde, Audre. 1984. *Sister Outsider*. Crossing Press.

Mangan, Katherine. 2024. "The End of Inclusion? Campus Leaders Struggle to Deliver on a Core Ideal." *Chronicle of Higher Education*, February 26. https://www.chronicle.com/article/the-end-of-inclusion.

Moraga, Cherríe, and Gloria Anzaldúa, eds. 1981. *The Bridge Called My Back: Writings by Radical Women of Color*. Kitchen Table: Women of Color Press.

Mucciaroni, Gary. 2017. "Whither the LGBTQ Movement in a Post-Civil Rights Era?" In Brettschneider et al., *LGBTQ Politics*.

Murib, Zein. 2017. "Rethinking GLBT as a Political Category in U.S. Politics." In Brettschneider et al., *LGBTQ Politics*.

PEN America. 2023. "The Culture Wars Are Coming for College Accreditation." July 13. https://pen.org/the-culture-wars-are-coming-for-college-accreditation/.

Phelan, Shane. 1989. *Identity Politics: Lesbian Feminism and the Limits of Community*. Temple University Press.

Piven, Frances Fox. 2006. *Challenging Authority: How Ordinary People Change America*. Rowman and Littlefield.

Piven, Frances, and Richard Cloward. 1977. *Poor People's Movements: Why They Succeed, How They Fail*. Vintage Books.

Rosenberg, Gerald. 1991. *The Hollow Hope: Can Courts Bring About Social Change?* University of Chicago Press.

Rubin, Gayle. 2011. *Deviations. A Gayle Rubin Reader*. Duke University Press.

Stein, Marc. 2012. *Rethinking the Gay and Lesbian Movement*. Routledge.

Stodolka, Jason. 2017. "You Don't Belong Here, Either: Same-Sex Marriage Politics and LGBT/Q Youth Homelessness Activism in Chicago." In Brettschneider et al., *LGBTQ Politics: A Critical Reader*.

Thompson, Mark, ed. 1991. *Leatherfolk: Radical Sex, People, Politics, and Practice*. Alyson Publications.

Vaid, Urvashi. 1995. *Virtual Equality: The Mainstreaming of Gay and Lesbian Liberation*. Anchor Books.

Vaid, Urvashi. 2012. *Irresistible Revolution: Confronting Race, Class, and the Assumptions of LGBT Politics*. Magnus Books.

Valocchi, Stephen. 2020. *Capitalisms and Gay Identities*. Routledge.

Ward, Jane. 2008. *Respectably Queer: Diversity Culture in Activist LGBT Organizations*. Vanderbilt University Press.

Warner, Michael, ed. 1993. *Fear of a Queer Planet: Queer Politics and Social Theory.* University of Minnesota Press.

Warner, Michael. 1999. *The Trouble with Normal: Sex, Politics, and the Ethics of Queer Life.* Harvard University Press.

Contributor Biographies

Julian Applebaum (he/him) received his Master of Philosophy in socio-legal research from the Centre of Socio-Legal Studies at the University of Oxford. His research investigated the disparate impact of municipal licensing on LGBTQ nightlife. Julian previously worked for the American Civil Liberties Union where he focused on LGBTQ+ rights issues.

Daryl J. Barker is an academic librarian whose work focuses on pedagogy, instruction, and the digital humanities, with a particular focus on working with nontraditional students and preparing academic librarians to be effective instructors. Much of his focus as a librarian occurs at the intersection of the social sciences, queerness, and library/information science. Daryl has experience working at a community college, a liberal arts college, and a large research library as well as working with justice-oriented nonprofit organizations. Daryl is currently a community college librarian and is completing a PhD in information studies. There his research interests include humanistic inquiry of digital technologies, the role of data in society, and critical information science.

Dorothee Benz (she/her) is a writer, organizer, and strategist who has spent decades on the front lines of social justice struggles in the United States. She holds a PhD in political science from the City University of New York with an expertise in social movements and an MDiv from Union Theological Seminary with a concentration in social ethics. Following a long communications career in the labor movement and civil rights litigation, she is now an ordained Christian minister dedicated to the urgent task of fighting white Christian nationalism.

Royal G. Cravens III (he/him) is a senior research analyst at the Southern Poverty Law Center. His book, *Yes Gawd! How Faith Shapes LGBT Identity and Politics in the United States*, is available from Temple University Press. He has previously held fellowships with the Social Science Research Council and the Public Religion Research Institute. He regularly contributes to public conversations at the intersection of LGBTQ politics, policy, and religion, having appeared in *Rolling Stone, Axios, NPR, USA Today*, and *Agence France-Presse*, among other outlets. Along with multiple scholarly publications, his public-facing scholarship has appeared in *The Washington Post, Religion News Service*, and *SPLC's Hatewatch*.

Maria J. D'Agostino is a professor of public administration in the Department of Public Management at John Jay College of Criminal Justice, CUNY, and the founding co-director of the Initiative for Gender Equity in the Public Sector. Her expertise is applied in practice through various public sector partnerships including the NYC Gender Equity Commission and the United Nations Gender Equity in Public Administration group.

Nicole M. Elias is an associate professor in the Department of Public Management at John Jay College of Criminal Justice, CUNY, and founding co-director of the Initiative for Gender Equity in the Public Sector at John Jay College. Her research focuses on equity in public administration and policy, with an emphasis on the ethics of administration, management of human resources in public organizations, and public policy impacts on SOGIE populations. Dr. Elias is the author of numerous journal articles, book chapters, government reports, and practitioner training modules aiming to foster greater diversity, equity, and inclusion in public service. She regularly collaborates with practitioners in government agencies and nonprofit organizations.

Andrew R. Flores (he/him) is an associate professor of government at the School of Public Affairs and a visiting scholar at the Williams Institute at the UCLA School of Law. His research focuses on attitude formation, attitude change, and public policies affecting LGBTQ populations. His research has appeared or is forthcoming in *Science Advances*, the *Proceedings of the National Academy of Sciences, Journal of Politics*, the *American Journal of Public Health, Policy Studies Journal, Political Behavior, Public Opinion Quarterly, Political Psychology*, and other peer-reviewed journals. Dr. Flores is an associate editor of *Political Research Quarterly*. Dr. Flores served as a member of the National Academies of Sciences, Engineering, and Medicine Consensus Committee on the Well-being of Sexual and Gender Diverse Populations in the US.

Elena Gambino (she/her) is an assistant professor of political science at Rutgers University in New Brunswick, New Jersey, working at the intersections of feminist, queer, and critical race theories. Elena's work has been published in *Political Theory* and *Contemporary Political Theory*, and she is the recipient of the 2020 Leo Strauss Award, presented by the American Political Science Association for the Best Dissertation in Political Philosophy. Her paper "Politics as Sinister Wisdom: Reparation and Responsibility in Lesbian Feminism" was also selected for the Best Paper Award by APSA's Women, Gender, and Politics section in 2020.

Cyril Ghosh is an associate professor and the Lloyd B. Politsch '33 Chair of Law at Clark University. He is the author of, among other things, *The Politics of the American Dream: Democratic Inclusion in Contemporary American Political Culture* (2013), *De-Moralizing Gay Rights: Some Queer Remarks on LGBT+ Rights Politics in the US* (2018), and (with Elizabeth F. Cohen) *Key Concepts in Political Theory: Citizenship* (2019). In the past, he has taught at several institutions, including Wagner College, Mount Holyoke College, Smith College, and Reed College.

Jyl J. Josephson (she/her) is professor of political science and women's and gender studies at Rutgers University–Newark. She is the author of *Rethinking Sexual Citizenship* (2016) and co-editor with Cynthia Burack of the Queer Politics and Cultures series for SUNY Press. She writes on democracy as well as on gender, sexuality, and public policy, primarily regarding the US with some collaborative research on Iceland. Her work has been published in journals such as *Politics and Gender*, *New Political Science*, *Perspectives on Politics*, *Trans Studies Quarterly*, *Urban Affairs Review*, and *Feminist Formations*. She is completing a manuscript on democracy and higher education and has ongoing projects on community organizing and on feminist, queer, and trans activism in Iceland. She can be reached at **jylj@rutgers.edu.**

Edward F. Kammerer Jr. (he/him) is an associate professor in the Political Science Department at Idaho State University. His research and teaching are in American politics, focusing primarily on LGBTQ politics and the judicial system. He also publishes extensively on political science pedagogy. He earned his PhD in law and public policy from Northeastern University and his JD from Suffolk University Law School. He worked as a public defender in Massachusetts before beginning his teaching career. His work has been published in *PS: Political Science & Politics, Journal of Political Science Education, JAMit: The Journal of American Studies in Italy, The New England Journal of Political Science*, and in edited volumes.

Whitney Ross Manzo is currently an associate professor of political science at Meredith College in Raleigh, North Carolina. She also serves as the pre-law advisor, director of undergraduate research, and assistant director of the Meredith Poll. Dr. Manzo holds a PhD from the University of Texas at Dallas in political science and methodology. Her general field is American politics, and her primary expertise is in the areas of public opinion, constitutional and electoral law, elections, and gender issues in politics. She also holds a MEd from the University of North Carolina–Charlotte in learning, design, and technology. Dr. Manzo's research agenda focuses on imbalances of power and issues of representation. She has recently published on unaffiliated voters in North Carolina politics and is currently working on a couple of projects on women in appointed office. She also studies higher education pedagogy and has published on the teaching of research methodology and proper assessment of learning objectives.

Erin Mayo-Adam (she/her) is the director of the LGBTQ Policy Center at Roosevelt House, an associate professor of political science at Hunter, and a member of the Roosevelt House Public Policy Faculty and Curriculum Committee. She is the author *of Queer Alliances: How Power Shapes Political Movement Formation* and has published in numerous academic outlets, including the *Law & Society Review, Law & Social Inquiry*, and the *Oxford Encyclopedia of LGBT Politics and Policy*. She specializes in American politics, law and society, and political theory and bridges scholarship on social movements, interest groups and public policy, intersectionality, gender and sexuality, and migration and labor politics.

Seth J. Meyer (he/him), LMSW, PhD, is an associate professor of public administration in the Department of Political Science at Bridgewater State University. His work focuses on social equity, LGBTQIA+ communities, and Jewish communities within public administration and nonprofit studies. He also has worked as a consultant for LGBTQIA+ organizations across the world. Dr. Meyer's is the author of *Lessons in Social Equity: A Case Study Book*.

Zein Murib is associate professor of political science and women's, gender, and sexuality studies at Fordham University. Their work focused on sexuality, gender, and race in US politics. Their first book, *Terms of Exclusion: Rightful Citizenship Claims and the Construction of LGBT Political Identity* (2023), won the Best LGBTQ Politics Book Award from the American Political Science Association's Sexuality & Politics section.

Haley Norris (they/them) holds a PhD in political science from Rutgers University–New Brunswick. They previously taught at both Rutgers University–New Brunswick and Bryn Mawr College. From 2023 to 2024, they served as an American Political Science Congressional Fellow. They are currently a policy analyst on LGBTQI+ rights in Washington, DC.

Anthony Perez (he/him) received his Bachelor of Science in psychology from Fordham University. He later received his personal training certification from the National Academy of Sports Medicine and later became a certified adaptive special needs trainer. He currently works with individuals who have developmental, intellectual, and/or physical disabilities.

Jamie Putnam (they/them) is a writer and most recently development worker for *Democracy Now!* They use their dreams of border and PIC abolition to inform their various volunteer work, including with Black and Pink NYC, New Sanctuary Coalition, and Proyecto Dilley. They received their bachelor's degree in political science from Fordham College at Lincoln Center in 2019.

Richard S. Price is the College of Social and Behavioral Science Endowed Professor of Political Science at Weber State University in Ogden, Utah. Their research explores obscenity, censorship, and queer educational activism. They are currently working on *The Perils of Queer Literature* exploring the suppression of LGTBQ stories since the 1940s.

Patrick Schmidt (he/him) is a professor of political science and co-director of legal studies at Macalester College (St. Paul, Minnesota). His research and teaching interests center on the history of American constitutional politics and range into regulatory policy, bureaucracies, and the legal profession. His books include *Lawyers and Regulation: The Politics of the Administrative Process* and *Conducting Law and Society Research: Reflections on Methods and Practices* (with Simon Halliday).

C. Heike Schotten (she/her) is professor of political science and affiliated faculty in women's, gender, and sexuality studies and teaches courses in political theory, feminist theory, and queer theory. Her research interests lie at the various and unlikely intersections of queer theory and Nietzsche studies, which ground a wide array of publications focusing, most recently, on the theoretical presuppositions animating right-wing ideologies, including but not limited to settler colonialism, anti-queerness, neoconservatism, "terrorism" policy and the "War on Terror," anti-Muslim racism, Zionism, and trans-exclusionary feminism. She is the author of *Queer Terror: Life, Death, and Desire in the Settler Colony* (2018), *Nietzsche's Revolution: Décadence, Politics, and Sexuality* (2009), and many articles and book chapters in Nietzsche studies, political theory, feminist theory, and queer theory.

Campbell M. Stevens (he/him) is an assistant professor of political science at a public regional university in the United States. His expertise is in the comparative politics of the post-Soviet region, and he has conducted qualitative fieldwork in the Russian Federation and Kyrgyzstan since 2008. As explained in his chapter and in work published in *PS: Political Science & Politics*, this work is published under a pseudonym for ethical considerations.

Fi Whalen (they/them) is an outdoor educator and Parks Department worker. They organize for better workplaces, homes, and worlds, most recently with the Met Council on Housing and City Workers for Palestine. In 2019, they received their bachelor's degree from Fordham University in Francophone studies and environmental studies.

Index

Note: Page numbers in *italics* indicate figures, **bold** indicate tables in the text, and references following "n" refer notes.

R. G. & G. R. Harris Funeral Homes Inc. v. EEOC, 194, 316
Rich, Adrienne, 288
Rivera, Sylvia, 367
Rizzo, Mary, 65–66
Robinson, Cedric, 376
Robinson, Russell, 107
Robson, Ruthann, 90
Roe v. Wade, 104, 381
Romesburg, Don, 52, 206
Rosenblum, Darren, 206
Rosky, Clifford J., 50
Roth v. United States, 85, 197
Rowling, J. K., 85
Rubin, Gayle, 144, 165–82, 295–96; academic production of theory, 170; conservative sexual morality, 178; democratic morality, 187n26; fascism within feminism, 188n28; feminist insight, 169, 179–80; inclusion of trans people, 181; "liberatory" and "radical" terms used by, 172; moral panics, theorization of, 169, 176; sex negativity, 174; sexuality theory, 161–72, 175; six ideological formations, 173; use of racism, 187n25
Rupp, Leila J., 4
Rutgers University-Newark, teaching LGBTQ politics in: approach to pedagogy, 65–68; assignment for oral histories, 68–69; community-engaged teaching, 71; core subject matter, 62–65; COVID-19 pandemic, 70; curriculum, location in, 62; features of course, 65–68; oral histories and LGBTQ politics, reflections on, 71–73; origin of course, 62; overview, 61–62; virtual instruction, adapting, 69–71

same-sex couples: adoption law for, 205; legal marriage recognition for, 243; marriage rights to, 193, 205–6; mimic heterosexual relationships, 206; political equality for, 80; same-sex marriage, 77–81, 87, 100, 105–6
Sarria, José, 352
Satter, Beryl, 65
Save Our Children, 186n20, 193
Save Women's Sports Acts, 49
say gay, 382
Scalia, Antonin, 81
Schilt, Kristen, 48
Schlafly, Phyllis, 315
Schmidt, Patrick, 12, 13
Schmitt, Arno, 125
scholarship, 218; in digital humanities, 348; on inclusive curricula, 2–4; LGBTQ political science, canon of, 22–28; queer and feminist, 183n4
schools in LGBTQ politics: curriculum, 50–52; overview, 33–34; straight school, 34–35; students, 42–49; teachers, 36–52
Schotten, C. Heike, 144
Schulenberg, Shawn, 21, 124
Schulman, Sarah, 70
Sears, Clare, 90–91
Sederbaum, Isaac, 106
Sedgwick, Eve Kosofsky, 120, 289, 290, 292–93, 332
Selective Service System, 314, 315
Serpe, Christine R., 123
Sex Is as Sex Does (Currah), 72, 267
Sex Perversion Elimination Program, 83
sex-segregated restrooms, 266
The Sexual Contract (Pateman), 184n10
sexual culture, 279
sexual identity, 181, 200, 372

www.ingramcontent.com/pod-product-compliance
Lightning Source LLC
Chambersburg PA
CBHW030856270326
41929CB00008B/441